INTERNATIONAL TRADE ISSUES

INTERNATIONAL TRADE ISSUES

ROBERT V. WEEKS
EDITOR

Nova Science Publishers, Inc.
New York

LIBRARY OF CONGRESS CATALOGING-IN-PUBLICATION DATA
Available upon request

ISBN 1-59454-621-5

Published by Nova Science Publishers, Inc. ✢ New York

CONTENTS

PREFACE

While some may dispute that economics is the driving force behind much of history, nobody can argue that trade is not a significant factor in international relations. In an increasingly globalized world, products are perpetually crossing borders, leading to both political and fiscal conflicts. Businesses have to face diverse markets and regions while worrying about protectionist government initiatives that hamper free trade. Even the ostensible champion of free markets, America, has its own streak of inhibiting the flow of goods; witness the recent steel tariffs which have angered European partners. No society, therefore, is immune to the pressures of world trade and the need to balance the free movement of products with the desire to preserve domestic industries.

This book assembles a collection of articles examining some of the most current and divisive issues in the international trade arena. They range from the tensions between the United States and Mexico in NAFTA to the war-fueled trade in diamonds in Africa. With such a broad range of issues discussed, this book serves as a needed tool for understanding the most important contemporary economic subjects.

The purpose of chapter 1 is to consider the role of network costs in a monopolistic competition trade model. I extend the Harris (1995) model with the global network to included local networks. It is shown that each country has unequal network expenses and no intra-industry trade occurs in the free-trade equilibrium, and there is some possibility that a smaller country will lose from trade.

Economic transformation leading to sustainable growth needs to be modeled taking into account geographic attractiveness for investment, infrastructure and trade linkages, trade regimes, and of course the entrepreneurial evolutionary process that drives the engine of productivity improvement. Chapter 2 attempts de novo a fusion of literatures, which perfectly well model one or the other element of a successful transformation process. The work presented in this chapter is based on an advanced economic version of earlier non-economic dynamic models worked on by regional scientists. Such dynamic models fall short by not incorporating price and microeconomic foundations. This work takes into account the recent work by Fujita by using an explicit price system and an explicit description of rational economic decision-making. Fujita type models are not rooted in identifiable physical space, rather they are a-spatial macro models. This chapter relies as much as possible on Allen's earlier spatial computer models. Theory is developed here in a way that it very much instructs practice, and maximizes transformation and development relevance of the work. The crucial difference that marks out evolutionary (complex) systems concerns assumption 3. This assumes that all firms of a given type, x say, are either identical, equal to the average *type,* or have a diversity that remains normally distributed around the average type. This means that for such models "sectors" or statistical aggregates of "firms" are used as variables reflecting the "average properties" of the included firms. But in reality, the micro-diversity of behaviours among individual firms in any particular part of the system is the *result of the history of local dynamics* occurring in the system. Economic transformation should really be modelled by these fully evolutionary models. Evolutionary trade theory as outlined in section 4 of the paper, establishes causal links from productivity gains to export success on a sector level. In the East German example the consequences of creative destruction at the micro level become apparent as sector change. One consequence is the relative increase in export unit values indicating greater export competitiveness as a result of changing productivity of firms. The empirical specification in the case of East German transformation reflects the model's population dynamics as well as the positive feedback elements apparent in the two model sections. Regression on East German technology and industry concentration data supports the evolutionary theory of trade. Population dynamics and the non-linear feedback elements are essential for an evolutionary trade model. A "complete evolutionary" model would generate this from the behaviour of co-evolving firms.

Where economic activity will locate in the future is one of the most important questions in economics as described in chapter 3. Even though advances in technology have reduced the cost of transport, communication and information gathering and processing, hence curtailing the 'distance penalty', local proximity (clusters) of firms that produce similar, competing and/or related products together with supporting institutions still matter. Economies of scale, activity-specific backward and forward linkages (indivisible production), accumulated knowledge and skills, innovation, existence of sophisticated customers and a fall in transportation costs play relevant roles in the 'protection' of clusters and absolute locational advantages of certain locations. 'Global' competitiveness often depends on highly concentrated 'local' knowledge, capabilities and common tacit codes of behaviour which can be found in a geographical concentration (cluster) of firms.

Chapter 4 analyzes empirically whether the European Union integration has promoted interdependent growth in its member countries. Employing spatial econometric techniques, and using trade data to measure integration, the authors find that trade has been a channel of diffusion of interdependent growth. Furthermore, the European integration, through successive enlargements, has reinforced this interdependence in EU countries. These results illustrate the idea that, by enhancing trade, the EU integration promotes more interdependent markets and non-pecuniary externalities. The EU integration has positive effect on the growth interdependence of its member countries. They find that if every trade partner of a given country experiences an extra growth of 1 percentage point, this economy will profit from an extra 0.5 point, and if this country belongs to the EU it will have an additional increase of its rate of growth of 0.17 point. Both figures illustrate that the EU integration promotes more interdependent markets, and therefore it can reduce the market fragmentation.

Chapter 5 investigates the impact of the euro adoption on commercial transactions of EMU countries. It refers to the abundant gravity-model literature about the effect of Currency Unions on trade originated by Rose (2000). The authors adapt this kind of modelling to the specific case of the European Monetary Union drawing from former literature some guidelines summed up as follows: distinction of "pure" common currency from exchange rate volatility effect; selection of sample of countries strictly focussed on EMU economies;

consideration of time as well as space dimension; inclusion of other political factors promoting integration. They add to these provisions the observation that the panel estimation of the gravity equation must be dynamic, because EMU is a young phenomenon; short run effects, like trade persistence, can hence play a crucial role. The main finding is that the euro adoption has had a positive but not exorbitant impact on bilateral trade of European countries (the estimated percentage increase ranges between 2.6 and 6.3%), much lower than that derivable from Roses's estimates referred to a larger and heterogeneous set of countries (providing a trade increase following the adoption of a common currency by as much as 200%). The results refer to short-run impacts; long-run effects could be stronger (but, in our opinion, not by the order of a doubling or a trebling effect indicated in the existing literature on currency unions), particularly if the structural change implied by the new currency regime (a fraction of foreign trade is potentially equivalent to domestic trade) becomes completely interiorised in the perception and the behaviour of Euroland citizens

The purpose of chapter 6 is to identify the variables that explain the real salaries and the desired salaries of retail executives in Brazil. To this end, it discusses the results of the application of a hedonic pricing model to input supplied by a sample of the said executives concerning the impact of different qualifications and characteristics (age, field of undergraduate degree, quality of MBA, number of language spoken, position in the company, etc.) on their worth (i.e., the remuneration they desire), vs. how retail companies actually "price" executives (i.e., characteristics and qualifications reflected in actual remuneration). These results were obtained by means of an econometric process that included a linear regression model of the demand for professional characteristics and involved 37 hedonic variables as applied to real salaries vs. desired salaries among retail executives. The input for the analysis was collected using a standard questionnaire answered by 215 executives. The main results show that: (i) certain job characteristics have a positive impact on wages, whereas others do not; (ii) many variables have a considerable impact on the level of remuneration that is sought, but not on actual remuneration; (iii) many companies disregard certain hedonic variables that represent academic achievement, such as MBAs and non-degree post-graduate programs, as a real reason to improve remuneration; (iv) workers understand that study and intellectual development can improve their wages; and (v) if the remuneration and hedonic prices connected with certain characteristics rise, then workers will prefer to devote their available time to developing these attributes.

The North America Free Trade Agreement (NAFTA) took effect in January 1994. From that year to 2000, Mexican exports grew three times faster (15%) than in the previous six years. Contrary to widespread beliefs, the cointegration analysis in chapter 7 finds no connection between the two facts. The evidence about imports is less conclusive. The results also suggest that the opening up of the Mexican Economy during the eighties is more likely to have caused a structural change in the trade flows. The boost from the American economy accounts for 96% of the growth of the equilibrium level of Mexican exports from 1994 to 2000.

Chapter 8 examines the extent to which exchange rate fluctuations affect sectoral employment and wages in the United States. It introduces a theoretical rational expectation model that decomposes movements in the exchange rate into anticipated and unanticipated components. The model demonstrates the effects of demand and supply channels on the response of the nominal wage and labor employment to changes in the exchange rate. The evidence indicates that the deflationary effect dominates on industrial nominal wage in

Manufacturing and Transportation industries in the face of dollar appreciation. More importantly, there is evidence of a decrease in employment growth in several industries in response to dollar appreciation, which is statistically significant in Construction and at the aggregate level. This evidence is consistent with a decrease in labor demand given the loss of competitiveness of U.S. products following dollar appreciation. Nonetheless, dollar appreciation is consistent with an increase in employment growth in the Mining sector where the share of imports is the largest among U.S. industries. There is also evidence of a positive spill over effect on employment in Transportation in the face of currency appreciation. Decomposing shocks in the exchange rate into appreciation and depreciation components yields symmetric, mostly insignificant effects, on employment and wages. Hence, the variability of the exchange rate appears to be neutral on employment growth and wage inflation.

Chapter 9 provides a systematic analysis of the impact of cross-border investment and exporting on firm level employment growth in the U.K manufacturing industry for the period 1990-1998. Economically significant employment growth effects are identified following entry into export markets, whereas the job creation effects of foreign direct investment are found to be more modest.

Chapter 10 sets forth the foundations for a transactional approach for the performance of arbitrage in foreign exchange markets. Firstly, the chapter reviews both the standard model of financial arbitrage and the so-called covered-interest arbitrage environment, and also lays bare striking shortcomings in these points of view, mainly grounded on a wide- ranging empirical evidence. Next, it moves on to what has been labeled in previous research working papers a transactional algebra, from which it expands on its main tools of analysis, namely differential rates, residual information sets, arbitrage gaps and transaction costs functions. Afterwards, the establish and prove the minimal conditions under which a successful arbitrage can be carried out within a transactional algebra.

There is much literature on the link between international trade, productivity growth and wage differential of skilled and unskilled labour. The theoretical and empirical research is mainly based on the Heckscher-Ohlin framework. Chapter 11 constructs a dynamic intertemporal general equilibrium (DIGE) model incorporating endogenous skill formation. Both the short- and long-run transition with shocks can be illustrated. The result supports the argument that trade has a responsibility for an increased wage differential. A cut in government education investment tends to enlarge the wage differential. Productivity growth may not be the cause of an enlarged wage differential in the long run.

In: International Trade Issues
Editor: Robert. V. Weeks, pp. 1-10
ISBN 1-59454-621-5

Chapter 1

COMMUNICATIONS NETWORKS, MONOPOLISTIC COMPETITION, AND INTERNATIONAL TRADE

Toru Kikuchi*
Graduate School of Economics,
Kobe University

Abstract

The purpose of this paper is to consider the role of network costs in a monopolistic competition trade model. I extend the Harris (1995) model with the global network to included local networks. It is shown that each country has unequal network expenses and no intra-industry trade occurs in the free-trade equilibrium, and there is some possibility that a smaller country will lose from trade.

1 Introduction

As the technology of communications has rapidly improved, the role of communication networks in economic activity has become more and more important. As a consequence of these changes, economic analysis of networks has become of general interest and several articles have been devoted to this topic.[1] In particular, Harris (1995) first noticed the relation between trade and communication networks. Harris (p. S47) points out that the distinguishing characteristic of globalization is the importance of communication costs which are largely *fixed* in nature, unlike specific transport costs.[2] Harris presents two models. The

---

*E-mail address: kikuchi@econ.kobe-u.ac.jp. This paper is a substantially revised and enlarged version of Kikuchi (2002). The author is grateful to Professors David Anderson, Fumio Dei, Nori Nakanishi, Peter Rosendorff, Katsuhiko Suzuki and Makoto Yano for their comments on earlier versions of this paper. Of course, I am solely responsible for all the remaining errors and shortcomings.

[1]See Economides (1996) and the reference cited therein.

[2]Harris suggests that, unlike transport costs, communication networks are characterized by (1) low marginal and high fixed costs; (2) a supplying industry that displays elements of a natural monopoly and produces goods that are quasi-public in nature; and (3) the presence of significant 'network externalities.'

first (Sec. 2) emphasizes the coordination of factor services geographically. On the other hand, with the second model (Sec. 3), which is the monopolistic competition trade model, he analyzes how a reduction in communication network costs affects the volume of trade. This paper extends the second model to consider both trade patterns and trade gains. I refer to the second model as the Harris model.

This research extends the Harris model in two ways: (1) it analyzes the 'local' network case in which each firm utilizes its own country's network while Harris analyzes the 'global' network case in which each firm utilizes the worldwide common network services; and (2) it introduces a homogeneous good which does not utilize the network.

Let us consider the first point. Much of network services consists of information. It is assumed that the information is disseminated freely at no additional cost; in reality, however, geographic distance or cultural and linguistic gaps require additional costs for transmission of information among different countries. Furthermore, markets for services are among the most regulated markets of a country, and it is therefore reasonable to argue that the extent to which a coherently and efficiently operating market for network services exists depends crucially upon how stringent the regulation barriers are. Thus it is important to consider not only the case of a global network but also that of local networks in which each country has its own network.

Turning to the second point, Harris (1995, p. S49) suggests that the communication costs associated with exchange are related to the complexity of the product sets being exchanged, and approximates it by the number of product varieties (i.e., the number of firms). The Harris model consists of symmetric differentiated products, and the volume of network services required by each product (i.e., each firm) is assumed to be constant. In reality, however, the level of required network services is not always constant. That is, the degree of utilization of network services may be different across goods. To consider this aspect, goods must be ranked according to their degree of utilization of network services. However, this is too involved a subject to be treated in detail here. Thus, as a step toward full analysis of the differences in the utilization of network services across goods, I introduce a homogeneous good which does not utilize network services into the Harris model. It is assumed that the homogeneous good need not utilize services because the information being exchanged is quite simple. I identify the homogeneous good as the non-network good.

Of course, in reality there are all sorts of gradations both in the tradability of network services and the degree of utilization of network services.[3] I analyze a simple two-country monopolistic competition trade model in which both a local network and a non-network good exist.

The structure of the paper is as follows. The next section presents the basic model. Following Harris, I assume the network services provider is a natural monopoly with average-cost pricing. Trade patterns are considered in Section 3. Section 4 turns to the question of trade gains. Section 5 presents some conclusions.

[3]Rauch (1996) considers the relation between the degree of product differentiation and the trading networks such as Japan's *Sogo Shosha*, extended family, etc. He suggests that the role of trading networks is less important in the less differentiated producer goods. This paper does not consider this kind of trading network.

2 The Model

Consider an economy that has two categories of goods: a homogeneous good and differentiated products. We treat the former as the 'non-network good', while the latter as the 'network good'. It is assumed that the only one factor of production, say labour, exists and that L units of labour endowed. The representative consumer has Cobb-Douglas preferences between the network good and the non-network good: $U = X^s Y^{1-s}, 0 < s < 1$, where Y is the amount of consumption of the non-network good, and X is the index for the consumption of the network good. The index takes the form,

$$X = \Big(\sum_{i=1}^{n} c_i{}^{\theta}\Big)^{1/\theta}, \quad 0 < \theta < 1,$$

where c_i is the amount of consumption of the i-th product and n is the number of varieties. We can also obtain the aggregate price index for the network good that is dual to X:

$$P = \Big(\sum_{i=1}^{n} p_i{}^{-\theta/(1-\theta)}\Big)^{-(1-\theta)/\theta}, \tag{1}$$

where p_i is the price of the i-th differentiated product. Solving the utility maximization problem, we have the following demand functions:

$$c_i = \frac{p_i{}^{-1/(1-\theta)} sI}{P^{\theta/(1-\theta)}}, \quad i = 1, ..., n. \tag{2}$$

where I is the national income.

The non-network good is produced with constant returns to scale technology. We let the non-network good be the numeraire and choose units such that one unit of labour produces one unit of output. Conversely, firms in the network good sector have increasing returns to scale technology. Production of the i-th product is characterized by the following linear cost function:

$$TC_i = \alpha + \beta x_i + \gamma, \quad i = 1, ..., n,$$

where TC_i and x_i are the total cost and output level of the i-th firm, respectively. Each firm has to commit α as fixed costs and has constant marginal cost β. This cost function is very popular in the analyses of monopolistic competition trade models. In this study, however, the main stress falls on γ, which we call the 'network cost'.[4] It consists of payments for network services from a provider with average-cost pricing.[5] Thus, we can think of the network cost as the kind of hook-up cost for network services. For tractability, we assume

[4]We can also interpret γ as the 'quasi-fixed cost'. 'Quasi-' implies that each firm perceives this cost as a fixed cost, while the level of it depends on the number of firms.

[5]As Ishikawa (1992, p. 58) notes, a single provider with average cost-pricing has been discussed in the context of contestable markets. Also, the government may force the monopolistic provider to price at average costs. Telecommunication services are a good example. These services are homogeneous and their production involves a huge fixed cost, such as for the construction of a telecommunication network.

a simple cost function for the provider: $K(n) = F + gn$, where F and g are fixed and marginal costs and n is the number of users (i.e., the number of firms). Because of average-cost pricing, the level of network costs is determined as follows:

$$\gamma(n) = \frac{K(n)}{n} = \frac{F}{n} + g, \quad \gamma' < 0, \quad \gamma'' > 0, \tag{3}$$

which implies that the network cost per firm falls as the number of firms in the network good sector increases: as the number of user increases, a *cost-sharing effect* works.[6]

The producer of the i-th product chooses the profit maximizing price,

$$p_i = p = \beta/\theta, \quad i = 1, ..., n. \tag{4}$$

With n firms, the profit of each firm, π, is given as: $\pi = px - [\alpha + \beta x + \gamma]$. Thus the level of output that generates zero profits with n firm is given by[7]

$$x(n) = \frac{[\alpha + \gamma(n)]\theta}{\beta(1-\theta)}, \quad x' < 0. \tag{5}$$

Now we can obtain the equilibrium number of varieties. Substituting (4) into (2), we obtain the relation between the product varieties and the demand for a product:

$$c(n) = \frac{\theta s I}{\beta n}. \tag{6}$$

By equating (5) and (6), we obtain the equilibrium number of varieties,[8]

$$n^A = \frac{(1-\theta)sL - F}{\alpha + g}, \tag{7}$$

where $[A]$ refers to the equilibrium value in autarky. If there is an increase in the labour force, the number of varieties increases and the level of output per firm decreases.

3 Trade Patterns

Suppose that two countries (home and foreign) open their goods markets and have a trade relationship. Throughout this paper, we assume that network services cannot be traded. Countries are assumed to be identical except for the size of their labour forces. Without loss of generality, the foreign country is assumed to be larger than the home country.

[6]Harris (1995) suggests that the network services may be subject to congestion effects so that K is ultimately increasing in n. Here to keep things simple, we suppose that there are no congestion effects. For the discussion of congestion effects, see Mackie-Mason and Varian (1995), Kikuchi and Ichikawa (2002), Kikuchi (2003).

[7]If there is no network cost, this level is independent from the number of firms. This corresponds to the results from standard monopolistic competition trade model. See, for example, Krugman (1981).

[8]In equilibrium, both firms in the network good sector and the network services provider earn zero profits. Therefore, the national income equals factor payments, L.

First, we must draw attention to the demand condition of the network good in the trading world. Since we have assumed homothetic preferences, we can aggregate both countries' demands for a product into one demand function. The worldwide demand function is given by

$$C(n, n^*) = \frac{\theta s(I + I^*)}{\beta(n + n^*)} \tag{8}$$

where $[*]$ refers to the foreign country.

Now turn to the equilibrium condition. Each value of n determines the supply quantity $x(n)$, as indicated in (5). There is some value of n^* which will equate the worldwide demand quantity in (8) to the home supply quantity. Following Ethier (1979, 1982), we call this relation between n and n^* the 'home allocation curve'.[9] Setting $x(n) = C(n, n^*)$ in (5) and (8) gives the implicit formula for the home allocation curve:

$$\frac{\alpha + \gamma(n)}{1 - \theta} = \frac{s(L + L^*)}{n + n^*}. \tag{9}$$

Similarly the foreign allocation curve can be obtained:

$$\frac{\alpha + \gamma(n^*)}{1 - \theta} = \frac{s(L + L^*)}{n + n^*}. \tag{10}$$

Equation (9) and (10) require the demand quantity to equal the supply quantity in the two countries. But equilibrium is consistent with $C(n, n^*) > x(n)$ if the home country specialized in the network good, and with $C(n, n^*) < x(n)$ if it specialized in the non-network good, so the allocation curve must also take this into account. The same is true for the foreign country. Figure 1 illustrates two possible cases.[10] The graphs of (9) and (10) are given by OAC and OAB.[11] The allocation curves are bounded from above by $n = N$ and $n^* = N^*$, where $N(N^*)$ is the number of varieties when the home (foreign) country completely specializes in the network good:

$$N = \frac{(1 - \theta)L - F}{\alpha + g}, \quad N^* = \frac{(1 - \theta)L^* - F}{\alpha + g}. \tag{11}$$

Thus, the full home (foreign) allocation curve consists of N*O plus OAC (NO plus OAB) in Figure 1(a), and N*O plus OAHN (NO plus OAGN*) in Figure 1(b). These curves intersect in three places: at A, B, and C in Figure 1(a), and at A, N, N* in Figure 1(b).[12] At such intersections the supply quantity of an individual product in each country is equal to a common world demand quantity, so the world is in the free-trade equilibrium.[13] In Figure

[9]Note that Ethier (1979, 1982) analyzes the case of two homogeneous goods.

[10]Figure 1(a) corresponds to the case where $(1 - s)/s > (L^*/L) > s/(1 - s)$ holds. This implies that the expenditure share for the network good is relatively small and diversification occurs. On the other hand, Figure 1(b) corresponds to the case where $(1 - s)/s < (L^*/L) < s/(1 - s)$ holds.

[11]Values of parameters underlying the figures are given in the Appendix A.

[12]The coordinate of points A, B, C is $([(1 - \theta)s(L + L^*) - 2F]/(\alpha + g),\ [(1 - \theta)s(L + L^*) - 2F]/(\alpha + g))$, $(0, [(1 - \theta)s(L + L^*) - 2F]/(\alpha + g))$, $([(1 - \theta)s(L + L^*) - 2F]/(\alpha + g), 0)$, respectively.

[13]This corresponds to Proposition 2 in Ethier (1979) and Proposition 5 in Ethier (1982).

1(a), equilibria B and C both involve complete specialization by one country (in the non-network good) and diversification by the other country, whereas A implies diversification by both countries. At A, there is intra-industry trade in the network good. In Figure 1(b), equilibria B and C both involve complete specialization by each country. By taking into acount the entry-exit process, it is clear that the equilibrium at A is unstable, while the other two equilibria are stable.[14]

To examine specialization patterns we need to know where the autarky equilibrium is located on the $n - n^*$ plane. By allowing L^*/L to vary while keeping $L + L^*$ constant at $\overline{L}$, we can depict all pre-trade situations. This is shown by the dotted line DE in Figure 1.[15] As the relative size of foreign country increases, the point which represents the autarky situation moves along the segment DA toward point D.[16] If the world enters free trade from autarky, the actual trading equilibrium at B in Figure 1(a) and at N* in Figure 1(b). The foreign country will export the network good while the home country will exporter the non-network one. We shall discuss the dynamic process in detail. By the opening of trade, there appears to be an opportunity for enter into the foreign country's network good sector because there is a competitive advantage in the sense that, through the cost-sharing effect, the level of the network cost per firm is lower. On the other hand, the home firms will not be able to cover their higher fixed costs, $\alpha + \gamma$, and will be pushed out of the market. Thus the scale of the home provider will contract, while the foreign one will expand. The differences in the zero-profit quantity will be reinforced with this entry-exit process. That is, there is a cumulative process in which the export of the network good brings an opportunity for entry, and the entry promotes exports. This cumulative process continues until the home country's network vanish.

As we saw in Section 2 firms in the larger country's differentiated products sector produce less than those in the smaller country. Thus we can predict trade patterns by using the relative autarky production scale instead of prices: the country with a relatively low scale of firms in the differentiated products sector will export those products. In our example, $x^{*A} < x^A$ and the foreign country will export differentiated products. Furthermore, if we regard the price of each differentiated product as $\rho = px$, we can say that the relative autarkic prices of varieties in the two countries correctly predict the trade patterns: $\rho^{*A} < \rho$ implies that the foreign country will export differentiated products.[17] In sum, the scale economies associated with network services imply that the larger country has comparative advantage in differentiated products, and the free trade equilibrium is efficient in the sense that only one network exists.

Proposition 1: *If the two countries commence free trade from autarky, the larger country completely or incompletely specializes in the network good and the smaller country completely specializes in the non-network good.*

[14]In the Figure the directions of motion are shown by arrows.

[15]This line is represented by $n^A + n^{*A} = [(1-\theta)s\overline{L} - 2F]/(\alpha + g)$.

[16]At the same time, the point F also moves along line IJ, which is represented by $N + N^* = [(1-\theta)\overline{L} - 2F]/(\alpha + g)$.

[17]For this approach, see Dixit and Norman (1980, ch. 9).

4 Gains and Losses from Trade

Now turn to the normative issue of whether individual countries will gain from trade. Consider, first, the larger (foreign) country side. By Proposition 1, this country will be driven to increase its production of the network good, possibly with completely specialization, by opening international trade. If the larger country does not specialize (the case of point B in Figure 1(a)), it produces some of the non-network good and the price of each network good does not change (see (4)). Since the price remains constant and the number of varieties increases, the larger country necessarily gains from trade. This gain will come solely through increased product variety.

If free trade induces completely specialization (the case of point N* in Figure 1(b)), the price of each foreign variety, p^{*T}, will be $p^{*T} = \beta sL/\theta(1-s)L^*$, where [T] refers to the equilibrium value in free trade.[18] For both countries to specialize, Figure 1(b) reveals that $sL > (1-s)L^*$ is necessary,[19] and then,

$$p^{*T} = \frac{\beta sL}{\theta(1-s)L^*} > \frac{\beta}{\theta} = p^{*A}. \tag{12}$$

The larger country gains from trade in this case also: by selling each network good, the larger country obtains more of the non-network good with trade than in autarky situation. There are gains both from the availability of a greater variety of products and from improvement in the terms-of-trade.

Proposition 2: *The larger country will gain from trade. In the equilibrium that is attained as a result of a movement autarky to free trade.*

Now turn to the smaller (home) country. The smaller country exports the non-network good and in fact specializes in it. If the larger country does not completely specialize, then the price of each network good does not change and the number of varieties will be increased. Therefore the smaller country will gain. The gain will come through increased product varieties.

Consider, then, an equilibrium in which both countries specialize. Since we chose the non-network good as numeraire, (12) shows that the terms-of-trade for the smaller country will deteriorate. However, we cannot conclude that the smaller country loses from trade without taking the changes in the number of varieties into account. In the free-trade equilibrium with both countries' specializing, the number of varieties will be N^* (see (11)). To consider these two effects, we can use the price index for the network good, P (see (1)).[20]

[18]In the complete specialization equilibrium, the countries' wage rates will diverge. We denote the foreign wage rate in terms of numeraire, w^*. By using international market equilibrium condition for the non-network good ($(1-s)w^*L^* = sL$), we can calculate w^*. Then, by substituting w^* into the firm's pricing rule, we can obtain p^{*T}.

[19]See footnote 10.

[20]Since we chose the non-network good as the numeraire and the smaller country produces it both before and after trade, the national income of the smaller country, L, does not change. To see the welfare changes, we

It is easy to verify that the smaller country will lose if and only if

$$(n^A)^{-(1-\theta)/\theta} p^A < (N^*)^{-(1-\theta)/\theta} p^{*T}.$$

By substituting (4), (7), and (11) into the above condition and taking the natural logarithm of each side, we can obtain the following expression:

$$\frac{1-\theta}{\theta} ln \left[\frac{(1-\theta)sL - F}{(1-\theta)L^* - F} \right] + ln \left[\frac{sL}{(1-s)L^*} \right] > 0. \quad (13)$$

The first term represents the *variety effect* which comes from the increase in the number of product varieties. Since the smaller country will face the greater variety of products, the first term will be negative. The second term represents the *terms-of-trade effect.* If two countries completely specialize, the second term on the left-hand side of condition (13) has a positive sign. Evidently there are some cases where two countries completely specialize and the condition (13) does not hold. In these cases, the gains from increased product diversity outweigh the conventional terms-of-trade effect, and the smaller country gains from trade.

Proposition 3: *If condition (13) holds, the smaller country will lose from trade.*

Three points deserve explicit emphasis. First, the smaller country will lose if L is sufficiently close to L^*. This corresponds to the conclusion of Ethier (1982): the smaller 'the smaller country' is, relative to the larger country, the greater the likelihood that it will gain. The reason is simply that a sufficiently large size disparity renders the switch of network activity to the larger country the dominant consideration.

Second, the normative implication is quite different from the one in the usual monopolistic competition trade models. In popular analyses, sufficiently small differences in countries' sizes or factor contents imply every country will gain from trade.[21] However, in this model, given condition (13) holds, the closer resemblance in size becomes, the more the smaller country will lose from trade. If two countries are quite similar in their sizes, the worldwide number of varieties does not increase so much by opening trade. This is because the number of missing varieties in the smaller country is relatively large. In contrast to the popular argument of trade gains between similar countries, a distribution of trade gains remains a matter of debate if we consider the case of competing local networks in those countries.

Finally, a sufficient relative importance of varieties, i.e., smaller θ, will reduce the likelihood of the smaller country losing by abondoning the production of varieties and network services seems reasonable enough. To put it another way, as θ converges to 1 and varieties matter less, the likelihood of the smaller country losing from trade will increase; this situation corresponds to Ethier's analysin of the model of homogeneous goods. Thus we see that our model covers lots of cases; not only the cases with differentiated products but also those with homogeneous goods.

---

must check the price index of the network good which indicates the minimum expenditure to obtain one unit of X.

[21]See, for example, Krugman (1981).

5 Concluding Remarks

This research incorporates both the specific features of a local network and the existence of a non-network good into a monopolistic competition framework to study the issues of trade patterns and gains.

Since there are increasing returns in the national communication network, the larger country exports the network good while the smaller one exports the non-network good (Proposition 1). Since the network cost for each firm is lower in the larger country than in the smaller country, the larger country exports the network good and there appears to be an opportunity for entry. This entry will, through the cost-sharing effect, reinforce the larger country's cost advantages and promote its exports further. That is, there is a cumulative process in which the export of goods brings an opportunity for entry, and the entry promotes exports. This cumulative process is crucially dependent on two assumptions in the model. First, since there is a *local* network, the cost-sharing effect works only domestically. This creates an incentive to increase the supply of the network good in the larger country where opportunities for cost-sharing are the greatest. Second, the existence of the non-network good sector allows the network good sector to draw labour out of the non-network good sector and realize the increase in the supply of the network good.

In this model, it is the interaction between the local network and an elastic labour supply that gives rise to the cumulative process. If the larger country, by opening trade, completely specializes in the network good, the latter factor disappears and the supply of the network good is bounded. This implies that the non-network good plays a crucial role in the cumulative process.

Depending on the extent of the cumulative process, trade patterns can be divided into two cases between which the welfare effects of trade differ. In the first case the larger country's incomplete specialization is induced by the cumulative process, i.e., it produces the non-network good in the trading equilibrium. At the same time, the smaller country completely specializes in the non-network good. In this case, the countries' wage rates will be equalized and both countries' consumers will gain from increased product variety. In the second case the cumulative process continues until the larger country completely specializes in the network good while the smaller country completely specializes in the non-network good. In this case, the countries' wage rates will diverge and the relative price of the network good will rise. Thus, the larger country will gain both from an increase in product variety and from an improvement in terms-of-trade. On the other hand, the smaller country will gain from increased product variety while losing from a deterioration in terms-of-trade. The net effect for the smaller country depends on the relative strength of these two effects.

In summary, the larger country will gain from trade (Proposition2) while the smaller country will lose from trade when both countries completely specialize and the negative terms-of-trade effect dominates the variety effect (Proposition 3).

A Parameter Values

In Figure 1(a), $F = 10, \quad g = 0.5, \quad L + L^* = 400, \quad s = 0.25,$
$\beta = 0.01, \quad \theta = 0.5.$

References

[1] Economides, N. (1996) 'The Economics of Networks,' *International Journal of Industrial Organization,* Vol. 14, pp. 673-699.

[2] Dixit, A. and V. Norman (1980) *Theory of International Trade,* Cambridge University Press.

[3] Ethier, W. (1979) 'Internationally Decreasing Costs and World Trade,' *Journal of International Economics,* Vol. 9, pp. 1-24.

[4] Ethier, W. (1982) 'Decreasing Costs in International Trade and Frank Graham's Argument for Protection,' *Econometrica,* Vol. 50, pp. 1243-1268.

[5] Harris, R. G. (1995) 'Trade and Communication Costs,' *Canadian Journal of Economics,* Vol. 28, pp. S46-S75.

[6] Helpman, E. and P.R. Krugman (1985) *Market Structure and Foreign Trade,*The MIT Press.

[7] Ishikawa, J. (1992) 'Trade Patterns and Gains from Trade with an Intermediate Good produced under Increasing Returns to Scale,' *Journal of International Economics,* Vol. 32, pp. 57-81.

[8] Kikuchi, T. (2002) 'Country-specific Communications Networks and International Trade in a Model of Monopolistic Competition,' *Japanese Economic Review,* Vol. 53, pp.167–176.

[9] Kikuchi, T. (2003) "Interconnectivity of communications networks and international trade," *Canadian Journal of Economics,* Vol. 36, pp. 155-167.

[10] Kikuchi, T., and T. Ichikawa (2002) 'Congestible Communications Networks and International Trade,' *Canadian Journal of Economics,* Vol. 35, pp. 331-340.

[11] Krugman, P. R. (1981) 'Intraindustry Specialization and the Gains from Trade,' *Journal of Political Economy,* Vol. 89, pp. 959-974.

[12] MacKie-Mason, J. K., and H. Varian (1995) 'Pricing Congestible Network Resources,' *IEEE Journal of Selected Area in Communications,* Vol. 13, pp. 1141–1149.

[13] Rauch, J. E. (1996) 'Trade and Search: Social Capital, Sogo Shosha, and Spillovers,' NBER Working Paper No. 5618.

In: International Trade Issues
Editor: Robert. V. Weeks, pp. 11-32
ISBN: 1-59454-621-5

Chapter 2

A REGIONAL DEVELOPMENT APPROACH TRANSPORT, INTERNATIONAL TRADE, AND INVESTMENT MODELED IN SPACE

Hans-Peter Brunner[*1]
Asian Development Bank
PO Box 789, 0980 Manila, Philippines
Peter Allen[2]
Complex Systems Mgt Ctr.
Cranfield University
Bedford, MK43 OAL, UK

Abstract

Economic transformation leading to sustainable growth needs to be modeled taking into account geographic attractiveness for investment, infrastructure and trade linkages, trade regimes, and of course the entrepreneurial evolutionary process that drives the engine of productivity improvement. This paper attempts de novo a fusion of literatures, which perfectly well model one or the other element of a successful transformation process. The work presented in this paper is based on an advanced economic version of earlier non-economic dynamic models worked on by regional scientists such as Allen (1997), and well summarized by Anas, Arnott and Small (1998). Such dynamic models fall short by not incorporating price and microeconomic foundations (Chen, 1996). This work takes into account the recent work by Fujita et al., by using an explicit price system and an explicit description of rational economic decision-making. Fujita et al. type models are not rooted in identifiable physical space, rather they are a-spatial macro models. This paper relies as much as possible on Allen's earlier spatial computer models. Theory is developed here in a way that it very much instructs practice, and maximizes transformation and development relevance of the work.

---

[*] The author alone in his personal capacity, not the Asian Development Bank, is responsible for the paper's content. The usual disclaimer applies

[1] E-mail address: Hbrunner@adb.org, Fax: ++632 -632 2337
[2] E-mail address: P.M.Allen@cranfield.ac.uk

The crucial difference that marks out evolutionary (complex) systems concerns assumption 3. This assumes that all firms of a given type, x say, are either identical, equal to the average *type*, or have a diversity that remains normally distributed around the average type. This means that for such models "sectors" or statistical aggregates of "firms" are used as variables reflecting the "average properties" of the included firms. But in reality, the micro-diversity of behaviours among individual firms in any particular part of the system is the *result of the history of local dynamics* occurring in the system.

Economic transformation should really be modelled by these fully evolutionary models. Evolutionary trade theory as outlined in section 4 of the paper, establishes causal links from productivity gains to export success on a sector level. In the East German example the consequences of creative destruction at the micro level become apparent as sector change. One consequence is the relative increase in export unit values indicating greater export competitiveness as a result of changing productivity of firms. The empirical specification in the case of East German transformation reflects the model's population dynamics as well as the positive feedback elements apparent in the two model sections. Regression on East German technology and industry concentration data supports the evolutionary theory of trade. Population dynamics and the non-linear feedback elements are essential for an evolutionary trade model. A "complete evolutionary" model would generate this from the behaviour of co-evolving firms.

JEL classification: F12, L11, O18, R12.

1 Introduction

Economic transformation leading to sustainable growth needs to be modeled taking into account geographic attractiveness for investment, infrastructure and trade linkages, trade regimes, and of course the entrepreneurial evolutionary process that drives the engine of productivity improvement. This paper attempts de novo a fusion of literatures, which perfectly well model one or the other element of a successful transformation process. The work presented in this paper is based on an advanced economic version of earlier non-economic dynamic models worked on by regional scientists such as Allen (1997), and well summarized by Anas, Arnott and Small (1998). Such dynamic models fall short by not incorporating price and microeconomic foundations (Chen, 1996). This work takes into account the recent work by Fujita et al., by using an explicit price system and an explicit description of rational economic decision-making. Fujita et al. type models are not rooted in identifiable physical space, rather they are a-spatial macro models. This paper relies as much as possible on Allen's earlier spatial computer models. Theory is developed here in a way that it very much instructs practice, and maximizes transformation and development relevance of the work.

The analysis of increasing return, agglomeration and network effects is important for their impact on trade, growth and development. The application of models that relate such positive externality effects to actual representations of physical and institutional infrastructure results in a powerful tool for the economic development of economic and trade corridors. It facilitates a definition of the role of government, and thus of the Asian Development Bank, in the provision of transport, communication, and institutional infrastructure. Accounting for location at a low level of resolution at a firm or other economic actor level, yields new insights into economic development phenomena that are normally analyzed in a-spatial, macro models.

Firms exist of course not in the abstract but are real, populated and run by people, who converge on a distinct place in time and on brick and mortar facilities. These facilities are served by infrastructure, for example roads to get to the factory and to move people and goods in and out. It is an important question how firms locate and invest in space when they are supposed to attract the most productive resources, and combine them under management for a competitive service or product to be sold in the domestic and foreign market. Surely firms will locate only in places where they have effective access to resources, markets, know-how and so on. Governments are often in the business of providing the public goods of access and location, learning and know-how to make sure the process of creative destruction is tilted towards the creative side. Generally research shows, that firms locate most productively where they have the best access to inputs and to markets on a per quality adjusted service or product unit mile / kilometer measure related to time. This depends also on the institutional arrangements for exchange and trade. One could of course say that knowledge intensive services and products are less geography and infrastructure dependent. Still they are even more people dependent, and qualified people want to live and work in an attractive location. Also, high-tech products tend to be more time-sensitive in delivery to customers, and even if roads may not be necessary for their transport, these services or products would have to be moved out and around, and across borders by electronic means or by air.

The first decade of the most dramatic economic transformation has passed in Eastern Europe. Looking at this experience, a successful pattern of transformation is emerging in the view of many that have intensively studied this process (Kornai, 2000). At the heart of such process lies a Schumpeterian style entrepreneurial transformation leading to higher quality adjusted labor productivity (Caballero and Hammour, 2000). A market driven creative destruction allocates resources from less productive firms to more productive ones (Brunner, 2001). Entrepreneurs pursue opportunities and invest in new firms. Firms which become uncompetitive are driven through competition to extinction. Creation and destruction often proceed at different pace leading to temporary dislocation of resources. Such dislocations are softened by the institutional frame that underpins the functioning of the market.

The process of creative destruction is most effective for economic development and growth when it allows the exploitation of positive externalities, involving increasing returns, agglomeration effects, or network effects. Increasing returns are prominent in knowledge intensive sectors, but not only there. The winner-take-all literature relates to this, when it shows the urgency for market players to corner market share for dominance (monopolistic competition). Agglomeration effects are prominent in spatial models, where productivity increases relate to a spatial convergence of resources in a critical mass. Overcrowding in mental or physical space can however lead to negative agglomeration effects, as many former inhabitants of ugly megalopoli can attest to. Network effects play a prominent role for entrepreneurs who produce network goods, where the utility for example to consumers rises with the increased and more geographically widespread use of the (standardized) product, or service delivered through an infrastructure.

The paper proceeds as follows. The paper introduces the approach of modelling complex growth and transformation. Then the first model section will develop a partial model of growth based on the notion of geographic *attractiveness*. The second model section will add to the model the evolutionary process that fuels the Schumpeterian process leading to productivity improvements and competitiveness increases. This model section will complete the integration of trade in economic technical and geographic space. A section illustrates the case of creative destruction and transformation with trade in East Germany. The final section draws conclusions on the applicability and practicability of the model in trade and growth, as well as transformation and development economics.

2 Introduction to Regional Growth with Complexity

Understanding "reality" and gaining knowledge about a problem requires us to reduce the real complexity of any particular situation to a simpler, more understandable one, by making specific simplifying assumptions. The hope is that there exists a representation that, while being sufficiently simple to be understood, remains sufficiently representative of reality to be useful. These assumptions have been discussed elsewhere (Allen, 1988, 1993, 1994,1997,1998) and we shall briefly summarize them here (Figure (1)).

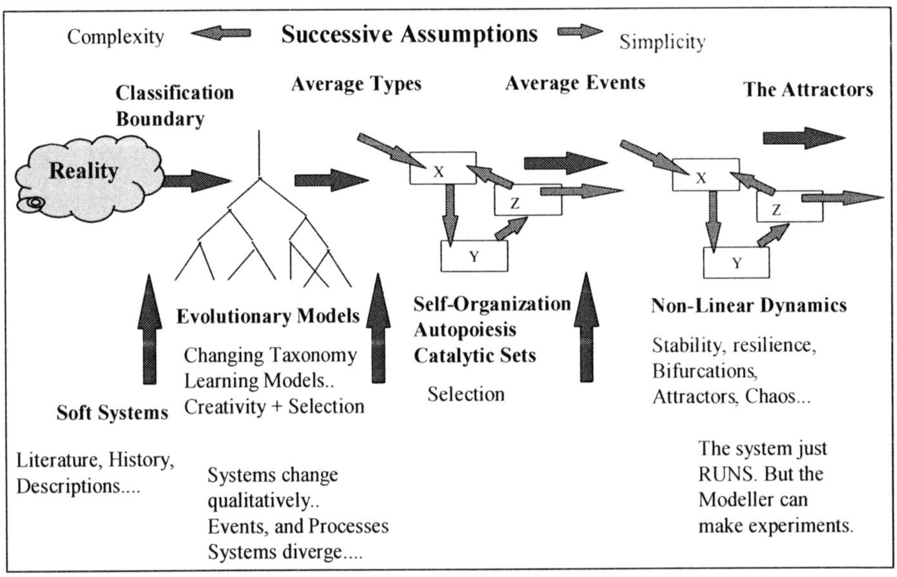

Figure (1) Assumptions made in reducing complexity to simplicity, in order to obtain understanding, and predictability – providing the assumptions hold.

2.1 The Assumptions Used to Reduce Complexity to Simplicity

These are:

1. That we can define a boundary between the part of the world that we want to "understand" and the rest. In other words, we assume first that there is a "System" and an "Environment".
2. That we have rules for the classification of objects that lead to a relevant taxonomy for the system components, which will enable us to understand what is going on. This is often decided entirely intuitively.

3. The *third* assumption concerns the level of description below that which we are trying to understand, and assumes are either all identical to each other and to the average, or have a diversity that is at all times distributed "normally" around the average.
4. That the individual behaviour of sub-components can be described by *average interaction parameters.*

2.2 The Modelling Outcomes of Different Assumptions

Clearly, the use of the assumptions above provides different interpretive frameworks of reality, some suppose far more constraints on what can happen than others. So different types of economic model can be developed in attempting to capture and predict changing patterns of trade and of development. In this paper we present some initial "transitional" and trade models that lead towards the goal of a full, evolutionary, spatial model of investment, changing productivity and patterns of employment and development.

Relating assumptions to outcomes in terms of types of model we have:

- Making all 4 assumptions plus stationarity gives either a static *equilibrium* model, or one corresponding to a cyclic or chaotic attractor
- Making all 4 assumptions leads to *System Dynamics*, a mechanical representation of changes
- Making 1 to 3 assumptions leads to *Self-Organising Dynamic* models, capable of reconfiguring their spatial and organisational structure.
- Making only assumptions 1 and 2 leads to mathematical models of *evolutionary* processes where the environment, system components and sub-components all co-evolve in a *non-mechanical mutual "learning" process.*

In order to understand the different type of models that are possible consider for example Figure (2). This shows a typical "map" of the possible behaviour described by a system of dynamical equations derived by making assumptions 1, 2, 3 and 4. Such a system would exhibit perfectly determined mechanical behaviour, in which the values of X and Y moved irrevocably to the "attractor" of the "attractor basin" they happen to be in initially. In traditional economic systems, it is assumed that there is a single attractor basin, and a general equilibrium state. However, with non-linear effects there may be multiple attractors, either different point equilibria (multiple equilibria), cyclic or chaotic attractors. However with the smooth average behaviour of all 4 assumptions, the system cannot ever "cross" over to a new attractor basin, unless it is pushed by external action. However, if assumption 4 is not made, and the reality of local fluctuations and variability are allowed into the description then the system of equations can spontaneously jump from one basin of attraction to another. It can therefore exhibit a range of different possible regimes and structures that may be seen as adaptive if the parameters of the situation and interactions (environment, technology, infrastructure etc.) are changing. However, in such a model, the interacting firms and actors do not change their parameters as a result of their experiences and no "learning" occurs. An improved model would therefore not make assumptions 3 and 4, leading to an evolutionary dynamic spatial model, driven by endogenous changes within the system and within the firms in interaction. The innovation and differential success that is encountered leads to selection and learning, and therefore to increasing productivity in some locations for some firms. This in turn leads to evolving patterns of investment, of employment, of consumption and of transport flows, and provides a "complete" model of the development of the economic system. The "map" of attractors would itself be changing as the system evolved.

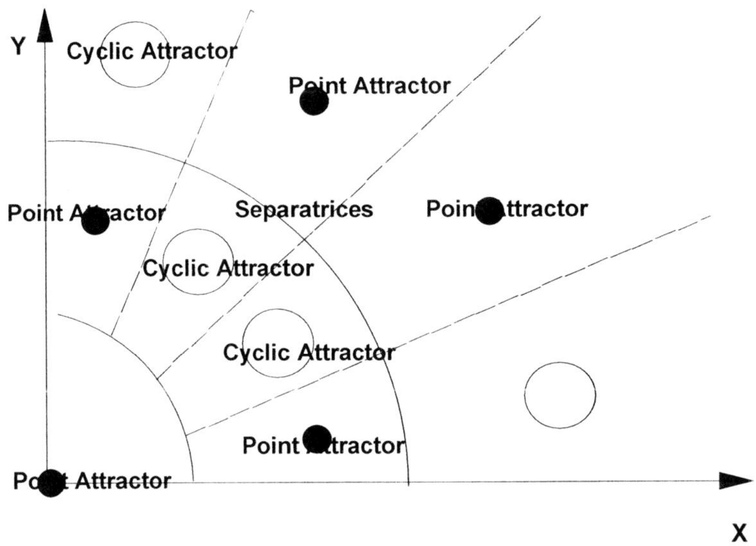

Figure (2). The different attractors (regimes of behaviour) for a particular set of dynamic equations. Such a picture would result from making assumptions 1, 2 and 3.

The crucial difference that marks out evolutionary (complex) systems concerns assumption 3. This assumes that all firms of a given type, x say, are either identical, equal to the average *type,* or have a diversity that remains normally distributed around the average type. This means that for such models "sectors" or statistical aggregates of "firms" are used as variables reflecting the "average properties" of the included firms. But in reality, the micro-diversity of behaviours among individual firms in any particular part of the system is the *result of the history of local dynamics* occurring in the system. This local history concerns the local mechanisms by which knowledge, skills, techniques and heuristics are passed on to new individuals over time. The existence of micro-diversity will necessarily lead to an evolutionary learning process of economic development. If there are firms with higher and lower productivity then the higher ones will be gradually amplified, while those with lower productivity are suppressed, and the "average" for the whole population of firms increases productivity. (Allen and McGlade, 1987, and Brunner 1994). This is the mechanism by which adaptation takes place. This demonstrates the *vital* part played by *exploratory, non-average behaviour*, and shows that, in the long term, evolution selects for firms with the ability to learn, rather than for populations with optimal, but fixed, behaviour. Economic transformation therefore should really be modelled by these fully evolutionary models. However, in this paper we shall present models that discuss separately the effects of changes in productivity of firms, and that consider the spatial processes of development using an "aggregate" exogenous increase in "sector" productivity.

3 The Co-evolution of Regional Dynamics and Geographic Attractiveness

From the view of spatial structure, variables in the modelling framework are disaggregated into those of different regions and sectors. The spatial structure that exists is generated by the interactions among regions and sectors. The interactions in spatial structure strengthen their non-linearities and feedback features. Therefore, the spatial structure of the system is not taken as being fixed necessarily, but instead as being the result of an ongoing evolutionary process. Most importantly, it introduces three behaviours through the use of 'attractiveness' which are the demand attractiveness, migration attractiveness and investment attractiveness. These are the mechanisms by which small differences in price, incentives and productivity can be amplified through self-reinforcing processes, eventually leading to a spatial re-structuring of the system. Economic incentives and investment attractiveness create the opportunity of employment, increase the vacancies and raise labour productivity, leading to increases in employment levels and wages. The improved income earning opportunity will alter relative economic conditions among the regions and increase migration of the workforce, which in turn will alter relative investment behaviour of sectors.

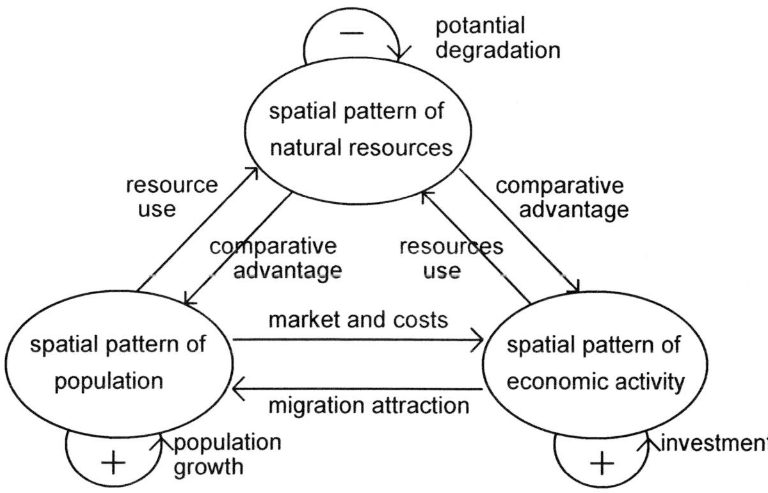

Figure (3). Basic modelling framework

One of notable characteristics of the modelling framework is that the economic model in it is built by an interregional input-output analysis, which is simply based on an input-output matrix. Most of economic variables, such as demand and supply, import and export, savings and consumption, depreciation, costs, wages and profits, link directly with the interregional input-output system, which differs from the conventional one. The flow equations of input and output are calculated in the simulation model. The flows of inputs from different sectors and regions per unit of time are converted by a productive sector and a distributive process into flows of outputs to different sectors and regions. In this complex converting process, the price of unit goods and services for different sectors and regions vary over the time according to difference between demands and supplies for different sectors and regions which will cause changes of productive costs, profit, investments and the spatial economic structure. It is obvious since the economic sectors of different regions are not generally the same there is a constant tendency to instability mediated by market mechanisms (mainly prices). So, this interregional input-output table which is suggested here establishes the relationship between the whole economy, regional/sector economy and local decision making process, that is the relationship between 'macro' economic behaviour and 'micro' economic structure.

3.1 Demand and Supply

Suppose the economic systems under consideration are split into regions (1, 2, 3 ...*i*, *j* ...*n*) and sectors (1, 2, 3 ...*l*, ...*m*). The core model describes the economic activities on the level of these sectors and regions. For every sector and every region, there is a similar set of variables in it.

It is useful to describe the model in detail by starting off with the notion of 'attractiveness' that is used to define conditions under which economic agents (for example, consumers, producers, investors) will be induced to alter their behaviour in specific ways. What factors will influence the demand behaviour of consumers in region j with respect to purchases of goods l from all regions i=1, 2, 3 ...n? We then define the attractiveness of goods and services produced in i and abroad from the standpoint of consumers in j as:

$$A^l_{ij} = \exp(-\rho \times (p^l_i + ts^l \times d_{ij})) \tag{1}$$

$$extA^l_j = \exp(-\rho \times p^l_{jw}) \tag{2}$$

where ρ represents a response rationality parameter, p^l_i = price of sector l in region i, $ts^l \times d_{ij}$ = unit transport costs for a unit of l between i and j, p^l_{iw} =world price of l including transport costs, $extA^l_j$ is the attractiveness of goods produced from abroad for the consumer j.

In order to find the relative attractiveness, we must now sum over all the potential sources of goods l for the consumer j, to give:

$$SA^l_j = \sum_i A^l_{ij} + extA^l_j \tag{3}$$

so that relative attractiveness is given by A^l_{ij} / SA^l_j and determines the proportion of the interregional demand for goods l that falls on region i, where SA^l_j= total economic attractiveness of for goods l for the consumer j.

The improved partial demand is calculated as a sum of three terms:

$$D^l_{ij} = \left| \frac{\Phi^l}{\sum_k \Phi^k} \times Wh_j + \frac{\Psi^l}{\sum_k \Psi^k} \times I_j + \sum_k x_{kl} \times J^k_j \times Py^k_j \times (P^l_i + ts^l \times d_{ij}) \right| \times \frac{A^l_{ij}}{SA^l_j} \tag{4}$$

where the intersector demand in j is given by :

$$SD_j^l = \sum_k x_{kl} \times J_j^k \times Py_j^k \tag{5}$$

where element x_{kl} of $m \times m$ input-output matrix X is defined as intersector demand for lower cost product l in order to produce unit product k of higher quality, J_j^k= employment for sector k in region j, Py_j^k= productivity for sector k in region j which is described by the following expression:

$$Py_j^k = Py_j^k * \{(1 + al(k) * t) + (1 + be(k) * J_j^k)\} \tag{6}$$

where al(k) and be(k) are the coefficients of productivity growth for sector k over time, and with concentration respectively.

The formula (4) is the partial demand D_{ij}^l for goods l falling on region i and generated by other region j (including i). The first term is the final consumption falling on l . This is a product of proportional function Φ and wealth Wh_j in region j. The second term is the investment falling on i which is a product of proportional function Ψ , and investment I_j in region j. The third term is the intersector demand falling on i from j.

Total demand falling on sector l and region i will then consist of partial demands falling on i from all region j and external demand from overseas (export):

$$D_i^l = Ext_i^l + \sum_j D_{ij}^l \tag{7}$$

where Ext_i^l= export or demand of abroad in region i for goods l.

We are now in a position to compare total demand falling on i (in sector l) with total supply of goods l in i. This is given by:

$$S_i^l = p_i^l \times J_i^l \times Py_i^l \tag{8}$$

It is now possible to model the change in economic activity that will result from any disequilibrium between supply and demand in terms of a rate of desired expansion and a rate of price change:

$$\frac{\partial p_i^l}{\partial t} = \eta^l \times p_i^l \left(\frac{D_i^l}{S_i^l} - 1\right) \tag{9}$$

where η^l = a rate per year of price change comparing supply and demand.

3.2 Costs, Profit and Income

The cost of per ton of goods from sector l in region i is calculated as the sum of three terms:

$$c_i^l = \sum_k \sum_j x_{lk} \times (p_j^k + ts^k \times d_{ij}) \times \frac{A_{ji}^k}{SA_i^k} + \frac{W_i^l + R_i^l + De_i^l}{Py_i^l} + \sum_k x_{lk} \times p_{jw}^l P_i^k \times \frac{extA_i^k}{SA_i^k} \tag{10}$$

where W_i^l = wages paid for sector l and region i, R_i^l =rent per job for sector l and region i, De_i^l = depreciation for sector l and region i. The first term is an expression of the unit production costs involved in the necessary base products k from the all region j. The second term is an expression of unit costs of wages, rent and depreciation in sector l and zone i. The third term is unit production costs of foreign exchange of the necessary base product k.

So, obviously, the profit is obtained by subtracting the total costs from the total revenue:

$$\pi_i^l = (p_i^l - c_i^l) \times J_i^l \times Py_i^l \tag{11}$$

Income are of two kinds, wages and rents for each of the zones which is calculated as a function of total wages earned by the labour force, plus the earnings obtained from renting space to each of the economic sectors in that region. That is, total disposable income in any zone are thus given by:

$$\mathrm{Y}_i = \sum_l J_i^l \times (W_i^l + R_i^l) \tag{12}$$

where wages are given by:

$$\frac{\partial W_i^l}{\partial t} = \gamma^l \times W_i^l \times \left(\frac{V_i^l}{J_i^l} - \theta^l\right) \tag{13}$$

where V_i^l = the vacancies (potential new jobs) for sector l in region i, γ= a change rate per year proportionally to itself and the excess of vacancies to jobs, θ= parameter of sensitivity of the wages to the job market.

Wages then determine regional income as described above, thus feeding back into the model and allowing it to continue to run. The end result is that the model generates continuous temporal data on economic output, jobs, land use and population.

3.3 Attractiveness of Investment

The investment is a complex decision-making, which involves many kinds of factors, such as limitation of land, benefit of investment, demand, labour market, profit of economic sector, scale of economic sector and so on. The dynamics of investment is one of the most important economic process. So, the attraction functions of investment have been added into the core model.

We define and compute the attractiveness of investment in the sector and region according to the profit as well as the limitation of land, that is, available land. Of course, many more factors can be added into the attractiveness. Simply, only two factors are considered here. The more the occupation of land or the less the available land, the less the attractiveness of investment. The greater the expectation of profits the greater the attractiveness of investment. So, the sector and regional attractiveness of investment are described as follow:

$$IA_i^l = \exp(\mu^1 \times (1 - \frac{space^l \times J_i^l}{area_i^l}) + \mu^2 \times (1 - \frac{p_i^l - c_i^l}{p_i^l})) \quad (14)$$

where $1 - \frac{space^l \times J_i^l}{area_i^l}$ is a proportion of available land for sector l in region i, $1 - \frac{p_i^l - c_i^l}{p_i^l}$ is a relative unit profit for sector l in region i, μ^1, μ^2 are the parameters of importance related to investment which weigh up profit against land.

In order to find the relative attractiveness of investment, we must now sum over all the potential attraction, to give:

$$IA_i = \sum_l IA_i^l \quad (15)$$

$$IA = \sum_i \sum_l IA_i^l \quad (16)$$

so that relative attractiveness of national investment is given by IA_i^l / IA, relative attractiveness of regional investment is given by IA_i^l / IA_i. Furthermore, we have investment for sector l and region i:

$$I_i^l = I \times \frac{IA_i^l}{IA} + I_i \times \frac{IA_i^l}{IA_i} \quad (17)$$

where I= total available national investment for the all sectors and regions, I_i= total available regional investment for the all sectors in that region.

The capital accumulation is obtained by:

$$\frac{\partial K_i^l}{\partial t} = I_i^l - De_i^l \quad (18)$$

3.4 Labour and Migration

In the model there is an important question: how much profit creates how many new jobs, and how many new jobs cause how much migration between regions? The model calculates the number of new jobs in each region according to how well its sectors are, generating profits per unit of output and how much its sectors are attracting investment from nation and region. At this stage, we are able to generate an expansion or contraction of the jobs that could potentially be filled. When the profit is positive, the investment will increase, so the vacancies will grow. When the profit is negative, the investment will fall, so the vacancies will decline. The modified equation relates changes in vacancies as a function of relative investment and past trends in the labour market. The equations should be distinguished from different cases of profit and vacancy.

When the profits are positive and the vacancies are also positive, the equations of jobs and vacancies should be:

$$\frac{\partial J_i^l}{\partial t} = \sigma^l \times V_i^l \times \frac{Ue_i}{\sum_k J_i^k} \text{ and } \frac{\partial V_i^l}{\partial t} = \frac{I_i^l}{\upsilon(Py_i^l)} - \sigma^l \times V_i^l \times \frac{Ue_i}{\sum_k J_i^k} \tag{19}$$

When the profits are positive and the vacancies are negative, a wise decision-maker should stop dismissing employees. On the contrary, when the profits are negative and the vacancies are positive, he should stop increasing employees. So, the equations should be:

$$\frac{\partial J_i^l}{\partial t} = 0 \text{ and } \frac{\partial V_i^l}{\partial t} = \frac{I_i^l}{\upsilon(Py_i^l)} \tag{20}$$

When the profits are negative and the vacancies are also negative, then the equations should be:

$$\frac{\partial J_i^l}{\partial t} = \alpha^l \times V_i^l \text{ and } \frac{\partial V_i^l}{\partial t} = \frac{I_i^l}{(Py_i^l)} - \alpha^l \times V_i^l \tag{21}$$

where σ, α = the change rate per year of vacancy, Ue_i = the number of unemployment, so $\frac{Ue_i}{\sum_k J_i^k}$ is a proportion unemployment to employment, producing the pressure on the labour market, $\upsilon(Py_i^l)$ = the capital per job as a function of productivity for sector l in region i.

The model then calculates a term called 'residential attractiveness', which reflects the relative attractiveness of each region to potential migrants from other regions. This is calculated as a function of the average wages earned in a region relative to the average wages earned in all other regions. Of course, the actual problem of migration could be quite complicated and involve many factors, but it is not difficult to add them into the equations.

$$RA_i = \exp(\lambda_i \times \frac{\sum_l W_i^l \times J_i^l}{\sum_l J_i^l}) \tag{22}$$

where λ_i represents a response rationality parameter, $\frac{\sum_l W_i^l \times J_i^l}{\sum_l J_i^l}$ = the average wages in region i, the relative residential attractiveness is $RA_i / \sum_i RA_i$.

4 Changing Productivity and the Evolutionary Process

The modelling framework set out above has been used in several examples (see Allen, 1997). However, the models are written in terms of "sectors" of activity, and only approximately located in spatial zones. The real situation is that within a zone, a "sector" is really made up of constituent firms, and these are located at specific locations within any zone. Furthermore, what is important for economic development is the change in productivity of these firms, that leads to greater competitiveness and to economic development and local specialisation. The issue of how the changes in productivity of firms can be treated properly within such dynamic spatial models has been addressed by Brunner (1994).

4.1 Technology Diffusion for Productivity Change in Firm Populations

An industry or economic sector k in region j (or i) is composed of a population of firms

$$q_j^{fk}(t) \in \{1,....,F\}, f = \{1,...,F\}$$

where each firm operates at time t at a distinct (that is non-average) level of technological productivity.

In taking equation (6) and writing on a firm level we get

$$Py_j^{fk} = Py_j^{fk} * \{(1 + al(k) * t) + (1 + be(k) * J_j^{fk}) + (1 + \text{var}(q_j^k) * ce(k) * q_j^k)\} \tag{23}$$

where ce(k) is the coefficient of sector concentration k over time. Firm productivity is influenced by the conditions of competition, expressed as a concentration index. Sector concentration changes over time, as the population of firms q_j^{fk} changes. The firm population changes over time with the difference between entry rate, and the exit rate. Both rates are dependent on the stock of firms at time t in a manner to be specified. This dependence is expressed by the *replication* coefficient ($A0_k$ - $B0_k$), A0 being the 'intrinsic' entry rate and B0 being the 'intrinsic' exit rate for a firm population k. Entry and exit rates are however nonlinearly dependent on the maturity or life cycle of an industry (Agarwal and Gort, 1996). In a new industry a large number of firms will enter at rate A1, attracted by high expected appropriation benefits from new technology. Increasing competition leads to a decline of appropriation. Relative fewer firms enter, a kind of *learning* effect. Entry exhibits thus a density dependence, when 'constrained' rate A1 increases first with the population and then decreases at a rate commensurate with the level of competition. Exit rates are low for a small industry population, but are rising rapidly with competition. *Self-inhibition* of population growth takes place at 'constrained' rate B1.

For now we can express the relationship between population stock and growth in a simple differential equation for the net birth rate

$$\bar{b} = \left(A0_k - B0_k\right) q_j^k(t) + \left(A1_k - B1_k\right) q_j^k(t)^2 \tag{24}$$

Population change relates to the net birth rate, is however subject to "carrying capacity" $q_i^{k'}$ based on either density of firms in the market, or density of firms of a sector in a region.

$$\frac{dq_i^k}{dt} = \sigma\left(q_i^{k'} - q_i^k\right) + \bar{b}q_i^k \tag{25}$$

where σ represents the speed of adjustment. Carrying capacity itself is determined over time by changes in the possibilities of employment, and productivities as they change.

A selection process sets in to amplify technologically and geographically successful firms and to induce exit of insufficiently successful ones. Most importantly the average sector rate of productivity change as expressed in (23) depends on the variance of all sector firms' productivity levels around the mean. The variance is

$$\operatorname{var} q_i^k = \int \left(Py_j^k - \mu_j^k\right)^2 f\left(Py_j^k\right) dPy_j^k \tag{26}$$

where $f\left(Py_j^k\right)$ is the density of an exponentially distributed random variable Py_j^k and μ its mean.

4.2 Trade in Economic-Technical and Geographic Space

The deficient representation of technological change distinguishes traditional and new trade theory from an evolutionary one. Technological change involves firm interaction, feedback and learning. Although some more elaborate new trade theory models include positive feedback (externalities) and learning economies, they generally assume homogeneity of technology on a sector level. Bounded rationality leads firms onto different technology trajectories. Technology is both costly and time consuming to acquire, and firms differ in their ability to do so. A firm's technological ability, or its capability to appropriate technological information from its competitive environment, has to be a function of its technological history. A satisfactory representation of technological change also has to include elements of serendipity, in a world where new technologies' creation is highly uncertain.

Markovian diffusion models can explain the technology transition of firms from one state of technological productivity to another. Spatial interaction implies that firm transition probabilities also depend on the number of actors in each state, as in interactive Markov chain models (John Conlisk, 1992). Brunner's (1994) model is based on Markovian technology diffusion processes among a population of firms.

The result of selective amplification is recognizable macroeconomic and spatial features, such as a tendency of a clustering of firms or other economic actors in economic-technical and geographic space to benefit from each other. Firms can save from proximity by exchanging ideas through people and employees, saving transport and communication costs. By building close supplier networks firms mutually increase their productivity. Such agglomerations can also be based on interregional and international trade and can also be accomplished by physical and institutional transport arrangements that enable the movement of people and goods in geography. Allen, Engelen and Sanglier (1986) have developed spatial dynamic models that simultaneously analyse the location determinants of populations (of firms), where populations interact and compete with each other via space constraints.

Trade flows emerge from cross-country differences in technology populations either in the price of a given performance in the same technology characteristic (e.g. intra-industry trade, such a as the import and export of telecommunications service) or because such differences exist for one industry characteristic that constitutes an input to other ones (inter-industry trade, such as relatively better computers that are exported from one country to the one that supplies telecommunication services). Shifts in trade flows in the full model[3] are determined by relative technological change (an indication of competitiveness) in *two* (or more) distinct *country* firm populations f and, f* in sector k, producing the same heterogeneous product at different productivity levels. Firms now compete for output and market shares in the "world market." The world market is divided into "domestic" markets and "foreign" markets. The domestic markets' size is Y_{ik}, and Yj_k for the two firm populations in their respective domestic markets. Each firm's output is:

$$y_i^{fk} = MS_i^{fk} Y_{ik} + ES_i^{fk} Y_{jk} \tag{27}$$

where MS_i^{fk} represents the domestic market share of firm f, and is ES_i^{fk} the export share of firm f from population i to all non-domestic markets. The total size of the domestic market is then the sum of all outputs over all firms f, minus their exports, plus their imports. The world market is simply the sum of all domestic markets.

A firm's change in output is not only related to the growth of the total market, but more importantly to the change of its market share, which now includes shares of the domestic and foreign markets. A change in the firm's domestic share MS_i^{fk} depends on its relative technological advance τ, related to sector average advance μ. A change in a firm's share in export markets ES_i^{fk} depends on the technological competitiveness $\tau *$ of the exporter relative to its competitors.[4]

$$\frac{dES_i^{fk}}{dt} = \tau * ES_i^{fk} \tag{28}$$

and

$$\tau * = \frac{\dfrac{dPy_i^{fk}(t)}{dt}}{\dfrac{dPy_i^{fk}(t)}{dt} + \dfrac{d\mu_j(t)}{dt}}; \qquad 0 \leq \tau * \leq 1 \tag{29}$$

5 The Example of East German Transformation: Evolutionary Trade

Recent evolutionary trade theory as outlined in section 4, establishes causal links from productivity gains to export success on a sector level. Neo-Schumpeterian theories see a restructuring and catching-up process of transition economies as intricately linked with the dynamics of technological change -- an advantageous dynamic process that is deemed to be promoted in a favorable sector and regional environment. Firms are the key actors in that process, whereas firms' external institutional and macroeconomic factors determine their abilities and opportunity for fostering technological change. The firms' international competitiveness stemming from technological change is in the medium- and long-run reflected in export (and import) shares of goods and services. A change in the sector structure and volume of goods trade is indicative of the success of the transformation process and the speed of the catching-up process. Trade structure and volume change analysis gives insight into the fundamental nature of East Germany's rapid transformation.

The evolutionary trade model suggests that the average changes in the relative technological capabilities of each country in each sector are a powerful determinant of export share changes of that same country in that sector on the world market. Following Amendola et al. (1993), the model could be tested by form of the following simple relationship

$$dES_i^k = f\left(\frac{\overline{dT_i^k}}{T_i^*}\right) \tag{30}$$

---

[3] An early, yet to be improved simulation version of the complete model is available with the author. The preliminary results show that growth and trade shares are higher for firms in sector populations that exhibit the highest level of average technological and competitiveness advance.

[4] For rare simulation models which use features of such relative firm competitiveness see Dosi and Freeman, 1992, p. 34; also Kwasnicki and Kwasnicka, 1992, p. 353-54.

where dES_i^k is the changing export share of country 'i' in sector k and $dT_i^k / \overline{dT_i^*}$ is a proxy for the change in technological capability of 'i' in k relative to an average change in capabilities of all *other* countries' sector k. Such a specification suggests that the technology factor dominates when proxies for different cost and wage levels or short-term swings in the exchange rates are accounted for. The model includes cost and wage differences by using price per unit of quality performance as a measure for technological capability.

One crucial aspect of an evolutionary trade model that cannot be neglected in the empirical specification is the population dynamics linking capability with market structure developments. Thus the technological change variable needs to be partitioned into a proxy for sector technology advance dP_y and one for firm population change dQ.

The specified model contains positive feedback elements with ES and output Y feeding on itself. Such a cumulative mechanism[5] can be considered in the econometric specification by an autoregressive structure in the dependent variable ES (Amendola et al. 1993). Accounting also for technology and population change, a general autoregressive-distributed lag can be derived.

$$ES_{it}^k = \sum_{l=1}^{f} \alpha_l ES_i^k(t-l) + \sum_{l=1}^{g} \beta_l \frac{Py_i^k(t-l)}{Py_i^k(t-l) + \overline{Py_i}(t-l)} + \sum_{l=0}^{k} \gamma Q_i^k(t-l) + \lambda_i^k + e_{it} \quad (31)$$

where Py (technological capability) and Q (turbulence and resulting change in concentration) are weakly exogenous variables, Py expressed as a ratio of one country's sector with respect to the average for all countries; λ stands for product-group-fixed effects such as sector characteristics as in Murrell (1990); and e is a random residual.

The independent variable Py, interpreted as measure of technological capability (TEC) in the regression that follows, is constructed here by comparing the home country's export unit values with the export unit values of OECD countries that are likely to represent world class technology in their exports. The best available price-performance ratio to compare the former GDR's before and after transition technology gap with the West and any changes in the gap, is the "kilogram-price" (Aiginger 1997, p.78). Such price can be calculated from trade data on the total quantity of a product category exported to 23 OECD countries and the total revenue thereby achieved.[6] Although factors other than technological sophistication determine these

[5] Empirically confirmed by Clerides, Lach and Tybout (1998).

[6] Because East European data is unreliable, before and after the transition process began in 1989, I have used mirror statistics for East Germany's OECD exports until 1989. Exports exclusively to OECD countries are used as a best quality indicator for technology capacity, thus excluding any vagaries that are associated with trade direction and data reliability before and after unification and result from exports into former CMEA and developing country markets. Moreover, until 1990, the 'inner-German' trade was a significant part of East Germany's hard currency exports. This is also reflected in the strong western orientation of GDR trade, with 57.4 percent in 1990. Only Hungary had a similarly intensive western orientation of its exports (Landesmann and Szekely, table 2.3). Since 1989, because of the German unification, East German trade can no longer be traced with mirror statistics since all OECD figures apply to the whole of Germany. Therefore, after 1991 East German analysis has to rely on the regional statistics of the German statistical office (Statistisches Bundesamt), which are put together by the regional statistical offices (Statistische Landesämter). Of course, there is no 'inner-German' trade to be recorded after 1989. In this study, I exclude the 'inner-German' trade before unification throughout the analysis to ensure comparability of results from before and after 1989. Trade data is continuous until 1995, when the industrial classification system was changed. The paper employs the time series including the data up to 1994.

prices, they reflect better technology in higher revenues. To calculate a proxy for the technology gap, the ratio of East German OECD exports has to be compared to a world standard, which I presume is established by the same 23 OECD countries' export unit values in the comparable product categories. The indicative ratio also improves with the homogeneity of the product groups for which they are calculated (Bentley, 1991). For example this work compares East Germany's 2-digit industry export unit values to a composite 2-digit unit value of 22 OECD countries' exports to the United States, Sweden and Switzerland. Three countries were chosen because in combination they represent very well overall OECD patterns of exports in sectors that are relevant for East Germany. The comparison is made in the same currency, US dollars.[7] The measure focuses solely on traded goods exports and excludes the unit value of non-tradeables. Relative changes in unit values of actually exported goods of a certain sector indicate changes in underlying product quality and technology. In competitive OECD export markets, higher prices reflected in unit values can be fetched only with a corresponding increase in product quality, reflecting technological change.

The following pooled (GLS cross section weight) regression examines the relationships between the dependent variable export share (ES), the lagged ES(-1), the independent variable technology level relative to OECD world standard (TEC), the Herfindahl index as all Germany's concentration and competition measure (H), and the product group dummies standing for MNC dominated (DUMNC), entry-sensitive (DUMEN), and Heckscher Ohlin goods sectors (DUMHO). Another dummy (DUMUNI91) was added to account for the first post-unification year, where export levels and shares are still strongly determined by GDR patterns, but dropped as it did not prove significant. The regression was first run with several other variables included: a transformed investment share by sector, a dummy for high-tech, and Ricardo goods, all of which where dropped as they were insignificant. The results of the analysis of the relationship among the remaining variables, shown in Table1, are both significant and surprising.

The results support the evolutionary theory of trade. East German export patterns after unification are determined by historical factors, as the significance of the lagged export shares shows. Technology as proxied in rising price performance ratios relative to world standards is a significant determinant of export share growth. Technology is indeed an East German engine of growth. There is thus evidence that East Germany has hesitantly moved towards a pattern of trade that increases the level of technology incorporated into goods.[8]

Industry concentration shows the theoretically right sign, with higher concentration leading to lower export share growth. Trade patterns reveal also an emphasis on sectors in which multinationals play a determining role, and a de-emphasis on sectors that are susceptible to entry pressure. Here the unique conditions of German unification come into play. The rapid adjustment from a closed economy to a completely open one was

[7] This study uses trade data at the 2-digit levels of the UN Standard International Trade Classification (SITC, Rev. 3). The raw trade data are all expressed in US dollars, using the exchange rates employed by the United Nations. Following Amendola et al. (1993), exports are considered in current value, so market shares are influenced by price movements. This specification is consistent with the notion of international competitiveness.

[8] The robustness of these results was tested, by eliminating TEC, and then running the regression with the transformed independent variable ITrans. The transformation was achieved through standardization of investment share by sector output, 1991-94. The result did not change significantly, with all independent variables continuing to show the same signs, yet ITrans remained insignificant with a negative sign.

accompanied by large, subsidized investment by western MNCs into the East. They brought management know-how, technology, and very important supply and marketing networks with them. Many supplier sectors with easy entry thus may have very quickly supplanted those firms in the east that were suppliers to former conglomerates bought in part by the investing MNCs.

Table 1: Results

Method: GLS (Cross Section Weights)
Dependent variable: Export Shares
Sample: 1991 1994
Included observations: 4
Total panel observations 56
Cross sections without valid observations dropped

Variable	Coefficient	Std. Error	t-Statistic	Prob.
C	0.034377	0.006630	5.184952	0.0000
H	-9.28E-05	5.15E-05	-1.802699	0.0776
TEC	0.025069	0.009364	2.677117	0.0101
ES(-1)	0.539963	0.086882	6.214930	0.0000
DUMEN	-0.021983	0.006896	-3.187802	0.0025
DUMNC	0.024043	0.007742	3.105686	0.0032
DUMHO	-0.016706	0.008335	-2.004381	0.0506

Weighted Statistics

R-squared	0.702673	Mean dependent var	0.078589
Adjusted R-squared	0.666265	S.D. dependent var	0.038245
S.E. of regression	0.022094	Sum squared resid.	0.023919
F-statistic	19.30025	Durbin-Watson stat	1.924463
Prob(F-statistic)	0.000000		

Unweighted Statistics

R-squared	0.748124	Mean dependent var	0.070357
Adjusted R-squared	0.717282	S.D. dependent var	0.045566
S.E. of regression	0.024228	Sum squared resid	0.028762
Durbin-Watson stat	1.654117		

From a neo-Schumpeterian and evolutionary theory point of view, trade flows are determined by relative technological change ("competitiveness"). They are also determined by changes in industry structure. Export shares tend to be significantly higher in sectors where East Germany has been historically strong, i.e., Meissen porcelain under miscellaneous manufactured goods, optics, or precision instruments. However contrary to the model predictions, sectors determined by high entry tend to have slower than standard export exposure in the East German case. Industry concentration tends to be negatively correlated to export success, but the prevalence of multinationals seems to induce extra export through their international access to market networks. MNC investment was an important driver of technology-induced export shares, i.e., in chemicals and road vehicles.

6 Conclusions on the Applicability and Practicability of Spatial Modelling to Transport, International Trade, and Investment in Regions

The paper has attempted to bring together the necessary parts to link the co-evolution and competition of firms at the micro level to the changing local economy and productivity, as an integrated set of processes that create the emergent macro-level spatial structure that characterizes the constituent zones of a region. In this way it provides the possibility of a policy support tool that can explore the complex consequences over time of particular policies or investments in such things as transport infrastructure. Underlying this, the sections devoted to the co-evolution of firms demonstrates how this leads to changing productivity of firms in the particular zone, and drives the competitiveness and attractiveness of the zone for investment. This results in "sector" change, which is then an aggregate figure, reflecting the internal dynamic. In the East German example the consequences of creative destruction at the micro level become apparent as sector change. One consequence is the relative increase in export unit values indicating greater export competitiveness as a result of changing productivity of firms. The empirical specification in the case of East German transformation reflects the model's population dynamics as well as the positive feedback elements apparent in the two model sections. Population dynamics and the non-linear feedback elements are essential for an evolutionary trade model. A "complete evolutionary" model would generate this from the behaviour of co-evolving firms.

However, despite these shortcomings the method already provides some basis for a poverty impact assessment. In addition, it provides a basis for an overall long-term assessment of the working of the economic spatial multipliers in the system, offering a basis for the policy and investment analysis that must precede any such large action. Changing patterns of traffic, of fuel consumption and of external trade could be explored on a coherent basis as issues connected with sustainable development were considered.

The complete model would link industrial and innovation policies to investments in infrastructure, allowing an improved integration and projection of possible futures. Also, the inclusion of migration models as part of the dynamic processes, it is possible to explore in a concerted way the changing spatial patterns of needs for services that accompany any particular evolutionary trajectory.

Symbols

Geography and space:

Sector k, l
Regions i, j
d_{ij} for distance matrix
w for World

Attractivities:
A for attractivity
SA for total economic attractivity

Economics
p for price (per quality unit)
r for resource endowment
c for total cost
fc for fixed cost
ts for transport costs
π for profit
q for producer population
x for input-output matrix
Py for productivity
De for depreciation
W for wages

λ, ρ for response rationality parameter
ω for input coefficients
υ for labor productivity
α, σ for speed of adjustment from actual to potential
τ for relative technological export competitiveness
b bar for net birth rate.
ES for export share
MS for market share
Φ for proportional function

ExtA for external attractivity
IA for regional attractivity
RA for residential attractivity of migration

K for capital
R for rent
Y for income
C for consumption
I for investment
J for employment
V for vacancies (new jobs)
Ue for unemployment
D for demand
S for supply
Ext for export demand
Q for turbulence

Ψ for proportional function
η for marginal rate of price change
γ for change rate in the job market
Θ for wage elasticity
μ for mean
al (k) for coefficient of productivity growth
be (k) for concentration coefficient
ce (k) for coefficient of sector concentration

References

Agarwal, Rajshree and Michael Gort. 1996. "The Evolution of Markets and Entry, Exit and Survival of Firms," *Rev. of Economics and Statistics*, **78** no.3, pp. 489-97.

Aiginger, Karl. 1997. "Unit values to signal the quality position of CEECs." In *The Competitiveness of Transition Countries*, Y. Wolfmayr-Schnitzer et al. (eds.), Vienna: WIFO.

Allen, Peter. 1998. "Selbstorganisation", in: *Modelling Complex Economic Evolution*, F. Scheiter and G. Silverberg (eds.), Berlin: Duncker and Humblot.

Allen, Peter. 1997. Cities and Regions as Self-Organising Systems: Models of Complexity. Gordon and Breach.

Allen, Peter. 1994. "Evolutionary Complex Systems: Models of Technology Change", in: *Evolutionary Economics and Chaos Theory*, Loet Leydesdorff and Peter Van den Besselaar (eds.), London: Pinter Publishers.

Allen, Peter. 1993. "Evolution: Persistent Ignorance from Continual Learning", in *Nonlinear Dynamics & Evolutionary Economics*, Oxford Univ. Press, Chapter III, 8, pp.101-12.

Allen, Peter. 1988. "Evolution: Why the Whole is greater than the sum of its parts", in: *Ecodynamics*, Wolff, Soeder and Drepper (eds.), Berlin: Springer.

Allen, Peter and J. M. McGlade. 1987. "Evolutionary drive: the effect of microscopic diversity, error making and noise", *Foundation of Physics*, **17** no.7, pp. 723-28.

Allen, Peter, G. Engelen and M. Sanglier. 1986. "Towards a general dynamic model of the spatial evolution of urban and regional systems", in: *Advances in Urban Systems Modelling*, D. Hutchinson (ed.), New York: Plenum Press.

Amendola, Giovanni, Giovanni Dosi and Erasmo Papagni. 1993. "The Dynamics of International Competitiveness." *Review of World Economics* **129**, no. 3, pp. 451-71.

Anas, Alex, Richard Arnot and Kenneth Small. 1998. "Urban Spatial Structure," *Journal of Economic Literature*, **36** no.3, pp. 1426-64.

Bentley, Raymond. 1991. Research and Technology in the former German Democratic Republic. Boulder, CO: Westview Press.

Brunner, Hans-Peter. 2001. "East German international trade during transition as reflection of the dynamics of competitiveness", *Eastern Economic Journal*, **27** no.3 (Summer), pp. 287-308.

Brunner, Hans-Peter. 1994. "Technological Diversity, Random Selection in a Population of Firms, and Technological Institutions of Government." In *Evolutionary Economics and Chaos Theory*, Loet Leydesdorff and Peter Van den Besselaar (eds.), London: Pinter Publishers.

Caballero, Ricardo J. and Mohamad L. Hammour. 2000. "Creative Destruction and Development: Insitutions, Crises, and Restructuring," MIT Working Paper, August.

Chen, Hsin-Ping. 1996. "The simulation of a proposed nonlinear dynamic urban growth model," *Annals of Regional Science*, **30**, pp. 305-19.

Clerides, Sofronis, Saul Lach and James Tybout. 1998. "Is 'Learning-by-exporting' important?" *Quarterly Journal of Economics* ,**113**, no.3, pp. 903-47.

Conlisk, John. 1992. "Stability and Monotonicity for Interactive Markov Chains," *J. Math. Sociology*, **17**, nos. 2-3, pp. 127-43.

Dixit, Avinash and Joseph Stiglitz. 1976. "Monopolistic Competition and Optimum Product Diversity," *American Economic Review*, **67** no. 3, pp. 297-308.

Dosi, Giovanni and Christopher Freeman. 1992. "The diversity of development patterns: On the processes of catching-up, forging ahead and falling behind." Paper prepared for the International Economic Association Meeting, Varenna, Italy, Oct. 1-3.

Fujita, Masahisa, Paul Krugman and Anthony Venables. 1999. The Spatial Economy. Cambridge, MA: MIT Press.

Grossman, Gene and Elhanan Helpman. 1991a. "Quality ladders in the theory of growth," *Review of Economic Studies*, **59**, pp. 43-61.

Grossman, Gene and Elhanan Helpman. 1991b. "Quality ladders and product cycles," *Quarterly Journal of Economics*, **108**, pp. 557-86.

Kornai, Janos. 2000. "Ten Years after 'The Road to a Free Economy': The Author's Self-Evaluation," Paper for the World Bank 'Annual Bank Conference on Development Economics - ABCDE', Washington, April.

Kwasnicki, Witold and Halina Kwasnicka. 1992. "Market, innovation, competition -- An evolutionary model of industrial dynamics." *Journal of Economic Behavior and Organization* **19**, no. 3, pp. 343-68.

Landesmann, Michael and Istvan Szekely. 1995. "Industrial structural change in Central and Eastern European economies." In *Industrial Restructuring and Trade Reorientation in Eastern Europe*, Michael Landesmann and Istvan Szekely (eds.), Cambridge: Cambridge Univ. Press.

Murrell, Peter. 1990. The Nature of Socialist Economies. Princeton: Princeton Univ. Press.

Taylor, Scott M. 1993. "Quality ladders and Ricardian trade," *Journal of International Economics*, **34**, pp. 225-43.

In: International Trade Issues
Editor: Robert. V. Weeks, pp. 33-85

ISBN: 1-59454-621-5

Chapter 3

LOCATION OF PRODUCTION: LOCAL VS. GLOBAL GAME[1]

Miroslav N. Jovanović[*2]
UN ECE, Transport Division, Palais des Nations,
1211 Geneva 10, Switzerland

Abstract

Where economic activity will locate in the future is one of the most important questions in economics. Even though advances in technology have reduced the cost of transport, communication and information gathering and processing, hence curtailing the 'distance penalty', local proximity (clusters) of firms that produce similar, competing and/or related products together with supporting institutions still matter. Economies of scale, activity-specific backward and forward linkages (indivisible production), accumulated knowledge and skills, innovation, existence of sophisticated customers and a fall in transportation costs play relevant roles in the 'protection' of clusters and absolute locational advantages of certain locations. 'Global' competitiveness often depends on highly concentrated 'local' knowledge, capabilities and common tacit codes of behaviour which can be found in a geographical concentration (cluster) of firms.

JEL: F15, F23, R12
Keywords: global, local, cluster, linkages, history, lock-in.

Does the eagle mount up at your command,
And make its nest on high?
Job 39:37

---

[1] An earlier version of this chapter was published in the Journal of Economic Integration in 2003.

[*] E-mail address: miroslav.jovanovic@unece.org, (Tel) +41 22 917 2493, (Fax) +41 22 917 0039

[2] Je tiens à remercier tout particulièrement Marinette Payot qui m'a beaucoup aidé sans que je le sache. I have benefited from discussions with and intellectual capital of many friends and colleagues, but I owe special gratitude to Amedeo Amato, Lisa Borgatti, Ron Boschma, Gioacchino Garofoli, Birgit Hegge, Jovan Jovanović, Jong Eun Lee, Antonio Majocchi, Marina Rossi, Bertram Schefold and James Wiltshire. Christopher Smith edited the text. The views expressed are my own and do not reflect the position of the organisation for which I work.

1 Introduction

Where economic activity will locate in the future is one of the most important and challenging questions in economics. Progress in technology, changes in demand and moves towards a liberal economic policy create new challenges for theorists, policymakers and business executives. As a number of economic activities became 'footloose' and highly mobile, one of the most demanding and intricate questions in such a situation is where firms and industries would locate, re-locate or stay.

Any society and each market oriented firm must first refer to the problem of what, for whom, how and where to produce. With this spatial distribution of economic activity in mind, the purpose of this chapter is to contribute to the debate about the 'local' versus the 'global' location of industries and firms. The approach employed is conceptual: the objective is to clarify and explain key tendencies, rather than to provide definite answers to the issue of the influence and consequences between local and global spatial distribution of production.

The spatial location of a firm is an issue only in a situation with market imperfections. Without market imperfections such as distance, transport costs and uneven distribution of natural resources (so that the location matters), there are no problems regarding deciding on the location of production. Without market failures firms may break up into units of any size and operate in any location with no cost disadvantage.

The structure of this chapter is as follows. Following this introduction, part 2 outlines principal theories regarding the location of national and international firms. Part 3 discusses the controversial term and impact of globalisation. Part 4 considers issues linked with the location of firms and industries in specific geographical areas such as clusters. Light is shed on the role of history, chances, accidents and wars in the selection of certain places for the location of production of goods and services. The conclusion is in part 5 that 'global' competitiveness often depends on highly concentrated 'local' knowledge, capabilities and a common tacit code or codes of behaviour which can be found in a spatial concentration (cluster) of firms.

2 Theories of Location

The study of the location of production (spatial economics) has a long, although somehow meagre history (Krugman, 1998, p. 7). In spite of the general interest, there is no consensus in the literature about the factors that influence the location of new businesses. The problem was noted, for example, by Ohlin who wrote that 'the theory of international trade is nothing but *internationale Standortslehre*' (teaching about international location) (Ohlin, 1933, p. 589). In the same vein, Isard wrote that 'location can not be explained without at the same time accounting for trade and trade cannot be explained without the simultaneous determination of locations. ...trade and location are the two sides of the same coin' (Isard, 1956, p. 207).

A country's or a region's level of income and it's structure of production (size, scope and variety of firms and industries) depend on at least two factors. The first includes a country's endowment of primary and derived stock of factors such as land, labour, capital, infrastructure, technology, as well as production, organisation and control skills and competences. The other element is how the country or region interacts with the external environment; in particular, the extent, level and form of its access to the international market for goods, services, capital and knowledge.

The creation of wealth used to depend in the distant past to a large extent on the local availability of natural resources. As the economy evolved, wealth creation started to depend more on physical assets (mainly equipment and finance). Prosperity of the modern economy and competitiveness of output depend not only on the physical, but also and increasingly on intangible assets such as knowledge, information processing, as well as on organisational and control potentials and capabilities.

Abundant natural resources may often be a problem for a country, not a benefit. A discovery of resources attracts gamblers, opportunists and crooks such as Francisco Pizzaro (Latin America), Robert Clive (East India Company) or Cecil Rhodes (South Africa). These resources provoke or contribute to civil wars: Angola, Congo or Nigeria. Elsewhere, abundant oil reserves and exports as is the case in Saudi Arabia, Bahrain or Kuwait keep local wages too high to permit the local development of the manufacturing industry. Foreigners from less well-off countries fill jobs in services in these countries. However, certain countries that are exceptionally poor in natural resources such as Switzerland, Austria or Japan are highly developed and amongst the wealthiest in the world. They base their prosperity on the most important resource: human capital.

Let us now turn to the principal theories of firm location. Realising the arbitrary character of our classification and its limits, we shall first look into the issue of how and where firms and industries locate in space without paying attention to the origin, control and ownership of the firm. Second, the issue of ownership and control is taken into consideration in order to get the full picture.

2.1 National Firm

A starting point in location (spatial) theory and economic geography is the national endowment of primary factors of production. *Adam Smith* and *David Ricardo* referred to the geography of production and spatial economics in an indirect way. A country specialises in the production of a good for which it has an absolute advantage in production. Hence, according to Smith, an *absolute advantage* determines the geographical location of production. Ricardo's argument is similar, but in his model a country specialises in the production of goods for which it has a *comparative advantage* in production. Regarding land, the fertile areas are put into cultivation first, while less productive land enters use only as demand for agricultural goods increases.

The models by Smith and Ricardo depend on constant returns to scale and on the assumption that competitive prices guide spatial resource allocation. Hence, free trade allows countries to gain, because they specialise in production that they carry out comparatively well. Such an assumption is challenged by the view that there are in reality important market distortions such as monopolies, externalities (pollution), controlled prices and rigid wages that do not tell the truth about social costs. As such, they send wrong price signals and may lead to the conclusion that trade liberalisation may make matters even worse! Thus some argued that protectionist policies were required for:

- the security of jobs, as was the case during the 1930s (and not only during this period), or
- the safeguard of infant industries, as during the 1950s, or
- rent shifting in oligopolistic markets, as during 1980s, or
- the safety of the environment, as is currently the case.

In addition to these classical models, in the standard neo-classical *factor endowment* or *Heckscher-Ohlin* model refers to locational fundamentals. The national endowment of factors (land, capital and labour) and their relative proportion decides the location of production. A relatively abundant national factor of production (compared with other factors) determines what a country produces and exports. Conversely, a country will import goods whose production requires factors that are scarce in the national economy. Considering cases of 'localisation' of industry in one or a few countries, Ohlin (1933, p. 133) simply argued that 'it must be shown that costs of production on the basis of existing factor prices are lower than in other countries: certain factors are cheaper here than abroad, which accounts for that condition'. In an empirical study of trade patterns of over a hundred economies, Leamer (1984) confirmed that the factor endowment model can explain these trade patterns rather well. This model elegantly assumes that there are no specific factors and that production functions are identical in all countries. As such, it does not give the answer to the whole issue, for it can not explain intra-industry trade. This type of trade (includes a large part of trade among developed countries) is not based on differences in factor endowments among countries.

The factor endowment model has been one of the two principal single-cause models in dealing with specialisation, trade and spatial location of production. The other approach takes account of differences in *technology, economies of scale* and learning by doing. It was conceived by Krugman (1979; 1980) and later developed and expanded both by him and by a host of others. In a nutshell, a variety of causes including history, expectations and changes in technology (not only factor endowment as before) influence a country's specialisation, geographical location of production and, hence, trade patterns. Differences in technology and increasing returns to scale change productivity levels. This in turn alters the bases for specialisation, spatial location of production and trade patterns. In the case where there are both increasing returns to scale and transport costs, there is an incentive to concentrate production. By spatially concentrating production near its largest market, a firm can both profit from economies of scale and minimise transportation costs. Economies of scale have a stronger impact on the location of modern, knowledge based production than was the case before the Industrial Revolution.

While one can not dispute the importance of factor proportions for the location of production and some processing of primary resources, this approach can not explain the location of footloose industry. In addition, this model does not consider market structure, economies of scale, demand conditions or trade costs. The Heckscher-Ohlin theory is not capable of explaining the location of an industry in regions with high mobility of factors such as the United States (US) or in countries with a broadly similar endowment of factors (France and Germany). A common feature in the standard trade theory is that it considers states, while it utterly ignores firm or regions, i.e. the distribution of economic activity within a country. This gap is filled by spatial economics.

In their survey of trade theory, Leamer and Levinsohn (1995, p. 1363) stated that 'one rather awkward assumption that cries out for change is that of equal numbers of commodities and factors. After all, we really don't know how to count either.' The existence of more goods than factors, trade costs and differences in technology present the principal obstacles for predicting the location of production and specialisation.

Harris (1954) argued that manufacturing firms tend to locate in places where they have favourable access to the market. He showed that the industrialised US regions were also the areas of high *market potential* (a large market attracts producers). The idea is that firms choose to locate in regions that have good market access. However, this access is good in areas in which many other firms exist and chose to settle. There is a self-reinforcing, snowball or herding effect in which the size of the market attracts still more firms. The underlining feature of this approach is, like in most models of spatial economics, that it is based on some kind of economies of scale that rely on a geographical concentration of certain production activities.

Countries tend to specialise and export goods for which they have a relatively large domestic market. It is this domestic demand or '*home market' effect* (Linder, 1961; Krugman, 1980) that induces production, rather than domestic factor endowment. The response by firms to strong local demand for a product is so powerful that it leads this country to export that product. Countries have a competitive edge in the production of these goods and thus gain an advantage in foreign markets, while they import goods demanded by a minority of the home population. The factor endowment or comparative advantage model would not predict the home market effect. However, economic geography would predict such effects. The US, Japan and Germany have the greatest comparative advantage in goods for which their home market is relatively big. These are standardised goods for mass consumption. Empirical investigation by Davis and Weinstein (2003) found support for the existence of home market effects, as well as for the role and importance of increasing returns in determining the production structure for the OECD.

At the heart of the location theory by von Thünen (1826) are differences in land rents and land uses. This model is primarily concerned with the *location of agricultural production.* While Ricardo focuses on the difference in the fertility of land, von Thünen studies how different agricultural lands around a city (marketplace) bid for various uses. The model assumes a given isolated city (one consuming centre) and surrounding agricultural hinterland, homogeneous land surface, free and costless mobility of labour and identical tastes at all income levels. Land rents are highest in the city. From there, they steadily decline to zero at the outermost limit of cultivation (beyond that limit, land is a free good). Hence the rent in a given location totals the difference between the value of its yield minus the sum of production and transport costs. Under the above assumptions the model explains the kind of crop that would be grown at places with different distances from the market. In other words, farmers decide on the type of production (dear to transport vegetables and cheap to transport grain) by taking into account land rent and cost of transport. As transport costs and yields differ among crops, the result is a spontaneous development of concentric circles of production around the city. Land is allocated among different crops in a (optimal) way that minimises production and transport costs of different crops.

Von Thünen's model is based on careful study of farming practices in northern Germany in the early 19th century. Such distribution of farmland is less obvious in the modern more intricate world, but there are certain remnants around large urban centres such as dairy production and gardening. This early model, however, does not consider the role played by economies of scale. There is no answer to the question if vegetables can be shipped in both directions: towards the city (in exchange for cloth) and outmost limits of cultivation (in exchange for grain). The model is, therefore, suitable for the analysis of a pre-railroad and a pre-industrial society.

The problem in von Thünen's model is to find which good to produce in the given location. In the optimal plant site model by Weber (1909) the branch of industry is given, so the problem is to get the spatial location for production. Weber's model takes the geographical location of markets, raw materials and population as given and assumes that there can be only one location for production. The objective of an individual producer is to *minimise the combined costs of production and delivery*. When the production costs are independent of location, the locational problem relates to the minimisation of transport costs for inputs and output.[3] This is the key condition in the decision-making process about the location of a firm. However, when there are key resources that are used on a large scale in certain industries and that are highly localised, this may affect the location of manufacturing industry. These industries would be attracted to locate near resource sites. Hence, this case is 'out of step' with the spatial uniformity and the underlying principle of central place location for some, but not for all kinds of manufacturing. The problem with this approach to the location of new firms is, however, that the initial, static locational needs of a firm may change over time as the firm, industry, technology, consumers' needs and tastes or markets change and develop. There is also a possibility for a historical accident which can be coupled with the economies of scale, lock-in effect and agglomeration.

Geographical remoteness can be a handy scapegoat to some, who may use it to explain why peripheral regions are marginalised in economic and certain social terms. Hummels (1999) argues that geographical factors remain an important determinant of both trade and location. He suggests furthermore that trade composition patterns and direct investment decisions can be sensitive to changes in the relative cost of different transport modes and information transfer. His proposition that international transportation costs have not declined significantly receives some support from Finger and Yeats (1976), who demonstrate that with the process of tariff liberalisation overseen by the GATT/WTO the effective rate of protection from transport costs exceeds that from tariff barriers for many commodities. It is, however, a shallow justification for many industries. Innovations in transport and communication technologies have made these costs rarely the most important determinant for the location of business. In addition, the cost of 'transport disadvantage' on exports is already included in the local factor prices. Hence, a peripheral location is not an insurmountable obstacle for a number of businesses as demonstrated in the cases of countries such as Japan, Australia, New Zealand, Finland or Ireland. Moses (1958) extended Weber's work and integrated location theory with the theory of production. This allowed investigation of the relation between substitution of inputs and geographical location of a firm.

Christaller (1933) wanted to clarify and explain the rationale for the number, size and spatial distribution of cities. The analysis of this geographer is based on the idea of market threshold and transport distance. He put forward the idea that cities form a *hierarchy of central places*. This hinges on the supposition that larger cities can sustain a wider variety of

[3] In the case with one market and two deposits of resources, the optimal firm location would fall inside the triangle area which links these three different spots.

activities relative to smaller (low order) cities and villages. Economies of scale are the source of such uneven distribution of production. The consequence of Christaller's model is that if there exist economies of scale, then the size of the market matters for the location of business. The concern is here, therefore, about the most 'national' product below which are other products. The hidden idea in this model is based on the minimisation of transport costs by rational consumers that make multi-purpose trips. In spite of its obvious value for the analysis of urban growth and distribution of services, this rigid application of the impact of market size neglects the consequences of unequal distribution of natural resources, changes in technology and negative externalities that come from agglomeration.

Developing the central-place theory and the issue of how the economy fits into space further, the economist Lösch (1940) started with a useful, but most unrealistic assumption, that there is a perfectly even distribution of raw materials and population. He starts his consideration of the economic landscape with a 'local' good and seeks to *minimise transport costs* for a given density of central places. In such a space, centres specialise in different products, hence there is a diversification of economic landscape. An efficient pattern of central places would have the shape of nested hexagonal (honeycomb) market areas with no empty corners.[4] This means that certain economic activities can be done only at a restricted number of locations. It was subsequently demonstrated that there is a wide range of geographical configurations of firms. The spatial arrangements that can satisfy the equilibrium condition include squares, rectangles and regular and irregular hexagons (Eaton and Lipsey, 1976, p. 91). Even though based on unrealistic assumptions, the model of central places need not be easily disregarded. A coherent general equilibrium model found certain justification for the central-place theory (Krugman, 1993, p. 298).

While the background theory in Christaller's model of central places is implicit, Lösch's separate approach made it explicit. When they seek to find synchronised locations for many kinds of goods and services they use different arguments. Lösch's model is more becoming for the analysis of the manufacturing sector, while Christaller's hierarchies are more relevant for the tertiary sector (retail services). In any case, it appears that Christaller and Lösch deal with planning problems, rather than with considerations of market results.

The theory of central places points to the factors that need to be examined during the decision making process about the location of an industry or a firm. These factors are sources of supply, intersections of traffic routes and the centre of gravity.[5] In order to reduce inaccuracy in such 'technical' process (suitable for the centrally planned system) one needs to

---

[4] If one imagines a geometrically even distribution of centres across flat and homogeneous surface and the corresponding circles (representing ranges of goods) around them, then if one wants to cover all the space with circles, there would be an overlap between the two adjoining circles. If one draws a straight line between the points where the two adjoining circles intersect, one would get a hexagonal market space of identical size around each centre without empty corners, as consumers would purchase goods from cheapest (nearest) producer.

[5] Paris and Madrid have relatively central geographical location in France and Spain, respectively. The same holds for Munich in Bavaria. In 1998 the capital of Kazakhstan was transferred from Almaty to Astana precisely because the latter city lies at the intersection point of major North-South and East-West transport routes. One of the reasons why Peugeot-Citroën announced in 2003 that it intends to invest and to locate a large (€700 million) car assembly factory in Slovakia (over alternative locations in Poland, the Czech Republic and Hungary) is that this country has good access to transport links and that it is 'in the centre of Europe' (*The Financial Times*, 15 January 2003). The factory would start production of around 300,000 small cars in 2006. The management intends to be closer to fast growing markets in the EU accession countries and to profit from wage rates that are a fifth of the rates paid in the EU(15) for similar industrial operations.

consider additional elements that are parts of a market based economy. They include actions of other functionally related firms, competitors, consumers and government policies.

The classical German location theory dealt with the locational decisions of firms which are in essence reduced to two issues: homogeneous distribution of natural resources over a flat space and optimum cost of transport. This literature was obsessed with the geometrical shape of market areas in an idealised landscape or with the optimal production site with given resources and markets. It ignored the crucial issue of market structure and competition. This was 'doing things in the wrong order, worrying about the details of a secondary problem before making progress in the main issue' (Krugman, 1992, p. 5). Organisational issues such as institutional reality and policies were put aside. Institution-free theoretical models avoid the problem of the impact of various policies on the location or reallocation of firms and industries.

Perroux (1950; 1955; 1961) introduced a predominantly intuitive concept of *growth poles* in spatial economics. The idea was discussed in the context of controversy between balanced and unbalanced regional growth during the 1950s. Geographical agglomeration, significant production linkages (with the key industry) and strong human contacts are necessary for the growth of a pole. A firm is located in a space consisting of poles. Each pole has both centrifugal and centripetal forces. Hence, each pole has its zone of influence (it attracts and repulses firms) and interacts with other poles. If, however, a certain pole does not have a degree of flexibility and adaptability to new technologies and changes in the market, it will stagnate and decline. For instance, France selected eight urban areas and bolstered their growth during the 1960s in the expectation that such policy would counteract the growth of Paris. Hence, the policy of geographical concentration of investments was diluted over time as it was coupled with political snags. Many other national 'areas' exerted pressure to be included in the select group of geographical poles for special treatment. The evaluation of the policy of geographical growth poles is beset by difficulties, as it was not vigorously implemented in practice.

Multiple equilibria create a situation for welfare ranking and set up many temptations to try to pick winners. The selection problem, however, remains unresolved, hence a *historical accident* (chance, arbitrariness) remains the unique deciding factor of the location. If governments want to tip markets towards a preferred solution, then it is timing and, to an extent, instruments that are crucial. There is only a narrow window of opportunity during which the policy may be effective. Otherwise, governments with their limited knowledge, instruments and resources try to stabilise artificially a 'naturally' unstable and evolving process.

Arthur (1989; 1990; 1994a and 1994b) argued that certain models of production geography give weight to differences in factor endowment, transport costs, rents and competition. In such case, the pattern of production locations is an equilibrium outcome. Hence, in these models history does not matter. The locational system is determinate and predictable (Arthur, 1994a, pp. 49-0). However, if one includes increasing returns and multiple equilibria into consideration, the new model has four properties that cause serious difficulties in analysis and policymaking. These features are (Arthur, 1989, pp. 116-7):

- *Multiple equilibria (non predictability)*: ex ante knowledge of firms' preferences and potentials of technologies may not be sufficient to predict the 'market outcome'. The outcome is indeterminate.[6]
- *Potential inefficiency*: increasing returns (*i*-activities) may uplift the development of technology with inferior long run aptitude.[7] Basically, a superior technology may have a bad luck in gaining early adherents. For example, the American nuclear industry is dominated by light-water reactors as a consequence of the adoption of such reactor to propel the first nuclear submarine in 1954. Engineering literature asserts, however, that gas-cooled reactor would have been a superior choice (Arthur, 1989, p. 126). If the claim by engineers is that Betamax is a technically superior system for video recorders, then the market choice of the VHS did not represent the best outcome. Similar arguments could be used for the triumph of DOS over Macintosh during the mid-1980s. In addition, the 'qwerty' arrangement for the typewriter keyboards was designed in the 19th century. Its name refers to the first six top line letters. Even though it has repeatedly been shown that this distribution of letters was suboptimal, the 'qwerty' system continues to be the standard for keyboards.
- *Inflexibility*: once an outcome such as a dominant technology begins to surface it turns out to be more 'locked in' and persist for a long period of time.
- *Path dependence (non-ergodicity)*:[8] small, unpredictable, random and arbitrary events (chances and accidents), path dependence and economies of scale in a non-ergodic system may set in motion mutations in economic structures and irreversibly decide the final outcome. These events are neither normalised, nor averaged away, nor forgotten by the dynamics of the system.

In this model history matters, but the system's dynamics, increasing returns, multiple equilibria, lock-in effect and path dependence generate theoretical and practical limits to predicting the future spatial location of an industry with a high degree of certitude.

The probability of the location of an industry resulting from a historical accident is shown in highly stylised, graphical form in Figure 1. If the distribution of potential locations of an industry is concave (Figure 1a), with a single minimum and a corresponding single outcome, the location is not influenced by a historical chance. This type of distribution is exemplified by the mining and steel-making industries, which are normally located close to their source of raw materials. If, however, the distribution is convex (Figure 1b), with two minima, then there are two potential outcomes, each resulting in a different location which may depend on the historical chance. The third case represents a sphere in which there are *n* solutions for the location of footloose industries (Figure 1c). Hence, multiple equilibria make policy analysis

---

[6] Murphy *et al.* (1989) discuss multiple equilibria with respect to the process of industrialisation, postulating that a certain critical mass of industries may have to be involved in order for industrialisation to be successful. A parallel could be drawn with location theory, and a role for government policy to aid the 'take- off' of a particular location, and encourage firms to move to the location.

[7] Positive feedback economics may also find parallels in non-linear physics. For example, ferromagnetic materials consist of mutually reinforcing elements. Small perturbations, at critical times, influence which outcome is selected (bifurcation point), and the chosen outcome may have higher energy (that is, be less favourable) than other possible end states (Arthur, 1990, p. 99).

[8] An ergodic system (a pendulum, water in a glass) returns at the end to its original state, no matter the disturbances between the starting and ending points in time.

conceptually difficult. This type of distribution is exemplified by corner shops, bakeries and petrol stations. However, firms in most industries need to be close to each other (i.e. they tend to agglomerate and create towns and cities), not only to be close to common suppliers of inputs, but also to foster competition and to facilitate exchange of information, which can be hampered if firms are spatially dispersed.

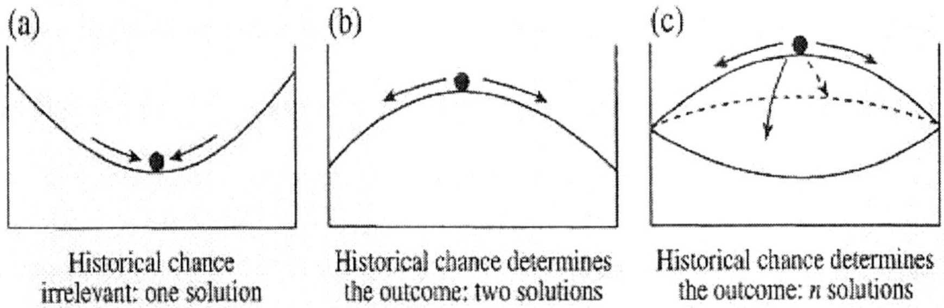

Figure 1. Concave (a), convex (b) and spherical (c) distributions of potential industry locations

Entrepreneurs (sometimes seen as 'maniacs with a vision') often have genuine ideas, but many of them do not have the necessary knowledge about how to run a business. Some of them may know, but cannot persuade those with funds to support their projects. Why is this so? Reasons include a number of cultural factors (risk lovers or risk averse investors) and the lack of knowledge and understanding to recognise and seize the opportunity. For example, a century ago a man went to a Belfast bank and asked for a loan to start a company. He explained to the bank managers that his invention was a mechanical horseless device that would replace horses in ploughing. This was too risky for the bank as it could not foresee that happening at all with a commercial success. Hence this man by the name of Ferguson went to Canada. He met another men by the name of Massey, they teamed up, and the rest of the story is generally known. Massey Ferguson became one of the major world producers of tractors and agriculture-related machinery. The moral of this story is that one needs to recognise and seize the opportunity at a critical time.

If agglomeration forces based on increasing returns are unbounded, then a single geographical location monopolises the industry. Which region is selected depends on its geographical attractiveness and the historical accident of firm entry, in particular early preferences of first entrants. If, however, agglomeration forces that come from increasing returns are bounded, then various regions may share the industry as if agglomeration economies are absent (Arthur, 1990a, p. 249). Locations with large number of firms cast an 'agglomeration shadow' in which little or no settlement takes place. This causes separation of an industry. Agglomeration occurs at a certain level of trade costs, while at another level of these costs, the spread of activities takes place. With bounded agglomeration economies, neighbouring locations cannot share the industry, but sufficiently separated regions can. In France, for example, Lyon lies between Paris and Marseille. Bounded agglomeration economies caused separation and dispersion. Again, 'which locations gain the industry and which become orphaned is a matter of historical accident' (Arthur, 1990a, p. 247).

2.2 International Firm

Ownership and control of the firm was neglected in the analysis by an implicit assumption that these do not matter or by the supposition that all assets are domestically owned. The presence of transnational corporations (TNCs) increases the mobility of capital, expands the availability of information and new products, changes competition structure and alters substitution of labour for capital. A TNC has different locational considerations than a comparable national firm engaged in the same type and scale of activity. A tendency is that strictly national firms expand where they already are, while TNCs enter where they think they may profit from access to the largest and growing market, favourable costs of labour, transport and/or taxes and subsidies. TNCs have 'organisational capital', i.e. a common set of rules, practices, routines and values which help them overcome various barriers while operating in different geographical, social, legal and other environments.

There are at least eight basic theories that explain certain aspects of why firms engage in trans-border business activities and become TNCs.[9] First, the motivation to control foreign firms may not come from the need to employ assets in a prudent way in foreign markets, but rather to remove competition from other enterprises. Hymer (1976) advocated such a *market-power* approach by TNCs. Reuber (1973, pp. 133-4) argued in a similar vein that long-term strategic factors for foreign direct investment (FDI) include the desire to eliminate competitors from foreign markets, to be within a protected foreign market, to secure low-cost source of supply and to lock the target country to a specific technology for a long time. Such a longer-term strategic view overshadows possible short-run variations in the profitability of FDI. The problem with this argument is that most of the TNCs (measured by their number) are small and medium sized. There were around 65,000 parent firms with around 850,000 foreign affiliates in 2002 (UNCTAD, 2002, p. 14). This shows that to become a TNC, a firm need not be a monopolist or an oligopolist at home and try to exercise that power abroad. If there is strong competition in the market for differentiated goods and services and if there is a high degree of substitutability between products (perfumes, soaps, watches, clothing, vehicles, passenger air transport on certain lines, to mention just a few examples), then the market-power argument for the transnationalisation of business is weakened.

Second, while the market-power model excludes potential rivals from competition, the *internalisation* theory holds that an arm's-length relation among individual firms is in some cases less efficient (e.g. trade in technology) than an intra-firm cooperative association. Profits may be maximised by means of an efficient and friendly intra-firm trade in intermediaries that eliminates sometimes excessive transaction costs (middlemen, exchange-rate risk, infringement of intellectual property rights, bargaining costs) which occur when the business is conducted through the market. In these circumstances a hierarchical organisation (an enterprise) may better reward parties in the longer term, as well as curb bargaining and incentives to cheat, than markets and external contractors. Payments of around 80 per cent of fees and royalties for technology 'take place between parent firms and their foreign affiliates' (UNCTAD, 1997, p. 20). This is an indication that TNCs play a key role in disseminating technology around the world (at least in the locations where they operate).

---

[9] In an early study, Weber (1909) offered two basic reasons why firms 'go to produce abroad'. The primary determinant is the achievement of lower labour and transport costs, while the secondary element is the benefit of large-scale production.

While Reuber and Hymer conceive TNCs as vehicles for reaping monopoly profits and for the internalisation of pecuniary externalities, the internalisation model looks at TNCs as a mode of business organisation that reduces transaction costs and internalises non-pecuniary externalities. This model of FDI may be convincing in some cases, but it may not explain the structure and location of all FDI flows. In addition to the internalisation possibilities, there ought to be ownership-specific and locational advantages for FDI.

Markusen (1984) tried to integrate TNCs into general-equilibrium trade models and locational patterns of firms that horizontally or vertically integrate across national borders. Intangible assets, as sources of multi-plant economies, are often firm-specific, rather than plant-specific. They include organisation, management, control, R&D, advertising, marketing and distribution. Many of these activities are centralised (finance) and present a 'joint input' across all production units. A TNC avoids replication of these activities that would be necessary if these units operated as independent national firms. This brings a 'technical' advantage to a TNC. However, if these advantages are transformed into market power, then the welfare effects of TNCs may not be clear.

Third, the *eclectic paradigm* (Dunning, 1988, pp. 42–5; 1999, pp. 1-3) explained the trans-border business activities of TNCs as a joint mix and interaction of three independent factors:

- In order to locate production abroad and be commercially successful, a TNC must have or control internationally mobile income-generating *ownership*-specific (O) advantages, assets, capabilities or skills. These firm-specific advantages include tangible and intangible advantages such as better technology, brand name, access to wide markets, monopoly, competence of managers, ability to innovate etc. that are superior to the ones that are available to local firms (including other TNCs) in the potential target country. This is to say that a firm needs to operate either on a different production function than other firms or that it operates at a different point on the same function.
- *Locational* (L) (non-mobile) advantages refer to the comparative or location-specific advantages of the target country. They refer both to the geographical distribution of resources and to those created by the government.[10]
- There must be opportunities for the *internalisation* (I) of ownership-specific advantages (management and quality control, protection of property rights, avoidance of uncertainty of buyers, etc.). It should be in the interest of the firm to transfer these advantages abroad within its own organisation, rather than sell the right to use these advantages to other firms located in the country of intended production. Fixed exchange rates or a single international currency provide a degree of stability necessary for longer-term business planning with a high degree of confidence.

The eclectic paradigm claims that the exact mix of the OLI factors facing each potential investor depends on the specific context. If a firm possesses or controls ownership-specific advantages, then it may use licensing in order to penetrate foreign markets. If it has both

[10] For example, governments may change over a certain period of time the availability, quality and cost of the domestic factors. The disposable tools for this policy include training of labour and education of management, R&D, science, transport and communication infrastructure and tax policies.

ownership-specific and internalisation advantages, such an enterprise may use exports as a means of entering foreign markets. Only when a firm is able to take *simultaneous* return of OLI advantages, it will employ FDI as a means of locating and operating in foreign markets. This model, however, does not apply to diversified and vertically integrated TNCs (Caves, 1996, p. 5).

Fourth, the *product-cycle* model reasons that mature (and, perhaps, environmentally unsound) lines of production of goods (there is no explicit reference to services) are passed on to developing countries (Posner, 1961; Vernon, 1966). Such spatial reallocation of production is based on the experience of Anglo-Saxon firms and depends a lot on low factor costs.

The product-cycle argument as the major explanation for the location of business abroad and with a rather vague timetable for this spread of production can not pass the test of recent developments. Asian firms, however, do not replicate this pattern of location of production abroad on a large scale. The Japanese auto companies invest at home and in the US and Europe at about the same time for a similar type of production. There is a heavy concentration of FDI in developed countries (70 per cent of the world stock), while the majority of developing countries are relatively neglected in FDI flows. In addition, countries start investing abroad at a much earlier stage of their development than before. The newly industrialised countries and many other developing countries are investing abroad. In many cases these investments are in the developed world. Such developments may be prompted by the desires:

- to be present in the developed countries' markets (closer to wealthy customers)
- to be near the source and cluster of the principal technological developments in manufacturing, distribution, management and already existing infrastructure (to have a foreign 'listening and learning post')
- to participate in R&D programmes
- to avoid the dangers of protectionism in target countries
- to win public contracts
- to exploit the strength of host country's domestic currency

Fifth is the *follow your leader* hypothesis. Oligopolists are risk minimisers. They would like to protect their own market position and avoid destructive competition. Therefore, they typically try to minimise risk and follow each other into the new (foreign) markets (Knickerboker, 1973, p. 100). A study of timing of FDI by US TNCs in manufacturing seems to support this snowball or 'herd behaviour'. The Japanese TNCs in automotive and consumer electronic industries were 'following their domestic leader' when they located their manufacturing facilities in the EU and US during the 1980s and 1990s. This type of investment location behaviour is quite relevant during the opening phases of new markets. If a TNC has no previous experience in a certain new market, then the actions of competitors in that market may be quite informative. Examples of this 'herd behaviour' are the actions of TNCs in China and to an extent to eastern Europe at the start of 1990s. In addition, mergers and acquisitions 'mania' of 1990s in the EU and US shows how assets-seeking by one TNC may be followed by others.

Such 'catastrophic' relocation of industry as a result of the predicted behaviour of rival firms is one feature of the core-periphery model, one of the key new economic geography models. It is postulated that when trade costs lie in a certain range all firms in an industry may relocate *en masse*, although this would not be the optimum strategy for an individual firm were it to relocate on its alone.

While relatively low labour costs in China could have been the reason to start to locate certain operations there at the start of 1990s, things have changed. It was reported that China's Pearl river delta attracted $1 billion of FDI a month. Microwave ovens are produced in Shunde. Just one of its giant factories produces 40 per cent of global output of microwave ovens. Shenzhen produces 70 per cent of world's photocopiers and 80 per cent of artificial Christmas trees. Dongguan has 80,000 people working in a single factory making running shoes for the world's teenagers. Flextronics is a Singapore electronics maker that produces for Microsoft, Motorola, Dell and Sony. The manager of its Chinese plant in Doumen said that 'It is a myth that companies are coming here just for the cheap labour. It is the efficiency of the supply chain that drives them here as more and more of worldwide demand is consolidated in this area'.[11]

Sixth, the competitive international industry model for the location of business abroad refers to oligopolistic competition and rivalry within the same industry. This is basically *exchange of threats* (tit for tat strategy) to business moves by foreign rivals (Graham, 1978). Large firms keep an eye on the actions of their rivals, i.e., they act strategically (pay attention to the likely reaction of their competitors to their own actions). What Texaco does in Europe, Shell will (try to) do in the US. Competition is not 'cut-throat', but rather 'stable' among several oligopolies. Other examples of this rivalistic trend include FDI in the manufacturing of cars and tyres or supply of services such as hotels and advertising. Small and medium-sized enterprises (SMEs) such as gas stations in the middle of nowhere may in their business, act independently. However, SMEs in a cluster keep a vigilant eye on the actions of the competitors.

Seventh, is the *diversification of portfolios* model of foreign investment (Brainard and Tobin, 1992). This approach considers uncertainty. Fluctuations in the rates of return on capital invested in various countries introduce an element of risk. This inconvenience may be reduced by a diversification of portfolios.

Firm-specific assets and exchange rates may be the eighth basic reason for FDI. Suppose that there is a target firm in the US with an innovation (a firm-specific asset) that can make the acquiring firm's assembly line 10 per cent more productive (10 per cent more output for the same level of input). If a US firm wants to acquire the target firm, then a change in the rate of exchange makes no difference as its gains will continue to be denominated in dollars. If, however, the acquiring firm is in Japan, the gains will be denominated in yens. A depreciation of the dollar relative to the yen will increase the Japanese firm's reservation bid, while the US firm's bid would remain unchanged. It is more likely that the Japanese firm would acquire the asset in this situation. The actual evidence about this taking place is rather mixed. The price of US assets needs not matter, only the rate of return: when the dollar depreciates, both the price of a US asset and its rate of return will go down. However, Blonigen (1997) found connection between exchange rate movements (weak dollar) and higher levels of Japanese acquisitions in the US in industries which involve firm-specific assets. This refers to the Japanese acquisitions in the US during 1975-92.

[11] J. Kynge and D. Roberts, 'The Pearl river delta is attracting $1bn of investment a month amid one of the fastest bursts of economic development in history', *The Financial Times*, 4 February 2003.

In addition to the above basic theories on why firms locate abroad, three other dimensions are relevant for coming to grips with the issue: cost minimisation, available technology and taxes. First, Kravis and Lipsey (1982, p. 222) argued that the location of foreign affiliates of TNCs is decided on the basis of *cost minimisation*. However, the intensity of this determinant varies from industry to industry. Second, Yamawaki (1993, pp. 19-20) did not dispute the importance of a relative difference in factor costs, the *availability of technology* in the target country is an additional and equally important factor for the location of Japanese FDI in the EU. A Japanese TNC from a certain industry decided to locate in the EU country which has a certain advantage over other EU countries in the same industry. Britain is preferred by the Japanese TNCs for the location of production of cars and electrical/electronic equipment, Germany for precision instruments and machinery, Belgium for stone, glass and clay products, while TNCs from the chemical industry prefer Germany, the Netherlands, Spain and France (Yamawaki, 1993).

Third come differences in *taxes and fiscal incentives*. While there are many 'tax havens' that attract quite a few firms (mainly from finance) and many countries offer different fiscal incentives to firms in order to attract them, is this enough by itself? Are tax incentives a bit more than 'corporate welfare'? Politicians use usually only three reasons to justify a local incentive programme. These three reasons are: jobs, jobs and jobs!

The importance, influence and evidence of taxes on the location of firms is still controversial. Investors may avoid locations that offer financial incentives as evidence of a region's non-competitiveness. Limited survey information reveal that fiscal variables matter little regarding business location. However, business executives often lobby hard for fiscal incentives. One can understand that attitude as firms have no incentives to forego such direct and indirect subsidies, even if they do not affect location decisions to a significant degree (Wasylenko, 1991). This was a confirmation of the results of an earlier study by Carlton which found that tax variables usually have a 'very small and always statistically insignificant' (Carlton, 1983, p. 447) impact on locational choice. Mody and Srinivasan (1998, p. 795) found that corporate tax rates do not have a major influence over FDI either by the American or by the Japanese TNCs.

A study into the effect of the elimination of a tax on paper for printing news (which accounted for about a half of the production costs) in the Netherlands in 1869 revealed that this assisted in the creation of new newspaper firms. Two thirds of these new entries took place in cities that already had other newspapers, while a third of new entries occurred in provincial towns that previously did not have a newspaper. Even though a cut in a weighty tax played an important role, the principal reason for this type of the location of firms was the size and growth of the local market. Hence, there is no basic difference in the rationale for a firm's location between a century and a half ago and now (Pfann and van Kranenburg, 2002).

Although many surveys give state and local taxes a low ranking on the list of location determinants, many locations in various states within the US can be close substitutes. In such a situation, even a small difference in production costs can play a key role for a particular decision about the location of business (Bartik, 1991, p. 8). As far as FDI by the American firms were concerned during 1984-92, they have become more sensitive to difference in host country taxes towards the end of that period (Altshuler *et al.* 1998).

This continues to be a controversial research area. There is a lack of consensus as the results of academic literature on the issue are still mixed. High(er) taxes may be preferred to low taxes by firms if the tax proceeds are used to finance local services useful for the business sector. In any case, high quality infrastructure is preferred by foreign investors to tax incentives. Transfer pricing and tax deductions in the home country provide other ways to minimise the tax burden on profit (Wheeler and Mody, 1992, pp. 71-2).

No single theory or model can provide a completely satisfactory answer to each issue related to trans-border investment activities of the firms. Motives for foreign production are different and they change over time in response to changes in the market, technology, tastes, management strategy, actions of rivals and economic policy. However, if taken together, these theories may provide useful elements for the understanding of the issue.

3 Globalisation

Liberalisation in the national and international economy is a policy choice of *governments*, primarily in the developed world. It is linked with privatisation and downsizing of the activities of the public sector and the expansion of the activities of the private sector. *Globalisation* of the economy and production is a fact. It is the outcome of the behaviour of *firms* (TNCs), their organisation, changing technology in production and distribution, control and finance, as well as economies of scale and takeovers. In part, it is also the consequence of a change in the behaviour of consumers (fickleness and declining loyalty to national producers and certain national products)[12] and liberalisation of national and international economies for trade, production and finance.

As a process primarily driven by technology and actions of TNCs (power is shifted from states to firms),[13] globalisation lacks two important components: transparency and accountability.[14] This process deals with the change in the geography of (integrated international) production and consumption as it reduces the importance of proximity to inputs or markets. It widens boundaries and deepens space for the geographical location of production and consumption because of the declining costs of getting goods and services to the market. A rapid expansion of FDI is the key component of this process. Capital market liberalisation and increased capital mobility have radically reduced the influence of governments in the monetary sphere. However, governments have gained increased control in other areas. For example, computers and information technology have greatly increased potential for data collection and processing, and consequently control over firms and citizens which is relevant for tax and other purposes.

[12] One should not accord an absolute value to the decline of consumer loyalty to local brands. Regional, rather than 'global' strategies in certain food and health-care products may offer a superior business outcome. However, there was a certain 'global success' by, for example, Coca-Cola, which succeeded in replacing a part of the consumption of milk and healthy natural fruit juices for an artificial and sweet liquid that has a questionable impact on health and weight.

[13] It was the church that once determined our life, than the state and now it is corporations. Governments court firms (TNCs) to come and locate within the confines of their control. Critics say that the protection of the vulnerable in society or safeguarding of the environment is weakened, even that it is left at the mercy of big businesses. This may be the case in certain lines of production, but it all depends on specific circumstances. In some cases the regulatory framework facing TNCs was strengthened, while in others it was loosened.

[14] The same holds for the increase in the power of special influence groups such as non-governmental organisations. Do these unelected groups of people with sometimes questionable accountability represent a risky shift of power towards special vested interests? Or do they represent a move towards the new 'civil society' (does anyone know the definition of this type of society)? Why does the general public believe sometimes more to these organisations that often lack resources for rigorous analysis than to the governments?

Regionalisation is increasing in importance in the world economy. This was exemplified in the inability of 135 member countries of the WTO to agree even on the agenda for the 'Millennium Round' of global trade negotiations that took place in Seattle in 1999. Well-organised, vociferous and strong world-wide protests by environmentalists, farmers, enemies of genetically modified food and big business, labour unions, anti-capitalists and animal rights activists just added to the problems of that meeting and many others that followed worldwide. Therefore, the creation of integrated global economic policies is likely to be a very hard task for quite some time to come. It seems that the regional approach to economic problems will call the tune at least in the medium term.

The rapid international expansion of TNCs made them the most visible feature of globalisation. Being foreign, making sometimes visible and highly publicised mistakes and being often big, TNCs are easy targets for non-governmental organisations (NGOs) which can run successful campaigns to disgrace a mighty TNC. A number of NGOs are relatively small players who would like to 'punch above their weight' because of the urgency of the matter.[15] Examples of their campaigns include valid targets such as land mines, HIV/Aids or poverty and third world debt. NGOs increased public awareness and pushed through agreements on the control of 'greenhouse gases' in the United Nations Conference on Environment and Development, the 'Earth Summit' in Rio de Janeiro in 1992. They also helped in torpedoing the Multilateral Agreement on Investment in 1998 and made a big ado in Seattle in 1999 (and many other subsequent meetings), which contributed to the failure to start a new WTO round of global trade negotiations before the meeting in Doha in 2001. No matter how justified the reasons for the campaign, these 'civil society' protestors against global capitalism demonstrated that the tide of globalisation could be checked and even turned back.

The anti-globalisation movement is moving beyond its radical, protest-driven even anarchist legacy (which might have worked against it) towards a movement with a concrete agenda. Rock-throwers, like Luddites (1811-16) that were smashing factory machines, were ineffectual and irrelevant in the long term. The strategy of the anti-globalisation movement is to address four weaknesses of the globalisation process:

- a lack of legitimacy,
- a lack of accountability,[16]
- a lack of organisation and
- a lack of transparency.

The idea is not to be against globalisation, but rather to put limits on it. The question is what kind of 'globalisation' is desirable and how to achieve it? The World Social Forum (Porto Alegre, Brazil) attempts hard to put under one umbrella hundreds of disparate groups. This Forum recommends a range of activities from limiting power of TNCs to adding new responsibilities and regulatory powers to the established international organisations such as

[15] NGOs often consider that it may be better to be just about right and make a big ado now in order to put an issue on the policy agenda, than to wait long for a firm scientific evidence and miss the political opportunity.

[16] The same holds for the increase in the influence of special influence groups such as NGOs. Do these unelected groups of people with sometimes questionable accountability represent a risky shift of power towards special vested interests or causes? Or do they represent a move towards the new 'civil society' (does anyone know the definition of this type of society)?

the UN, the International Labour Office and the World Health Organisation. In this way the anti-globalisation movement may be able to gain more leverage on national and international scene.

The anti-globalisation campaigners have shown that governments are not powerless. The authorities can just as easily dismantle old trade and investment barriers, as they can introduce new ones. New technology, in particular the Internet, telecommunications, computing and data processing can offer some of the greatest economic opportunities ever for increasing living standards in all countries. Governments and the national elite in all countries (due to incompetence or indifference) have failed to explain this. However, the process needs to be coupled with balanced policies both in the rich and poor world. Even though global economic integration may be the best end point for the future of the world economy for the proponents of globalisation, it is more likely that other outcomes may be chosen for the time to come. Globalisation may be favourable for economic efficiency, but it can be harmful for social goals.

Apart from a partial integration of international production, globalisation brings risks and disruptions. Volatile capital flows, speculative attacks on currencies, financial crises and unpredictable reallocation of jobs are obvious examples of increased economic and social vulnerability of many countries, in particular in the developing world. To wrap up the issue, Henry Kissinger labelled globalisation as 'another name for the dominant role of the United States'.[17]

The vogue term 'globalisation' has not yet been well or clearly defined. Hence, this fuzzy, but powerful metaphor is overused; often abused and very often misleading. For some it basically refers to the choices and strategies, as well as the shape, extent, direction and significance of activities of TNCs. 'Globalisation has been defined in business schools as the production and distribution of products and services of a homogeneous type and quality on a worldwide basis. Simply put – providing the same output to countries everywhere' (Rugman and Hodgetts, 2001, p. 333).[18] 'Thanks' to al-Quaeda many realised that globalisation goes well beyond links that bind TNCs, producers, traders and bankers. For others, globalisation is linked with and invigorated by new technologies in communications and information processing. It is a sum of techniques that are at the disposal of private players and states. Yet for others, globalisation is an incentive to the reform process in economic strategy in many countries as outward-looking economic models replace inward-looking and TNC-hostile economic policy approaches. Others look at globalisation as a process that alters interactions among agents across space; still others equate globalisation with economic integration.[19]

The Internet symbolises the borderlessness brought about by globalisation. Physical presence in a specific location is not necessary. In the invisible continent of cyberspace, the users are 'everywhere and nowhere' at once. They use the Internet as a meeting place, a

---

[17] H. Kissinger, 'Globalisation: America's role for the millennium', *The Irish Independent*, 13 October 1999.

[18] Uniformity and homogeneity in the modern world may be a heavy price to pay for new or 'better' standardised things we consume. This introduces an ever present potential for the neo-communist danger that everyone eats and drinks the same, is dressed the same, uses homogeneous (perfectly substitutable) goods and services and ends up or is forced to, perhaps, even think 'the same'. If someone is not 'in step' with these global developments (no matter their democratic appearance and sugar-coating), well, then … the concerned may 'court trouble' from the central 'politburo'!

[19] 'Globalisation is no more than an (admittedly ugly) name for the process of integration across frontiers of liberalising market economies at a time of rapidly falling costs of transport and communications' (M. Wolf, *The Financial Times*, 3 October 2001, p. 15).

market, a distribution device, a library, and the like. This alters the geography of production, at least for certain products. Persons spend more time by working at home or 'on the road', hence certain office space (in congested cities) is vacated. However, one does not need to give an absolute value to globalisation. In spite of this process, localisation and clusters still matter. Firms that went furthest in 'globalisation' report that face-to-face contact is essential for the smooth organisation of business within the firm and marketing outside it. In addition, just try to tell that this is a 'borderless world' to someone that that wants to enter the EU or North America from outside. Borders continue to matter a great deal as people from different locations are prevented from crossing them without a cumbersome, costly and uncertain administrative procedure.

The Internet is based on communication and data that are located in computers that exist in the real world. Initially, this parallel universe of pure data existed everywhere freely in a 'lawless' world. The Internet was breaking barriers and eliminating physical distance. However, computers exist in an identifiable geographical space. If they can be located together with their users, then they are subject to law. Now governments are increasing their control over the cyberspace. For example, France prohibited the sale of Nazi memorabilia on the Internet; Iran banned access to immoral or anti-Iranian information; while South Korea prohibited access to gambling websites. There is also increased international police cooperation in combat against child pornography or computer viruses and hackers that attack major computer networks. Hence, borders are being created in the Internet. Even though the economic impact of geographical distance is being reduced, the local economic geography is keeping its strength.

The imposition of 'global' standards may have its justification for relatively new and standardised goods and services such as copiers, fax machines, computers, mobile phones or better medicines, otherwise communication and exchange of information might be difficult and costly. However, the imposition of such standards for traditional goods (e.g., food) with the exception of health and the environment may not be easily justified. If needs and tastes for certain types of food are strongly locally specific (even the thickness of pizzas throughout Italy differs) why should one favour or impose global Pizza Hut type standards?

John Gray of the London School of Economics said that faith in globalisation melted down and that 'led by the United States, the world's richest states have acted on the assumption that people everywhere want to live as they do. As a result, they failed to recognise the deadly mixture of emotions - cultural resentment, the sense of injustice and a genuine rejection of western modernity - that lies behind the attacks on New York and Washington... The ideal of a universal civilisation is a recipe for unending conflict, and it is time it was given up'.[20] It is not that the people that live outside the Western world are unable to have liberal mind, rather there are social, cultural and institutional barriers that prevent a fast transfer of Western values, culture and institutions elsewhere. Then there are also 'recipients' choices. Do they really want and need what is exported or 'imposed' on them?

There was a faulty premise and vision that all people are culturally homogeneous that they think, act and most of all, shop alike (or like Americans); that there exist institutional bases for political democracy; and that the citizens are aware of their duties to one another and to the state. Checks and balances are mixed; there is mistrust vis-à-vis the government and state administration which has often deep roots in dictatorship, authoritarian and

[20] *The Economist*, 29 September 2001, p. 14. The reference here is to the attacks of 11 September 2001.

bureaucratic conduct, as well as in corruption. Without a very long term reform, education and trust-building, any attempt to transfer fast 'global' (social) standards would fail, and fail miserably, in many parts of the world. Lest it should be forgotten that 'it took 400 years for England to develop from that stage to its present one. To do the same elsewhere in half the time of 200 years would be a tremendous achievement; to aspire to do it in 25 or 50 years may be to court disaster' (Lipsey, 1992, p. 755).[21] There are stubborn local differences. Until the world becomes homogeneous, adaptation towards the local preferences and capabilities will be necessary. Problems regarding globalisation that appeared in the form of troubles regarding progress in the WTO or in the Multilateral Agreement on Investment illustrate signals of regional (triad: US, EU and Japan) or even local power.

It is true that the greatest and matchless advantage of free markets and globalisation is that they give free choice to consumers. Economic interactions are voluntary, so consumers are free to choose, for example, between local and global goods and services. But, this is only on the surface. If global products are advertised by large TNCs aggressively, including campaigns that are often beyond the financial capacity of local competitors, then the 'free choice' by consumers may be restricted and the local producers (and certain dimensions of the local culture) may be damaged. Critics of such unchecked global capital movements say that global TNCs put 'profits before people'. When these TNCs 'start talking about how they will no longer put profits first, people (rightly) think they are lying'.[22]

The critics of globalisation have certain valid points. 'The promise of export-led growth has failed in too many places. In particular, Latin America has signally failed to replicate Asia's success: Latin nations have liberalized, privatised and deregulated, with results ranging from disappointing (Mexico) to catastrophic (Argentina).'[23] In addition, India still remembers the moment when first ships of the East India Company arrived at the port of Surat. The Company came to India as a trader in 1608 and ended up virtually owing the country.

Another cost of globalisation can be found in the examples of countries such as Mexico, Thailand, Indonesia, South Korea and Russia. Globalisation led these countries into financial crises in the second half of the 1990s. Without the exposure to global capital markets, the crises would not have developed as they did. The critics of this view argue that these countries would not have developed fast prior to crisis without such exposure. In any case, one ought to be fair and observe that certain 'global tendencies' were present in the past well before the current wave of globalisation. For example, there was (for whatever reason and means) a spread of certain European languages outside Europe; spread of Islam in Africa, Asia and Europe; or spread of Christianity in Latin America.

Trade and foreign investments (globalisation) are partners, not adversaries of social agendas, but they ought to be coupled with effective national and international institutions that ease adjustment problems (such as the polluter-pays principle). Globalisation may bring

---

[21] Institutional elements such as clear property rights are very important for foreign investors. However, the mere transfer of these solutions from the developed countries elsewhere is not a sufficient condition for a successful economic performance. For example, while Russia has introduced a system of private property rights, China guarded the general socialist legal system. Nonetheless, domestic and foreign investors regarded China as a promising location for investment and this country became one of the prime locations for investment. There was a strong credibility that investments would be protected. In contrast, this credibility was lower in Russia in spite of the property rights system. Hence, this was one of the elements why Russia continued to score much lower than China as a location for investment.

[22] *The Economist*, 'A survey of globalisation', 29 September 2001, p. 4.

[23] P. Krugman, 'The Good News', *The New York Times*, 28 November 2003.

adjustment costs in the affected industries and labour markets, but this may be only transitory. The gradual opening up of markets in Japan during the 1970s, and later in south-east Asia during the 1980s and in China during the 1990s, demonstrates that as a country grows wealthier, it ceases to be competitive in the production of labour intensive goods. Such a country becomes an importer of these goods and concentrates its production on higher value-added activities.

Child labour, begging, theft and prostitution in poor countries would certainly decline if globalisation opened advanced countries' markets to the products made by their parents. Even though globalisation spreads symbols of highly dubious value such as Coca-Cola, McDonalds, MTV, Halloween or chewing gum,[24] it also spreads profound values such as the rights of women and children. However, it is unfortunate that this takes place at a much slower pace. A still unresolved problem is that under globalisation human rights may sometimes be more important than state sovereignty.

The debate about globalisation is often about jobs (social dimension). Supporters argue that it is beneficial and that it creates jobs, while critics argue the opposite and say that jobs migrate to trading partners and competitors. Certain segments of labour in all countries are suspicious of globalisation, as they no longer perceive the national government as a sure protector of their concerns against external threats. To counter these fears, the best long-term policy response may be to advance possibilities for education and training, as technical progress has a strong bias against unskilled workers.

As far as firms are concerned, there is the search by efficiency-seeking enterprises, particularly some TNCs, for seamless and wide international markets regarding trade and investment. On the one hand, the *globalisation* of economic activity is making national frontiers less divisive than was the case 'ever before'.[25] Such worldwide economic integration and integrated international production of goods and services whereby competitors are in each other's backyard are made possible by the expansion of information and telecommunication technologies.[26] That process is sometimes inverted, on the other hand, by the spread of *regionalism* pushed by relatively inefficient firms and governments that are driven by short-term election interests, even though the conditions for a relatively successful integration process, such as that in western Europe, may be largely absent.

Regional integration (a second best solution) may be a promising form of supranational governance in areas where there is a strong case for coordination and harmonisation of national policies. Integration may resolve conflicts through positive cooperation within a cosy group but, if pushed to the limit, it may undermine multilateral (first best) trade and investment systems and fragment the world economy into conflicting regional blocs. Regionalism and multilateralism (globalisation) need not necessarily conflict. If the regional blocs cooperate and if they adopt liberal external trade and investment policies, the outcome may be an overall welfare improvement. The pace of international trade liberalisation since

[24] One thinks of the particular consequences of chewing gum for the cleanness of elevators and chairs.

[25] Increased international mobility of factors, increased international intra-firm transactions, expanding international cooperative arrangements between firms, the increasing importance of knowledge, as well as a reduction in transport and communication costs, support the process of globalisation and are constituent parts of it. In these circumstances, individual actions of national governments may not increase global welfare (pollution is an example) and certain supranational rules may be necessary in order to deliver more beneficial outcomes.

[26] Trade is relatively more concentrated within regions than FDI. This suggests that trade plays a more prominent role in intra-regional integration arrangements, while FDI has a greater influence on global integration (UNCTAD, 1993, p. 7).

the 1960s, as well as the extension of the GATT into new areas such as services and agriculture, might have been much slower in the absence of challenges posed by the progress in integration in the EU. The debate should not be between regionalism and multilateralism, but rather between liberalism and interventionism (Blackhurst and Henderson, 1993, p. 412).

It is often forgotten that the spirit of 'globalisation' does not bring anything essentially new. The need is for more freedom for trade in goods and services and for capital mobility (FDI). The economic role of national frontiers declines as national economies merge in a single 'global' unit. In a nutshell, the idea is to return to the essentials of the system that was prevailing before 1914. Re-globalisation may be a more appropriate term.

An enlarged market is an important gain for efficiency-seeking firms in a small country. In a situation without integration, foreign countries can simply threaten a small country that they will introduce protectionist measures or 'sanctions' against it (frequent threats by the US to many countries). Such a warning can seriously undermine the quality of all economic decisions in a small country. Integration enhances and secures market access for partner countries, as well as increases the potential for long-term competitiveness of a small country's goods and services. A common market may eliminate or harmonise national incentives to foreign TNCs to locate in partner countries (which were previously subject to countervailing duties). It also mitigates non-economic considerations, such as political pressures on third country investors to locate in a particular country.

Transnational corporations behave like other firms: they primarily follow the opportunities for maximising profit while staying within the law. Size and growth of the local market, including privileged access to international markets (instead of mere differences in the cost of labour), are the most prominent motivators for their trans-border business operations. In addition, in a situation where market liberalisation became a widely accepted policy choice, there is an increase in the importance of created assets and structures (technology and ability to create it, business culture, capability to organise and control production and marketing, communications infrastructure, marketing networks) as determinants for FDI. Those are the reasons why 65 per cent of the activities of TNCs were located in developed market economies (measured by the stock of FDI in 2002) (UNCTAD, 2003). In spite of the talk about 'globalisation,' on average, a significant part of the output of affiliates is still sold on the local market.[27] In this situation the developing countries and those with the economy in transition face very tough competition to attract TNCs.

Foreign investors will locate their activities in a country that offers the most favourable mix of cost of operation (production and marketing), provided that this factors well into the longer-term vision about potential profit. FDI can be made simpler by regionalisation of the world economy and international economic integration. However, integration/regionalisation is only a supporting tool for the tendencies that bring globalisation of international business. Modern competitive firms are usually TNCs that 'globalise' their business in the search for seamless and widest markets. Therefore, an increasing share of domestic output even in the developed countries is under the control of foreign TNCs. The same holds for an increasing share of foreign output of domestic TNCs. Strong FDI relations may exist even though the countries or groups of countries are not formally integrated. Just take a look at the example of two-way FDI flows between the US and the EU.

---

[27] 'Over 90 per cent of products produced in each of the triad regions is sold within that region. There is no global car. ... well over 90 per cent of MNE manufacturing is intra-regional rather than global' (Rugman, 2002, p. 5).

Glue holding transatlantic relations together is not principally trade, but FDI. Large global interpenetration of FDI reduces the chance that regional arrangements may turn into closed blocs. A 'hostage population' of TNCs may reduce the fear of retaliatory measures. Extensive FDI links between the US and the EU helped reduce any potential conflict between the two partners regarding market access. The same is not yet true of Japan. There is a hope that Japan will mature as a foreign investor in future and that potential conflict with that country will be defused.

In order to avoid the weakening of the competitive position of EU firms in global markets, the EU may follow two courses, although there may be a strong appeal to employ a mix of the two. First, the EU may increase protection of domestic firms against foreign TNCs through measures such as rules of origin, local content requirements and other trade related investment measures. Second, the EU may open its domestic market and welcome foreign, in particular high-technology, TNCs to locate their manufacturing operations in the EU. As widely argued, EU firms in a sizeable part of its manufacturing industry are less efficient than their counterparts in the US and Japan. Suppose that the EU adopts a liberal economic policy; if the EU firms adjust and withstand competition from foreign TNCs, they may, in relative terms, gain more from market liberalisation than their foreign competitors.

A caveat for developing countries is that sometimes they use tariff proceeds for investment purposes. If that is the case, a customs union may dry up an important part of domestic investments by lowering tariff revenue. In a situation with many market imperfections, the opportunities for gains and losses are numerous. Hence, long-term gains in growth that originate in international economic integration may offset this loss of tariff revenue. However, the question asked by the public choice theory is: are we sure that the government of the day in a developing country cares or can afford to care about long-term gain?

4 Localisation

4.1 History and Expectations

a. Background

As already noted, the Heckscher-Ohlin theory is inadequate to provide the reason for the location of an industry in regions with high mobility of factors (US) or in the countries with broadly similar endowment of factors (France and Germany). Patterns of regional specialisation and location of firms and industries are often created by a historical accident. Ohlin noted that 'Chance plays a significant part in determining the localisation of industry... A different distribution of inventions would have caused a different localisation' (Ohlin, 1933, p. 137). More recently Krugman wrote: 'I at least am convinced that there is a strong arbitrary, accidental component to international specialization; but not everyone agrees, and the limitations of the data make a decisive test difficult' (Krugman, 1992, p. 9). In any case, chance and economies of scale are strong forces that influence the spatial location of firms.

When there are multiple equilibria, various spots for the location of business are substitutable ex ante ('putty'). After the investment is made, these locations can not be easily substitutable for quite some time ('clay'). Once a business is established at a specific geographical location, it is then 'locked in' through learning, path dependence, sunk costs, circular and cumulative causation effects (for examples of this putty-clay locational model). In this sense '...history matters in a way that it does not in neo-classical theory...' (Eaton and Lipsey, 1997, p. *xxv*). Two questions are relevant here:

- Are there inherent differences among locations that create predestination for certain activities?
- How can a small historical accident, a chance (something that is beyond the prior knowledge of an investor), alter the economic fate of an industry, region or a country?

Meaningful multiple equilibria exist when firms make independent profit-maximising decisions about output, prices and location. Sources of this multiplicity are pecuniary externalities that originate in (large) fixed costs and imperfect competition. The question is which equilibrium gets established? Will it be stable in the long-run? Since a particular space has only a limited influence on the location of new economic activity (especially footloose industries), what are the options for policy makers in this situation?

On the one hand, there is a belief that the choice is basically resolved by history. Past events set preconditions that move the economy from one steady state to another. This reasoning, found in the traditional literature, argues that history matters because of increasing returns and lumpiness (inseparability) and activity specific knowledge and capital goods (Eaton and Lipsey, 1997, pp. *x-xi*). The same idea is also behind promotional campaigns or 'location tournaments' (David, 1984) among countries to attract international footloose capital (TNCs). The idea is that once an activity starts in a place, it perpetuates itself and related businesses gravitate towards it. However, this 'self-reinforcing aspect of foreign investment begins to operate only after a certain development threshold has been reached' (Wheeler and Mody, 1992, p. 71). This is to say that spillovers on the local economy are not a direct consequence of the location of a TNC. Gains that come from these externalities can be achieved only if the local firms have, or can be motivated to take on, new (foreign) technologies and skills. The structure of the local economy, attitude of the private sector and policies of the government that promote change play a key role. In addition, there is evidence in the case of the US foreign investors that 'past investment in the country was a strong predictor of new investment. That persistence was attributed to the favourable effects of agglomeration' (Mody and Srinivasan, 1998, pp. 780-1).

There is, on the other hand, a view that the choice of equilibrium is determined by expectations. This observation is based on the belief 'that there is a decisive element of self-fulfilling prophecy' (Krugman, 1991, p. 652). Let us consider both views in turn.

b. Historical lock-in effect

The non-linear probability theory can predict with some certitude the behaviour of systems subject to increasing returns. Suppose that balls of different colour are added on a table. The probability that the next ball will have a specific colour depends on the current proportion of colours. Increasing returns occur when a red ball is more likely to be added when there is already a high proportion of red balls (Arthur, 1990, p. 98). Equilibrium depends on the initial point and latter arrivals. Hence, history as a series of (random) arrivals sets the final result.

The national rate of growth of capital stock (without FDI and foreign loans) depends on home savings and investment. Suppose now that one region/country initially accumulates more capital than the other does. In the following period both regions grow, but the one with more capital grows faster than the one with less capital. As manufacturing capital grows, the relative prices of manufacturing goods fall. After certain period of time, there is a point where the lagging region's industry can not compete internationally and it begins to shrink. Once this process begins the new theory of trade and strategic industrial policy suggests that nothing can stop agglomeration for a long time. Economies of scale may drive prices down in the capital-abundant region and at the same time the lagging region's manufacturing industry disappears. In this model, relatively small beginnings can have large and irreversible final consequences for the manufacturing structure of a country, its trade and competitiveness of its output (Krugman, 1990, pp. 99-100).

The dynamics of capital accumulation makes the region that starts with a higher capital stock than the other regions, end up with a dominant industrial position. If this is reinforced with a learning process and cumulative causation (strong internal production links where extension of one activity increases the profitability of others), than the existing pattern of comparative advantage is reinforced over time even if the overall structure of the economy has changed. This process-dependent development adds new layers of firms and industries on the inherited production structure. If output is concentrated within a relatively small spot, firms can benefit from economies of scale and linkages (growth of one activity increases the profitability of other). If this spot is close to a larger market, there are additional benefits in the form of lowered trade (including transport) costs. Hence, the current state of the economy determines its future shape.

The investment decisions and trade policy of a country in the current period will have an impact on the shape of the national economy in the future periods. For example, at the end of the 19th century Argentina and Sweden were relatively comparable backward farming-based economies. At about the same time, Argentina invested in the education of lawyers and priests, while Sweden invested in the education of engineers. The impact of such choice (coupled with other economic policies) on the material standard of living between the two countries is obvious.

Once the structure of an economy becomes unsustainable, there are certain critical branching points (bifurcations), at which the qualitative behaviour of the economy changes. New production geography either evolves or is triggered. This history dependent development can follow different paths, hence it is unpredictable. A long period of stability is broken up by an event of change (equilibrium is punctuated). For example, nearly all big cities are ports. However, it is a long time since New York or Boston ceased to be primarily harbour cities. One may find examples of punctuated equilibrium elsewhere. In biology, for instance, many species (crocodiles, crabs, turtles or monotreme animals) remain stagnant for a very long period of time. However, there are crucial, relatively brief and unpredictable moments (bifurcations) when new species arrive and old ones disappear. These include change in climate 64 million years ago caused by the fall of a meteor that provoked an enormous volcanic activity and fires, water and atmosphere were polluted, while smoke and dust prevented the penetration of heat from the Sun. Hence a very big part of life on Earth was frozen, burned, starved or suffocated. This change in climate caused the extinction of dinosaurs.[28]

More than a century ago Alfred Marshall spelled out the idea of 'backward-looking dynamics' or external economies (named in the modern jargon). In his analysis, factors of production are moving towards those industries in which they earn the highest current rate of return. If there are several meaningful equilibria in which the returns would be equalised, then the initial conditions determine the outcome. History matters together with factor endowment, tastes and technology (Krugman, 1991, pp. 653-4).

Marshall also described the concentration of specialised industries in particular localities in the following way. 'When an industry has once chosen a locality for itself, it is likely to stay there long: so great are the advantages which people following the same skilled trade get from near neighbourhood to one another. ... if one man starts a new idea it is taken up by others and combined with suggestions of their own; and thus becomes the source of yet more new ideas' (Marshall, 1890, p. 332). Contemporary jargon refers to these processes as externalities of innovation.[29]

Somehow similar 'first mover advantages' (to use the term from analysis of competition) may be found in biology as many bits and pieces of the past can be found long after their functions were lost. For example, 'embryonic birds and mammals still have gill arches, which have been useless for 400 million years. Why are the vestiges not eliminated by natural selection? The usual answer is that baupläne and the vestiges are developed early in the embryo and hence are most difficult to modify than features that develop later. The genetic programs controlling embryonic development were formed in the early days and have been frozen ever since' (Auyang, 1998, p. 195). A similar example can be found in the appendix in the human body. However, a question immediately comes to mind: why cannot newly created adaptive features be also frozen?

One of the chief causes for the localisation of industries can be found in physical conditions of the area. Metals producers located either near mines or close to sources of cheap energy. First-rate grit (for grindstones) was found near Sheffield, England, therefore it became the place for manufacturing of cutlery too. Another cause for the localisation of production has been the support of a court. In the Middle Ages many rulers in Europe have been constantly changing their residences (partly for sanitary reasons). They have frequently invited artisans from a distance and settled them in a group near the royal court. Once the court left, if the town survived, it continued the development of a specialised industry in many cases (Marshall, 1890, pp. 329-30).

Thus, cities often began to develop around royal courts and bishops' sees (concentration of consumers). Later on, the administrative, defence and educational dimension of towns and cities reinforced their function as consumers, but industrial production also started evolving in the cities. Today, many cities produce more value added than they consume.

Certain recent research provided some evidence that general government policy can indeed influence the location of firms and industries. Since 1947, a number of manufacturing industries in the US migrated to southern states because of the wish to escape unions. This was, however, only one of the reasons for the change in the location of certain business in the

[28] One has to recall that dinosaurs probably came into being after an earlier fall of a meteor 251 million years ago.

[29] Because of the availability of wood, Sweden developed mighty pulp and paper industry. Strong links with the suppliers contributed to the replication of the success in the machinery that handles wood, pulp, making and drying paper.

US. Others included innovation and change in transport (substitution of trucking for rail which contributed to a spread in production), as well as the advent of air conditioning that 'made the climate in the South relatively more attractive than the climate in the North' (Holmes, 1998, p. 670).

Firms cluster together in order to benefit, among other reasons, from the availability of a close network of suppliers. They usually, but not necessarily, cluster in locations with large local demand. This demand will be large in the areas where most producers chose to locate (a process of circular interdependence or cumulative causation). 'There is a degree of indeterminacy in the location of activities – firms locate where they do because of the presence of other firms, not because of underlying characteristics of the location' (Venables, 1996, p. 57).[30] For example, there are around 600 tanneries in Arzignano (Vicenza, Italy), most of which employ just a few dozen workers. The region, however, produces 40 per cent of Europe's leather supply. The area around Vicenza does not only soak, dye, stretch, stamp, cut and ship material used for Gucci handbags, Louis Vuitton luggage, Nike sneakers and BMW car seats, but also produces gold chains, clothing and machine tools, many of them for exports. The major problem of a small or a medium-sized enterprise is often not in its 'smallness', but rather in its isolation which is eased in a cluster.

Should one in such an indeterminate situation search for answers to the questions on the geography of production elsewhere? Should it be outside standard economics? Should it be in non-linear dynamics (popularly known as chaos theory) which examines unstable behaviour with multiple dynamic equilibria, lock-in effects, bifurcations and extreme sensitivity to initial conditions; or in self-organisation (spontaneous appearance of order)[31] so common in complex systems; or in the new evolutionary economics[32] that has open frontiers, keeps an interdisciplinary dialogue and considers the role of history, technical change, institutions and development of human capital; or in evolutionary biology (evolution and hybridisation)[33] or elsewhere?

'Organisms are vulnerable, but they are not passive; they dig holes, build dams, modify the environment, and create their own niches of survival. Thus organisms and their environment interact, and together they form an ecological system that is better treated as a whole' (Auyang, 1998, p. 61). Similarly, the effects of externalisation are also pronounced in economics. Consumers' tastes and institutions, both public and private, interact, evolve and alter over time. Consumers, for example, in similar situations make different choices (recall the diversity of breakfast cereals, painkillers, cigarettes, chocolate bars, T-shirts, shoes, cars,

[30] 'Japanese business firms operating in Germany have an unexplainable attraction to Düseldorf rather than Frankfurt' (Beckmann, 1999, p. 61).

[31] Think of theatre when the audience applauds. After a brief period of time, it will all of a sudden start clapping at the same tempo without any conductor. Such self-organisation happens when many initially uncorrelated actions lock into each other's rhythm and create a strong collective group.

[32] Mainstream economics deals with decision-making within given structures. Evolutionary economics is concerned with decision-making and long-term changes of the structure. The interested reader is invited to consult a classical article on the issue by Boschma and Lambooy (1999).

[33] Information in the physical world is transmitted via flows of particles such as electrons or photons and density gradients. In the social world (and to a lesser extent in the biological) 'there are the controls of information flows from the exercise of the *principle of optimum loss of detail* and use of *near-decomposability* within hierarchical structures - and even more so within the intricate interconnections of complicated hierarchical structures that may be embodied in an heterarchical model conceived by a human mind' (Isard, 1996, p. 357). Even though there are difficulties to apply biological analogies to social phenomena, they were widely used in the analysis of firms. The examples include the 'life cycle' theory of the firm, 'viability' of the firm and 'homeostasis' (habitual return to the initial equilibrium) (Penrose, 1952).

cameras or bicycles). Hence, complex systems keep on moving from one pseudo-stable situation to another.

c. Expectations

Resources move gradually from one location and/or industry to another in response to differences in current earnings. If this shift is only gradual, then there must be certain barriers that increase the cost of the move. If there are costs, then the resource owners will be interested in expected returns in the future, rather than in current returns. However, future returns also depend on the decisions of owners of other factors and their expectations about future earnings. For instance, when a new technology is introduced, multiple equilibria cause expectations of potential action from competitors. In this model, expectations (rather than history) determine the future shape of the economy.

A river may, over centuries, bolster its bed and reinforce the work of natural forces over time. However, a strong earthquake (a bifurcation point) may instantaneously ruin such a long history. That was the case with the mechanical cash registers that were made obsolete by digital ones. Subsequently, optical scanners that read bar codes replaced digital cash registers. Those changes were all based on totally different technologies.

Other examples may be found in an almost overnight disappearance of the market for film cameras after the appearance of video cameras; the redressing of the market for mechanical watches after the invention of digital and quartz ones; a shift from dot matrix to bubble jet and laser printers; or fibre optics that evolved independently of the telecommunication technology. A good encyclopaedia has always been a must if the parents wanted their children well educated. A door-to-door salesman of Encyclopaedia Britannica has been replaced by Microsoft's cheap CD-ROM encyclopaedia Encarta produced first in 1993. In addition, Amazon is taking business from real world retail booksellers.

A new product (or service) has to be at least several times superior to the well established product, be it in convenience of use, price, size, shape and/or speed in order to remove the entrenched product from the market. No single source of advantage appears to last for very long. Even unique raw materials can be replaced by synthetic substitutes. Innovation is threatening firms from every side, hence the lock-in effect is not forever. High business concentration of a cluster/town on a single line of production can leave it highly vulnerable on external shifts in demand and technology. Rational entrepreneurs ought to treat bygones as bygones. Being a key player and staying on the top is not a state, but a process.[34] Hence, one needs to recall one of the main lessons from the two century long growth theory: it is innovation, rather than capital accumulation that is the real source of growth in the long term.

Even though they may be important, one may not wish to give an absolute value to external shocks. For example, the nuclear bombs dropped on Hiroshima and Nagasaki in 1945 had no long run impact on the size of these two cities. 'Within the space of just 20 years, they recovered from the devastation to return to their former place in the constellation of the cities' (Davies and Weinstein, 2002, p. 1283). Similarly, the impact of the bombardment of German cities during the Second World War on the city place in the economy and its growth was significant, but temporary (Brakman *et al.*, 2002, p. 28). There

[34] Australians were stopped from selling their wines under French names such as champagne, chablis or claret. So they simply rebranded their products as sparkling wines, cabernet sauvignon and chardonnay. The French were subsequently forced to rebrand obscure labels with varietal names to compete with the Australians on the British market (*The Financial Times*, 28 July 2003).

may be a stronger resilience to shocks in the locational fundamentals than one may expect a priori.

A clear example of how expectations shape the national geography of future production can be found if one considers the case of debt in the developing countries.[35] Back in the 1980s, these countries found themselves unable to repay huge debt owed to the big international banks. Had they all gone into default together, they threatened to damage or even sink the global economic system. The US Secretary of Treasury Nicholas Brady, developed a scheme for refinancing this debt, with the International Monetary Fund (IMF) playing the role of the financial policeman of developing countries by linking lines of credit to painful austerity programmes. This was taken to be a victory for the IMF and international institutions. It could have been, but only in the short run.

During the 1970s, the world saw a massive increase in the price of oil and other internationally traded commodities. The conventional wisdom (expectation) was that commodity prices would only go higher. The Club of Rome and other similar observers of history pointed out that the world was running out of scarce resources. The world was compared to a space ship: resources were being exhausted by growing populations and intensified industrial use. It followed that the price of commodities such as oil, copper and wheat could only increase. If this were the case, a rational expectation was that the best business area to invest in was in commodities. Correct?

The primary producers of commodities were developing countries that lacked manufacturing capability, but controlled natural resources so much demanded by the industrial world. Any sane investor in the 1970s knew that investing in industries that purchased raw materials was dumb, while investing in production of raw materials was smart. So everyone, particularly the international banking community and the World Bank, began investing billions of dollars into ventures designed to produce raw materials in developing countries such as Mexico over Nigeria to the Philippines. As the crucial commodity such as oil was expected to cost 40, 50 or even 100 dollars a barrel in the future, the cost of production was not a critical element in decision-making about investment. The price of commodities was going up and it was important to get into this business early. All of the technocrats simply knew this and the entire international economic system became skewed towards investing and lending to commodity producers in the developing countries.

As a consequence of the above process, the inevitable happened. It turned out that while the world may have a finite amount of oil or copper, there were still huge untapped reserves and progress in technology (which saves in the use of resources). When these megaprojects in the developing world started operating, the price of commodities collapsed. When prices fell below the cost of production, projects went bankrupt because of unsustainability. The outcome was the debt crisis. Nicholas Brady and the IMF stepped in to rectify the trouble. The debt crisis coming from beliefs in commodity scarcity led to an avalanche of investment decisions that has left a legacy of misery. The simplistic and linear projection of future in which commodity producers dominated industrial commodity consumers was rendered false by the collapse in commodity prices and made irrelevant by another phenomenon in the early 1980s. It is related to Microsoft and similar companies that came out of nowhere.

Microsoft, and the endless number of other software and related companies that appeared during the 1980s, altered the equation that had obsessed the World Bank and most other

[35] *Stratfor*, 'IMF's Camdessus misses the point', 15 November 1999.

serious economic thinkers. The emergence of computing technologies and 'brain imports' in the US meant that it was possible to increase economic growth without having similar increase in commodity consumption. Microsoft and creators of ideas, after all, produce wealth without consuming commodities in proportion to growth.

A sharp increase in productivity[36] based on knowledge and innovation is in the core of the new economy. Investments by US firms in shorter-lived assets such as information and communication technology (supposedly important contributors to an increase in productivity) were very high during 1995-2000. After 2000, these investments shrank, but productivity growth accelerated. What is the reason for such type of growth? Are studies about productivity flawed? These studies may arbitrarily include or exclude depreciation. They may also assume that new computers have a direct impact and full impact on production from day one. In reality, however, it takes quite some time to master new equipment.[37] Or, are invisible and intangible activities such as formal and informal computer-related training and reorganisation of business methods more important than measurable investments in new equipment which show only tip of an iceberg? These intangible assets helped American companies produce more output with fewer production workers. As far as Europe is concerned, it had the worst performance in industries that are heavy users of information and communication technology, especially retail trade (where the US productivity is growing strongest which is obvious in retail chains such as Wal-Mart).[38] In addition, the US energy consumption in 1997 and 1998 was almost unchanged, while the US economy grew by 9 per cent during those two years.[39] Those economies that are successful in reducing energy consumption per unit of output can comparatively benefit a lot from increases in the price of energy in the future. The reason is that their competitors that have not done similar adjustments will suffer.

The extraordinary growth of the US economy has many causes. There is no doubt that the persistent growth of productivity in the US is due to the improvement in efficiency introduced by computing and 'brain imports'. Even Federal Reserve Chairman Alan Greenspan has acknowledged this, while also recognising that it is hard to calculate the impact. This much is apparent. At a time when productivity should be falling, inflation and interest rates soaring and the economy moving towards recession, growth in productivity (driven by the effects of computing, as well as new ideas) is keeping long term growth trend.

At the start of 1980s Japan produced cars and cameras at lower prices, smaller in size and better quality than the US. Two decades later the ability to produce cars, copiers and cameras is much less interesting than the ability to write software. The structure of production has shifted in a way that is almost beyond recognition. The hardware that runs a web server is much less valuable than the immaterial intellectual property that resides on the server. Perhaps the Japanese industrial targeting was superior during the age of fax machines, while the US liberal (unplanned) economic system and alert financial markets that force firms to adjust rapidly to shifting markets and changing technology are more becoming for the age of

[36] Increased productivity (growth in output per hour) is the basis for an increase in living standard and economic progress in long term.

[37] The performance of computer chips doubles every 18 months (Moore's law). However, this does not mean that the impact of computers on productivity follows this trend in a linear way. It depends who, how, when and for what purpose uses computers: management of stocks or computer games.

[38] R. Gordon, 'America wins with a supermarket sweep', *The Financial Times*, 19 August 2003.

[39] *The Economist*, 19 August 2000, p. 9.

Internet (Krugman, 2000, p. 174). To put it bluntly, the Japanese bet on hardware, while the Americans bet on software. The decoupling of value from physical production, its shift to intellectual production, is a millennial shift whose full meaning will not unfold for many generations.

The firms that will define the next twenty years of economic history and production geography are probably completely unknown to anyone today. Uncertainty and risk are very high and the way forward is not always clear. Therefore, it is very difficult to know with high degree of confidence where is really going the world's economy. Deep changes that occur little by little (such as transformation in the economy and life that was brought by Microsoft) may be noticed only long after they happen. Therefore, the greatest danger is in 'linear thinking': the belief and expectation that what exists today will also exist tomorrow, but only with a higher degree of intensity.

The old industrial regions in advanced countries exhibited relatively long periods of growth. They were highly specialised in products that serve as basic inputs (coal, steel and chemicals) in the production of other goods or in the manufacture of goods for mass consumption (clothing or cars). However, competition from relatively low-labour cost Asian countries contributed to the economic decline of such clusters in the western countries from the 1970s. According to a dated model this process may find a parallel in the life cycle of a product. A more modern 'network' explanation adds to the economic aspects of over-specialisation a socio-cultural and institutional dimension to explain the meagre ability of old industrial clusters to learn, innovate, apply, absorb, spread and adjust to new realities (Boschma and Lambooy, 1999).

Technological, institutional and political lock-in in old agglomerations places the region in rigid trajectories. This path dependency, routine, a narrow focus on a specific activity and cosy relations between public authorities, business community and labour unions which safeguard the current structure, may often prevent the region from adjusting to new technologies and changes in demand, tastes and market situation. It is still not clear if dealing with such a situation calls for local institutional 'thickness' or 'thinness' in order to revive the local economy. There are at least two ways to address this problem:

- The neo-classical policy advice on this situation would be to enhance factor mobility.
- The evolutionary approach to counter this situation would be to increase local networking, learning and innovative capacity, to reduce dependence on various local 'lock-ins' and to stimulate new start-ups.

Even though there is a certain pessimism regarding the large-scale revival of old industrial clusters, it is often overlooked that new footloose industries do not need to establish ex ante local linkages in order to develop. They often rely to a large extent on their own skills to create conditions for growth. For example, new environment-related industries are emerging in the Ruhr (the connection may be the solution of the pollution problem). In addition, there is little technological continuity between the textile machinery complex in New England of the 19th century and the current electronics cluster (Boschma and Lambooy, 1999).

4.2 War and Location of Firms

Unexpected political events (chances, accidents) such as wars, their start, intensity and length can not be predicted by everyone with a high degree of certitude. Nonetheless, wars decisively influence development, expansion, location, dislocation and spread of certain industries. There are numerous examples that support such arguments. For instance, as a late comer in the colonial era and because of post war(s) external sanctions, Germany had the 'incentives' (was forced by events) to produce various chemicals as substitutes for natural inputs that were not available either in colonies or through 'normal' trade. Self-sufficiency has often been of vital national importance. Germany's success was remarkable as the country developed world-leading chemical[40] and related industries such as pumps, sophisticated precision measurement and control instruments. Let us consider other examples.

- There was a recession in Seattle (Washington) after the First World War. The economy of the region was based on fishing, production of timber and ship/boat building. At about the same time demand for aircraft (made of wood) started to emerge. There were unemployed boat-builders and other inputs. Workers had talents in making wooden boats, they could easily make a fully covered boat (the body of an aeroplane), they also knew how to fix a propeller, which lead to the emergence of Boeing. The US was the country that took advantage of airmail on a large scale, large purchases of military aircraft and large demand for fast travel, which in turn provided domestic producers with early incentives to lower production and learning costs per aircraft as compared with foreign competitors.
- The first commercially successful motor scooter, the Vespa, was produced by the Italian company Piaggio in 1946, although the idea for it was conceived during the Second World War.[41] During the war, Piaggio, at Pontandera, near Pisa, made aircraft engines. After RAF bombing destroyed the factories, warehouses and roads at the site, it became difficult and tiring to get around the site on foot. The company owner, Enrico Piaggio, asked one of his engineers, Corradino d'Ascanio to come up with a simple and economical two-wheel personal vehicle. D'Ascanio built the prototype using his imagination, the leftovers from small two-tact motors used to start the aircraft engines, aircraft wheels (note the shape of wheels on a Vespa when you next see one) and whatever else he could find in the warehouse (or what remained from it), such as metal sheets. It also incorporated a shield on each side to protect the rider's legs from injury. The prototype was ready within a few weeks and once in production, the Vespa became an immediate hit. It was extremely popular and fashionable in the 1950s and 1960s and was rediscovered by another generation in the 1990s because of increasing traffic congestion in cities.
- The Swiss chemical and heavy industry had certain benefits during the world wars. On the one hand, the German industry did not have access to the international market, hence the Swiss entrepreneurs filled the gap where they could. On the other

---

[40] The German chemical industry was based on domestic deposits of salt and coal, as well as talents.

[41] The first of many attempts to produce a small, economical runaround vehicle early in the 20th century resulted in the Auto-Ped. Introduced in New York in 1915, this looked like a child's scooter: it had no seat and there was a platform for the rider to stand on. A two-horsepower motor gave the Auto-Ped a maximum speed of 55 km/h.

hand, the Swiss benefited from the inflow of funds, talents and invalidation of German patents by the Allies.

- Caterpillar went from the US abroad during the Second World War in order to service machines that were used by the US Army. Following the War, the machinery that remained abroad had to be serviced. Hence, Caterpillar became an international company on a larger scale. Coca-Cola also followed the US Army during the Second World War to keep up the morale of the soldiers, and also remained abroad after it. Mars Bars were also distributed to armed forces all around the world during the War.[42]
- Sialkot is a provincial town in the Punjab, Pakistan. It had a military garrison and a mission hospital during the British period a century ago. This created a demand for repair and, later on, production of surgical instruments, tennis rackets and footballs. The area had had a local tradition of producing swords and daggers for several centuries. When the military technology changed, the need for surgical instruments from the local hospital provided demand for sharp scalpels. Later on, around the Second World War, the supply of surgical instruments was necessary for the war efforts. Technology and experts were brought from Britain in order to support the production of those goods. Currently, a core of around 300 family-run firms (almost all have less than 20 employees) in Sialkot produce a range of 2,000 surgical instruments. They are, together with firms in Germany, major world exporters of surgical instruments. As Sialkot has no airport and as it is located over 1,500 km from the nearest sea port, a private self-help action created the Sialkot Dry Port Trust which brought 'the port to Sialkot'. The Trust offers a range of collective services such as customs clearance, warehousing and transport. The success of this, as well as all other clusters is based on two factors. First, the demand driven approach and, second, competition based on collective efficiency. However, not all is ideal in Sialkot. Infrastructure is still rather undeveloped. Power supply is inadequate, communications are poor and roads are covered with ankle deep mud during the monsoon season. Health and safety standards are insufficient and child labour is a serious problem in Sialkot's football making industry (Nadvi, 1998).
- Italian motor car racing companies such as Alfa Romeo, Ferrari and Lancia dominated the market in the period immediately after the Second World War. Within several years, however, a cluster of small firms from around Oxford became another dominant world player. There were several fortuitous events that prompted this evolution. First, there was a huge surplus of abandoned airfields in southern England after the War. Second, Mercedes withdrew from motor racing in 1955 after an accident in Le Mans in which 183 spectators were either killed or injured. This left room for the British racing car builders. Third, large and vertically integrated manufacturers such as Ferrari and Porsche built cars for their own racing teams, while the British were selling cars to everyone that wanted to buy them. Even though the British were not winning races, they dominated the staring grids with the number of cars. Fourth was the ban on cigarette advertising on TV in Britain in 1965.

[42] In an attempt to eliminate the textile waste during the Second World War, the US government reduced by one-tenth the amount of fabric allowed for women's swimwear. The chain of events that resulted in the ever decreasing amount of material necessary for the bikini was set in motion.

Tobacco companies became sponsors of motor racing with vast sums of money in return for having their logos on the racing cars. Pinch and Henry (1999) argue that although the success of the British constructors may have been influenced by a few accidents, it was only to a small extent. Other more important causes such as accumulated knowledge, its circulation through the companies by the means of transfer of personnel, as well as skilled labour, are the origins of the British success. The British have a tradition of expertise in engines and lubricants, aerodynamics and composite materials. In particular, the national aerospace industry was bigger and more sophisticated after the War than the one in Italy. This could, according to Pinch and Henry, probably have encouraged the production of racing cars even without the Mercedes crash and without the money from cigarette manufacturers.

- Another example about the impact of war on the change in the spatial distribution of production deals with the end of 'Cold War' around 1990. Huge defence cuts hit hard the military aerospace cluster in southern California.

4.3 Clusters

Industrial clusters often determine what a country exports. Their success often establishes the competitive position of a country's goods and services on international market. Prior to the Industrial Revolution high transport costs splintered production in many units throughout space. The Industrial revolution reduced costs of transport, but brought high fixed costs that contributed to the development of new and expansion of the existing agglomerations.

A promising point of departure for the analysis of clusters is to consider two basic forces which, through their tension and interplay, influence the spatial distribution (concentration or spread) of firms. They are centripetal and centrifugal forces that also assist to explain the agglomeration and dispersion forces of the 'core-periphery'[43] development model.

- *Centripetal forces* promote agglomeration. They concentrate production and employment in specific geographical areas. These 'snowball' or herding forces include: economies of scale, forward and backward linkages in production, trade costs, increasing returns in transport, concentration of firms and consumers, existence of suppliers, limited spread of information and embodied knowledge, as well as thick labour market (especially for certain skills so that employers can find workers and workers can find jobs). Centripetal forces take the production system towards the equilibrium.
- *Centrifugal forces* push the other way and test if the equilibrium is stable. These dispersion (comparative advantage) forces discourage further spatial concentration of business. They favour a geographical spread of firms and include factor immobility, regional or international wage differentials, relative height of land rents, competition for factors and consumers, commuting costs, pollution, congestion, traffic accidents, crime, infectious and other diseases, sewage and waste disposal.

---

[43] A core region may be taken to mean the one that has capabilities and potentials to create, attract and employ resources and ideas. A periphery region may be taken to be the one that has the economic path determined chiefly by the developments in the core region(s).

The final result depends on the balance between these two forces, on what factors are mobile and what immobile, on barriers to the reallocation of resources, on demand and its change and on public policy. In essence, three outcomes are possible. First, economic activity may spread so that each region becomes specialised in certain activity. This type of clustering does not mean polarisation as is exemplified in North America. The US economy is less geographically polarised than Europe. Second, activity may agglomerate in core regions leaving others without production potentials and without people. Finally, a long run polarisation may split the country or an economic grouping into advanced regions with high incomes and low unemployment and depressed regions with low income and high unemployment (Braunerhjelm *et al.*, 2000, pp. 29-30).

A concentration of functionally related business activity within a relatively small area (agglomeration; 'thick' market effects; benefits of co-location; and non-ergodicity) provides firms with collective gains that would not be available if the firms operated in a remote place. These shared benefits or externalities are different from the ones that are created within and available to a single firm. In essence, clusters create economies that are external to individual firms, but internal to a network of firms in a cluster, which are exchanged and enriched in a non-market way. Hence, a great deal of individual firm's competitive advantage is outside it, but inside the location where it operates.

A firm locates in an area where there are firms from the same or related industry (in a cluster) because:

- it has production links with other firms,
- it may benefit from the already existing pool of suppliers,
- there are services such as finance, information, consulting and maintenance,
- there may be a pool of trained and experienced labour,
- firms may reduce cost of transport,
- there may be a concentration of consumers (proximity to the major growing markets is often the most important reason for the selection of a particular location) and
- they may jointly negotiate contracts with transporters and organize export promotion boards and the like.

Manchester (England) in the 19th century provides the example of such type of cluster specializing in textile manufacturing. Subsequently, the manufacturing of looms and their reparation; bleaching, dying and finishing facilities also located there. In the course of time, the town set up a technical college in order to train people for the manufacture of machinery, textile design and other skills related to the local industry. All this was supported by marketing organizations such as the Cotton Exchange (Smith, 1981, pp. 60-1). A similar story can be told for Reutlingen in Germany. However, even the most recent industries rely on the 'old rule' of geographical concentration (clustering). That is why there is a Silicon Valley in California or Route 128 in Boston (because of the existence of the best universities in the vicinity).

A more recent example of similar developments in the manufacturing of surgical instruments and certain sports goods can be found in the town of Sialkot (Pakistan). This town is the leading world spot for exports of surgical instruments and hand-sawn balls for football. The success of this, as well as of all other clusters is based on two factors. First, demand driven approach and, second, competition based on collective efficiency (Schmitz, 1998, p. 6). An example of a joint action can be found in the surgical-instruments manufacturing cluster the Tuttlingen (Germany). The cluster produced joint publications on various topics of common interest. They include booklets on: quality requirements in the surgical-instruments-making industry; guide on how to use correctly the instruments; and a guide which gives the customer arriving in Tuttlingen the list and profile of firms that produce surgical instruments.

Technical advances in transportation, information technology, organisation and control of production and distribution reduce production time and costs. They 'do away' with distance. 'Globalisation' (integrated international production) creates possibilities to disperse production and ownership. In such circumstances already established spots face tougher times anchoring income-generating activities. At the same time, strong centripetal forces make certain spots remain 'sticky places in slippery space' (Markusen, 1996, p. 293). Spatial barriers for the location of businesses are becoming less important, but capital is more sensitive to the choice of location.

Up until the 1960s it seemed to be more efficient to move people to jobs by migration. The footloose element of many modern industries supports production in relatively small and flexible units. Hence, there is an arbitrary and uncertain element (multiple equilibria) in the location of firms that have footloose industrial character. Locations that are close to consumers save in transport costs of final output, while other locations may save in the cost of production. Due to costs of inputs, economies of scale and forwarding outlays, one business may favour peripheral locations, while for another a preference may be for locations nearest to the consumers.

A cluster is a relatively large group (a critical mass) and system of formal and informal functionally related specialised firms, knowledge, skills and competences, as well as specialised institutions (standards-setting bodies, schools, universities, research institutes, trade associations), in a particular geographical location. This functional relation among firms may be downstream (suppliers), horizontal (competitors and collaborators), upstream (clients) and/or through the circulation of accumulated knowledge, skills and competences by means of turnover of personnel.

Clusters, as spatially limited business incubators, are a part of the new industrial order named alliance capitalism in which continuous collaboration and networking with related knowledge and experience-rich firms are sources of competitiveness. It is also associated with the complex and dynamic 'new economy' based on knowledge and continuous innovation, as firms that operate in clusters are usually innovative. In addition, a vibrant dialogue is continuously taking place among all players in a cluster. The reason why this view fails to define a clear geographical boundary for a cluster is because the structure of a cluster may change over time. It does not refer either to the specific industrial boundary of a cluster, as this may overlook the complex relationship among different industries that support each other's competitiveness.

Agglomeration and the spatial clustering of firms and industries are motivated by efficiency considerations within a network. They are based on economies of scale in production and transportation, as well as on transaction costs. For example, the Massachusetts General Hospital in Boston is among the largest in the world in terms of R&D funds. Industrial managers come to the R&D Department of the Hospital because all the specialists and all the needed knowledge is 'within 20 minutes walking' (Lambooy, 1997, p. 298). This

cluster of more than 400 firms linked to medical devices is invisible as it is concealed in business categories such as electronic equipment and plastics products.

Agglomeration does not apply only to private businesses. Because of the complexity of action and need for a fast response to changing and uncertain events, Simon Jenkins wrote that 'Britain is a centralised state. Two thirds of the top 100 powerful people in Britain work within 300ft of the Prime Minister and Chancellor of the Exchequer' (*The Times*, 11 December 2002).

Marshall (1890) considered the issue of why it is beneficial for producers from the same industry to be located together. He offered three basic reasons for the producers to concentrate (to form a cluster). These are:

- *Knowledge spillovers*: proximity eases exchange and spread of information.
- Advantages of *'thick markets' for specialised skills*: firms may easily find the necessary labour and workers may get promotion or work if the current employer does poorly. There is no need to create the human capital from scratch. The 'mysteries of trade' (craft secrets) are no mysteries at all as they are 'in the air' and children learn many of them unconsciously. Knowledge, experience and values are 'stored'. In addition, tacit knowledge and shared culture of beliefs and practices is difficult to transfer without labour mobility.
- Backward and forward *linkages* associated with large markets: links may clarify and explain a part of the concentration story only if there are economies of scale. Otherwise, a firm would set up a separate production unit to serve each distinct market. A concentrated industry provides market for specialised local suppliers of components, as well as private and public suppliers of various services (institutional thickness).

These economies, external to individual firms in a cluster, but internal to a network of firms in a cluster, are essential, but not sufficient to explain the basic reason for the strength of firms in a cluster. Conscientiously pursued joint action and horizontal and vertical cooperation by firms in a cluster (sharing equipment, developing a new product, various consortia) enhance collective efficiency and improve the competitive advantage of the participating firms. When there is a problem (market failure), it can be resolved by government intervention and/or by private self-help (as was the case in Sialkot, Pakistan)[44] (Schmitz, 1999, pp. 468-70). However, relations between firms in a cluster may take different forms. Take a look, for example, at shoe producing clusters in Italy and Mexico. While cooperation is more common in Italy, market rules prevail in Mexico.

There are, however, additional reasons for the spatial clustering of firms and industries. They include the following:

- Owing to the changed situation in competition and technology, the past arm's-length and hierarchical organisation of a firm can be replaced by a flexible network of business organisation in a cluster. Inter-firm competition is based on innovation.
- Firms may reduce transaction costs.

---

[44] See section on the war and location of firms.

- Presence of one firm/industry creates direct or indirect market for another firm/industry. One industry output is used exclusively as other industry's input (tyres and cars).
- Firms use common services (marketing, storage, accounting, repair, transport).
- Two industries use a common resource.
- Firms may create entry barriers.
- Labour markets of two unrelated industries may be complementary: one industry (metal or car assembly) uses male labour, while other(s) (textile or food processing) employs female labour.
- Firms use common social infrastructure (schools, health, roads).
- The more there are the potential firms that can use infrastructure, the more likely that infrastructure would be built. Each user in a cluster assists other users in this situation, hence the fixed cost of an infrastructure project (such as educational and training centres, power plant, railway or airport) can be recovered and the project can come close to profitability. These are relatively standard projects, hence the government can be easily involved as the specific local knowledge is not always essential for the success.

The presence of a relatively large concentration of demanding consumers in an agglomeration, coupled with technologies with economies of scale, agglomeration forces can bring certain economic advantages through the interrelationship of functionally connected, as well as competing firms. Competition forces firms to employ state of the art technology, hence there are no low-technology industries, but only low-technology firms within various industries.

The clustering of firms selling identical goods (competitors) such as ice cream on the beach was thought to be welfare-inefficient from a social standpoint (Hotelling, 1929, p. 53). However, the clustering of firms often occurs in response to consumers' desires to make comparisons between goods (e.g., in shopping malls). They usually visit more than one store prior to making a purchase. Department stores often demand that certain space is made available in shopping malls to small shoe and apparel retailers. The reason is to assure clients that the offered goods are balanced by other competitive offers (i.e., that a minimum differentiation exists) for comparison. Clustering of *identical* firms can serve a socially-useful purpose because they lower transportation costs (Eaton and Lipsey, 1979, pp. 422-3). The same holds for clustering of *heterogeneous* firms. A rational consumer would connect purchasing activities such as search, purchase and transport. Multipurpose shopping assists in the lowering of shopping costs (Eaton and Lipsey, 1982, p. 58).

If the firms are similar, they seek comparable if not identical features for the spatial location of business. If this is true, then the outcome may be a cluster in such an industry. For example, the US film industry started a century ago in California, around Los Angeles. The concerned firms were similar. They were looking for comparable locational features such as dry weather and excellent daylight conditions. Although modern filming and lighting technology does not depend on natural light at all, the clustering of film and entertainment industry in California continued. Homogeneous initial needs of firms created the film cluster rather than input-output production relations. Hence, functional production links and agglomeration economies are not a necessary condition to create a cluster.

In spite of a few global TV stations such as the BBC or CNN and newspapers such as *The International Herald Tribune* or electronic media, one may easily find that most of the stories that the editors still publish or broadcast are indeed local. The proximity of firms in the same industry increases both the visibility of the course of action of competitors and the speed of the spread of information. 'Popular luncheon spots are patronized by executives from several companies, who eye each other and trade the latest gossip. Information flows with enormous speed' (Porter, 1990, p. 120). This 'cafeteria effect' breaks the spatial boundaries to information flow and gives incentives for the creation of matching improvements by other firms in the cluster. It also offers a partial confirmation that there is a spatial limit to knowledge spillovers. Information may be freely available notwithstanding distance, but the charge for the spread of embodied knowledge, in particular tacit, complex, changeable and 'sticky', goes up with the distance.[45]

The high speed of information diffusion is one of the major strengths of clusters. Entrepreneurs often prefer to enter or stay in a cluster even though they may be able to appropriate a higher return on their innovation elsewhere. The reason for the preference to stay in the cluster is that the firms are there not only providers of information, but also recipients (Schmitz, 1999, p. 475). In the fields where technology changes often, personal contact may be the preferred way of communication rather than the less timely sources such as professional journals, fairs and conferences. 'Human capital accumulation is a *social* activity, involving *groups* of people in a way that has no counterpart in the accumulation of physical capital' (Lucas, 1988, p. 19). This all supports progress in technology (creation of knowledge).

Personal contacts and informality are essential for the exchange of tacit knowledge. '*Tacit knowledge*, as opposed to *information*, ... can only be transmitted informally, and typically demands direct and repeated contact. The role of tacit knowledge ... is presumably the greatest during the early stages of the industry life cycle, before product standards have been established and a dominant design has emerged' (Audretsch, 1998, p. 23).[46] 'Companies that have gone furthest towards linking their global operations electronically report an increase, not a decline in the face-to-face contact needed to keep the firms running well: with old methods of command in ruins, the social glue of personal relations matters more than ever' (*The Economist*, 30 July 1994, p. 11). Such a durable social network that shortens the learning curve, informality in contacts and local embeddedness are essential to identify user requirements, proper installation, operation and service of the product.[47] Therefore, operation of firms within clusters makes firms relatively less sensitive to local taxes. This provides the local authorities with opportunities to tax them more heavily than would otherwise be the case.

---

[45] Audretsch and Feldman (1996) found evidence that the US industries in which new knowledge spillovers are relevant (semiconductors and computers in California; pharmaceuticals in New Jersey) have a greater propensity to cluster innovative activity, than industries where these spillovers are less important. Bottazzi and Peri (2002) reported that the benefits of R&D in generating innovation were extremely localised.

[46] Information are simple structured and unstructured data. Knowledge is the capability to process those data, to analyse and to evaluate them and, possibly, to deepen and to extend them. Tacit knowledge is something that is within a knowledgeable person, but something that one cannot put in a manual.

[47] Personal contacts, face-to-face communication, proximity and trust with a partner are emphasised by Henderson *et al.* (2001), Venables (2001, p. 24), Crafts and Venables (2001, p. 32), Porter (2000, p. 262), Gordon and McCann (2000, p. 520), Sternberg and Tamásy (1999, p. 374), Porter and Sölvell (1998, pp. 445-6) and Kleinknecht and ter Wengel (1998, pp. 645-6), but were well known also to Perroux (1955, p. 317 and 1961, p. 152).

The principal key of success in clusters of related firms in northern Italy ('Padania') is their ultra specialisation and family run type of business. Relatives support each other in business so there is no need for supervision, they relentlessly upgrade skills and they have opportunities for invention. Common values and local consensus is preserved. This reduces the possibility for business sclerosis, so common in large, vertically organised firms. For example, in Lumezzane (near Brescia) which produces two thirds of the national output of bottle openers: one family is strictly specialised in the production of screws, other has expertise in covers, etc. A similar situation is in Cadore (near Austria) with the production of spectacles. In general, company strategy is friendly with fast changes, customised products and niche marketing.

A summary of properties of such industrial districts would include (Garofoli, 1991, p. 52):

- a high level of division of labour between the firms and closer input-output relations;
- a high level of specialisation which stimulates accumulation of knowledge and introduction of new technologies;
- a high level of skills of workers as a result of a very long-term accumulation of knowledge at a local level;
- a large number of local competitors which leads to the adoption of 'trial and error behaviour' and fast imitation process;
- efficient local informal (and formal) system for the exchange of information; and
- an increased emphasis on face-to-face relations.

The existence of the following elements could also be added:

- entrepreneurs,
- innovators,
- financial institutions with venture capital and
- demanding clients.

The growing importance of intangible assets, particularly intellectual capital together with complexities and changeability of information and uncodified knowledge, increases the importance of knowledge externalities (spillovers) and frequent face-to-face contacts among the relevant players. They need to exchange uncodifiable knowledge, to be involved in interactive learning, to have feedback and suggestions, as well as to have a dialogue about risk and changing situation in the market and technology. Clear-cut, routine and simple activities based on codified and standardised knowledge can be managed and controlled from a distance. They can be easily located in regions with lower wages. However, successful handling of more elaborate activities still requires a high degree of exchange of information and face-to-face contacts.[48] This is highly important in complex activities with no or little codified knowledge and where market changes and uncertainty require a fast response (contracts are incomplete). 'Knowledge is the most important resource and learning is the most important process' (Pinch and Henry, 1999, p. 820).

---

[48] Do you know someone that learned to cook a good French or a Chinese dish only by reading a cookbook?

Knowledge externalities are among the key reasons for the existence and success of clusters. Hence, clusters may also be seen as networks for information gathering, facts processing and network production places. 'Almost every internationally successful Italian industry has several if not hundreds of domestic competitors. Frequently, they are all located in one or two towns. ... Where domestic rivalry is absent Italian firms rarely succeed internationally' (Porter, 1990, p. 447). Toyota in Japan, for example, is cultivating suppliers in it's own 'back yard'. Toyota independent suppliers are on average 94 km away from its assembly plants. They make nine deliveries a day. By contrast in North America, GM's suppliers are on average 683 km away from plants they serve to which they make fewer than two deliveries a day. One of the results is that Toyota and its suppliers keep inventories that are a quarter of GM's.[49] While just in time delivery and logistics method may be technically possible, organisationally feasible and financially desirable for a firm, an area that asks for further research includes environmental and social costs of this type of logistics. The just in time delivery method is often linked with half loads and more transport journeys than are the more traditional delivery methods.[50]

The existence of competitors in the vicinity serves a useful business and social purpose. If one imagines a cluster in the shape of an input-output matrix for information, then the direct and indirect functional relations are 'diffused' through rows and columns. Competition increases productivity which is the key ingredient of prosperity. Firms do not chase every chance to ruin rivals. This is contrary to the standard story in every introductory economic textbook.[51] Every firm in a cluster perceives its survival, growth and success in terms of collective growth. These firms learn and prosper collectively. The learning process in a cluster is not only interactive, but also cumulative as it persists over time (once it exists it does not cease to exist, experience and discovery builds on experience and discovery). Turnover of labour, technical staff and management among these firms reinforces the transfer of tacit knowledge, cross-fertilising research, collective learning process and regional competitive advantage.

The underlying general operations within a cluster can be seen from another example. 'New York City's garment district, financial district, diamond district, advertising district and many more are as much intellectual centers as is Columbia or New York University. The specific ideas exchanged in these centers differ, of course, from those exchanged in academic circles, but the process is much the same. To an outsider, it even *looks* the same: A collection of people in similar activities, each emphasizing his own originality and uniqueness' (Lucas, 1988, p. 38). Continuous and straight dealings among players allow tacit and accumulated knowledge to be exchanged within a network of players. Social closeness in such cases may be equally, if not more, relevant than the geographical proximity.

Established locations can be vulnerable to 'technological lock-in' in certain cases. New ideas may need new space. 'When IBM developed its own personal computer, the company located its fledgling PC capacity in Boca Ratton, Florida, way outside of the manufacturing

---

49 *Fortune*, 8 December 1997, p. 43.

50 There was an estimate that empty trucks were making about 60 billion kilometres in the EU at an approximate annual cost of €45 billion. A better organisation of transport could radically reduce these figures (*The European Voice*, 29 January 1998, p. 15).

51 Even though Siemens is a dominant firm in the Munich high technology cluster, it does not threaten or absorb SMEs in the cluster, but rather develops ties with SMEs that are characterised by collaboration (Sternberg and Tamásy, 1999, p. 375).

agglomeration in the North-east Corridor' (Audretsch, 1998, p. 24). This is an example of a bifurcation point. In addition, certain industrial regions may become victims of own past success. Institutional sclerosis, vested interests of large firms, labour unions and public authorities may oppose changes and adjustment to new circumstances. For example, the German Ruhr region was led into the 'trap of rigid specialisation' (Grabher, 1993, p. 275). The Belgian Walloon region is in the same situation. However, it is sometimes overlooked that in certain cases new footloose industries often create own conditions for growth. For example, new environment-related industries are emerging in the Ruhr (the connection may be the solution of the pollution problem). In addition, there is little technological continuity between the textile machinery complex in New England of the 19th century and the current electronics cluster (Boschma and Lambooy, 1999, p. 394).

The existence of a good university or a research institute is not enough alone for the overall economic success of an area. During the period of central planning in the former Soviet Union, Akademgorodok (near Novosibirsk) was essentially a town full of research institutes financed by the Soviet Academy of Sciences. It remained an 'isolated island' as it has not developed functional links with industries. During the centrally planned period, the Soviet enterprises depended primarily on the respective ministries and the central plan.

Sophia-Antipolis was developed in vacant space at the end of 1960s in the south of France. It did not develop around an established university as was the case in Cambridge. A lot of time and effort, such as the establishment of the University of Nice, was necessary to create the necessary links among the high technology firms in the Sophia-Antipolis cluster. In general, it is hard to find any plan of action or best practice to promote a cluster that could have an instantly recognisable success. However, there is a rare general agreement on one point. To have a commercial success, one needs to build on already existing competences in the target location.

The cluster of high technology firms around Cambridge (England) offers a different story. The common tacit code of behaviour among the high technology firms in the region includes trust and cooperation. The cluster is based on two local 'collective agents'. They are Cambridge University and consulting firms in R&D. In contrast to most other British universities which have formally regulated links with the industry, Cambridge has rather liberal rules governing such type of links. In fact, faculty members were allowed to work part time in the private sector. All this had a strong and positive spillover effect on the regional cluster of high technology firms.

There is also a view that 'clusters often emerge and begin to grow naturally. Government policy had little to do with the beginning of Silicon Valley or the concentration of mechanical firms around Modena, Italy. Once a cluster begins to form, however, government at all levels can play a role in reinforcing it. Perhaps the most beneficial way is through investments to create specialized factors, such as university technical institutes, training centres, data banks, and specialized infrastructure' (Porter, 1990, p. 655). In fact, many governments impeded the 'natural' development of clusters on behalf of regional policy and subsidised firms to locate in the areas with high unemployment and without supporting infrastructure (rather than to encourage migration of labour from these regions).

It was thought up until the 1960s that production costs were not sensitive to regional location. It does not come as a surprise that firms located in such areas became white elephants that demanded subsidies to continue operations later on. The importance of endogenous technological change became appreciated only in the following decades, so the policy of regional decentralisation became suspect (Bekar and Lipsey, 2001, p. 1). However, universities have always been established in cities. Children and students had to be assembled. Only relatively recently have universities become established in the countryside.

Governments and big TNCs often have nothing to do with the establishment of clusters (Silicon Valley, clusters in Italy, City of London financial district). They were created out of 'thin air'.[52] However, governments may easily support their growth through the provision of education, infrastructure, tax policy, public procurement, as well as through sponsoring of R&D.[53] All this ought to build on existing local specialties and competences, rather than to create entirely new ones. The private sector needs to lead the process, while the government needs to play a flexible catalytic role as one-size policy does not fit all clusters. There may not be a mechanical transfer of policy instruments from one cluster to another. Positive experiences from other clusters ought to provide more a source of inspiration and less a prescription for a general action.

Papageorgiou (1979) demonstrated that agglomerated firms can achieve higher aggregate profit, lower prices per unit of output and face increased demand than more dispersed firms. In addition, firms located in a cluster tended both to introduce more innovations and to grow faster than more isolated firms (Beaudry *et al.*, 2002, p. 191). Relative to the rest of the economy, clusters could have higher productivity, higher profitability, they may create more new jobs and new firms. On the cost side, land rents may increase in and around clusters and so can pollution and congestion. Labour costs can inflate, while institutions and specialisation may suffer from a path dependence and lock-in effect which may be unfriendly with adaptation to changes in technology that is not directly related to the specialisation in the cluster, but may easily alter the structure of general demand.

What are the implications for policy towards clusters? Well, new and successful clusters may appear. The examples of Ireland and costal region of China provide evidence for this statement. Economic integration and liberal treatment of trade and foreign investment may also assist. Many non-spatial policies such as education and training may have a stronger and more important impact than openly 'spatial' policies. A select list of clusters in the US, Italy and Germany is given in the Annex.

---

[52] The emergence of a cluster may be based on a historical accident such as the existence of certain skills or raw materials or a crossroad. Its evolution may enter into the second phase with the agglomeration of firms and the arrival of externalities that may have cumulative features. Next step in the growth of a cluster may include creation of supporting bodies such as business associations and knowledge related institutions (schools and research centres). The next stage includes the spread of the non-market relations. Firms and institutions create and maintain the spirit of strong non-market collaboration which is external to individual firms, but internal to the cluster. Such clusters may be highly specialised and may have success with their output on the market. However, they may easily become victims of their own success. They may get into a 'trap of rigid specialisation' as the final period in their life. They may be locked in their own technology, specialised output and spirit. If there is another, competing and new good, service or technology elsewhere, which is demanded, than the cluster may decline and demise.

[53] Public policy and administrative areas in which the authorities collect statistics are usually not equal to clusters. That is the reason why it is hard to determine the exact economic significance of clusters with a high degree of reliability.

5 Conclusion

Where a firm or an industry should locate is not a question with a straightforward answer. Rich nations fear the relocation of firms and industries to low-wage nations; poor nations worry that the production of goods and services will migrate to developed countries; while small countries are concerned that businesses will move to large countries.

At the time and age of 'globalisation' of business, one might expect the importance of firm location to be diminishing. Some argue that distance is dead in terms of production and business because of astonishing changes in communications and computers. 'Time zones and language groups, rather than mileage, will come to define distance' (Cairncross, 2001, p. 5). But this may be relevant only for certain manufacturing and services activities that are simple, routine and with codified knowledge. However, local proximity (clusters) of firms that produce similar, competing and/or related products together with supporting institutions still matters for complex activities, with no or lightly codified knowledge and where market changes and uncertainty require a rapid reaction. Economies of scale, activity-specific backward and forward linkages (indivisible production), accumulated knowledge, innovation, lock-in effects, existence of sophisticated customers and a fall in transportation costs play relevant roles in the protection of clusters and the absolute advantage of certain locations. 'Global' competitiveness often depends on highly concentrated 'local' knowledge, capabilities and a common tacit code of behaviour which can be found in a spatial concentration (a cluster) of firms. Hence, successful managers must often think in regional and act in local terms.

Availability of highly skilled and educated workers is becoming an increasingly important determinant for industrial location. This is reinforced by the limited spatial spillovers of knowledge, hence in certain industries 'local' clusters matter for the 'global' competitiveness of firms. National economic policies concerning investment, industrial change, R&D, mobility of people, skills and knowledge, investment in human capital (education) that develops and extends skills, experience and organisational competencies is crucial for the efficiency of the economy. Regional and social affairs also play a role as sometimes regional and social policies impede the development of clusters on behalf of equity considerations among national regions.

A century ago, even a half of a century ago economic theory looked at the location of firms and industries in a rather technical and deterministic way. Subjects and causes were separated from objects and effects, and everything ended up in equilibrium. Parts of modern spatial economics and the new geography of production consider the location of firms in an evolutionary way where the state of equilibrium is only temporary special case as everything is in an unstable organic process.

The new economic geography differs from the traditional model in several important dimensions. The new model makes a case that production specialisation in a given locality is not only based on certain comparative advantages, but rather on a self-reinforcing lock-in effect, path dependence, accumulated knowledge, agglomeration, clustering and linkages (indivisible production). In addition, while the traditional models reason that a reduction in trade costs among locations favours local specialisation, the new economic geography claims that the effect on local specialisation is ambiguous. The final outcome is industry specific and depends on the functional intra-industry production linkages, market structure, consumer preferences (homogeneity of tastes) and factor market (availability and mobility of factors and flexibility in prices). In general, the choice of location for a new investment or a new firm that produce tradable goods and services depends on a complicated interplay of at least three elements: factor intensity; transport intensity; and each in relation to the already established firms and their activities and (re)actions. Remote places do not necessarily need to be poor locations for firms as their remoteness is already reflected in their factor prices (Venables and Limão, 2002, pp. 260-1).

At the end, one may reason that there is an important lacuna in our understanding of spatial economics. It comes as no surprise that there are many disagreements and perhaps only four theoretical agreements:

- First, if one wants to start a new activity in a specific location, one has to build on already existing expertise and specialisation of that location.
- Second, if one wants to use policy intervention to influence the location of firms, this is most effective only very early in the process.
- Third, economies of scale and functional linkages in production have a certain impact on the location of firms and industries.
- Last, success or failure of a region or a policy sometimes depends on uncontrollable factors and events that are located outside regions themselves.[54]

The analysis of spatial economics depends on special assumptions. It is often a detective-type study and a collection of particular cases. Generality is often abandoned for discovery. This should not come as a surprise as spatial economics is simultaneously charged with some of the most difficult problems in economic theory: multiple equilibria, economies of scale, externalities, imperfect competition (which kind?), linkages and path dependence. Nonetheless, many useful things can be learned from exceptional cases. The examination of the issue is still elastic and highly suggestive (in particular how a historical accident may shape the production geography) than conclusive, convincing and general. A coherent theory of the subject is not yet in sight. However, there are various approaches that contribute to the raising of new questions and understanding of the issue. This leaves the topic subject of further theoretical and empirical analysis.[55]

Annex

The production geography of the US is particularly interesting as it is a country without important internal borders and it is so big that it may serve as an example for economic comparison with an integrated Europe.[56] Even a superficial look at US production geography

---

[54] Coalmining regions weakened and declined when liquid fuels started to be used as principal sources of energy.

[55] Topics for further research include: spillovers, externalities and linkages as they are so poorly understood; local interactions; monopolistic competition; cross-fertilisation with industrial organisation and urban economics, trade and growth; cost benefit analysis that can include linkages; services as research was mainly concentrated on the manufacturing sector; the speed of (exponential?) weakening of the effect of spillovers and information relative to distance especially in developing countries; and agglomeration and spread of innovative activities.

[56] One has to be careful regarding comparisons between the current, post Second World War European integration and the evolution of integration in the US. To integrate the country, the American Civil War (1861-65) took the lives of around 620,000 persons in a nation of 35 million. (This loss would be comparable to a loss of 6.7

reveals a high concentration of industries. The implication is that the US clusters profit from large scale production for an almost homogenised large national market. For example, the following industrial clusters come to mind:

- aviation around Seattle
- finance on Wall Street
- insurance in Hartford (Connecticut)
- pharmaceuticals in central New Jersey
- medical equipment in Mineapolis
- electronics in the Silicon Valley and Boston's Route 128
- advertising on Madison Avenue in New York City
- optics related industries in Rochester (New York)
- cars around Detroit
- paints and coatings in Cleveland (Ohio)
- entertainment in California
- office furniture in western Michigan
- orthopaedic devices in Warsaw (Indiana)
- hosiery and home furnishings in North Carolina
- carpets in Dalton (Georgia)
- wine in Napa Valley (California)
- shoes in Massachusetts
- gambling in Las Vegas and Atlantic City

In Europe, production of knives is clustered in Solingen, watches in Geneva and the Swiss Jura, financial services in London, fashion garments and motorcycles in northern Italy, pleasure in Paris, flowers in Holland, sex/prostitution[57] in Amsterdam, carpets in Kortrijk (Belgium), but the European car industry has never created a cluster similar to Detroit.

Italy is an often quoted example of a country with distinct manufacturing clusters. A select group of those clusters include the following:[58]

- motorcycles in Bologna [2,370]
- electronics, mainly alarms for cars in Varese [100]
- jewellery in Valenza Po [1,400] (Alessandria); Vicenza [1,100]; Arezzo [1,300] (Florence)
- spectacles in Cadore [930] (Belluno)
- textiles and clothing in Sempione [3,900] (Varese)
- textiles around lake Como; Prato [8,481] (Florence); Olgiatese [2,614] (Varese); Biella [1,300] (Piedmont); Valdagno (Pisa)

million people in the EU of 2003.) During this war, more persons died of disease and sickness such as dysentery, diarrhea, measles, malaria and typhoid than on the battlefield; the ratio was about 4:1.

57 This has always been an urban 'activity' because cities 'sell' anonymity and tolerance.

58 The list is based on data for 1996; if available the number of related firms in the cluster is given in square brackets; and a bigger city in the vicinity or province is given in 'normal' brackets. Source: "Quanti sono i distretti industriali in Italia?", *Newsletter Club dei Distretti Industriali* n° 9, Novembre 1998, Club dei distretti industriali Prato, p. 9.

- clothing in Val Vibrata [1,150] (Pescara); Empoli (Florence); Treviso
- female underwear in Castel Goffredo [280] (Mantova)
- silk in Comasco [2,600] (Como)
- wool in Biella
- knitwear in Carpi [2,054] (Modena)
- shoes in Fermo, Montegranaro, Porto Santelpidio, Sanbenedetto, San Benedetto del Trono (Ancona); Lucca, Santa Croce Sull'Arno [1,749] (Pisa); Ascoli [3,100]; Riviera del Brenta [886] (Padova)
- sports footwear in Montebelluna [623] (Treviso); Asolo (Treviso);
- tannery in Arzignano [600] (Vicenza) and Solofra (Naples)
- ceramic tiles in Sassuolo [199] (Bologna)
- marble in Apuo-Versiliese [1,161] (Carrara)
- taps and valves in Alto Cusio [300] (Novara)
- furniture in Brianza Comasca Milanese [6,500] (Milan); Cantù [7,200] (Milan); Alto Livenza [2,000] (Udine); Poggibonsi [1,294] (Siena); Bovolone-Cerea [3,000] (Verona)
- kitchens in Pesaro [1,200]
- chairs and tables in Udine [1,200]
- wood machinery in Rimini [1,345]
- agricultural machinery in Modena [100]
- foodstuffs in Parma [215]
- saucepans and valves in Lumezzane [1,008] (Brescia)
- packaging machinery in Bologna
- musical instruments in Castelfidardo [400] (Ancona)

Clusters in Germany:

- steel in Dortmund, Essen and Düsseldorf
- locksmith's products in Velbert
- cutlery in Solingen
- surgical instruments in Tuttlingen
- chemicals in Leverkusen, Frankfurt and Ludwigshafen
- jewellery in Pforzheim
- cars in Wolfsburg, Stuttgart, Munich, Ingolstadt, Neckarsulm and Regensburg
- machine tools in Stuttgart
- pens and pencils in Nuremberg
- printing presses in Heidelberg, Würzburg and Offenbach
- optics in Wetzlar
- tool-making in Remscheid

References

Altshuler, R., H. Grubert and T. Newlon (1998). 'Has U.S. investment abroad become more sensitive to tax rates?', NBER Working Paper No. 6383.

Arthur, B. (1989). 'Competing technologies, increasing returns, and lock-in by historical events', *Economic Journal*, pp. 116-131.

Arthur, B. (1990). 'Positive feedbacks in the economy', *Scientific American* (February), pp. 92-99.

Arthur, B. (1990a). 'Silicon Valley locational clusters: when do increasing returns imply monopoly', *Mathematical Social Sciences*, pp. 235-251.

Arthur, B. (1994a). 'Industrial location patterns and the importance of history', in *Increasing Returns and Path Dependence in the Economy* (ed. B. Arthur). Michigan: University of Michigan Press, pp. 49-67.

Arthur, B. (1994b). 'Urban systems and historical path dependence', in *Increasing Returns and Path Dependence in the Economy* (ed. B. Arthur). Michigan: Michigan University Press, pp. 99-110.

Audretsch, D. (1998). 'Agglomeration and the location of innovative activity', Oxford *Review of Economic Policy*, pp. 18-29.

Audretsch, D. and M. Feldman (1995). 'Innovative clusters and the industry life cycle', CEPR Discussion Paper No. 1161.

Auyang, S. (1998). Foundations of Complex-system Theories in Economics, Evolutionary Biology and Statistical Physics. Cambridge: Cambridge University Press.

Bair, J. and G. Gereffi (2001). 'Local clusters in global chains: the causes and consequences of export dynamism in Torreon's blue jeans industry', *World Development*, pp. 1885-1903.

Bartik, T. (1991). Who Benefits from State and Local Economic Development Policies? Kalamazoo: Upjohn Institute.

Beaudry, C., S. Breschi and P. Swann (2002). 'Clusters, innovation and growth', in *Multinational Firms* (eds J. Dunning and J. Mucchielli). London: Routledge, pp. 190-213.

Beckmann, M. (1999). Lectures on Location Theory. Berlin: Springer.

Bekar, C. and R. Lipsey (2001). 'Clusters and economic policy', Simon Fraser University, Vancouver, mimeo.

Bernstein, J. and D. Weinstein (2002). 'Do endowments predict the location of production? Evidence from national and international data', *Journal of International Economics*, pp. 55-76.

Blackhurst, R. and D. Henderson (1993). 'Regional integration arrangements, world integration and GATT', in *Regional Integration and the Global Trading System* (eds K. Anderson and R. Blackhurst). New York: Harvester Wheatsheaf, pp. 408-435.

Blonigen, B. (1997). 'Firm-specific assets and the link between exchange rates and foreign direct investment', *American Economic Review*, pp. 447-465.

Bottazzi, L. and G. Peri (2002). 'Innovation and spillovers in regions: evidence from European patent data', CEPR, Working Paper, No.215.

Brainard, W. and J. Tobin (1992). 'On the internationalization of portfolios', Oxford Economic Papers, pp. 533-565.

Brakman, S., H. Garretsen and M. Schramm (2002). 'The strategic bombing of German cities during World War II and its impact on city growth', CESifo Working Paper No. 808.

Braunerhjelm, P., R. Faini, V. Norman, F. Ruane and P. Seabright (2000). Integration and the Regions of Europe: How the Right Policies Can Prevent Polarization. London: CEPR.

Boschma, R. and J. Lambooy (1999). 'The prospects of an adjustment policy based on collective learning in old industrial regions', *GeoJournal*, pp. 391-399.

Cairncross, F. (2001). *The Death of Distance* 2.0. London: Texere.

Carlton, D. (1983). 'The location and employment choices of new firms: an econometric model with discrete and continuous endogenous variables', *Review of Economics and Statistics*, pp. 440-449.

Caves, R. (1996). Multinational Enterprise and Economic Analysis. Cambridge: Cambridge University Press.

Christaller, W. (1933). Die Zentralen Orte in Süddeutschland, Jena: Gustav Fischer. [Translated from German by C. Baskin Central Places in Southern Germany (1966), Englewood Cliffs: Prentice-Hall].

Crafts, N. and A. Venables (2001). 'Globalization in history: a geographical perspective', London School of Economics, Centre for Economic Performance.

David, P. (1984). 'High technology centers and the economics of locational tournaments', Stanford University, mimeo.

Davies, R. and D. Weinstein (2002). 'Bones, bombs and break points: the geography of economic activity', *American Economic Review*, pp. 1269-1289.

Dunning, J. (1988). Explaining International Production. London: Unwin Hyman.

Dunning, J. (1999). 'The eclectic paradigm as an envelope for economic and business theories of MNE activity', Discussion Paper No. 263, Department of Economics, University of Reading.

Eaton, C. and R. Lipsey (1976). 'The non-uniqueness of equilibrium in the Löschian location model', *American Economic Review*, pp. 77-93.

Eaton, C. and R. Lipsey (1979). 'Comparison shopping and the clustering of homogeneous firms', *Journal of Regional Science*, pp. 421-435.

Eaton, C. and R. Lipsey (1982). 'An economic theory of central places', *Economic Journal*, pp. 56-72.

Eaton, C. and R. Lipsey (1997). On the Foundations of Monopolistic Competition and Economic Geography. Cheltenham: Edward Elgar.

European Commission (1998). Foreign Direct Investment. London: Kogan Page.

Finger, J. and A. Yeats (1976). 'Effective protection by transportation costs and tariffs: a comparison of magnitudes', *Quarterly Journal of Economics*, pp. 169-176.

Fujita, M., P. Krugman and A. Venables (1999). The Spatial Economy. Cambridge: MIT Press.

Garofoli, G. (1991). 'Industrial districts: structure and transformation', in *Endogenous Development and Southern Europe* (ed. G. Garofoli). Aldershot: Avebury, pp. 49-60.

Gordon, I. and P. McCann (2000). 'Industrial clusters: complexes, agglomeration and/or social networks?', *Urban Studies*, pp. 513-532.

Grabher, G. (1993). 'The weakness of strong ties: the lock-in of regional development in the Ruhr area', in The Embedded Firm (ed. G. Grabher). *London: Routledge*, pp. 255-277.

Graham, E. (1978). 'Transatlantic investment by multinational firms: a rivalistic phenomenon?', *Journal of Post Keynesian Economics*, pp. 82-99.

Harris, C. (1954). 'The market as a factor in the localization of industry in the United States', *Annals of the Association of American Geographers*, pp. 315-348.

Henderson, J., Z. Shalizi and A. Venables (2001). 'Geography and development', *Journal of Economic Geography*, pp. 81-106.

Holmes, T. (1998). 'The effects of state policies on the location of manufacturing: evidence from state borders', *Journal of Political Economy*, pp. 667-705.

Hotelling, H. (1929). 'Stability in competition', *Economic Journal*, pp. 41-57.

Hymer, S., (1976). The International Operations of National Firms: A Study of Direct Foreign Investment. Boston: MIT Press.

Isard, W. (1954). 'Location theory and trade theory: short run analysis', *Quarterly Journal of Economics*, pp. 305-320.

Isard, W. (1956). Location and Space-Economy. Cambridge: Technology Press of MIT and London: Chapman & Hall.

Isard, W. (1996). Commonalities in Art, Science and Religion: An Evolutionary Perspective. Aldershot: Avebury.

Jovanović, M. (1998). International Economic Integration: Limits and Prospects. London: Routledge.

Jovanović, M. (2001). Geography of Production and Economic Integration. London: Routledge.

Jovanović, M. (2003). 'Spatial location of firms and industries: an overview of theory', Economia Internazionale, pp. 23-81.
http://papers.ssrn.com/sol3/papers.cfm?abstract_id=451800

Jovanović, M. (2003a). 'Local vs. global location of firms and industries', *Journal of Economic Integration*, pp. 60-104.
http://papers.ssrn.com/sol3/papers.cfm?abstract_id=394760#Paper%20Download

Jovanović, M. (2005). *The Economics of European Integration*. Cheltenham: Edward Elgar.

Jovanović, M. (2006). *The Economics of International Integration*. Cheltenham: Edward Elgar.

Kleinknecht, A. and J. ter Wengel (1998). 'The myth of economic globalisation', Cambridge *Journal of Economics*, pp. 637-647.

Knickerboker, F. (1973). Oligopolistic Reaction and Multinational Enterprise. Boston: Harvard University.

Kravis, I. and R. Lipsey (1982). 'The location of overseas production and production for export by U.S. multinational firms', *Journal of International Economics*, pp. 201-223.

Krugman, P. (1979). 'Increasing returns, monopolistic competition and international trade', *Journal of International Economics*, pp. 469-479.

Krugman, P. (1980). 'Scale economies, product differentiation and the pattern of trade', *American Economic Review*, pp. 950-959.

Krugman, P. (1990). Rethinking International Trade. Cambridge MA: The MIT Press.

Krugman, P. (1991). 'History versus expectations', *Quarterly Journal of Economics*, pp. 651-667.

Krugman, P. (1992). Geography and Trade. Cambridge MA: The MIT Press.

Krugman, P. (1993). 'On the number and location of cities', *European Economic Review*, pp. 293-298.

Krugman, P. (1998). 'What's new about the new economic geography', *Oxford Review of Economic Policy*, pp. 7-17.

Krugman, P. (2000). 'Can America stay on top?', *Journal of Economic Perspectives*, pp. 169-175.

Lambooy, J. (1997). 'Knowledge production, organisation and agglomeration economies', *GeoJournal*, pp. 293-300.

Leamer, E. (1984). Sources of International Comparative Advantage. Cambridge: The MIT Press.

Leamer, E. and J. Levinsohn (1995). 'International trade theory: the evidence', in *Handbook of International Economics* (eds G. Grossman and K. Rogoff). Amsterdam: Elsevier, pp. 1339-1394.

Linder, S. (1961). An Essay on Trade and Transformation. Uppsala: Almquist & Wiksells.

Lipsey, R. (1992). An Introduction to Positive Economics. London: Weidenfeld and Nicolson.

Lösch, A. (1940). Die Räumliche Ordnung der Wirtschaft, Jena: Gustav Fischer [Translated from German by W. Woglom and W. Stolper, The Economics of Location (1973), New Haven: Yale University Press].

Lucas, R. (1988). 'On the mechanics of economic development', *Journal of Monetary Economics*, pp. 3-42.

Markusen, A. (1996). 'Sticky places in slippery space: a typology of industrial districts', *Economic Geography*, pp. 293-313.

Markusen, J. (1984). 'Multinationals, multi-plant economies and the gains from trade', *Journal of International Economics*, pp. 205-226.

Marshall, A. (1890). *Principles of Economics*. London: Macmillan.

Maurseth, P. and B. Verspagen (2002). 'Knowledge spillovers in Europe: a patent citations analysis', *Scandinavian Journal of Economics*, pp. 531-545.

Midelfart-Knarvik, K., H. Overman, S. Redding and A. Venables (2000). 'The location of European industry', *Economic Papers*, No. 142, European Commission.

Mody, A. and K. Srinivasan (1998). 'Japanese and U.S. firms as foreign investors: do they march to the same tune?', *Canadian Journal of Economics*, pp. 778-799.

Moses, L. (1958). 'Location and the theory of production', *Quarterly Journal of Economics*, pp. 259-272.

Murphy, K, A. Shleifer and R. Vishny (1989). 'Industrialization and the Big Push', *Journal of Political Economy*, pp.1003-1026.

Nadvi, K. (1998). 'International competitiveness and small firm clusters – evidence from Pakistan', *Small Enterprise Development*, pp. 12-24.

Ohlin, B. (1933). Interregional and International Trade. Cambridge: Harvard University Press.

Papageorgiou, G. (1979). 'Agglomeration', *Regional Science and Urban Economics*, pp. 41-59.

Penrose, E. (1952). 'Biological analogies in the theory of the firm', *American Economic Review*, pp. 804-819.

Perroux, F. (1950). 'Economic space: theory and applications', *Quarterly Journal of Economics*, pp. 89-104.

Peroux, F. (1955). 'Note sur la notion de, <pôle de croissance>', *Économie Appliqué*, pp. 307-320.

Perroux, F. (1961). L'Économie du XXe Siècle. Paris: Presses Universitaires de France.

Pfann, G. and H. van Kranenburg (2002). 'Tax policy, location choices and market structure', Institute for the Study of Labor (IZA), Bonn, Discussion Paper No. 499.

Pinch, S. and N. Henry (1999). 'Paul Krugman's geographical economics, industrial clustering and the British motor sport industry', *Regional Studies*, pp. 815-827.

Porter, M. (1990). The Competitive Advantage of Nations. New York: The Free Press.

Porter, M. (2000). 'Locations, clusters and company strategy', in *The Oxford Handbook of Economic Geography* (eds G. Clark et al.). Oxford: Oxford University Press, pp. 253-274.

Porter, M. and Ö. Sölvell (1998). 'The role of geography in the process of innovation and the sustainable competitive advantage of firms', in *The Dynamic Firm* (eds A. Chandler et al.). Oxford: Oxford University Press, pp. 440-457.

Posner, M. (1961). 'International trade and technical change', *Oxford Economic Papers*, pp. 323-341.

Reuber, G. (1973). Private Foreign Investment in Development. Oxford: Clarendon Press.

Rugman, A. (2002). 'Multinational enterprises and the end of global strategy', in Multinational Firms (eds J. Dunning and J. Mucchielli). *London: Routledge*, pp. 3-17.

Rugman, A. and R. Hodgetts (2001). 'The end of global strategy', *European Management Journal*, pp. 333-343.

Sachs, J. (2000). 'Globalization and patterns of economic development', *Weltwirtschaftliches Archiv*, pp. 579-600.

Schmitz, H. (1998). 'Fostering collective efficiency', *Small Enterprise Development*, pp. 4-11.

Schmitz, H. (1999). 'Collective efficiency and increasing returns', *Cambridge Journal of Economics*, pp. 465-483.

Smith, D. (1981). *Industrial Location – An Economic Geographical Analysis*. New York: John Wiley.

Sternberg, R. and C. Tamásy (1999). 'Munich as Germany's no. 1 high technology region: empirical evidence, theoretical explanations and the role of small firm/large firm relations', *Regional Studies*, pp. 367-377.

UNCTAD (1993). World Investment Report: Transnational Corporations and Integrated International Production. New York: United Nations.

UNCTAD (1997). World Investment Report: Transnational Corporations, Market Structure and Competition Policy. United Nations: New York.

UNCTAD (2002). World Investment Report: Transnational Corporations and Export Competitiveness. United Nations: New York.

UNCTAD (2003). World Investment Report: FDI Policies for Development – National and International Perspectives. United Nations: New York.

Venables, A. (1996). 'Localization of industry and trade performance', *Oxford Review of Economic Policy*, pp. 52-60.

Venables, A. (2001). 'Geography and international inequalities: the impact of new technologies', London School of Economics, Centre for Economic Performance.

Venables, A. and N. Limão (2002). 'Geographical disadvantage: a Heckscher-Ohlin-von Thünen model of international specialisation', *Journal of International Economics*, pp. 239-263.

Vernon, R. (1966). 'International investment and international trade in the product cycle', *Quarterly Journal of Economics*, pp. 190-207.

von Thünen, J. (1826). Der Isolierte Staat in Beziehung auf Landtschaft und Nationalökonomie. Hamburg: Perthes. [Translated from German by C. Wartenberg, von Thüunen's Isolated State (1966), Oxford: Pergamon Press].

Wasylenko, M. (1991). 'Empirical evidence on interregional business location decisions and the role of fiscal incentives in economic development', in *Industry Location and Public Policy* (eds H. Herzog and A. Schlottmann). Knoxville: The University of Tennessee Press, pp. 13-30.

Weber, A. (1909). Über den Standort der Industrien, Tübingen: J.C.B. Mohr [Translated from German by C. Friedrich, *Theory of the Location of Industries* (1962), Chicago: University of Chicago Press].

Wheeler, D. and A. Mody (1992). 'International investment location decisions: the case of U.S. firms', *Journal of International Economics*, pp. 57-76.

Yamawaki, H. (1993). 'Location decisions of Japanese multinational firms in European manufacturing industries', in *European Competitiveness* (ed. K. Hughes), pp. 11-28.

In: International Trade Issues
Editor: Robert. V. Weeks, pp. 87-106
ISBN: 1-59454-621-5

Chapter 4

INTERDEPENDENT GROWTH IN THE EU: THE ROLE OF TRADE

Maria Garcia-Vega[*]
Universidad Complutense de Madrid, Spain
Jose A. Herce[**]
Universidad Complutense de Madrid, Spain and FEDEA.
Mail Address: FEDEA. c/ Jorge Juan,
46. 28001 Madrid. Spain

Abstract

We analyze empirically whether the European Union integration has promoted interdependent growth in its member countries. Employing spatial econometric techniques, and using trade data to measure integration, we find that trade has been a channel of diffusion of interdependent growth. Furthermore, the European integration, through successive enlargements, has reinforced this interdependence in EU countries. These results illustrate the idea that, by enhancing trade, the EU integration promotes more interdependent markets and non-pecuniary externalities. The EU integration has positive effect on the growth interdependence of its member countries. We find that if every trade partner of a given country experiences an extra growth of 1 percentage point, this economy will profit from an extra 0.5 point, and if this country belongs to the EU it will have an additional increase of its rate of growth of 0.17 point. Both figures illustrate that the EU integration promotes more interdependent markets, and therefore it can reduce the market fragmentation.

JEL classification: F15, F43, O47, R11
Key words: Interdependent growth, trade, EU integration

---

[*] E-mail address: mlgarcia@ucmail.ucm.es
[**] E-mail address: herce@fedea.es, Phone: +34- 914350401.

1 Introduction

Interdependence among countries can provide positive non-pecuniary externalities. Bigger markets can lead firms to produce more efficiently and face more competition, allowing them to lower the prices, raise quality and gain competitiveness (Baldwin and Wyplosz, 2002). Additionally, more interdependence is especially relevant for EU (European Union) countries because with the launch of the Euro monetary policies are tied up. As the debate on the policy implications of asymmetric shocks for monetary unions has illustrated[67], it is important to promote policies that enhance interdependence in countries forming these unions. European integration has gradually reduced trade barriers, and this has increased trade, especially among EU members[68]. Has this fact had any influence on the interdependence of the growth patterns in the EU countries? We study this question by exploring the growth pattern relationship for 14 EU countries[69] and 7 non-EU OECD countries from 1970 to 1997.

While there is a large literature[70] on measuring productivity spillovers, and the new growth economic models[71] emphasize the idea that trade can induce convergence of growth rates across countries when there are technological externalities, there are few studies that have empirically examined the importance of trade-driven interdependent growth across countries. Ben-David (1993, 1996) has shown that per capita incomes tend to converge as a result of economic integration and trade. Some authors have considered the links among different sectors of the economy, or the domestic transmission of technology through input-output relations. For example, Miller and Spencer (1977) and Grinols (1984) use general equilibrium approaches to reflect interdependence, DeBressons (1996) measures intersectoral dependence in firms. However, these papers do not propose an explicit relationship among countries (exceptions can be found in Keller, 2002, where the transmission of technology among industries affects productivity via trade flows within and among countries, or in Ciccone, 1996, where it is estimated the existence of externalities across countries depending, among other factors, on their physical distance). The article that is closest in spirit to ours is Goicolea et al.(1998) which shows that trade among Spanish regions enhances their interdependent growth. We adopt their approach to apply it to the EU integration process.

Using spatial econometric techniques[72] and bilateral trade data, we examine how growth in a current EU country affects the growth in another EU country depending on their trade links. We then consider the limitations of this approach. The effect of the EU integration on interdependent growth is not reflected in our estimation, since the EU composition has changed during the analyzed period. Moreover, the growth interdependence can have been reinforced if countries belonged to the same economic block. We address these concerns in two ways. First, we include other OECD countries in our estimations. Second, we control for the fact that two countries can belong to either the EU or the EFTA[73] in a particular year. In

---

[67] See for example Bayoumi and Eichengreen (1997).
[68] See for example Srinivasan et al. (1993) for a survey of the literature on the effects of regionalism.
[69] Belgium and Luxembourg data are added all through this paper.
[70] See Bernstein and Mohnen (1998), Branstetter (2001), Coe et al. (1997), Eaton and Kortum (1996), Meyer (2001) among others, and for a survey of the recent literature see Keller (2001)
[71] Grossman and Helpman (1991), Rivera-Batiz and Romer (1991)
[72] See for example Anselin (1988)
[73] EFTA: European Free Trade Association

this way, we measure how the rate of growth of a particular country is affected by the weighted rate of growth of the other countries in the sample. The weights are, on the one hand, the bilateral trade flows between OECD countries and, on the other hand, the bilateral trade flows between countries that belong to the EU or the EFTA in the corresponding year. One natural concern is that the EU countries' rates of growth could be positively related to a third unobserved factor, the coordination of macroeconomic policies. In order to control for this possible problem, we add an inflation variable (GDP deflator) to the regression. Arguably, the EU has emphasized the control of the inflation to its members. Therefore, this variable might reflect that there has been an inflation convergence among EU countries and that there is a common macroeconomic coordination.

The results suggest that EU integration has positive effect on the growth interdependence of its member countries. We find that if every trade partner of a given country experiences an extra growth of 1 percentage point, this economy will profit from an extra 0.5 point, and if this country belongs to the EU it will have an additional increase of its rate of growth of 0.17 point. Both figures illustrate that the EU integration promotes more interdependent markets, and therefore it can reduce the market fragmentation.

In the last part of the article, we measure the scope of the trade intensity to generate growth interdependence. As the literature of technological spillovers has shown[74], the diffusion of technology depends on the level of economic integration and on the geographic distance and location of countries. We analyze the extent of trade to promote interdependent growth. Our results indicate that below a certain threshold of trade intensity, the growth externality turned out to be non significant.

The rest of the article is organized as follows. Section 2 explains a simple model of interdependent growth. Section 3 describes the data that will be used. The estimation of interdependent growth externalities using spatial econometrics is carried out in Section 4, which contains the paper's central result concerning trade, growth and economic integration. Finally, Section 5 summarizes the results obtained.

2 Interdependence in a Standard Growth Equation

Our theoretical framework follows closely that of Garcia-Vega and Herce (2001). We consider the standard growth model (Solow). Suppose that there are J countries indexed: $i = 1, 2, ..., J$, at any time $t = 1, 2, ..., N$; this model states that output in country *i* at period *t*, Y_{it}, is produced using technology, A_{it}, capital, K_{it} and labor, L_{it}.

$$Y_{it} = A_{it} K_{it}^{\alpha} L_{it}^{\gamma} \qquad (1)$$

We assume that interdependence among countries can be expressed as follows:

[74] See Keller (2001) for a survey of this literature.

$$\mathrm{A_{it}} = \eta_{it} \left(\prod_{j=1}^{J} Y_{jt}^{\omega_{ijt}} \right)^{\rho_i} \quad ; \text{with } i \neq j \tag{2}$$

where *Ait* reflects both technology for country *i*, through η_{it}, and a "thick markets" externality, $Y_{jt}^{\rho_i \omega_{ijt}}$, that emerges as markets expand. This part of equation (2) thus implies that the output in country *i* benefits from the fact that the market is growing, as well as bilateral relationships, as economic integration proceeds. This positive effect is due to larger markets that are more densely populated by firms and consumers, displaying a larger variety of goods and services. As countries trade more, they become more interrelated what reinforces the previous effect. Also in equation (2), ρ_i, translates a growth externality that becomes larger the larger bilateral relationships are, measured through ω_{ijt} (trade, investment flows, distance, etc).

The externality set-up assumed in (2) has been proposed by Bertola (1992) where interdependence is established through private capital. It is also retaken in Goicolea et al. (1998) where ouput (market) in other regions or countries replaces capital as the explicit context where externalities emerge and bilateral relationships constitute the channel through which they flow.

Replacing (2) into (1) and taking logarithms one obtains:

$$\mathrm{y_{it}} = \log \mu_{it} + \rho_i \sum_{j=1, j\neq i}^{J} \omega_{ijt}\, \mathrm{y_{jt}} + \alpha\, \mathrm{k_{it}} + \gamma\, \mathrm{l_{it}} \quad ; \text{with } j \neq i \tag{3}$$

where $\mathrm{y_{it}} = \log \mathrm{Y_{it}}$; $\mathrm{k_{it}} = \log \mathrm{K_{it}}$; $\mathrm{l_{it}} = \log \mathrm{L_{it}}$. Taking differences in (3) we get:

$$g_{\mathrm{yit}} = + \rho_i \sum_{j=1, j\neq i}^{J} \mathrm{w_{ijt}}\, g_{\mathrm{yjt}} + \alpha\, g_{\mathrm{kit}} + \gamma\, g_{\mathrm{lit}} + \varepsilon_{it} \quad ; \text{with } j \neq i \tag{4}$$

where $g_{\mathrm{yit}} = \mathrm{y_{it}} - \mathrm{y_{it-1}}$; $g_{\mathrm{kit}} = \mathrm{k_{it}} - \mathrm{k_{it-1}}$; $g_{\mathrm{l}} = \mathrm{l_{it}} - \mathrm{l_{it-1}}$; $c + \varepsilon_{\mathrm{it}} = \log \eta_{it} - \log \eta_{it-1}$ with *c* being a (constant) technological growth parameter, $\varepsilon_{\mathrm{it}}$ and error term, and $\mathrm{w_{ijt}}$ can be interpreted as a moving average of ω_{ijt} over the medium run adopted in order to simplify the procedure to obtain equation (4)[75]. This variable will be given a more precise role latter on.

Equation (4) applies to every country *i*. If we furthermore assume that $\rho_i = \rho$ for all *i*, we end up with a general formulation for interdependent growth equation of the sort:

$$g_{\mathrm{y}} = c + \rho\, \mathrm{W}\, g_{\mathrm{y}} + \alpha\, g_{\mathrm{k}} + \gamma\, g_{\mathrm{l}} + \varepsilon \tag{5}$$

[75] We could have assumed ω_{ijt} to be independent of time. This can be true in the short run but not in the long run. This idea of a smooth process for ω_{ijt} relative to the process for output, at least, seems to us to be a convenient way to simplify the derivation of equation (4).

where c is a constant ($NJ \times 1$) column vector (with all the elements equal), g_y, g_k, and g_l gl are ($NJ \times 1$) column vectors for output, capital and labor growth rates for all years and countries; ρ, α and γ are parameters and W is a block diagonal ($NJ \times NJ$) matrix with the following structure:

$$W = \begin{bmatrix} W_1 & 0 & \dots & 0 \\ 0 & W_2 & \dots & 0 \\ \dots & \dots & & \dots \\ 0 & 0 & \dots & W_N \end{bmatrix}$$

where each W_t is a ($J \times J$) matrix of bilateral trade flows for that particular year whose elements are defined as follows:

$$\omega_{\text{ijt}} = \begin{cases} \dfrac{x_{ijt}}{\sum_{s=1}^{J} x_{ist}} & \text{if i} \neq \text{j} \\ 0 & \text{if i} = \text{j} \end{cases}$$

where x_{ijt} are exports from country *i* to country *j*. Note that the weights have been normalized (dividing by the total exports that country *i* has with the rest of the countries) in order to avoid biases due to the absolute size of trade flows or variation of their measurement unit across time. The arrangement of the W matrix implies that only contemporary spatial dependence is assumed (the elements out of the main diagonal are null).

There are basically two reasons for considering such specification. First, it makes explicit how relationships among countries generate a pattern of interdependent growth. Second, it permits the application of spatial econometric techniques to a specification based on a theoretical model. Spatial econometric techniques (Anselin, 1988), permit to study cross-section data with dependency relationships in space. This spatial dependence can be caused by measurement problems or because there exits complex dependence and interrelations in the studied phenomena based on "physical transfer of commodities, people, information", "background geography" or "relates to more volatile levels of spatial regularity", (Haining, 1986). In particular the parameter ρ measures the importance of the "spatial lagged variable" (in spatial econometrics that makes reference to the variable that is the product of the weights matrix W with the dependent variable) or in our case the strength of the influence of trade dependence on growth. In other words, it indicates the extent of trade autocorrelation, after the other variables have been controlled for. Therefore, following this specification we test whether there is growth dependence among countries due to trade interactions[76]. Or in other words, we are trying to explain the growth of each country through factors that depends on

[76] We explored different ways to construct these weights without significatively different results. Some of the alternatives where indicative that, below a certain level, trade does not influence growth patterns.

each country, such as the labor and capital growth, a constant factor equal for all countries and years, and finally, through the weighted growth of the rest of the countries. The weights in our analysis are the normalized bilateral trade flows between countries. Those countries with higher trade interrelations are expected to have higher growth dependence.

3 Trade between EU Countries

What do the data tell us about trade evolution in EU countries? In this section we give a statistical overview of bilateral trade flows from 1970 to 1997 between EU countries.

Changes in the incentives to trade can be documented through data on bilateral trade from IMF's "*Directions of trade*". To obtain a measure of how the EU integration has modified the incentives to trade of EU countries, we calculate the openness ratio that each of the EU countries has with the other thirteen EU countries[77] minus its openness ratio with the rest of the world. This differential, shown in Table 1, indicates whether a country has a more oriented trade towards the EU rather than towards the rest of the world. The openness ratio is computed as imports plus exports over a country's GDP. GDP data come from the OECD "*Statistical compendium*" database.

For most of the countries this differential is positive and especially large for Belgium+Luxembourg and the Netherlands -the founding Benelux countries. For some countries this differential has increased in the period close to their accession to the EU. This is the case for Spain, Portugal and Greece, while, in the UK, the gap is reduced with its accession to the EU.

More telling about trade flows, however, there is a measure that corrects for the fact that most of the EU countries had different trade agreements between them prior to their accession to the EU (that is the case of the EFTA countries or Spain). Hence in Table 2 and 3 we report trade flow intensities between the EU countries as the flows between any two countries i and j, relative to total flows of these countries with the EU. Defining $x_{i,j}$ as exports of i to j (or imports of j from i), a trade flow intensity measure currently used is just:

$$\text{Trade flow intensity} = \frac{1}{4}\times\left[\left(\frac{x_{i,j}}{x_{UE,i}}\right)+\left(\frac{x_{j,i}}{x_{i,UE}}\right)+\left(\frac{x_{j,i}}{x_{j,UE}}\right)+\left(\frac{x_{i,J}}{x_{UE,J}}\right)\right]$$

With these data we can see who are the main EU trade partners of each of the present EU countries on average between 1970-1997 as shown in Table 4.

This table reflects the huge weight of Germany in the EU economy for it figures regularly among the three main trade partners with the rest of the EU countries. Table 5 shows the main changes in trade flow intensities in the last thirty years. Looking at the pattern in Table 5 some features can be pointed out.

[77] Belgium and Luxembourg have been added all through this article.

Table 1. Differential between EU openness ratio and rest-of-the-world openness ratio For present EU countries 1970-1997

	Aus.	BL	DK	D	Gr.	Irl.	Spain	Fran	Italy	NL	Port.	Fin.	Sw.	U.K
1970	0.12	0.38	0.15	0.04	0.04	0.38	-0.02	0.05	0.02	0.33	0.06	0.12	0.10	-0.09
1971	0.12	0.44	0.14	0.06	0.06	0.47	0.00	0.06	0.03	0.33	0.04	0.14	0.10	-0.08
1972	0.14	0.46	0.13	0.07	0.07	0.39	0.00	0.06	0.04	0.34	0.06	0.14	0.12	-0.06
1973	0.17	0.49	0.15	0.06	0.07	0.43	0.01	0.06	0.04	0.36	0.08	0.15	0.16	-0.06
1974	0.12	0.48	0.15	0.05	0.04	0.52	-0.03	0.05	0.00	0.37	0.06	0.11	0.15	-0.08
1975	0.10	0.43	0.14	0.05	0.05	0.49	-0.03	0.03	0.00	0.33	0.04	0.06	0.10	-0.07
1976	0.11	0.47	0.16	0.05	0.02	0.51	-0.04	0.04	0.02	0.33	0.05	0.06	0.08	-0.06
1977	0.13	0.44	0.14	0.05	0.03	0.53	-0.02	0.05	0.01	0.32	0.06	0.04	0.08	-0.05
1978	0.14	0.44	0.16	0.05	0.04	0.59	-0.02	0.06	0.03	0.31	0.08	0.05	0.08	-0.03
1979	0.15	0.48	0.18	0.06	0.07	0.62	-0.02	0.06	0.03	0.36	0.10	0.07	0.10	0.00
1980	0.15	0.46	0.19	0.06	0.04	0.58	-0.04	0.04	0.02	0.35	0.07	0.04	0.10	-0.02
1981	0.12	0.43	0.16	0.05	0.09	0.50	-0.06	0.02	-0.02	0.36	0.05	0.00	0.07	-0.02
1982	0.12	0.51	0.18	0.05	-0.0	0.47	-0.05	0.05	-0.01	0.38	0.06	-0.01	0.08	-0.01
1983	0.14	0.54	0.18	0.06	-0.0	0.45	-0.04	0.06	0.00	0.40	0.07	0.00	0.10	0.00
1984	0.14	0.55	0.16	0.06	0.00	0.44	-0.03	0.06	-0.01	0.43	0.08	0.02	0.10	0.01
1985	0.15	0.58	0.17	0.07	-0.0	0.45	-0.02	0.07	0.01	0.46	0.10	0.03	0.11	0.02
1986	0.18	0.55	0.16	0.08	0.04	0.41	0.05	0.08	0.05	0.39	0.19	0.06	0.12	0.03
1987	0.20	0.60	0.12	0.09	0.07	0.44	0.07	0.10	0.06	0.43	0.25	0.08	0.13	0.04
1988	0.21	0.63	0.16	0.10	0.09	0.47	0.08	0.10	0.07	0.45	0.29	0.09	0.12	0.04
1989	0.23	0.64	0.18	0.11	0.14	0.48	0.08	0.11	0.07	0.48	0.30	0.08	0.14	0.04
1990	0.22	0.65	0.17	0.10	0.13	0.47	0.10	0.12	0.07	0.47	0.31	0.10	0.14	0.04
1991	0.22	0.63	0.18	0.09	0.10	0.46	0.10	0.12	0.08	0.48	0.29	0.11	0.10	0.05
1992	0.20	0.59	0.18	0.09	0.11	0.46	0.11	0.12	0.07	0.44	0.29	0.13	0.11	0.05
1993	0.19	0.40	0.11	0.03	0.06	0.34	0.11	0.09	0.04	0.23	0.26	0.10	0.12	0.01
1994	0.18	0.46	0.15	0.06	0.07	0.33	0.12	0.10	0.04	0.28	0.27	0.11	0.10	0.02
1995	0.16	0.47	0.14	0.05	0.10	0.17	0.14	0.11	0.05	0.27	0.30	0.10	0.12	0.03
1996	0.17	0.46	0.11	0.05	0.08	0.24	0.14	0.10	0.04	0.27	0.31	0.09	0.10	0.02
1997	0.15	0.48	0.17	0.05	0.08	0.22	0.15	0.11	0.04	0.33	0.34	0.09	0.12	0.00

Source: Own computations

Table 2. Trade flow intensities (in %) between EU countrie 1970

	Austria	**B-L**	**DK**	**Germ.**	**Greece**	**Ireland**	**Spain**	**France**	**Italy**	**NL**	**Port.**	**Fin.**	**Sw.**	**UK**	
Austria		1.5	2.6	28.3	1.9	0.2	1.2	2.7	8.3	2.8	1.9	1.7	4.3	6.5	Austria
B-L	1.5		2.1	22.3	3.3	1.2	3	22.1	6.5	22.6	2.4	1.8	4.1	7.2	B-L
Denmark	2.6	2.1		13.5	0.8	0.7	1.4	3.1	3.3	3.1	2.2	4.9	19.5	16.4	Denmark
Germany	28.3	22.3	13.5		18.6	3.4	12.5	28.9	27.7	30.5	30.5	11.7	15.2	11.4	Germany
Greece	1.9	3.3	0.8	18.6		0.1	1.2	6.2	8.9	3.8	0.4	0.9	2.2	6.8	Greece
Ireland	0.2	1.2	0.7	3.4	0.1		0.6	2.1	1.2	1.6	0.3	0.7	0.9	44.4	Ireland
Spain	1.2	3	1.4	12.5	1.2	0.6		12.4	7.3	4.3	4.2	1.1	3	11.2	Spain
France	2.7	22.1	3.1	28.9	6.2	2.1	12.4		20.7	10.8	5.8	3.3	5.2	9.4	France
Italy	8.3	6.5	3.3	27.7	8.9	1.2	7.3	20.7		7.5	4.2	2.2	3.8	7.4	Italy
Netherlands	2.8	22.6	3.1	30.5	3.8	1.6	4.3	10.8	7.5		2.3	3.4	5.2	10.9	Netherlands
Portugal	1.9	2.4	2.2	10.4	0.4	0.3	4.2	5.8	4.2	2.3		1.6	4.2	16.7	Portugal
Finland	1.7	1.8	4.9	11.7	0.9	0.7	1.1	3.3	2.2	3.4	1.6		16.9	14.6	Finland
Sweden	4.3	4.1	19.5	15.2	2.2	0.9	3	5.2	7.4	5.2	4.2	16.9		16.3	Sweden
UK	6.5	7.2	16.4	11.4	6.8	44.4	11.2	9.4	3.8	10.9	16.7	14.6	16.3		UK

Table 3 Trade flow intensities (in %) between EU countries 1997

	Austria	**B-L**	**DK**	**Germ**	**Greece**	**Ireland**	**Spain**	**France**	**Italy**	**NL**	**Port.**	**Fin.**	**Sw.**	**UK**	
Austria		2.2	1.4	33.2	1.3	0.5	2.2	4.1	8.7	3.3	0.9	1.4	2.0	3.6	Austria
B-L	2.2		2.7	18.7	2.4	3.4	4.1	18.5	6.5	19.4	2.4	4.3	4.7	10.9	B-L
Denmark	1.4	2.7		17.8	1.4	1.5	1.9	4.9	4.0	5.7	1.2	5.1	16.1	7.4	Denmark
Germany	33.2	18.7	17.8		14.2	7.8	14.1	22.9	22.6	24.9	10.4	12.0	13.9	19.2	Germany
Greece	1.3	2.4	1.4	14.2		0.5	3.1	6.0	14.3	4.0	0.4	1.1	1.5	5.2	Greece
Ireland	0.5	3.4	3.4	7.8	0.5		2.1	6.0	2.9	4.8	0.6	1.2	1.8	28.4	Ireland
Spain	2.2	4.1	1.9	14.1	3.1	2.1		18.9	11.6	5.0	15.0	2.0	2.3	8.9	Spain
France	4.1	18.5	4.9	22.9	6.0	6.0	18.9		18.6	10.2	7.4	4.4	5.5	15.6	France
Italy	8.7	6.5	4.0	22.6	14.3	2.9	11.6	18.6		7.5	4.4	3.5	3.8	10.6	Italy
Netherlands	3.3	19.4	5.7	24.9	4.0	4.8	5.0	10.2	7.5		2.9	4.5	7.3	11.3	Netherlands
Portugal	0.9	2.4	1.2	10.4	0.4	0.6	15.0	7.4	4.4	2.9		0.9	1.3	14.8	Portugal
Finland	1.4	4.3	5.1	12.0	1.1	1.2	2.0	4.4	3.5	4.5	0.9		14.0	8.6	Finland
Sweden	2.0	4.7	16.1	13.9	1.5	1.8	2.3	5.5	3.8	7.3	1.3	14.0		10.0	Sweden
UK	3.6	10.9	7.4	19.2	5.2	28.4	8.9	15.6	10.6	11.3	14.8	8.6	10.0		UK

Table 4. Main EU partner between 1970-1997 and major recent changes

	1 partner	**2 partner**	**3 partner**	**Recent changes**
Austria	Germany (31.9%)	Italy (8.9%)	France (3.5%)	
B-L	Germany (21.6%)	Netherlands (20.6%)	France (19.5%)	
Denmark	Sweden (16.3%)	Germany (16.2%)	United K. (11.2%)	
Germany	Austria (31.9%)	Netherlands (27.9%)	France (25.9%)	
Greece	Germany (16.1%)	Italy (11.4%)	France (7.2%)	
Ireland	United K (34.3%)	Germany (6.1%)	France (4.3%)	
Spain	France (16.2%)	Germany (13.5%)	United K. (9.2%)	Portugal (8.4% av.) is a 2 partner since 1992 (15%)
France	Germany (25.9%)	Italy (21.4%)	B-L (19.5%)	Spain (16.2% av.) is 2 partner since 1995 (18.9%)
Italy	Germany (24.7%)	France (21%)	Greece (11.4%)	
Netherlands	Germany (27.9%)	B-L (20.6%)	United K. (12.9%)	
Portugal	Germany (11.1%)	United K. (10.9%)	France (8.5%)	Spain (8.4% av.) is 1 partner since 1988 (15%)
Finland	Sweden (17%)	Germany (12.2%)	United K. (10.9%)	
Sweden	Finland (17%)	Denmark (16.3%)	Germany (14.8%)	
United K.	Ireland (34.3%)	Germany (17.2%)	France (13.7%)	

Table 5. Changes in trade flow intensities between 1970-1997

	Austria	B-L	DK	Germ.	Greece	Ireland	Spain	France	Italy	NL	Port.	Fin.	Sw.	UK.	
Austria		≈	≈	↑	≈	≈	≈	≈	≈	≈	≈	≈	↓	↓	Austria
B-L			≈	↓	≈	↑	≈	↓	≈	↓	≈	≈	≈	↑	B-L
Denmark				↑	≈	≈	≈	↑	≈	↑	≈	≈	↓	↓	Denmark
Germany					↓	↑	≈	↓	↓	↓	↑	≈	≈	↑	Germany
Greece						≈	≈	≈	↑	≈	≈	≈	≈	≈	Greece
Ireland							≈	↑	≈	≈	≈	≈	≈	↓	Ireland
Spain								↑	↑	≈	↑	≈	≈	↓	Spain
France									↓	≈	↑	≈	≈	↑	France
Italy										≈	≈	≈	≈	↑	Italy
Netherlands											≈	≈	≈	↑	Netherlands
Portugal												≈	≈	↓	Portugal
Finland													≈	↓	Finland
Sweden														↓	Sweden
United K.															United K.

Note: This matrix, like the one in Table 4, is symmetric and in order to ease exploration by the reader the symbols below the diagonal have been deleted.

For founder countries (EUR-6), in general, trade flows intensities between themselves decrease or remain stable. For non EU-6 countries, flows intensities increase. As for the United Kingdom, Denmark and Ireland, all joiners in 1973, the first two countries belonged to EFTA-7, therefore they had a particular trade agreement before their entry in the Community. With their accession to the EU their trade flows intensities have decreased (from 16.5% to 7%), increasing mainly those with Germany and France. Ireland has increased its trade flows intensities about one point with almost each country of the Community except with the United Kingdom with which it has decreased its flows (from 44% to 27%). All these countries have clearly diversify their trade patterns since their entry in the EU. The two Iberian countries trade considerably more between themselves since their accession to the EU in 1986. At the same time, Portugal and the United Kingdom reduce their trade intensities (from 16% to 6%). There are also important increases in trade flow intensities between Spain and France and Spain and Italy for almost each period since the seventies and between Greece and Italy since the Greece entry in the Community. The picture is one of a Europe that on average switches its trade partners, trading more with geographically closer countries.

4 Estimation of Interdependent Growth among EU Countries

4.1 Interdependent Growth and Trade

We estimate equation (5) for EU countries using labor and gross fixed capital investment data from 1970 to 1997 (388 observations) from the OECD "Statistical compendium". Data for capital are obtained using the perpetual inventory method[78]. A first step is to test whether there is spatial dependence for the data of trade and growth. This can be done using the scatterplot of Moran (Vayá et al. 2000) (figure 1).

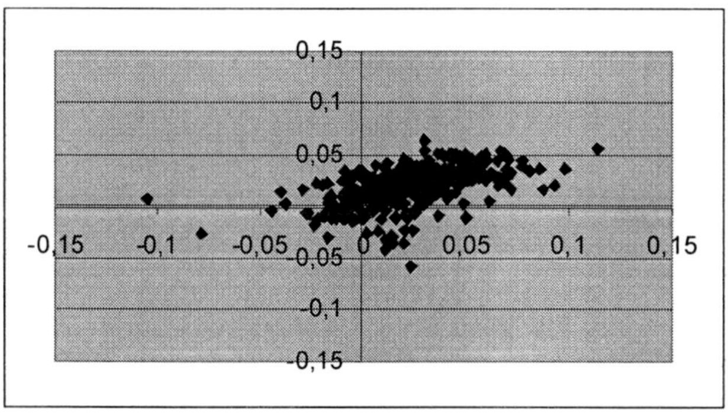

Figure 1. Moran scatterplot for the EU countries: Growth in one country against trade weighted growth in the other countries

[78] Perpetual inventory method measures the stock of capital (K_t) in year t as follows: $K_{t+1} = K_t\,(1-\delta) + I_t$, where δ is the rate of depreciation of capital (we assumed 5%; calculations done with 7% and 3% do not change the results) and I_t is the gross fixed capital formation in period t. To obtain the value of the stock of capital at 1969, somewhat arbitrarily, we assume a capital output ratio of 3 for every country.)

In this graph the dependent variable, g_{yit} is plotted in the x axis whereas the explanatory variable, Wg_{yt} is plotted in the y axis. One can determine whether there is spatial dependence in the data and what structure is as follows. If the observations are dispersed in the four quadrants, there is not spatial dependence. On the contrary, if the set of points lies mainly in upper-right and lower-left regions this indicates that there is a positive spatial correlation.

From figure 1 one can observe that there is positive spatial correlation. Consequently the next step is the estimation of the interdependent growth equation (5). However in our specification we can overestimate the parameter of the interdependent growth if we do not control by other characteristics that are similar among EU countries. EU countries arguably can be in similar stage of development and they can be growing faster until their arrival to their technological frontier. In order to control by those convergence issues, we add to the regression the variable y_{-1}, that is the logarithm of per capita GDP lagged one year. One would expect that the parameter β has a negative sign indicating that; other things equal, richer countries grow less than poorer ones. Equation (5) can then be rewritten as:

$$g_y = c + \rho\, W g_y + \alpha\, g_k + \gamma\, g_l + \beta\, y_{-1} + \varepsilon \qquad (6)$$

In estimating equation (6) the errors are not independent therefore OLS estimation would be inconsistent. Rather, we employ maximum likelihood, as usually done in spatial econometric literature. These estimations are reported in columns (iii) and (iv) of Table 6.

Table 6 Estimation of the interdependent growth spillover for EU countries (t-statistics between brackets)

	(i)	(ii)	(iii)	(iv)	(v)	(vi)
Intercept	0.01 (3.3)	0.008 (6.2)	-0.003 (-1.3)	0.02 (2.6)	-0.004 (-1.7)	0.01 (2.3)
Capital stock	0.73 (8.4)		0.54 (7.8)	0.58 (8.4)	0.57 (8.0)	0.6 (8.5)
Labour	0.36 (7.9)		0.32 (10.3)	0.32 (10.5)	0.3 (9.6)	0.3 (9.9)
Growth spillover ρ_{all}		0.75 (16.1)	0.6 (10.9)	0.57 (10.3)	0.52 (7.8)	0.51 (7.8)
Growth spillover for EU members ρ_{eu}					0.11 (1.5)	0.08 (1.1)
Growth spillover for EFTA members ρ_{efta}					0.14 (1.6)	0.12 (1.5)
Convergence term β				-0.01 (-3.4)		-0.01 (-3.3)
Adjusted R-squared	0.32	0.28	0.46	0.47	0.46	0.47
Sample	388	388	388	388	388	388

We find that the "growth externality" has a positive and statistically significant influence whether we include controls or not, confirming that there can be trade-driven linkages of across countries in the EU. This growth dependence among EU countries, enhanced by trade, enters with a coefficient of around 0.6. This suggests that if every trade partner of a given country experiences an extra growth of 1 percentage point, this country's economy will grow around an extra 0.6 point as implied by the value of ρ in the third column of table 6. While the main result in table 6 indicates that trade interactions affects the pattern of growth for countries of the EU, we cannot deduce an effect from the EU process itself. Of course, one can conclude that as the EU process has helped to increase trade amongst its members it has also promoted interdependent growth for a natural interpretation of the ρW coefficient of the g_y independent variable is that it increases with trade.

In order to assess the influence of the EU process more precisely, we account for the fact that, along the period analyzed, more and more countries have become members of the EU. We consider that growth interdependence among countries could happen in a reinforced way if, among other factors, any two countries belong to the same economic block, the EU in our case. This idea can be formally expressed modifying expression (2) as follows:

$$\mathrm{A}_{it} = \eta_{it} \prod_{\mathrm{R}} \left(\prod_{j=1}^{J} Y_{jt}^{(\omega_{R,ijt})} \right)^{\rho_{R,j}} \quad ; \quad \text{with } i \neq j \text{ and R} = All, EU \text{ and } EFTA \qquad (2')$$

where the different regimes of R refer to all countries, those belonging to the EU and those belonging to the EFTA.

After replacing (2') into (1) and following the same process leading to expression (5) we obtain:

$$\mathrm{g_y} = \mathrm{c} + \rho_{\mathrm{All}} \mathrm{W_{All}}\, \mathrm{g_y} + \rho_{EU} \mathrm{W_{EU}}\, \mathrm{g_y} + \rho_{EFTA} \mathrm{W_{EFTA}}\, \mathrm{g_y} + \alpha\, \mathrm{g_k} + \gamma\, \mathrm{g_l} + \varepsilon \qquad (5')$$

where W_{EU} and W_{EFTA} are block diagonal matrix like W, where:

$$w_{R,ijt} = \begin{cases} \dfrac{x_{R,ijt}}{\sum_{r=1}^{J} x_{R,ijt}} & \text{if } i \neq j\text{; and both i and j belong to R at year t} \\ 0 & \text{otherwise} \end{cases}$$

The results of estimation of equation (5') are reported in columns (iv) and (v) of table 6. The results indicate that belonging to the EU or EFTA increases the growth dependence of its members. This effect seems to be greater for EFTA countries. The coefficients are, however, not very significatively different from zero due to the fact that the variables $W_{All}\, g_y, W_{EU}\, g_y$ and $W_{EFTA}\, g_y$, present high correlation amongst them.

We also explore the possible lags in the "growth externality" estimating the equation (6) with different specifications for the term Wg_y. In particular, we assume, on the one hand, that the growth interdependence between countries can depend on the lagged bilateral trade flows, and on the other hand, that the growth of one country can depend on the lagged growth of the rest of its trade partners. The estimations of the variation of equation (6) are reported in Table 7.

Table 7 Estimation of the nterdependent growth S pillover EU countries with lags (t statistics between brackets)

	(i)	(ii)
Intercept	0.01 (5.28)	0.00 (-0.45)
Capital stock	0.44 (7.84)	0.35 (6.88)
Labour	0.49 (23.4)	0.43 (15.4)
$W_{-1}gy_{-1}$	0.03 (0.57)	
W_{-1} gy		0.58 (12.5)
Adjusted R-squared	0.34	0.45
R-squared	0.33	0.45
Sample	567	567

$W_{-1}gy_{-1}$is the result to multiply the trade weighted matrix lagged one period times the growth of the EU countries lagged one period
W_{-1} gy is the result to multiply the trade weighted matrix lagged one period times the growth of EU countries

The results indicate that there are not significant differences when lags are included in the matrix of weights, although there are when lags are included in the growth of the trading partners of a given countries. These estimations suggest that the interdependence between countries can have a contemporarily factor.

To solve the problem of the high correlation among the variables $W_{All}\, g_y, W_{EU}\, g_y$ and $W_{EFTA}\, g_y$, we re-estimate equation (5') including other non EU OECD countries: United States, Canada, Japan, Norway, Switzerland, Australia and New Zealand. We have in this case 588 observations (21 countries and 28 years). The Moran scatterplot for this new set of countries (figure 2) shows that there is again spatial dependence for the data.

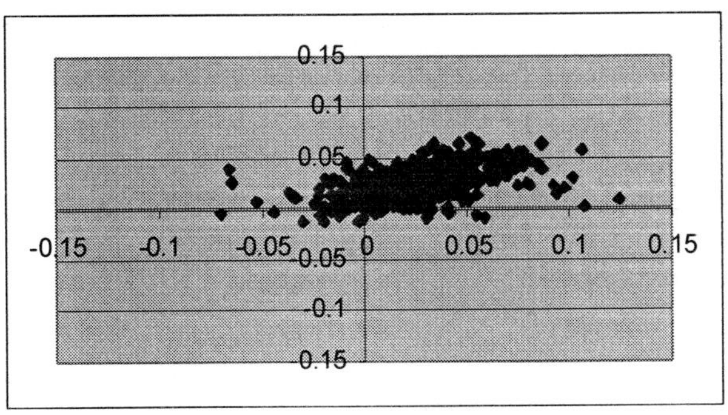

Figure 2. Moran scatterplot for the OECD countries: Growth in one country against trade weighted growth in the other countries

The results of re-estimating equation (5') for this larger set of countries are shown in table 8. As in the estimation for EU countries, we find that trade relations promote an interdependent growth and that belonging to a trade club or other type of trade union (the EU or EFTA) affects positively the growth of the country members.

Table 8 Estimation of the interdependent growth spillover for OECD countries (t-statistics between brackets)

	(i)	(ii)	(iii)	(iv)	(v)	(vi)	(vii)	(viii)	(ix)	(x)
Intercept	0.01	0.03	0.01	-0.002	-0.003	-0.004	0.02	-0.01	-0.005	0.02
	(4.2)	(5.8)	(5.6)	(-1.2)	(-1.8)	(-2.2)	(4.6)	(-2.9)	(-2.5)	(4.7)
Capital stock			0.50	0.40	0.44	0.46	0.43	0.46	0.49	0.46
			(8.3)	(8.6)	(9.3)	(9.8)	(9.4)	(10.0)	(10.3)	(10.1)
Labour			0.48	0.41	0.41	0.41	0.42	0.41	0.41	0.43
			(11.5)	(14.3)	(14.2)	(14.5)	(15.4)	(14.8)	(15.4)	(16.6)
Growth spillover	0.8	0.78		0.59	0.54	0.49	0.47	0.48	0.51	0.49
palll	(14.6)	(14.0)		(12.9)	(11.5)	(9.6)	(9.3)	(9.5)	(9.9)	(9.7)
Growth spillover					0.11	0.17	0.15	0.16	0.19	0.17
for EU members ρ_{eu}					(2.0)	(2.9)	(2.6)	(2.7)	(3.2)	(3.0)
Growth spillover						0.16	0.18	0.2	0.19	0.21
for EFTA members ρ_{efta}						(2.8)	(3.2)	(3.4)	(3.2)	(3.7)
Convergence term β		-0.01					-0.01			-0.01
		(-4.7)					(-5.7)			(-5.9)
Convergence term								-0.01		
with the US. β_{us}								(-4.3)		
Inflation									-0.02	-0.02
									(-2.6)	(-3.0)
R-squared	0.23	0.25	0.34	0.45	0.46	0.46	0.48	0.47	0.47	0.49
Adjusted R-squared	0.23	0.25	0.33	0.45	0.45	0.46	0.48	0.47	0.46	0.49
Sample	588	588	588	588	588	588	588	588	588	588

Our estimates suggest (column (vi) in table 8) that that if every trade partner of a given country experiences an extra growth of 1 percentage point, this country's economy will grow around an extra 0.5 point as implied by the value of ρ_{All} . Moreover, if this country belongs to the EU there is an additional 0.17 percentage point of growth added to the previous figure or an additional 0.16 point if its belongs to the EFTA. The collinearity problem that we detected in the previous estimation has now almost disappeared. The overall growth externality seems now to be larger when more countries are added to the sample, with this increase due to a larger "club effect". Without loosing significance, these results hardly change when we control by convergence issues[79] (columns ii, viii, ix and x). In columns (ix) and (x) we add an inflation variable (GDP deflator) to the estimation in order to control for other unobserved characteristic, in particular, that there has been a co-ordination of macroeconomic policy that possibly has affected the growth co-movement, particularly in the case of the EU. The results show that growth externalities remain statistically significant and about the same size than in previous estimations.

4.2 The Scope of the Trade to Generate Growth Interdependence

In this section, we examine what is the scope of trade to promote growth interdependence. In order to do that, we divide the trade flows matrix W_{All} in different

[79] The parameter β measures the convergence of the country to its technological frontier, whereas β_{USA} measures the catching up with the U.S. This last variable is defined as the difference between the logarithm of per capita GDP of any country with the logarithm of per capita GDP of the U.S.

subgroups depending on the degree of trade between countries[80]. In this way, we modify the equation (5) in order to estimate:

$$g_y = c + \rho_1 W_1 g_y + \rho_2 W_2 g_y + \rho_3 W_3 g_y + \rho_4 W_4 g_y + \\ + \rho_5 W_5 g_y + \rho_6 W_6 g_y + \alpha g_k + \gamma g_l + \varepsilon \qquad (6)$$

where $W_1, W_2, \ldots, W_n, \ldots, W_6$ are block diagonal matrix like W, where trade flows have been grouped in n different classes such that those trade flows belong to the interval $[a_n, b_n)$. In particular, each element in each W_n matrix is constructed in the following way:

$$w_{n,ijt} = \begin{cases} \dfrac{1}{m_{r,ijt}} & \text{if } i \neq j; \text{ and } w_{ijt} \in [a_n, b_n) \\ 0 & \text{otherwise} \end{cases}$$

where $m_{r,ijt}$ is the number of countries that have a bilateral trade flow that belongs to the interval $[a_n, b_n)$ in one particular year.

The different intervals have been defined depending on the data availability to obtain a balance distribution of data in each W_n matrix[81]. The results of the estimation of equation (6) are reported in Table 9.

Table 9 Estimation of the extent of trade to promote interdependent growth (t-statistics between brackets)

	(i)	(ii)	(iii)	(iv)	(v)	(vi)
Intercept	0.00 (0.35)	0.00 (-1.2)	0.00 (-1.38)	0.00 (-1.91)	0.00 (-1.99)	0.00 (-2.46)
Capital stock	0.42 (9.19)	0.41 (8.6)	0.39 (7.7)	0.39 (7.81)	0.39 (7.79)	0.37 (7.19)
Labour	0.43 (15.9)	0.41 (14.2)	0.41 (14.0)	0.42 (14.7)	0.42 (14.75)	0.43 (14.54)
ρ_1	0.45 (11.4)	0.34 (8.5)	0.30 (6.5)	0.27 (5.93)	0.27 (5.73)	0.27 (5.81)
ρ_2		0.25 (6.8)	0.21 (5.2)	0.14 (3.12)	0.13 (2.92)	0.12 (2.54)
ρ_3			0.12 (2.2)	0.05 (0.96)	0.04 (0.78)	0.01 (0.18)
ρ_4				0.18 (3.98)	0.17 (3.64)	0.16 (3.30)
ρ_5					0.03 (0.75)	0.03 (0.74)
ρ_6						0.11 (2.83)
Adjusted R-squared	0.43	0.45	0.45	0.46	0.46	0.47

[80] We follow the Botazzi and Peri (2003) approach. They analyze the extend of physical distance to promote technological spillovers among European countries.

[81] Each W_n matrix has approximately 1700 elements different from zero. The different trade flows intervals are in decreasing order as follows: (0.1,0.89], (0.05, 0.1], (0.02,0.05], [0.02,0.01), (0.008,0.01], (0.004,0.008], (0,0.004].

In this specification a result emerges, growth interdependence decays as trade flows decrease. For trade flows below certain threshold the effect of growth of one country over the rate of growth of its trade partner is insignificant, although this threshold is very low[82].

5 Conclusion

This article examines the impact of the EU integration process on interdependent growth. The European integration can transmit output co-movement through several channels, although we have opted for trade. In particular, increased output in one country leads to increased supply for its trading partners, and therefore, it can increase the other countries' output. Our analysis suggests that EU integration, by enhancing trade among its members, has lead to a more interdependent growth. Averaging across our regressions, we come up with an estimate for the impact of trade on mutual growth for all the countries in the sample of 0.5 percentage point. Countries that belong to the EU can profit from an additional 0.17 percentage point. These estimates suggest that if every trade partner of an EU country experiences an extra growth of 1 percentage point, this country will grow around an extra 0.77 percentage point. Further, the fact that the estimate for the EFTA countries is similar to the one for the EU countries indicates that belonging to an economic block is an important element that promotes interdependent growth.

The results obtained in this article suggest that even if there is some specialization in EU regions, a higher interrelation between countries, through its bilateral trade flows, induces the diffusion of asymmetric shocks. Therefore, it is necessary a higher coordination[83] of economic policies among EU countries. This conclusion is consistent on the one hand, with the theoretical studies of Miller and Spence (1977), Grinols (1984), DeBressons (1996) and Backus et al. (1994), among others, where it is explained the economic dependence among sectors, firms or countries, and on the other hand, with the literature about the correlation of economic cycles. The increasing integration in the EU countries and economic policies that decrease the fragmentation of the markets may allow firms to have access to bigger markets, and this can produce a growth externality that we have measure through the evolution of trade flows. The growth model presented in the paper captures the idea that integration and trade have a positive effect on the participating countries because the market size increases. However, we have an incomplete understanding of the phenomenon. As an extension, it would be interesting to perform a more detailed analysis by sectors and regions, in order to, on the one hand, obtain some insight on agglomeration patterns, that is, where clusters of interdependence are located and which regions profit more from the growth generated in other regions, and on the other hand, evaluate what has been the contribution of the EU process on the productive structure of its members.

Furthermore, whereas this paper has focused only on trade as the element that makes economies interdependent, we think that the analysis of other aspects that are becoming increasingly important in the EU such as financial integration, the Euro or EU-wide policies can provide a deeper understanding about the linkages between integration and growth.

[82] In particular, for trade flows below 0.05.
[83] See Kray and Ventura (2003).

References

Anselin, L. (1988), *Spatial Econometrics: Methods and Models.* Kluwer Academic Publishers.

Baldwin, R. and C. Wyplosz (2002), *The Economics of European Integration* McGraw Hill forthcoming, available on http://www.unige.ch/~baldwin/papers/BW/hw.thm

Bayoumi, T and B. Eichengreen (1997) "Ever closer to heaven? An optimum-currency-area index for European countries" *European Economic Review* April 1997

Ben-David, D. (1993) "Equalizing exchange: Trade liberalization and income convergence" *Quaterly Journal of Economics*, August, pp. 653-679

Ben-David, D. (1996) "Trade and convergence among countries" *Journal of International Economics*, **40**, pp. 279-298

Bernstein, J. and P. Mohnen (1998) "International R&D Spillovers between U.S. and Japanese R&D Intensive sectors" *Journal of International economics* **44**: 315-38

Bertola, G. (1992), "Models of economic integration and localized growth" Discussion Paper 651 CEPR.

Branstetter, L. (2001), "Are knowledge spillovers national or international in scope?. Microeconomic evidence from the U.S. and Japan" *Journal of International Economics* **53**: 53-79.

Botazzi, L. and G. Peri (2003) "Innovation and Spillovers in Regions: Evidence from European Patent Data" *European Economic Review* **42/4** pp. 687-710

Ciccone, A. (1996) "Externalities and interdependent growth: Theory and Evidence" in http://www.econ.upf.es/eng/research/onepaper.php?id=194

Coe, D. and Helpman, E. (1995), "International R&D spillovers" *European Economic Review*, **39**, 859-887.

DeBresson, S. (1996) *Economic interdependence and innovative activity: an input-output analysis.* Aldershot, Edgar.

Eaton, J., and S. Kortum (1996) "Trade in ideas: patenting and productivity in the OECD" *Journal of International Economics* **40**: 251-278.

Garcia-Vega, M., and J. A. Herce (2002) "Integration and growth in the EU: the role of trade" *Información Comercial Española* No. 796

Goicolea, A., J. A. Herce and J. J. de Lucio (1998), "Regional integration and growth: The Spanish case" FEDEA D. T.. 98-14.

Grinols, L. (1984), "A thorn in the lion's paw: Has Britain paid too much for Common Market membership?" *Journal of International Economics*, **16**

Grossman, G. and E. Helpman (1991), *Innovation and growth in the global economy.* Cambridge M.A. M.I.T. Press.

Haining, R. (1986), "Income diffusion and regional economics" in *Transformations through space and time* edited by Griffith and Haining Dordrecht: Martinus Nijhoff.

Keller, W. (2001) "International technology diffusion" webpage: http://www.eco.utexas.edu/~keller/s110901.pdf

Keller, W. (2002) "Trade and the transmission of technology" *Journal of Economic Growth* **7**, 5-24

Meyer, J. (2001), "Technology diffusion, human capital and economic growth in developing countries", UNCTAD working paper #154, Geneva, June.

Miller, M. and J. Spencer (1977), "The static economic effects of the UK joining the EEC: A general equilibrium approach" *Review of Economic Studies*, **44**

Rivera-Batiz, L., and P. Romer (1991), "Economic integration and endogenous growth", *Quaterly Journal of Economics* **106**: 531-555.

Srinivasan, T., Whalley, J. and I. Wooton (1993) "Measuring the effects of regionalism on trade and welfare" in Kym Anderson and Richard Blackhust eds, *Regional Integration and the Global Trading System*, New York: Harvester

Vayá, E. and R. Moreno (2000), "La Utilidad de la Econometría Espacial en el ámbito de la ciencia regional" FEDEA D. T. 2000-13.

In: International Trade Issues
Editor: Robert. V. Weeks, pp. 107-121
ISBN: 1-59454-621-5

Chapter 5

THE IMPACT OF EURO ON TRADE: THE (EARLY) EFFECT IS NOT SO LARGE*

Sergio de Nardis and Claudio Vicarelli
ISAE, Rome
Institute for Studies and Economic Analyses

Abstract

We investigate the impact of the euro adoption on commercial transactions of EMU countries. We refer to the abundant gravity-model literature about the effect of Currency Unions on trade originated by Rose (2000). We adapt this kind of modelling to the specific case of the European Monetary Union drawing from former literature some guidelines summed up as follows: distinction of "pure" common currency from exchange rate volatility effect; selection of sample of countries strictly focussed on EMU economies; consideration of time as well as space dimension; inclusion of other political factors promoting integration. We add to these provisions the observation that the panel estimation of the gravity equation must be dynamic, because EMU is a young phenomenon; short run effects, like trade persistence, can hence play a crucial role.

Our main finding is that the euro adoption has had a positive but not exorbitant impact on bilateral trade of European countries (the estimated percentage increase ranges between 2.6 and 6.3%), much lower than that derivable from Roses's estimates referred to a larger and heterogeneous set of countries (providing a trade increase following the adoption of a common currency by as much as 200%). Our results refer to short-run impacts; long-run effects could be stronger (but, in our opinion, not by the order of a doubling or a trebling effect indicated in the existing literature on currency unions), particularly if the structural change implied by the new currency regime (a fraction of foreign trade is potentially equivalent to domestic trade) becomes completely interiorised in the perception and the behaviour of Euroland citizens

JEL Classification No. F4; F15; C230. Key words: Bilateral, Economic Integration, Dynamic Panel data.

---

* The opinions expressed in this paper are the authors' own and do not reflect those of ISAE.

1 Introduction

As widely discussed in the literature on monetary unions, the elimination of national currencies and their replacement with a single (international) currency brings both benefits and costs to countries that give up their monies and their independent monetary policies. The degree of optimality of currency areas depends on the structural characteristics of member economies that make benefits prevail on costs or not. While costs are essentially related to the loss of an important instrument of macroeconomic policy to adjust to asymmetric shocks, benefits mainly deal with potential gains in economic efficiency, several of which deriving from the elimination of both transaction costs, associated with the use of different monies, and uncertainty deriving from fluctuations of exchange rates.

As a side effect of the adoption of a common currency, many observers also expect a boost to the volume of trade among member countries. The argument generally goes as follows: transaction costs and, especially, currency risks constitute a barrier to trade by dampening the volume of exchanges of goods and services that would otherwise take place. Hence, zeroing these costs and the exchange-rate variability with the introduction of a unique currency, produces an expansion of cross-border transactions and a deeper integration in the monetary area.

This vision, although widespread, is not at all undisputed among scholars of monetary unions. Particularly, sceptics underline that, even in a turbulent currency environment, there exist several financial instruments that allow exporters and importers to hedge against exchange risks, so that the potential increase in trade coming from the elimination on national currencies, is at best small. The counterargument, is that hedging against exchange rate risks cannot be complete and it is, at any rate, costly, especially for small-size exporting firms that typically do not have sufficiently developed financial branches able to efficiently manage the risk in currency markets.

These disputes, focused exclusively on the abatement of the variability of exchange rates, may miss the most relevant point in the analysis of the trade effects of currency unions. As a matter of fact, the elimination of uncertainty is only part – and probably not the most relevant one – of the whole story. The same result could be equally obtained through a credible regime of fixed exchange rates. A currency union is, qualitatively, a different thing. It entails a modification of perceptions and expectations of economic agents which end up dealing with an institutional arrangement whose degree of transparency (all prices across member countries are named in the same currency) and of irrevocability/commitment (breaking up a currency union is different from breaking up an exchange rate mechanism) is incommensurably larger than that of any fixed-exchange-rate regime. As a consequence of these important peculiarities, a significant fraction of foreign trade of the countries adopting a common currency may become, to the eyes of economic agents, equivalent to domestic trade. In this perspective discussions of the repercussions o monetary unions on trade acquire quite a different qualification.

This paper investigates the impact of the euro adoption on commercial transactions of EMU countries, trying to specifically disentangle the effects attributable to the annihilation of exchange rate volatility, and to other policy factors acting in promoting integration, from the influence properly related to the emergence of the European currency union. Section 2 surveys the empirical literature on currency unions and trade, largely developed over the past few years, in which our paper is inserted and from which the main general indications and methodological instruments for the analysis are drawn. Sections 3 and 4 expose the characteristics of the model adopted. Illustration and discussion of the results of the estimates are made in Section 5. Conclusions are reported in Section 6.

2 Currency Union and Trade: A Survey of the Empirical Literature with an Eye to the EMU

Despite widespread convictions that exchange rate volatility dampens trade, scant empirical evidence has been produced to support this view until the mid-nineties. The results of these older studies generally showed a relation between exchange rate and trade either with the "wrong" sign (e.g. Brada and Mendez ,1988), or statistically insignificant (e.g. Belanger et alii, 1992) or at best weak (e.g. Frankel and Wei, 1993).

Given the rather inconclusive state of the literature, great attention was paid at the beginning of this decade to the seminal work of Rose (2000) who - explicitely considering in a gravity model the effect of common currency distinct from that of exchange rate variability - found an extremely large positive impact of currency union on trade: according to his estimates, two countries sharing a common currency trade three times as much as they would with different currencies. Such a striking result remained substantially unchallenged in a conspicuous set of subsequent sensitive analysis aimed at checking the robustness of the finding to different specifications and methods of estimation of the basic equation (Rose 2001; Frankel and Rose 2001; Rose and Engel 2000).

Having the goal to test the effect on trade of the most ambitious experiment of currency union ever tried – since such is the EMU experiment – the obvious question is to what extent these findings are relevant to infer on the consequences of the euro on the transactions between Euroland economies. Quite disappointingly, the answer is "not much". Although there is no benchmark from this literature, the magnitude of the effect proposed in this new vintage of studies (a tripling impact!) seems implausibly large in general and, in particular, for the peculiar experience of EMU countries.

Starting from the general implausibility of the effect, several authors have criticised under different points of view these original findings[1] and tried to obtain (among them, Rose himself) lower estimates. We go through this literature with a special eye to the EMU case, picking up the contributions that seem most promising in shedding light on how to proceed to detect the impact of the euro which is a more limited case (and a special case as we will see) than the common currency effect considered in Rose's universe[2]. In what follows, we try to single out some major directions of route that prove useful for subsequent analysis.

---

[1] See, for example, Lockwood (2000) and Quah (2000), the report of the general discussion on Rose (2000) and Persson (2001)

[2] Limiting the field of observation to the euro area only, we avoid some of the criticism to Rose's works, like those concerning the aggregation bias (see Levy Yeyati, 2001). For a recent survey of the empirical works on the topic of monetary union, see Rose (2002).

Heterogeneity of the Sample Countries

The sample of countries in the dataset of Rose (2000) was extremely heterogeneous. It included 186 countries, dependencies, territories, overseas departments, colonies and so forth: there was a number of currency unions comprising one large and developed country with a number of much smaller countries or territories. It is a world completely different from that represented by the subset of European countries that gave rise to the European Monetary Union. As stressed by Lockwood (2000) and Rose (2000), it is not possible to extrapolate relevant information about the trade repercussions of the euro from this kind of sample[3]. We derive from these observations that, to infer the impact of the euro on the transactions of EMU countries it is necessary to refer to a sample somewhat narrowly defined around a core consisting of the Euroland economies.

Time versus Spatial Dimension

Rose (2000) exclusively focused on a spatial dimension. He estimated a gravity equation on a very ample cross-section of countries; the large estimate of the common-currency parameter measures the variation of trade between member countries of a currency union with respect to trade between countries that maintain their national monies. But, as underlined by Rose (2002), a time-series rather than a cross- cross-section approach would allow to address the more relevant policy issue of the measurement of the variation of trade of countries before and after the creation (or the destruction) of a monetary union, As a matter of fact, this is precisely the issue we want to deal with when testing the consequences of that very specific and (up to now) short-lived currency union which is the EMU. However, not to loose the equally important information conveyed by the spatial dimension, the best strategy to follow seems to be, even in the case of EMU, resorting to panel estimations.

Working with panel estimates generally allows to treat properly all the time-invariant (but space-variant) factors. Rose (2000), working on cross-section data, considers a set of space (geographical, cultural and historical) factors that are actually independent of time. Yet, in spite of the many time-invariant variables one adds to the regressors, there always remains the possibility to omit some, which are difficult to proxy, thus seriously running the risk of a spurious regression. Conversely, in the case of panel estimation, a fixed-effect method allows to control for all the possible time-invariant factors specifically affecting bilateral trade of each pair of countries, including those factors for which it would be impossible to find an explicit approximation[4].

---

[3] This is for example a criticism carried out by Lockwood (discussion on Rose, 2000), but Rose himself said that" In 330 observations two countries trade and use the same currency. Many of the countries involved are small, poor, or both, unlike most of the EMU-11. Thus, any extrapolation of my results to EMU may be inappropriate since most currency union observations are taken from countries unlike those inside Euroland", see Rose (2000), p. 15.

[4] Besides, the fixed-effect estimation also allows to avoid a number of problems of mispecification created by the measure of geographical distance. This problem is well known in empirical works adopting gravity equation. Distance can be a poor measure of transport costs. Usually, it is measured by miles or kilometres between two single points, i.e. the capital cities, under the implicit assumption that all citizens concentrate in the capital; trading costs are quite different if people are spatially distributed within the country. Recently, Melitz (2001) has demonstrated that a measure of distance can reflect comparative advantages. The latter depends on differences in climate and seasons, factors that are simply reflected in differences in latitude between

Rose (2000)[5] noted that a fixed-effect estimation would in many ways be preferable to estimation techniques based on cross-sectional evidence; the very few regime changes in his data (countries entering or leaving common currencies) did not enable him to adopt this method[5].

Resorting to a different dataset – a panel whose time series go back to 1948 – and to a modified specification of the gravity equation, Glick and Rose (2002) obtain, with a fixed-effect method, the reduction by about one third of the original threefold-trade-increase estimation.

Distinguishing Common Currency from Other "Political" Effects

Lower and more plausible estimates of the trade effect of common currency require a keen separation of the currency union from other political factors, whose influence on trade may get improperly confused with that of the single-currency. Melitz (2001), using the heterogeneous dataset of Rose (2000) and making a distinction between the different political effects, came to a lower quantification of the impact of currency union that would raise trade by a factor of 2 (rather than 3). This result was basically obtained distinguishing Political Union and Free Trade area from the currency-union effect. The rationale for this differentiation is apparent: in general, countries that tend to form a monetary union already enjoy particularly close trade or political ties. When not controlling for these links, (most) part of the coefficient of a currency union variable is likely to catch the influences attributable to other political factors.

In the already-mentioned study, Glick and Rose (2002) separated a "*within*" from a "*between*" estimate for the impact of common currency: the former relates to the effect of entry into (or exit from) currency union for a specific country pairs; the latter concerns cross-section or different pairs. While the former does not mix a currency union effect up with political-ties or close-trade effects, the latter can be supposed to do so. The results of the "*within*" estimate showed a smaller influence of currency (a twofold increase of trade), in line with the findings of Melitz (2001).

On a rather different ground, Rose and Van Wincoop (2001) considered the cases of new currency unions between countries that already trade a lot with each other, as it in the case of EMU economies. Introducing a multilateral-trade-resistance index, drawn from Anderson and Van Wincoop (2001), which varies positively with the intensity of trade barriers between each country and with all its trading partners, the authors estimate an increase by "only" 59% in trade between Euroland members: a significantly smaller impact than previous estimates, but, still, a large effect.

---

countries. If this holds true, it is not clear which sign is expected for this variable: an increase in distance might raise, not diminish, trade, if differences in comparative advantage prevail. A fixed-effect estimation allows to bypass this kind of problems, including distance in bilateral constant term.

[5] Probably for this reason, the results addressed by Pakko and Wall (2001) might be biased. In fact, they start from the original dataset adopted in Rose (2000); using trading pair specific fixed effects to control for time-invariant factors, they show an opposite result: a common currency may lead to significant reductions in trade; indeed, this result is statistically insignificant. The authors point out that "..the pooled cross section estimates are not reliable because they are biased by the exclusion or mis-measurement of trading pair-specific variables". This is probably true, but the original Rose's dataset shouldn't permit to apply this estimation method.

3 Short Term Dynamics in Euroland Trade: The "Persistence Effect"

From the former discussion we extract four main guidelines for our work:

1) distinction must be made between euro adoption and exchange rate variability effects, since the former should entail different implications for the economic agents' behaviours;
2) the sample of countries has to be selected by focusing on the group of economies that entered EMU, so that this case is adequately weighted in the whole sample;
3) time as well as space dimensions must characterise the analysis to be able to address the most relevant policy issues, provided the time dimension includes enough years of the euro experience;
4) an explicit consideration must be made on the political and economic ties between Euroland economies that pre-existed or accompanied the formation of EMU and gave rise to an independent increase of the share of intra-area trade.

Before facing estimation issues, a further observation should be added to the former guidelines in order to better adapt the findings of the literature to the special monetary union we are dealing with. When considering the time dimension, one should not forget that EMU is quite a young phenomenon. The European common currency replaced the member countries' national currencies on January 1, 1999, even though only in a "virtual" form[6]. Taking into consideration that "irrevocable" decisions concerning the "euro club" founding members, their exchange rates and their macroeconomic policies were taken in 1997, at best it is possible to scale the beginning of the influence of the (future) new common currency back to 1998. Given the novelty of EMU, traditional static gravity models, that generally deal with long-run relationships, do not fit well to interpret the repercussions of the euro. To this aim, we need to make the gravity equation more short-run oriented, by explicitly introducing dynamics, controlling for the lagged effects of the dependent variable and detecting the short-term influences of the euro and of all other variables affecting bilateral trade in Euroland.

Indeed, "short run" can be generally very relevant in trade analyses, since countries that trade a lot with each other normally tend to keep on doing so. Such inertia mainly derives from the sunk costs exporters have to bear to set up distribution and service networks in the partner country, leading to the emergence of substantial entrance and exit barriers (see Eichengreen and Irwin, 1996). This sticky behaviour seems all the more important in the EMU case, where trade relationships are affected not only by past investments in export-oriented infrastructures, but also by the accumulation of invisible assets such as political, cultural and geographical factors characterising the area and influencing the commercial transactions taking place within it. It is worth noticing that, notwithstanding the general importance of the "persistence effects", quite few studies, based on a panel estimation of gravity equations, have considered the possibility to control for them (among the few, see Egger, 2000, De Grauwe and Skudelny, 2000; Bun and Klaassen, 2002)

[6] The single currency was officially introduced on January 1, 2002.

4 Model and Dataset

The estimation methodology adopted is hence a dynamic panel data approach. We consider 11 exporter countries (European countries now joining the euro, data for Belgium and Luxembourg aggregated) and 30 importer countries (the 11 euro countries plus 19 other countries[7]). The estimate refers to the period 1980-2000.

The introduction of dynamics in a panel data model raises an econometric problem. If trade is a static process, the "*within*" estimator (fixed-effect estimator) is consistent for a finite time dimension T and an infinite number of country-pairs N. But if trade is a dynamic process, the estimate of a dynamic panel such as our model (a static one with the lagged dependent variable) is more difficult. The reason is that the transformation needed to wipe out the country-pair fixed effects[8] leads to correlation between lagged dependent variable and the transformed error term that (for a finite T and an infinite N) renders least square estimator biased and inconsistent.

There are alternative estimators to bypass this inconsistency problem[9]. We focus on that proposed by Arellano and Bond (1991). They suggest to transform the model in first differences and run it by using the Hansen two-step generalised method of moments (GMM) estimator. First differencing the equation removes the random effects that are independent and identically distributed over the individuals, and produces an equation that is estimable by instrumental variables[10].

We are interested in distinguishing the "pure" currency union effect on trade from other political effects (free trade area, exchange rate volatility) that are specific to the case of EMU. To this aim, two distinct monetary variables were considered: a measure of exchange rate volatility and a dummy variable for countries that adopted the euro[11]. Our assumption is that countries sharing the same currency have an additional positive effect on trade with respect to countries sharing a fixed-exchange-rate regime. *De facto,* the assumption is that a common currency can affect trade by the elimination of exchange rate volatility and by another, different influence that we might call "currency union" effect, the latter including a structural change in the perception of agents due to the irreversible choice of adopting a common currency[12]. Since exchange rate volatility between Eurozone countries was reduced during the last decade thanks to the EMS and, lately, to the convergence process leading to the common currency, the distinction between the two effects seems important. Beside, the specific effect on trade deriving from bilateral free trade agreements is taken into account introducing a dummy variable to this scope.

The estimated equation is:

---

[7] They are: Argentina, Australia, Brazil, Canada, China, Czech Republic, Korea, Hong Kong, Japan, Mexico, Norway, Poland, Romania, Russia, Sweden, Switzerland, Turkey, United Kingdom, United States.

[8] The "within"estimator consists of removing the country-pair effects by taking deviations from country-pair means and then applying least squares on the centered variables.

[9] See Baltagi (2001).

[10] Arellano and Bond (1991) identified how many lags of the dependent variable and of the pre-determined variables were valid instruments and how to combine these lagged levels with first differences of the strictly exogenous variables into a potentially very large instrument matrix

[11] Considering that countries decided to join the single currency in May 1998, we consider that year as the start of the common currency period.

[12] "Sharing a common currency rate is much more serious and durable commitment than a fixed rate", see Rose (2000), pp. 10-11

$\Delta Ln(Exp_{ijt}) = b1\ Ln(Exp_{ijt-n}) + b2\ \Delta EURO_{ijt} + b3\ \Delta VOL_{ijt} + b4\ \Delta FTA_{ijt} + b5\ \Delta ln(MASS) + b6\ \Delta RFE$ *(1)*

where:

ln is the natural logaritm, i is the exporter country, j is the importer country and t is the year, n is a lag structure for the dependent variable;

Exp_{ijt} are the exports in volume from country i to country j;

$EURO_{ijt}$ is a dummy variable describing the adoption of the same currency by the 11 European countries: it assumes value 0 for trade between all the pairs of countries in which at least one is not member of EMU, and value 1 for trade between Eurozone countries from 1998 to 2000; in doing so, we assume that the euro started to exert its influence in 1998, before its actual introduction, after decisions were taken (in 1997) about the countries entering the union and endorsing the commitments on exchange rates and macroeconomic policies.

VOL_{ijt} is the exchange rate volatility between countries ì and j at time t; it has been measured by the standard deviation of the first-difference of monthly natural logarithm of the bilateral nominal exchange rate at the current year t.

FTA_{ijt} is a dummy variable that assumes value 0 for absence of free trade agreement or custom unions, 1 if these agreem1ents are present

MASS is the bilateral real GDP of a country pair, as in traditional gravity applications, where

$MASS= ln(GDP_{it} \times GDP_{jt})$

GDP_{it} is the gross domestic product in volume of exporter country, GDP_{jt} is the gross domestic product in volume of importer country;

RFE is an index for relative factor endowments, proxied by *per capita* GDP (GDPPC). The index takes the following form:

$RFE = \left| ln(GDPPC_{it}) - ln\ (GDPPC_{jt}) \right|$

with RFE ≥ 0; The index takes its minimum for countries with identical factor endowments.

The sources of these variables are showed in Table A1 in the Appendix.

Bilateral export flows were expected to be positively influenced by:

a) the euro effect. We expect a positive effect of the euro adoption on trade: considering historical trade relationships between European countries, we expect a smaller impact compared to Rose's results.
b) the product of GDPs of exporter and importer countries (i.e. the sum of their values expressed in logs); in gravity models, trade flows are positively influenced by the dimensions of the origin and destination countries ("mass effect"), proxied by GDP.
c) the presence of custom unions or bilateral free trade agreements. Considering all the European countries joining the euro, the implementation of a Single Market should have caused an important effect on bilateral trade within the area. On the other hand, in the period under examination, European countries have signed regional trade agreements with most non-European countries of our dataset. We expect an economically large impact on trade from this variable.

d) the lagged endogenous variable. Trade relationships between industrialised countries and, in particular, among European countries, have been characterised by very tight economic and political links. We expect that countries trading a lot with each other continue to do so, thus reflecting entrance and exit barriers due the sunk costs.

Bilateral export flows were expected to be negatively correlated

e) with the exchange rate volatility indicator. We expect an increase in bilateral trade when uncertainty regarding bilateral exchange rate fluctuations diminishes[13].
f) with the RFE index. This index is a proxy of differences in factor endowments: a negative correlation with bilateral trade indicates that countries with similar levels of development (small value of the index), like those in our sample, trade a lot, reflecting the importance of intra-industry trade; the correlation could indeed be positive if the sample included economies characterised by very different levels of development and predominance of inter-industry trade.

5 The Results

Arellano and Bond (1991) propose a test of the hypothesis that there is no second-order serial correlation in the disturbances of the first differenced equation. This is a necessary condition for a valid instrumentation; if it is confirmed, then the GMM estimator is consistent. A test for the hypothesis that there is no first order serial correlation is also reported: the rejection of the null hypothesis (i.e. the presence of first order serial correlation) indicates the inconsistency of the OLS estimator.

Table 1 reports the results of these tests and the estimates of the equation by the Arellano-Bond procedure. The tests show the consistency of the GMM estimator and the inconsistency of the OLS procedure. Hence, by introducing dynamics, the proper estimation method is the former[14]. A test of over-identification (Sargan test) is also reported: the statistic shows that the hypothesis that all moment restrictions are satisfied for dynamic specification is not rejected at 5% significance level.

All the regressors are statistically significant and show the expected sign. In particular, the positive impact of the euro adoption is confirmed, as is the negative influence of bilateral exchange rate volatility and the positive effect of being part of a free trade agreement.

---

[13] Among more recent works, also De Grauwe and Skudelny (2000) find a negative relationship between the variance of nominal exchange rate and trade.

[14] Bun and Klaassen (2002) show that trade is a dynamic process and that panel gravity models should allow for that; they also show that, for a T large, the LSDV estimator is a better tool than the GMM one. In other words, there is a consistency problem but also a bias problem. For T large, the bias of the GMM estimator is higher than that of the OLS one. In their sample T=48, we have a T=21. It is well known that the bias increase when T becomes smaller. For a smaller T than in the Bun and Klaassen dataset, the bias will be higher for both estimators. We are interested to the relative bias. We know that finite sample bias of the GMM estimators increase as the number of momentum conditions gets larger, in other words, as T gets larger. It is reasonable to suppose than for a T smaller than the Bun and Klaassen dataset, the bias of the GMM will be lower than their figure and the bias of the OLS estimator is higher. To evaluate with more precision the accuracy of the estimators, a Monte Carlo experiment should be performed.

Table 1

Estimation results
Dependent variable: Total-EMU countries' bilateral exports
Time period: 1980-2000

Lnexp	Coef.	Std. Err.	z	P>|z|	[95% Conf. Interval]	
Exp_{ijt-1}	.3791956	0.021174	17.91	0	0.337695	0.420697
Exp_{ijt-2}	.059718	0.014563	4.1	0	0.031174	0.088262
Exp_{ijt-3}	.0313784	0.012558	2.5	0.012	0.006765	0.055992
VOL_{ijt}	-.2887072	0.043723	-6.6	0	-0.3744	-0.20301
MASS	.6711997	0.051214	13.11	0	0.570823	0.771577
RFE	-.1874568	0.094771	-1.98	0.048	-0.3732	-0.00171
FTA	.1577987	0.027919	5.65	0	0.103079	0.212519
EURO	.0610236	0.026971	2.26	0.024	0.008161	0.113886
_const	.0038835	0.003836	1.01	0.311	-0.00364	0.011402

Sargan test of over-identifying restrictions: chi2(184) = 280.73 Prob > chi2 = 1.0000
Arellano-Bond test that average autocovariance in residuals of order 1 is 0: H0: no autocorrelation z = -1.98 Pr > z = 0.0473
Arellano-Bond test that average autocovariance in residuals of order 2 is 0:m H0: no autocorrelation z = -0.12 Pr > z = 0.9063

Let's have a closer look at the three different kinds of "political" influences (so defined because their values depend on political decisions). As currency variability, a hypothetical reduction of exchange rate volatility between Euroland countries and their partners by one standard deviation around its mean would increase total bilateral trade of Eurozone countries by around 4%.[15] Belonging to a free trade area or to a custom union increases total exports of the Eurozone countries (on average) by 17%[16]. After controlling for these two factors, the "pure" effect on total EMU trade produced by the euro adoption is an increase of 6.3%[17]; since no other country in our sample is member of a monetary union, such an effect ends up

[15] We perform the same simulation exercise proposed by Rose (2000). It consists of reducing VOL, the variable measuring the exchange rate volatility, by an amount equal to its standard deviation. Being the standard deviation of VOL 0.137295 (with a mean of 0.6435) and the estimate of its parameter –0.2887, the increase of trade following the fall of VOL by its standard deviation, i.e. $[(EXP_{\text{reducing VOL by one standard deviation}}/EXP)-1]x100$, is given, *coeteris paribus*, by $[(e^{-0.2887x(VOL-0.1372)}/e^{-0.2887xVOL})-1]x100$ and therefore by $[e^{(-0.2887)(-0.1372)}-1]x100$; since $e^{(-0.2887)(-0.1372)}=e^{0.03964}=1.0404$, the increase in bilateral trade following a reduction of volatility from one standard deviation to zero is around 4%.

[16] Since the parameter of the dummy FTA is 0.1577, the variation of trade induced by being part of a trade agreement (FTA=1) with respect to the case of not being part of any agreement (FTA=0), I.E. $[(EXP_{\text{BEING PART OF A TRADE AGREEMENT}}/EXP_{\text{NOT BEING PART OF AY TRADE. AGREEMENT}})-1]X100$, IS GIVEN, *COETERIS PARIBUS*, BY $[(E^{0.1577x1}/E^{0.1577x0})-1]x100=17.09\%$

[17] This result coincides with the average increase of intra-EMU trade both with respect to all countries that are not part of EMU and with respect to the trade of the EMU countries themselves considered before the creation of the monetary union. For the calculation method, see note 17.

coinciding with the increase of intra-EMU trade following the euro introduction. This result seems more reasonable than the previous ones obtained on the grounds of quite heterogeneous samples of nations.

On the whole, the estimated parameters seem to confirm our priors: the adoption of a common currency had a positive but nor exorbitant impact on the bilateral trade of European countries. This probably because trade links were already tight for several reasons. Trade relationships within Europe, historically intense for cultural and neighbourhood factors, were reinforced during the past 20 years by several (partially overlapping) policy decisions as the creation of the European Monetary System at the end of the seventies, the institution of the Single Market in the eighties, the euro adoption at the end of the nineties. Taking the estimates of the policy parameters at their "face value", one is led to attribute the largest impact on EMU transactions to the implementation of the Single Market (though the estimated effect also includes the influence of minor bilateral trade agreements with third countries outside Europe concluded in that period): the impact of the FTA dummy on trade is significantly higher than that of the EURO dummy and that of the exchange rate volatility.[18]

The lagged dependent variable is statistically significant until a 3-period lag; the value of the coefficient shows the importance of the "persistence effect".

The other "gravity" variables are generally in line with the expectations and the "tradition" of this kind of modelling. Trade directly varies with the size of importers and exporters and indirectly with the differences in *per capita* GDP of trading economies; the latter evidence seems to confirm the prevalence of intra-industry trade between industrialised countries.

The impact of the euro on the EMU trade, obtained in this estimation, measures the variation of transactions of EMU economies with respect to:

1) transactions with non-member countries;
2) transactions of EMU countries themselves before they entered the "euro club". Such a variation has hence both a spatial and a time dimension, with the complication that the latter includes a comparison with both EMU economies (for which there is a change in the currency regime in 1998) and non-EMU countries (for which there is no change in currency regime during the relevant time interval).

To have an evaluation of the effects of the euro on intra-EMU trade before and after the adoption of the single currency, we have re-estimated equation *(1)* considering a sub-panel only comprising EMU variables; hence, the dependent variable in this estimation is represented by intra-EMU exports. Results are shown in Table 2. Attention is drawn on the differences, compared with the estimation made on the whole panel, of the dimension of the so-called policy parameters (euro, Exchange rate volatility, FTA) and of the parameter of the lagged dependent variable. Starting from the latter, the lagged dependent variable shows a higher coefficient than in the complete-panel regression. This probably reflects the structurally tighter intra-area trade links that are mirrored in a higher degree of inertia in trade flows.

[18] It is worth noticing that the dimension of the exchange rate volatility parameter is in line with that found by De Grauwe and Skudelny (2000) in their first difference estimation.

Conversely, coefficients of the policy parameters favouring integration generally lead to estimate smaller impacts than in the complete-panel-regression case: this may be explained by the fact that variations are measured with respect to a "base" already characterised by a significant degree of commercial integration, higher than that denoting the larger panel. As for exchange rate volatility, the larger dimension of the parameter than in the previous estimate is more than offset by the lower variability of the variable, so that the impact of a currency volatility reduction gives rise to a very modest gain in intra-area trade: a volatility fall by one standard deviation around its mean would have increased on average intra-EMU trade by 0.8%[19]. In evaluating this figure one has to consider that this kind of exercise is counterfactual: it gives an indication of "what it would be like" compared to "what it actually is". In the case of EMU countries, bilateral exchange rate variability has been much lower than general volatility (in our panel it has been lower by a factor of 12), mainly because of the EMS functioning and, more recently, the process of macroeconomic convergence to meet the criteria to enter the monetary union. Given this evolution, the extra gain in trade from a further fall of exchange rate variability is necessarily limited.

Table 2

Estimation results
Dependent variable: Intra-EMU countries' bilateral exports
Time period: 1980-2000

LnexpEU	Coef.	Std. Err.	z	P>|z|	[95% Conf. Interval]	
Exp_{ijt-1}	0.638625	0.013505	47.29	0	0.612155	0.665095
VOL_{ijt}	-0.6832	0.102555	-6.66	0	-0.88421	-0.4822
MASS	0.521753	0.022367	23.33	0	0.477915	0.565591
RFE	-0.10094	0.025637	-3.94	0	-0.15119	-0.0507
FTA	0.059221	0.007416	7.99	0	0.044687	0.073755
EURO	0.025713	0.005209	4.94	0	0.015503	0.035922
_const	0.000895	0.000273	3.27	0.001	0.000359	0.001431

Sargan test of over-identifying restrictions: chi2(189) = 1840.22 Prob > chi2 = 1.0000
Arellano-Bond test that average autocovariance in residuals of order 1 is 0: H0: no autocorrelation z = -6.29 Pr > z = 0.0000
Arellano-Bond test that average autocovariance in residuals of order 2 is 0: H0: no autocorrelation z = -0.46 Pr > z = 0.6439

As far as the FTA dummy variable is concerned, in the EMU sub-panel it basically reflects the progressive enlargement of the European Union to new countries. Compared with

[19] The standard deviation is 0.01168 (with simple mean 0.00452) and the estimate of the coefficient is –0.6832; for the calculation method, s ee note 16.

the large- panel regression, the parameter dimension shows a smaller impact (by a factor slightly less than 3): according to this estimate, the effect on intra-area trade is 6.1%[20].

Finally, the coefficient for the EURO dummy is positive and statistically significant. Also in this case, the magnitude of the parameter is lower than in the estimate conducted on the complete panel. The adoption of the common currency, controlling for all the other factors, would have induced an intra-area trade increase by 2.6% with respect to the previous period[21]. This figure compares with the one obtained in the estimate conducted on the large panel (6.3%) which included both the time-dimension impact referred to the only intra-EMU trade and the space-and-time-dimension effect relative to trade with non-EMU countries.

6 Concluding Remarks

The goal of the paper is to estimate the impact of the euro adoption on trade of EMU countries. To this aim we referred to the abundant gravity-model literature originated by Rose (2000) which has provided estimates of the rise of trade due to the emergence of a currency union by a factor varying between 1.6 (i.e. 60%-increase) and 3 (i.e. 200%-increase). These figures seem to us implausibly large, even considering the lower end of the range, for the EMU case.

To adapt the gravity model to the specific case of the European Monetary Union, we draw some general guidelines from the literature that can be summed up as follows:

- distinction of "pure" common currency from exchange rate volatility effect;
- sample of countries strictly focussed on EMU economies;
- time as well as space dimension;
- consideration of other political factors promoting integration.

We add to these provisions the observation that the panel estimation of the gravity equation must be dynamic, because EMU is quite a young phenomenon, where short run effects, like trade persistence, may play a crucial role; this is particularly the case for European economies where persistence in commercial transactions is not only induced by physical investments in distribution and service networks, but also favoured by such "intangible" factors as policy, history, culture.

We performed two kinds of estimations to quantify the euro effect on the EMU trade. In the former, we calculate the variation of EMU trade with respect to both the intra-EMU trade before the introduction of the common currency and the EMU trade with other economies that do not share the European currency. Other things being equal, the euro causes an EMU trade increase by 6,3%; since the sample only includes the EMU case as monetary union, this rise coincides with an increase of intra-EMU trade. With the latter estimation we aim at exclusively detecting the variation of intra EMU-trade before and after the euro adoption. Not surprisingly, the more limited scope of the exercise leads to a lower impact estimate: this mainly depends on the fact that the trade variation is measured with respect to a "base"

[20] For the calculation method, see note 17.

[21] This result represents the increase of intra-EMU trade with respect to the situation of intra-area transactions before the adoption of the common currency. For the calculation method, see note 17.

characterised by an already high degree of trade integration (i.e. intra-EMU commercial transactions). According to this latter estimate - other things being equal - the euro has induced an increase of intra-EMU trade by 2,6% with respect to the behaviour of this kind of trade in the period before the euro adoption.

In conclusion, the order of magnitude of the positive euro effect on the EMU trade we have obtained seems more plausible than the (very large) measures proposed in a literature not specifically focusing on the EMU experience. One has to consider that, since we deal with dynamic panel estimation, our results mainly refer to short-run impacts; long-run effects might be stronger (but in our opinion they certainly are not by the order indicated in the existing literature), particularly if the structural change implied by the new currency regime (intra-EMU trade is potentially equivalent to domestic trade) becomes completely interiorised in the perceptions and the behaviours of Euroland citizens.

Annex 1

Table. A1

Variables	Source	Available years
Bilateral exports flows (US million $)	International Monetary Found, Direction of trade statistic database	1980-2000
Export deflator	Economist Intelligence Unit	1980-2001
GDP at costant price (billion US $ at 1996 prices)	Economist Intelligence Unit	1980-2001
Free Trade Agreement	WTO, Mapping of regional Trade Agreement, available at *http://www.wto.org/english/tratop_e/region_e/region_e.htm*	1980-2001
Bilateral exchange rate	International Monetary Found, International Financial Statistic database	1980-2001
GDP per head (US $ at PPP)	Economist Intelligence Unit	1980-2001

References

Anderson J. and van Wincoop E. (2001), "Gravity with Gravitas: a Solution to Border Puzzle", *NBER Working Paper* n.**8079**, January.

Arellano M. and Bond S., (1991), "Some Tests of Specification for Panel Data: Monet Carlo Evidence and a Application to Employment Equations", *Review of Economic Studies*, n.**58**, pp.277-297.

Baltagi B.H., (2001), *Econometric Analysis of Panel Data*, , John Wiley & Sons.

Belanger D., Gutierrez S. and Raynauld J. (1992), "The Impact of Exchange Rate Variability on Trade Flows: Further Results on Sectoral U.S. Imports from Canada", *North American Journal of Economics and Finance*, Spring, pp 888-892.

Brada J. and Mendez J. (1988), "Exchange Rate Risk, Exchange Rate Regime and the Volume of International Trade", *Kyklos*, **41**(2), pp 263-280:

Bun M.and Klaassen F.(2002), "The Importance of Dynamics in Panel Gravity Models of Trade", *Discussion Paper* presented at the European Economic Association Meeting, Venice, August 22, 2002, University of Amsterdam, April.

De GrauweP. and Skudelny F. (2000), "The Impact of EMU on Trade Flows", *Weltwirtshaftliches Archiv*, **136**, pp.381-402.

Eichengreen B. and Irwin D.A., (1996), "The Role of History in Bilateral Trade Flows" *NBER Working Paper* n.**5565**, May.

Egger P., (2000), "European Exports and Outward Foreign Direct Investment: a Dynamic Panel Data Approach", *WIFO Working Paper* n.**129**, Vienna

Frankel J. and Rose A.K. (2000), "Estimating the Effect of a Currency Unions on Trade and Output", *NBER Working Paper* n.**7857**, August.

Frankel J. and Wei S. (1993), "Trade Blocks and Currency Blocks", NBER Working Paper n.4335.

Glick R. and Rose A., (2002) "Does a Currency Union Affect Trade? The Time-Series Evidence", *European Economic Review*, **46**, June, pp.1125-1151.

Head K. And Mayer T., (2002), "Illusory Border Effects: Distance Mismeasurement Inflates Estimates of Home Bias in Trade", *CEPII Working Paper* n.**2002**-01, January.

Levy Yeyati, E., (2001), "On the Impact of a Common Currency on Bilateral Trade", Universidad Torcuato Di Tella, *Mimeo*, available at
http://www.utdt.edu/~ely/commoncurrency.pdf

Linnemann H. (1966), *An Econometric Study of International Trade Flow*, Amsterdam, North Holland.

Lockwood B., (2000), Discussion on "One Money, One Market: the Effect of Common Currencies on Trade", *Economic Policy*, **30**, April, pp 34-35

Melitz J. (2001), "Geography, Trade and Currency Unions", *CEPR Discussion Paper* n.**2987**, October.

Pakko M. and Wall H., (2001) "Reconsidering the Trade-Effects of a Currency Union", *Discussion Paper*, Federal Reserve Bank of St. Louis, September/October

Persson T. (2001) "Currency Unions and Trade: How Large is the Treatment Effect?", *Economic Policy*, **33**, October, pp.435-448.

Quah D. (2000), Discussion on: "One Money, One Market: the Effect of Common Currencies on Trade" *Economic Policy*, **30**, April, pp.35-38.

Rose A.K., (2000), "One Money, One Market: the Effect of Common Currencies on Trade", *Economic Policy*, **30**, April, pp.7-45

Rose A.K., (2001), "Currency Unions and Trade: the Effect is Large", *Economic Policy*, **33**, October, pp.449-461.

Rose A.K., (2002), "The Effect of Common Currencies on International Trade: Where do we Stand?", *Mimeo*, August.

Rose A.K. and Engel C.(2000), "Currency Unions and International Integration", *NBER Working Paper* n.**7872**, September.

Rose A. K. and van Wincoop E. (2001), "National Money as a Barrier to International Trade: The Real Case for Currency Union", *American Economic Review*, **91**, 2, May, pp.386-390.

In: International Trade Issues
Editor: Robert. V. Weeks, pp. 123-144
ISBN: 1-59454-621-5

Chapter 6

CAREER AND REMUNERATION IN BRAZILIAN RETAILING: AN APPROACH TO THE THEORY OF HEDONIC PRICES

Claudio Felisoni de Angelo[1], Luiz Paulo Lopes Fávero[2], João Paulo Lara de Siqueira[3] and Eduardo de Almeida Salles Terra[4]
Universidade de São Paulo
Address: Av. Prof. Luciano Gualberto, 908 – Sala G-121 – 1° andar.
Cidade Universitária – São Paulo – SP - Brazil
CEP: 05508-900

Abstract

The purpose of this article is to identify the variables that explain the real salaries and the desired salaries of retail executives in Brazil. To this end, it discusses the results of the application of a hedonic pricing model to input supplied by a sample of the said executives concerning the impact of different qualifications and characteristics (age, field of undergraduate degree, quality of MBA, number of language spoken, position in the company, etc.) on their worth (i.e., the remuneration they desire), vs. how retail companies actually "price" executives (i.e., characteristics and qualifications reflected in actual remuneration). These results were obtained by means of an econometric process that included a linear regression model of the demand for professional characteristics and involved 37 hedonic variables as applied to real salaries vs. desired salaries among retail executives. The input for the analysis was collected using a standard questionnaire answered by 215 executives. The main results show that: (i) certain job characteristics have a positive impact on wages, whereas others do not; (ii) many variables have a considerable impact on the level of remuneration that is sought, but not on actual remuneration; (iii) many companies disregard certain hedonic variables that represent academic achievement, such as MBAs and non-degree

[1] E-mail address: *cfa@usp.br*, Phone: (55 11) 3813-6467
[2] E-mail address: *lpfavero@usp.br*, Phone: (55 11) 3813-6467
[3] E-mail address: *jpsiq@usp.br*, Phone: (55 11) 3813-6467
[4] E-mail address: *eduterra@fia.com.br*, Phone: (55 11) 3813-6467

post-graduate programs, as a real reason to improve remuneration; (iv) workers understand that study and intellectual development can improve their wages; and (v) if the remuneration and hedonic prices connected with certain characteristics rise, then workers will prefer to devote their available time to developing these attributes.

Key words: Career, remuneration, hedonic prices, attributes, evaluation and retailing.

Introduction

In the current Brazilian economy, similarly to what occurs in some other developing countries, the wholesale, retail and services sector is the most important one, accounting for some 50% of Brazil's GDP. Among the many services it supplies, commercial activity stands out, more specifically the retail trade, whose relevance is not only due to its immense economic importance, but also to its being the final supply chain link. Thus, thanks to its direct contact with consumers, the retail trade serves as an indicator of the trends of the consumer market and of the distribution of goods in general.

For many decades, the operating aspects of retail management were neglected, given that the vast and profitable possibilities offered by the financial market allowed the sector's companies to easily offset operating income shortfalls with financial profits. Indeed, very little attention was paid to commercial activity in and of itself, since financial investments provided earnings several times greater than what could be obtained from the outwardly simple operation of buying and selling merchandise (BLECHER, 2001, p. 32).

The policy of drastically reducing inflation, introduced in 1994 through the Real Plan, however, fostered substantial changes in the entire dynamics of the Brazilian economy and promptly restructured the consumption market. Retailers, which until then drew their profits from financial operations, suddenly became unable to rely on this source of income. With their earnings severely curtailed, they now found themselves obliged to generate profit almost entirely from their commercial operations. The new economic reality, in conjunction with technological progress, globalization and the manifestation of new formats, substantially changed the way retail operated, providing room for questions and better management. Technology has been providing improved management methods, cost reduction, and better servicing of customer needs. Globalization caused the 90s to become the decade in which foreign concerns increased their presence in food retail; one can expect that the first decade of our current century will reflect a substantial expansion of the world's large non-food retailers in Brazil, this being a sector in which the country is far less developed than other countries. As for the new formats that have appeared, they have been reducing the life cycle of the more traditional institutions, which are obliged to give way for the development of new models. (PARENTE, 2000, p. 16-18).

The reasonable price stability in effect since 1994 strongly encouraged competition, which can be explained by the combination of several factors. The first relevant element was the expansion of the imports of consumer goods, an integral element of the Real Plan's rationale (SESSO FILHO, 2001, p. 21). The second element concerns the different perspective of consumer actions and positioning (RÉVILLION, 2000, p. 38-60), given the newly-found and much enhanced awareness of relative prices and value, as lower inflation rates and the occasional periods of deflation allowed consumers to develop a clearer idea of the true value of products purchased or services hired (RIBEIRO FILHO, 2000, p. 12). And finally, the need to sell increasingly unique products and services, as a means of increasing average sales margins, coupled with low opportunity cost fostered the expansion of the range of products and services offered by supermarkets, besides the ensuing expansion of their respective floor space and of the number of employees per store.

Although these thoughts possibly apply to all segments of Brazil's consumer market, supermarkets undoubtedly deserve special attention (ANGELO; SILVEIRA; SIQUEIRA, 2001, p. 3). At present, most of the goods marketed in Brazil are sold through this type of outlet. Supermarkets have been expanding the scope of their operations and the range of product offerings. Their activities, formerly limited to the sale of food, cleaning and personal care products, are now expanding into other segments, such as durable goods, semi-durable goods and textiles, among others.

The growth of the supermarket business in Brazil is not a recent phenomenon. In 1994 and 1995, Nielsen data indicated that traditional stores accounted form some 85% of the total number of retail outlets, although they accounted for a meager 15% of sales. Self-service stores, on the other hand, a segment dominated by supermarkets, accounted for only 15% of the outlets, but 85% of sales (NIELSEN, 1995). These figures show that supermarkets are currently the main source of food and personal care product distribution in the country, and that the population regards them as the outlets of choice for their shopping needs. Furthermore, one cannot fail to note that supermarket sales totaled roughly R$ 51.8 billion in 2002 (SUPERHIPER, 2003, p. 88).

Self-service, originally conceived as a means of cutting costs by using less manpower, brought new elements in its wake that allowed supermarket chains to increase sales by displaying a countless number of products directly to end consumers, contrary to sales conduced over a counter. On the other hand, defining what is the number of employees required and what their qualifications should be in this segment is an issue that continues to give rise to discussion.

The described transformations encouraged the growth of supermarket chains (SESSO FILHO, 2001, p. 22). However, the ways in which the remuneration of their executives was affected and the concrete benefits generated by the latter's innovative qualifications still give rise to doubts. Thus, this work used data collected through a structured questionnaire answered by retail executives in Brazil to evaluate the actual impact of each one of these qualifications, acquired as a result of the executives' own effort or of other encouragement, on their fixed or variable remuneration, in order to find out which are the attributes that best explain the make up of both their actual salaries and of the salary they desired, given the greater competitiveness of the job market over the last few years. To this end, we employed a hedonic pricing model, which enables an analysis of the relative importance of each attribute vis à vis the different positions and salaries found in the job market.

The results fulfill three main objectives, in that they allow one to assess: first, to what extent the semi-logarithmic hedonic model employed in this study is suitable; second, if the results are satisfactory for determining whether or not the data supply sufficient information on the attributes found in the market; and third, whether the analysis incorporates the differences in salaries and remuneration due to the presence or lack of a given characteristic.

This article opens with an explanation of the evolution of the retail sector in Brazil. Then, we present the classical theory of remuneration structure, relating it with the attributes. This is followed by a discussion of the concept of hedonic prices and its applicability in terms of remuneration. After this, we present the research method employed and the study's theoretical model. Finally, results are presented and analyzed. The implications of hedonic analysis and the possibility of future studies are discussed in the conclusion.

1 Evolution and Overview of the Retail Sector in Brazil

Brazilian retail has been exposed to increasingly major challenges, in terms of attaining operational and productivity excellence, as a result of the new reality that ensued from the 1994 Real Plan (MARQUES; NORONHA, 2001, p. 177). Prior to that year, these companies earned most of their income from financial investments. When these investments mirrored inflation, they could produce a yield of as much as 80% a month. Thus, there was little concern with trying to offer increasingly better and explicitly differentiated products and services. What consumers witnessed in the stores was a constant rise in the price of the merchandise and a total lack of coherence in the pricing of products from one day to the next. This drove them to visit stores only to do what was then known as "the month's shopping", an occasion in which large amounts of products were bought to be stocked at home, thereby allowing consumers to evade price increases during the course of that month. However, with inflation stabilized at a relatively low level, the yield of retail chains' financial investments dried up. The need to offer better and more unique products and services at logical and competitive prices to a consumer that started visiting stores more and more often obliged retail chains to focus on operations and on their offerings. One of the ways they found for dealing with the new reality was to expand their range of goods and services, as well as providing good quality customer care. Thus, customer satisfaction became extremely important for supermarket chains to achieve good performance (MARQUES; NORONHA, 2001, p. 177).

Whereas the 80s were a decade that in Brazil was characterized by political and economic instability, the 90s stood out for enormous competition in the industry. For some retail groups, this involved, among other things, major acquisitions and expansion (ROJO, 1998, p. 10-20). This process was very intense during the transition period leading from the 90s into the new century regarding both the incorporation of many domestic chains by foreign ones and the acquisition of small and medium-sized chains by larger domestic chains. The entire process resulted in a structural change and greater concentration of the retail market. (GHISI; CAMARGO; MARTINELLI, 2003, p.219). As for 2002, it was a year in which the acquisitions made by the sector's main companies settled down (SUPERHIPER, 2003, p. 66-67).

In an environment in which theoretical knowledge and practical experience need to be increasingly enhanced, an executive's distinguishing features lie in his professional and academic qualifications, which constitute a differentiation in a field that is competitive and has reflected a rising concentration of organizational power over the last few years. Table 1, below, shows the progress of the concentration of the ten largest retail chains in Brazil, in aggregate, over the last ten years. This is an indicator of the need for the sector's executives to have increasingly better qualifications, in order to be able to manage companies with bigger earnings and a level of demand never before encountered.

Table 1: Evolution of the concentration of the ten largest brazilian retail chains, as a percentage of gross sales

YEAR	RETAIL CONCENTRATION
1994	51.5%
1995	51.8%
1996	51.9%
1997	53.0%
1998	61.8%
1999	71.8%
2000	72.6%
2001	72.3%
2002	71.3%
2003	72.9%

OBS.: Within the universe of the 150 largest retail chains in Brazil.

In addition to the clear concentration of gross sales among just a handful of companies, there is also a concentration of the number of retail companies headquartered in the Southeast or South of Brazil, among the 150 largest ones. Graph 1 (below) shows the percentage of companies belonging to the 150 largest retail groups headquartered in each of the country's five geographical regions.

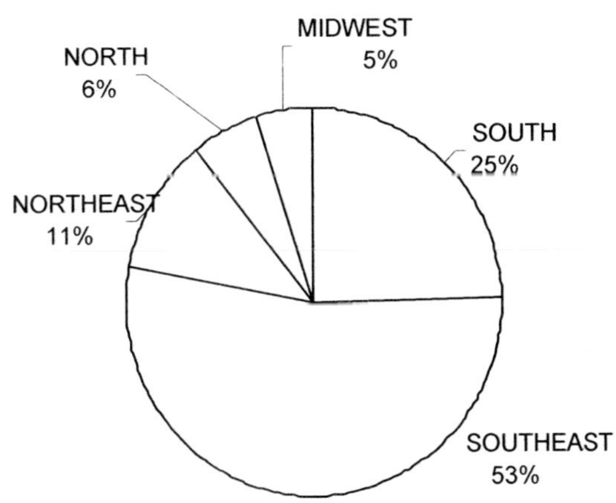

Graph 1: Percentage of the number of companies headquartered in each of the brazil's five geographical regions

Thus, the geographical concentration of retail companies increases the degree of competition and hence the pursuit of qualifications capable of standing out among the industry's executives, given the scarcity of job offers and their positioning throughout the country.

2 An Approach to the Structure of Remuneration

The definition of a market price structure has been studied recently using hedonic models of regression[5] that estimate the price of certain goods or services based on their features (LEEUW, 1993, p. 33).

According to SARTORIS NETO (1996, p. 2), "if, perhaps, the set of goods available to most consumers did not change throughout most of the 19th century, other than on occasion and under specific circumstances, today a comparison between certain entirely differentiated goods can be entirely devoid of sense, given the enormity of the perceived attributes."

In general terms, the organizational market is dominated by a major segment of agents that offer knowledge, such as executives, who compete amongst themselves on the basis of practical experience and theoretical knowledge, this being their offering of differentiated attributes (DANTAS, 1998, p. 10). Therefore, in order to analyze real salaries vs. the salaries desired as a function of the attributes offered, one must try to deal with themes that are connected with the vectors of pressure in market relations, so that the resulting element characterizes the "price" of each transaction. On the other side of the transaction, we have consumers, in this case companies and corporations, which try to maximize their satisfaction by choosing from a basket of attributes in the market, based on what they believe will provide them with the greatest amount of utility within the limits of their budgets (PINDICK; RUBINFELD, 1999, p. 83). Figure 1 (below) shows that the dividing line represents the interface between the consumer and the offering of a given set of attributes by a retail executive. This executive determines a price (PE) based on his characteristics, and an offering of utility (UE), represented by his attributes. The company and/or the market, on the other hand, indicate the maximum price they are willing to "pay" (this being determined their budget limitations and interests), in the form of remuneration, for an executive for a given job or position and for the perceived utility that the set of attributes offered would provide them with.

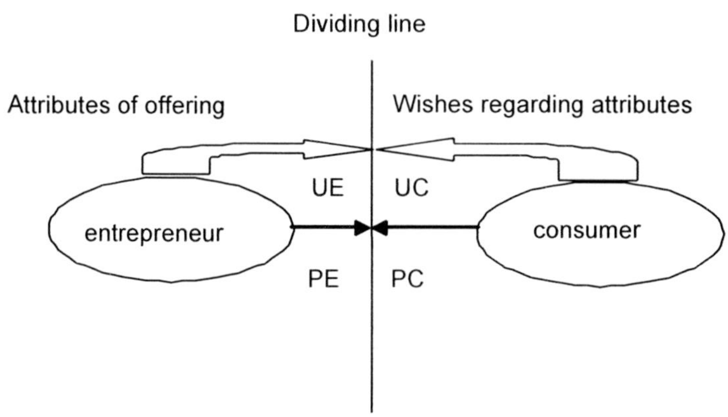

Source: lima júnior, 1993, p. 9.

Figure 1: Interface between the supply and demand for attributes

[5] According to GRILICHES (1971, p. 4), the best argument for using the analyses of hedonic models by regression is the simplicity that the latter provides.

3 Classical Theory and the Attributes Approach

Classical consumer theory considers that the choice of a given product or service is a feature intrinsic to it. According to HENDERSON and QUANDT (1988, p. 8), "the utility function is defined by reference to consumption over a specified period of time and the degree of satisfaction that the consumer derives from a given combination of products or services depends on the length of the period over which it is acquired. Normally, the consumer derives utility from the variety and diversity of the products and services he consumes. Thus, the utility function should not be defined for a period of time so short as to make it impossible to satisfy the desire for variety."

LANCASTER[6], as quoted by SARTORIS NETO (1996, p. 10), does not disregard the traditional approach to the utility function, but proposes instead a broader approach to Consumer Theory, according to which utility may be derived from the properties or characteristics of the products and services. Thus, the utility function has, as its underlying argument, the characteristics of the products and services, rather than the products and services themselves. One can therefore assume that consumption is an activity in which products and services, alone or combined, are "entries" that lead to "exits" that consist of a "package" of characteristics.

It is assumed that the product or service per se provides no utility to the consumer, but that it has characteristics that do. Similarly, the product and service generally has more than one characteristic, many of which can be found in more than one product or service. Furthermore, in combination, they can offer features that are different from those found in individual products and services.

Thus, the nature of this approach is more realistic with regard to goods and their characteristics (LANCASTER, 1966, p. 132-157) and makes the building of a model necessary.

Considering that zi and xj are, respectively, the quantity of characteristic i and the quantity of goods j, it follows that in a system of r characteristics and n goods, the "package" of characteristics that a series of goods (x1,..., xn) has is represented, in terms of a matrix, by:

$$z = B.x \tag{1}$$

where z = [zi] is the vector of characteristics, x = [xi] is the vector of goods, and B = [bij] is the matrix (r x n) of the coefficients that relate goods with characteristics.

The consumer obtains utility from the characteristics found in the goods he acquires, rather than from the goods themselves. Thus, the utility function has as its argument the characteristics of the goods, represented by vector z, rather then the goods themselves, as was the case in traditional theory (vector x), i.e.:

$$U = U(z1,..., zn) = U(z) \tag{2}$$

As the consumer acquires the characteristics he wants (the "package" of attributes) by means of the purchase of goods, strictly speaking, his budgetary restrictions depend on the vector of goods x, and the solution to the problem calls for correspondence between the two

[6] In LANCASTER (1966, p. 132-157).

vectors. Therefore, the proposed model is comprised of four parts that can be represented as follows:

$$U(z) \text{ --- maximized} \tag{3}$$

Where U is defined in the space of the characteristics (space C);

$$p.x \leq k \tag{4}$$

where budget restriction p.x is defined in the space of the goods (space G);

$$z = B.x \tag{5}$$

where the system of equations, represented by vector z, shows the transformation between space G and space C; and

$$x,z \geq 0 \tag{6}$$

which represents the non-negativity restrictions over x and z.

In traditional Consumer Theory, budget restrictions and the utility function are both defined in space G and, therefore, one may relate them as in a typical diagram of indifference curves. However, this approach, according to LANCASTER (1991, p. 17), offers two alternatives: the transformation of the utility function into space G, or the transformation of budget restrictions into space C. In the first instance, one can determine that:

$$U(z) = U(B.x) = u(x) \tag{7}$$

Therefore, one has a utility function u(x) that is defined directly in terms of goods, but whose properties depend on the structure of matrix B and lead to a far more complex situation than that found in traditional analysis. The second case also depends on the structure of matrix B.

Matrix B, represented by B = [bij], determines the coefficients that relate goods with characteristics. Thus, three possible cases may arise concerning the number of goods and characteristics.

First, when the number of characteristics equals the number of goods. In this case, we have a one to one relation between the goods and services vectors. Thus:

$$z = B.x, \text{ or } x = B\text{-}1.z \tag{8}$$

If B is a diagonal matrix, there is a relation of one to one between each component of z and each component of x and the model becomes identical to the traditional one. If, however, B is not a diagonal matrix, the objects of utility are not individuals goods, but combinations of goods, and the model starts to reflect significant differences versus the traditional model.

Second, if the number of characteristics is greater than the number of goods. The relations z = B.x contain more equations than xi variables, making it impossible, in general, to find a vector of goods x that gives rise to a vector of characteristics z, arbitrarily specified. Therefore, the number of characteristics is reduced to n, becoming equal to the number of goods. In this case, it is generally more practical to analyze consumer behavior by means of the transformation of the utility function into space G.

The third case is analyzed to verify a number of goods greater than the number of characteristics. Equation z = B.x shows fewer equations than variables, so that, for each point in the space of characteristics, the consumer can choose between the different goods vectors. Given, for instance, a price vector, this choice is characterized by being one of pure efficiency, if for all of the characteristics vector the consumer chooses the most efficient combination of goods for obtaining that collection of characteristics. The efficient selection for vector of characteristic z* will represent the solution to the following linear program:

$$\begin{gathered} p.x \text{ --- minimized} \\ z^* = B.x \\ x \geq 0 \end{gathered} \tag{9}$$

This last case represents the situation best suited to remuneration and the definition of careers (which is the purpose of this work), where the quantity of goods is represented by the number of executives active in the market and the quantity of characteristics is associated with the attributes of each one of them.

The complete choice made by a consumer who is subject to a budget restriction $p.x \leq k$ can be due to two factors: efficient choice, which determines the boundary between characteristics and efficient collections of goods, and private choice, which determines which is the point along this boundary of characteristics preferred by the consumer.

A simple case can be seen in figure 2, in which matrix B is composed of two goods and two characteristics:

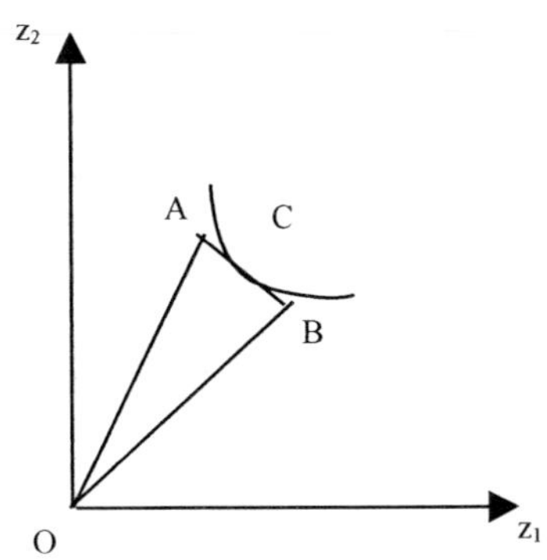

Source: Sartoris neto, 1996, p. 17.

Figure 2: Choice involving two goods and two characteristics

In figure 2, "characteristics z1 and z2 are found in two goods, a and b, represented by lines OA and OB, respectively. Line AB represents the boundary of characteristics for a given level of income and prices of goods a and b. The point of tangency between the indifference curve and the boundary (point C in the figure) determines the consumer's choice." (SARTORIS NETO, 1996, p. 16-18).

As for the specific situation of this study, in which more goods than characteristics are analyzed, a generic graph can be prepared, as shown on figure 3.

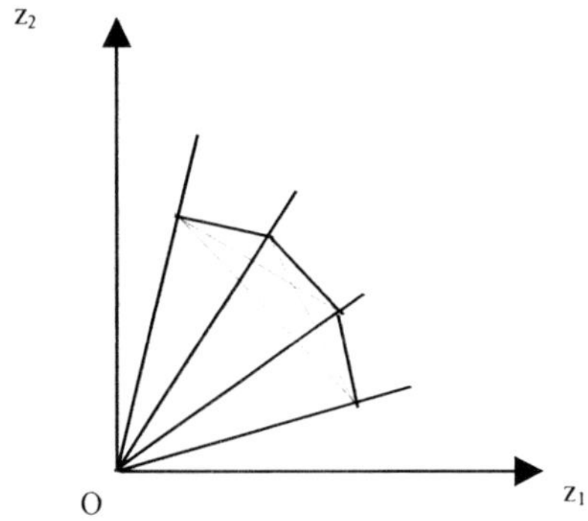

Source: Sartoris neto, 1996, p. 18.

Figure 3: Choice for more goods than characteristics (four goods and two characteristics)

The theoretical basis discussed in this section will not be entirely used for this work. The concepts related with attributes and the understanding of how these behave in the formation of "prices" and for decision-making on remuneration provide the groundwork for the application of hedonic prices. This being so, one should stress that this study will relate real salaries and desired salaries among executives active in the retail sector with their respective attributes and that their valuation will be worked out based on the concepts concerning characteristics proposed by LANCASTER (1966, p. 132-157), but using a hedonic prices approach.

4 The Hedonic Prices Approach

According to BESANKO, DRANOVE and SHANLEY (2000, p. 439), hedonic prices use market data to determine the value of the attributes of a particular product or service. For instance, the pricing of automobiles reflects the quantity, type and variety of attributes they carry (level of attributes), such as, for example, engine power and metallized paint. Through an analysis of how the pricing of automobiles varies as a function of different combinations of attributes, one can determine the price of another automobile with the same features. Still according to the said authors, hedonic prices have been used to identify the value of innovations for automobiles, computers, residential property and the prospects of professional careers in organizations. However, they require multiple regression analyses in order for one to estimate the impact of the attributes on the value of a product or service. The dependent variable of the regression is the price or value of the goods, whereas the predictors are the variables that measure the presence or absence of different attributes. If, for instance, the automobile market is being studied, an analysis of hedonic prices can identify to what extent the prices of automobiles will be affected by a 1% increase in engine power or the inclusion of air bags. Furthermore, hedonic price models can represent a tool for the evaluation of tradeoffs involving price and inclusion, improvement or exclusion of attributes (level of attributes). This analysis, ultimately, can help one to determine the slope of the "indifference curve" proposed by BESANKO, DRANOVE and SHANLEY (2000, p. 395), as shown on figure 4, below:

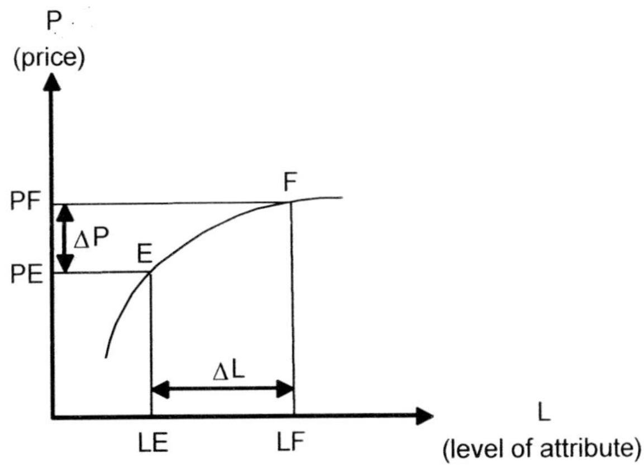

Source: Besanko, Dranove and Shanley (2000, p. 395).

Figure 4: "Indifference curve" and the tradeoff between price and level of attribute

It is necessary to criticize the authors mentioned above, since, according to PINDYCK and RUBINFELD (1999, p. 74), indifference curves are convex relative to the origin, because when larger quantities of attributes are consumed, it is expected that the consumer will prefer increasingly fewer units of a second attribute in order to obtain additional units of the first one. Thus, as one follows an indifference curve and the consumption of a given attribute increases, consumer desire for additional units of that attribute should fall. Therefore, the curve proposed by BESANKO, DRANOVE and SHANLEY (2000, p. 395) can be called a curve of isosatisfaction.

As figure 4 enables one to analyze, a price increment over the course of a curve of isosatisfaction corresponds to ΔP exactly, caused by the increment ΔL on the level of product attribute. The sharp slope of the curve for lower levels of attribute indicates that there is a greater possibility of increasing the price or the value of the product or service through an increment in the level of the attribute. When the curve's slope becomes less sharp, the possibility of increasing price becomes lower for extra levels of the attribute. It is important to stress that higher levels of attribute are connected with the increasing availability of amounts, different types and variety of attributes.

The construction of hedonic price models in the determination of market values has been used to evaluate automobiles, to determine the rates to be charged for electric power and for the evaluation of residential property (KRAVIS; LIPSEY, 1969, p. 233-246). In a historical context, the work of COURT (1939, p. 99-117) pioneered this type of analysis; it was motivated by practical issues that involved the automotive industry in the United States. In 1961, GRILICHES[7], as quoted by SARTORIS NETO (1996, p. 4), also employed a practical context for comparing the prices of different automobiles through the application of the several available characteristics.

[7] GRILICHES, 1961, p. 137-196.

However, in a theoretical way, LANCASTER (1966, p. 132-157) proposes an alternative type of approach, in which the arguments of the utility function are the characteristics of the goods, rather than the goods themselves. According to this approach, as we have already discussed, the consumer is willing to pay the price of goods, in order to acquire them, with a view to the utility that their characteristics will provide.

Starting with Lancaster, many other authors carried out several studies on the use of the hedonic prices approach, but the first one to put the problem within a market context was ROSEN (1974, p. 34-55). Item 5, below, presents several studies that originated from the work of Court, Griliches and Rosen.

5 Literature Review

The structuring of the concepts related with the decision to choose a product or service and the utility offered by the latter was structured theoretically, as already discussed, in the approach to Consumer Theory proposed by LANCASTER (1966, p. 132-157), according to whom the choice of a certain product or service does not occur spontaneously, but as a response to a package of characteristics associated with it, the utility function's arguments being these very characteristics, its being therefore assumed that consumption is an activity in which the product or service or a combination thereof are obtained with the purpose of acquiring a set of characteristics found in them (SARTORIS NETO, 1996, p. 10). Thus, LANCASTER (1966) did not replace traditional Consumer Theory, but proposed its expansion, in that he structured these concepts theoretically, taking into account the presence of the characteristics of the products or services, this being a practice also employed before LANCASTER (1966) by COURT (1939) and GRILICHES (1961), for instance.

Firstly COURT (1939, p. 99-117), in order to determine a hedonic equation capable of explaining the behavior of automobile prices as a function of their characteristics, proposed a simple procedure, involving a single equation that allows one to see how much each characteristic influences the end price of the vehicle, and that also enabled the creation of indices. This method, also adopted by GRILICHES (1961, p. 137-196), defines a hedonic equation and corresponds to the first stage of the procedure proposed by ROSEN (1974, p. 34-55), described below.

The works of KING (1976) are some of the few to be based solely on Lancaster's approach, King having been the first author to employ the term "Lancastrian". From the empirical standpoint, his method was not significantly different from the one used by Court and Griliches (SARTORIS NETO, 1996, p. 34).

The method proposed by ROSEN (1974), on the other hand, has the purpose of defining supply and demand equations, so that the market's equilibrium can be defined. Thus, two equations are proposed, representing supply and demand, as follows:

$$\text{Demand:} \quad p(z) = f(z1, z2, ..., zn, Y1, W) \tag{10}$$
$$\text{Supply:} \quad p(z) = f(z1, z2, ..., zn, Y2, W) \tag{11}$$

Where

p(z) represents the price as a function of the vector of attributes;

zi represents the model's intrinsic set of variables;

Y1 represents the vector of extrinsic variables that only affect demand;
Y2 represents the vector of extrinsic variables that only affect supply;
W represents the extrinsic variables found in both equations.

The work of ROSEN (1974, p. 34-55) has two stages. The first one refers to estimating p(z), without considering Y1 and Y2; in other words, one works out the regression of the prices found for the products differentiated by characteristic z. Rosen's second stage refers to the application of simultaneous equations methods, in which each of them is identified as a function of the composition of vectors Y1 and Y2 (SARTORIS NETO, 1996, p. 23).

One should stress that our study used Rosen's method as the basis for determining the hedonic regression models, as we will show under item 6, given that the hedonic equation that has the actual salary as a dependent variable refers to the demand equation (the company's point of view),whereas the hedonic equation that offers the desired salary as a dependent variable refers to the supply equation (the executive's point of view).

6 Research Method

The research conducted with retail executives was based on a sample. The tool employed for collecting data was a questionnaire developed by the technical staff of the Retail Management Program (PROVAR - *Programa de Administração de Varejo*) of the Management Institute Foundation (FIA – *Fundação Instituto de Administração*), an organization connected with the School of Economics, Administration and Accounting of the University of São Paulo, Brazil. This questionnaire, before being used, was pre-tested, after which it was fine-tuned until the final version used for online research was reached.

The universe of this investigation consisted of executives working for companies operating in the various segments of retail. As a census type of research calls for a very high budget, we chose to rely on a sample. For the case in point, the sample amounted to 215 answered questionnaires, obtained over the time span during which the research was explained on the PROVAR site (www.provar.org), i.e., October, November and December 2003.

Solely for the purposes of checking deviations relative to the population, given the number of questionnaires answered, one can calculate the maximum admissible error. As most of the questions were closed and of a dichotomic nature, and given that the dispersion of the population was not known beforehand, we admitted to the worst possible case regarding the sample's dimensions, namely, 50% positive responses and 50% negative responses. Adopting a level of correction of 95.5% in the establishment of the confidence intervals and being aware of the dimension of the sample (215 interviews), one reaches a sample error of plus or minus 6.8%. As the sample is far smaller than the population, it is unnecessary to use the correction factor for finite populations.

Formula employed for calculating the size of the sample:

$$n = (P.Q.\,Z^2) / D^2 \qquad (12)$$

Where:

- n is the dimension of the sample (215 completed interviews);

- P is the estimate of the proportion of the population favorable to a given result. In this case, P = 0.50 (50%);
- Q = 1 – P is the estimate of the proportion of the population unfavorable to a given result for the same question. In this case, Q = 0.50 (50%);
- Z is the abscissa of the standard normal distribution, with a given level of confidence being fixed. In this case. Z=2, because the level of confidence was 95.5%; and
- D is the sample error, i.e., the maximum difference admissible between P* (the real proportion of the population) and P.

7 Theoretical Research Model

As we mentioned above, the purpose of this article is to identify the variables that explain the real salaries and the desired salaries of retail executives working in the Brazilian market. Figure 5 proposes a better understanding of what was sought:

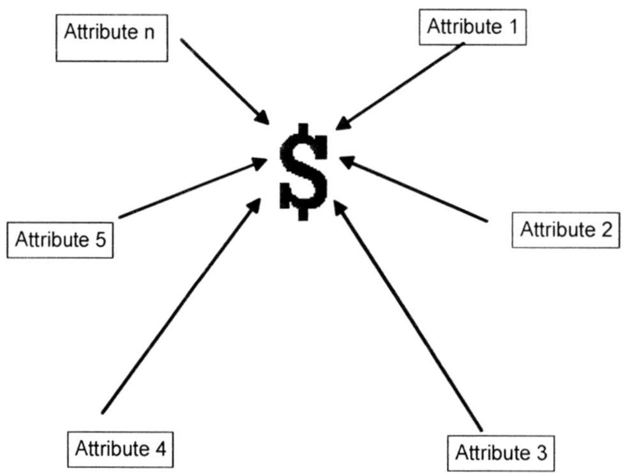

Figure 5: Explanation of the real salary & desired salary of a given retail executive through the presence of certain attributes

The model was specified based on the pioneering work of ROSEN (1974, p. 34-55). Real salaries and desired salaries were related to a set of attributes in the following way:

$$\text{Log } S = x_0 + x_1.\text{AGE} + x_2.\text{TIMEWORK} + x_3.\text{NCOMPANIES} + x_4.\text{CURRCOMPANY} + x_5.\text{ANALYST} + x_6.\text{CONTROLLER} + x_7.\text{MANAGER} + x_8.\text{SUPERINTENDENT} + x_9.\text{DIRECTOR} + x_{10}.\text{VICEPRES} + x_{11}.\text{PRESIDENT} + x_{12}.\text{ENGLISH} + x_{13}.\text{SPANISH} + x_{14}.\text{LANGUAGES} + x_{15}.\text{MKT} + x_{16}.\text{ADM} + x_{17}.\text{ECON} + x_{18}.\text{COMP} + x_{19}.\text{ENGIN} + x_{20}.\text{ACCTG} + x_{21}.\text{SOC} + x_{22}.\text{PSYCH} + x_{23}.\text{LAW} + x_{24}.\text{PEDAG} + x_{25}.\text{JOURN} + x_{26}.\text{STAT} + x_{27}.\text{MED} + x_{28}.\text{ARC} + x_{29}.\text{GRAD} + x_{30}.\text{FORGRAD} + x_{31}.\text{MBA} + x_{32}.\text{FORMBA} + x_{33}.\text{MAMSC} + x_{34}.\text{PHD} + x_{35}.\text{LATUSENSU} + x_{36}.\text{COURSE} + x_{37}.\text{FORHOME} + e \quad (13)$$

Where:

S: the executives' real or desired salary

AGE: age
TIMEWORK: length of time during which the person has been active in the job market
NCOMPANIES: number of companies worked for
CURRCOMPANY: length of time with the current employer
ANALYST: position of analyst (dummy)
CONTROLLER: position of controller (dummy)
MANAGER: position of manager (dummy)
SUPERINTENDENT: position of superintendent (dummy)
DIRECTOR: position of director(dummy)
VICEPRES: position of vice-president (dummy)
PRESIDENT: position of president (dummy)
ENGLISH: speaks English (dummy)
SPANISH: speaks Spanish (dummy)
LANGUAGES: number of languages spoken, other than English and Spanish
MKT: degree in marketing (dummy)
ADM: degree in administration (dummy)
ECON: degree in economics(dummy)
COMP: degree in computer science and IT (dummy)
ENGIN: degree in engineering (dummy)
ACCTG: degree in accounting (dummy)
SOC: degree in sociology (dummy)
PSYCH: degree in psychology (dummy)
LAW: degree in law (dummy)
PEDAG: degree in pedagogy (dummy)
JOURN: degree in journalism (dummy)
STAT: degree in mathematics and statistics (dummy)
MED: degree in medical sciences (dummy)
ARC: degree in architecture (dummy)
GRAD: number of undergraduate degrees
FORGRAD: undergraduate degree from foreign university (dummy)
MBA: MBA (dummy)
FORMBA: foreign MBA (dummy)
MAMSC: Master's degree (dummy)
PHD: Ph. D. (dummy)
LATUSENSU: non-degree post graduate specialization programs – *latu sensu* (dummy)
COURSE: number of professional training courses completed during the last year
FORHOME: has lived abroad for more than six (6) months

In the model presented, the logarithm of the real / desired salary is the dependent variable, whereas all other variables are possibly explanatory ones. We chose a semi-logarithmic specification, given that, as many of the independent variables are dummies, the definition of the natural logarithm of zero becomes impossible.

As the dependent variable is the logarithm of the salary, the coefficients resulting from regression may be interpreted as an estimated percent change in value for a unit change in a particular attribute (GRILICHES, 1971). Therefore, the partial derivative of these hedonic regressions, with regard to a given attribute, describes a marginal change in the total evaluation, associated with a change in one of the characteristics, other constants being maintained (LINNEMAN, 1980, p. 47-68). Thus:

$$DSh / dNk = Snk (Nk) \tag{14}$$

This determines the increment that applies to a given salary, whether this is the real one or the desired one, which starts to reflect an attribute Nk, all other things being equal.

The method adopted for this study has the purpose of estimating a model of the market for remunerating the careers of retail executives, taking into account 37 characteristics in the formation of salaries. Some of the independent variables were incorporated in the form of dummies; thus, 1 indicates the presence of a given attribute whereas 0 indicates the lack thereof. Table 1, below, shows a description of the independent variables.

Table I: Definition of the hedonic variables

ATTRIBUTE VARIABLE	DEFINITION OF THE VARIABLE
AGE	Age
TIMEWORK	Amount of time active in the job market
NCOMPANIES	Number of companies worked for
CURRCOMPANY	Amount of time with current employer
ANALYST	Yes = 1; No = 0
CONTROLLER	Yes = 1; No = 0
MANAGER	Yes = 1; No = 0
SUPERINTENDENT	Yes = 1; No = 0
DIRECTOR	Yes = 1; No = 0
VICEPRES	Yes = 1; No = 0
PRESIDENT	Yes = 1; No = 0
ENGLISH	Yes = 1; No = 0
SPANISH	Yes = 1; No = 0
LANGUAGES	Number of languages spoken, other than English and Spanish
MKT	Yes = 1; No = 0
ADM	Yes = 1; No = 0
ECON	Yes = 1; No = 0
COMP	Yes = 1; No = 0
ENGIN	Yes = 1; No = 0
ACCTG	Yes = 1; No = 0
SOC	Yes = 1; No = 0
PSYCH	Yes = 1; No = 0
LAW	Yes = 1; No = 0
PEDAG	Yes = 1; No = 0
JOURN	Yes = 1; No = 0
STAT	Yes = 1; No = 0
MED	Yes = 1; No = 0
ARC	Yes = 1; No = 0
GRAD	Number of undergraduate degrees

Table I: Definition of the hedonic variables (Continued)

ATTRIBUTE VARIABLE	DEFINITION OF THE VARIABLE
FORGRAD	Yes = 1; No = 0
MBA	Yes = 1; No = 0
FORMBA	Yes = 1; No = 0
MAMSC	Yes = 1; No = 0
PHD	Yes = 1; No = 0
LATUSENSU	Yes = 1; No = 0
COURSE	Number of professional training courses completed during the last year
FOREHOME	Yes = 1; No = 0

8 Results

In this section, we present the results obtained from the sample we collected. The hedonic estimates are analyzed in order to determine the suitability of the model, i.e., whether the data collected provide sufficient information to allow adequate hedonic estimates to be calculated (ARYEETEY-ATTOH, 1992, p. 183-198). We then analyze the coefficients, to find out which attributes have the greatest impact on real and desired salaries.

First, for better specification, the existence of problems related to the autocorrelation of residues was checked. According to VASCONCELLOS and ALVES (2000, p. 113), the problem of residue autocorrelation results from the fact that the residue incorporates the effects of a variable that was excluded from the model. Additionally, incorrect specification of the functional form of the model may account for the generation of autocorrelated residues. Figure 6, below, illustrates the problem of residue autocorrelation.

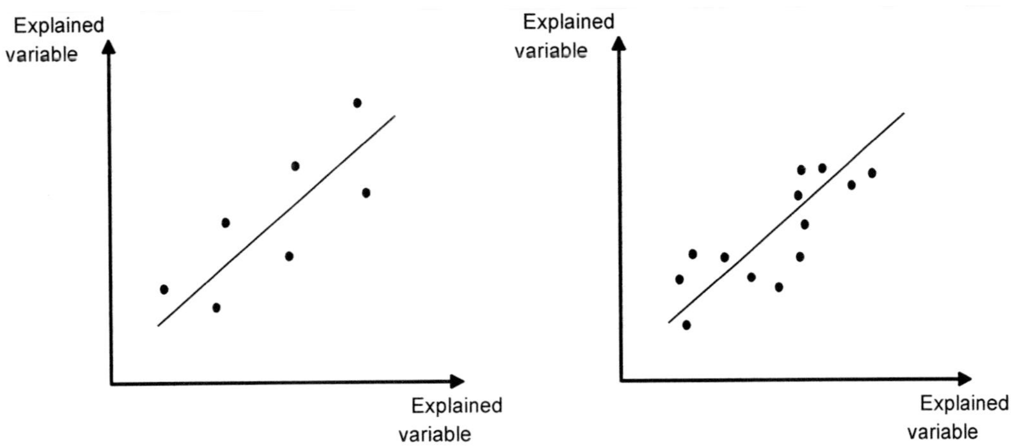

Source: Vasconcellos and Alves (2000, p. 31).

Figure 6: Residue autocorrelation

The presence of heterocedasticity must also be tested, given that flaws in the specification of the model can generate a heterocedastic residue; in other words, as an explanatory variable increases, there is an increase in point dispersion. This means that the variance of the random term will be greater the greater the value of the explanatory variable, or vice-versa. Figure 7, below, illustrates the problem of heterocedasticity.

One must also check whether multicolinearity is occurring, given that many of the explanatory variables taken into account in this study can produce similar behavior; in other words, there may be a greater correlation than theoretically expected between some of them, as a result either of the selection of a sample collected on the basis of convenience or of an insufficient number of observations (VASCONCELLOS; ALVES, 2000, p. 140).

With the modeling carried out, one can see, luckily, that there were no problems concerning the autocorrelation of residues, heterocedasticity or multicolinearity between the explanatory variables.

The results are therefore presented below.

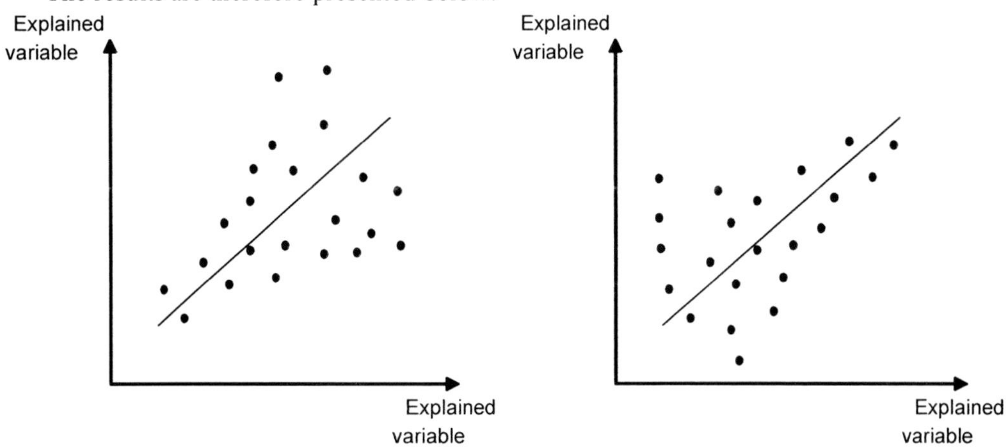

Source: Vasconcellos and Alves (2000, p. 119).

Figure 7: Heterocedasticity

9 Conclusions and Possible Extensions

As table 2 shows, some variables that explain the determination of desired salaries are not significant for the formation of real salaries.

A vertical analysis shows that the variables that best explain the behavior of real salaries are those connected with the executive's age, the amount of time he has been employed by his current company and fact that a position of director, vice-president or president is held. The educational variables that appear to be significant for explaining real salaries are speaking English, the number of undergraduate degrees and having a Master's Degree (but not an MBA).

Table 2: Regression results for the semi-logarithmic model

Attribute Variable	Dependent Variable = Real Salary	Dependent Variable = Desired Salary
AGE	0.273 *	0.374 **
TIMEWORK		
NCOMPANIES		0.118 **
CURRCOMPANY	0.135 **	0.123 **
ANALYST		
CONTROLLER		
MANAGER		
SUPERINTENDENT		
DIRECTOR	0.201 **	0.241 **
VICEPRES	0.123 **	0.115 **
PRESIDENT	0.125 **	0.190 **
ENGLISH	0.126 *	0.123 **
SPANISH		
LANGUAGES		0.134 **
MKT		
ADM		0.255 **
ECON		0.092 *
COMP		0.143 **
ENGIN		0.170 **
ACCTG		
SOC		
PSYCH		0.206 **
LAW		0.121 **
PEDAG		
JOURN		
STAT		0.095 **
MED		
ARC		
GRAD	0.127 *	0.132 *
FORGRAD		
MBA		0.140 **
FORMBA		
MAMSC	0.102 *	0.105 *
PHD		
LATUSENSU		0.072 *
COURSE		
FOREHOME		
R^2	0.488	0.684
R^2 - adjusted	0.373	0.617
F	4.257	10.230
Prob. (Est. F)	0.000	0.000
N	215	215

OBS.: The blank cells refer to the lack of statistical significance, at a level of 10%, for the hedonic variable in the referred income level.

* indicates a significance level of 0.10.

** indicates a significance level of 0.05.

N is the number of the sample.

When we analyze the variables that are significant in the formation of the salaries that executives desire, in addition to the ones mentioned above, the only addition is the one that refers to experience, which is related with the number of companies for which the executive has worked. On the other hand, many academic qualification variables, besides the ones mentioned in the paragraph above, are now factors that explain the desired salaries, such as the number of languages spoken, the field the undergraduate degree was in (business administration, economics, computer sciences, engineering, psychology, law and mathematics & statistics), and an MBA or a non-degree post-graduate specialization course.

Thus, one can see that, from the point of view of demand, there is a surplus of consumers (represented by the companies in the market), in that many of them fail to recognize the relevance of a post-graduate course or an MBA, even though their line of discourse contradicts this. Meanwhile, executives, who represent the supply point of view, believe that they should continue to pursue academic qualification and knowledge, since they highlight the importance of having degrees and theoretical skills in order to improve their salaries and remuneration. This becomes very clear when one compares the average actual salary with the average desired salary found in this study. Results show that, whereas the average actual salary is roughly R$ 5,100.00, the average desired salary, based on the qualities acquired by these executives, amounts to some R$6,980.00.

Thus, results indicate that: (i) certain attributes have a positive influence on increasing actual and desired salaries, whereas others do not; (ii) many variables have a considerable impact on the determination of desired salaries, but not of actual salaries; (iii) many retail sector companies fail to take into account certain hedonic variables that concern academic qualifications, such as an MBA or a non-degree post-graduate specialization program, as a real reason for improving remuneration; (iv) executives feel that intellectual development can enhance their remuneration; and (v) if there is a positive correlation between a salary increase and the presence of a given attribute, executives will invest a greater amount of time in developing these qualifications.

This having been said, one can see, first, the power of adaptation of the semi-logarithmic hedonic model used in this study. Furthermore, results are satisfactory, allowing one to state that the data supply sufficient information as to the attributes that can be found in the market. Finally, hedonic analysis ends up by incorporating the differences in salaries and remuneration that result from the presence or absence of certain attributes.

Although the results presented in this article may be used in different ways as regards defining priorities and strategies, it is necessary to continue to pursue the subject, as we did not use all the possible attributes that might have an impact on the subject at hand. Further data can be collected as variables, taking into account, for instance, the psychological profile and the degree of entrepreneurship of the executive, as well as family-related characteristics. The subject is truly vast and should be seen as input into the education of executives and the job market for the development and implementation of strategic recruitment and career remuneration actions.

References

Aryeetey-Attoh, S. An analysis of household valuations and preference structures in Rio de Janeiro, Brazil. *American Journal of Agricultural Economics,* Oregon, p. 183-198, August, 1992.

Angelo, C. F.; Silveira, J. A. G.; Siqueira, J. P. L. O comportamento de consumo nos supermercados. *PROVAR Research* – FIA Retail Management Program, 2001.

Besanko, D; Dranove, D.; Shanley, M. *Economics of strategy,* **2.** ed. Wiley, 2000.

Blecher, N. Quer preço ou quer marca? *Exame* magazine, year 35, n. 12, p. 32, 2001.

Court, A.T. Hedonic price indexes with automotive examples. *The Dinamics of Automobile Demand,* Nova York, The General Motors Corporation, p. 99-117, 1939.

Dantas, R. A. *Engenharia de avaliações:* uma introdução à metodologia científica. São Paulo: Pini, 1988.

Ghisi, F. A.; Camargo, S. V.; Martinelli, D. P. Redes de compras de supermercados de pequeno e médio porte: um estudo multicaso no interior do Estado de São Paulo. *Varejo Competitivo*, São Paulo, v. 7, p. 217-240, 2003.

Kravis, I. B.; Lipsey, R. E. International price comparisons. *International Economic Review,* v. 10, p. 233-246, 1969.

Griliches, Z. Hedonic price indexes for automobiles: an econometric analysis of quality change. The Price Statistics of the Federal Government, *General Series*, n. **73**, p. 137-196, 1961.

___________ Price indexes quality change. Cambridge: Harvard University Press, 1971.

Henderson, J. M.; Quandt, R. E. *Teoria microeconômica: uma abordagem matemática.* **2**. ed. São Paulo: Livraria Pioneira Editora, 1988, p. 5-49.

King, A. T. The demand for housing: a Lancastrian approach. *Southern Economic Journal,* v. 42, n. 2, October 1976.

Lancaster, K. A new approach to consumer's theory. *Journal of Political Economy,* n. **74**, p. 132-157, 1966.

_______________ *Modern consumer theory.* New York: Edward Elgar Publishing Company, 1991, p. 11-21.

Leeuw, F. A price index for new multifamily housing. *Bureau of Economic Research*, p. 33-42, February 1993.

Lima Júnior, J. R. *Planejamento do produto no mercado habitacional.* São Paulo: EPUSP-PCC, 1993. 26 p. Technical Bulletin.

Linneman, P. Some empirical results on the nature of hedonic price function for the urban housing market. *Journal of Urban Economics,* n. **8**, p. 47-68, 1980.

Marques, E. F.; Noronha, A. B. Avaliação e dimensionamento da percepção de excelência de serviços no setor supermercadista: uma abordagem quantitativa. *Varejo Competitivo*, São Paulo, v. 5, p. 173-197, 2001.

Nielsen. *Censo Nielsen de Serviços de Marketing 1994/1995*, 1995.

Parente, J. *Varejo no Brasil:* gestão e estratégia. São Paulo: Atlas, 2000.

Pindyck, R. S.; Rubinfeld, D. L. *Microeconomia.* 4. ed. São Paulo: Makron Books, 1999.

Révillion, A. S. P. Satisfação do consumidor com o setor supermercadista: o caso de Porto Alegre. *Varejo Competitivo*, São Paulo, v. 4, p. 38-60, 2000.

Ribeiro Filho, A. K. O professor em ação. *Super Giro*, São Paulo, ano 4, n. 48, p. 12, August 2000.

Rojo, J. G. *Supermercados no Brasil*: qualidade, marketing de serviços, comportamento do consumidor. São Paulo: Atlas, 1998.

Rosen, S. Hedonic prices and implicit markets: production differentiation in pure competition. *Journal of Political Economy*, v. 82, n. 1, p. 34-55, 1974.

Sartoris Neto, A. *Estimação de modelos de preços hedônicos:* um estudo para residências na cidade de São Paulo. São Paulo, 1996. 74 f. Master's degree thesis – School of Economics, Administration and Accounting, FEA - Universidade de São Paulo.

Sesso Filho, U. A. Crescimento e desempenho de redes de supermercado na década de 90. *Varejo Competitivo*, São Paulo, v. 6, p. 21-44, 2001.

Superhiper. *Revista da Associação Brasileira de Supermercados.* São Paulo, year 29, n.333, May 2003.

Vasconcellos, M. A. S.; Alves, D. (Coord.). *Manual de Econometria.* São Paulo: Atlas, 2000.

In: International Trade Issues
Editor: Robert. V. Weeks, pp. 145-169

ISBN 1-59454-621-5

Chapter 7

Õ“ □□Ã□ □¤ÿ “‹ Ãÿ¤ ” ¤» › □“ ¤» ––ŒÃ □ —” ¯ÔÁÁÏ ÛÓ ˜□

Daniel Garces-Diaz
Bank of Mexico, MEXICO

□æ¨Æ ¨

The North America Free Trade Agreement (NAFTA) took effect in January 1994. From that year to 2000, Mexican exports grew three times faster (15%) than in the previous six years. Contrary to widespread beliefs, the cointegration analysis in this paper finds no connection between the two facts. The evidence about imports is less conclusive. The results also suggest that the opening up of the Mexican Economy during the eighties is more likely to have caused a structural change in the trade flows. The boost from the American economy accounts for 96% of the growth of the equilibrium level of Mexican exports from 1994 to 2000.

Ô ¨Æº ´ ¨ ±

Free trade agreements among a few countries have become common as substitutes or intermediate steps for wider arrangements. A very important one that generated a great deal of expectations and controversy was signed by Canada, Mexico and the USA. The negotiations preceding the North America Free Trade Agreement (NAFTA) were long and difficult, in part because of the uncertainty about its ramifications. To assess the potential economic effects on the three countries involved, a lot of forward-looking research was carried out by means of computable general equilibrium (CGE) models. These models mostly anticipated large benefits for Mexico and less important ones for Canada and the USA.

In this paper, I concentrate in studying the impact of that accord on the value of trade flows and do not discuss any other aspects, such as changes in the composition of trade, income distribution or employment. I explain what role NAFTA played, if any, in the strong performance of Mexican foreign trade since 1994, the year of the inception of that agreement.[1]

The research about the effects of NAFTA is rather scant. Gould (1998) found that Canada's trade with the US and Mexico did not have perceptible effects, but that trade between Mexico and the US did show changes after NAFTA. He based his estimates on a gravity model of bilateral trade where the change in tariff and nontariff barriers due to NAFTA was approximated by a dummy variable that he found significant for the equations of trade between Mexico and the US; by contrast, I found a similar dummy variable to be nonsignificant in the error correction equations I derived.

Krueger (1999) observed that both Canadian and Mexican foreign trade have become more concentrated towards the US and wondered, also in the context of a gravity model, if that phenomenon was the result of trade creation or trade diversion. She concluded that NAFTA did not induce large effects with respect to other processes already underway, such as previous reduction of tariffs and the modification of the exchange rate regime; on the contrary, the results of this paper imply that the adoption of a new exchange rate system did not have any effects on the trade flows. I do find, however, that changes in Mexican trade policy carried out long before NAFTA had important effects on the behavior of the Mexican foreign trade sector. Finally, Gruben (2001) did not find an effect of NAFTA on employment in assembling plants (maquiladoras) in Mexico. This result is strongly consistent with the ones from this paper.

I examine the Mexican trade flows assuming that they are entirely determined by the demand side; i.e., both the import and export supply functions are perfectly elastic within the observable range or, equivalently, the country is a price taker in world markets. This is a reasonable assumption for Mexico. The analysis is based on the estimation of cointegration relationships. The results are robust enough so as not to depend on the estimation method.

The main results are the following: a structural change occurred during the eighties which makes it difficult to estimate cointegration relationships for the period that begins in 1980 and ends in 2000; therefore, I split the sample and estimated long-run relationships for exports and imports for the period 1990-2000. I obtained coefficients with the correct sign and reasonable magnitude. I also found that the equation for exports, as a function of the US index of industrial production and the real exchange rate, is very stable for that period. The US economy's upswing accounts for 96% of the growth of the equilibrium level of Mexican exports from 1994 to 2000. The net effect of the real exchange rate during that period is small because after the sharp 1995 devaluation it appreciated enough to return to its former level. The import demand (as a function of the Mexican index of industrial production, the level of exports and the real exchange rate) shows instability for the same period although the long-run equation fits the data very well, even without considering seasonality and short-run dynamics.

The analysis was extended to disaggregate data and it was found that only in a few

[1]From that year to 1999 exports grew on average almost three times faster than during the previous six years: 15.5% against 5.5%, annually. The degree of openness of the economy, (defined as the sum of exports and imports over GDP), for the year 2000 (0.77) is twice as big as that of 1993 (0.36).

individual categories of exports and imports can one find a cointegration vector valid for the whole twenty one years. For the 1990-2000 period I found a stable cointegration vector in all cases, which explains the result for aggregate exports and imports. I also obtained stable and constant error-correction models for the same period. These results imply that a structural change in Mexican foreign trade during the nineties was very unlikely and therefore NAFTA could not have caused the boom in Mexican exports. In most cases, a cointegration vector was also found for the 1980-1989 subsample although those vectors do not present the stability shown for the 1990-2000 period. This suggests that a structural change occurred during the time Mexico opened up its economy and joined the General Agreement on Tariffs and Trade (GATT). A likely reason for the lack of evidence in favor of NAFTA as a great catalyzer of trade is that many of the structural reforms that that agreement was supposed to bring about were already there when it started.

The rest of the paper is organized as follows: in section 2, I describe the data and test for the presence of unit roots; in section 3, I analyze the behavior of exports and imports at the most aggregate level; in section 4, I carry out the analysis for different types of exports and imports; in section 5, I derive and analyze the error correction models; section 6 concludes.

Ó ‹ª Æ¨± ø º Õø¨ ¨ ø¥–Æ ªÆª ± ¨ ª ‹ ø¨ø

The data is of monthly frequency. Mexican exports (X) and imports (M) are in constant US dollars.[2] Exports are also disaggregated in maquila ($X^{\{Q\}}$), oil-related ($X^{\{O\}}$) and the rest ($X^{\{-QO\}}$). Imports are disaggregated in consumer goods ($M^{\{cons\}}$), capital goods ($M^{\{cap\}}$) and intermediate goods ($M^{\{int\}}$). I also consider imports of intermediate goods for maquila ($M^{\{intQ\}}$) and the rest ($M^{\{int-Q\}}$). The unilateral real exchange rate peso/dollar (RER) is based on the respective consumer price indexes. The indicators of economic activity are the US index of industrial production (IVUSA) and the Mexican index of industrial production (IVPI). I will use small letters to represent logarithms of the series.

Table 1 presents two tests (with three and six lags) to classify the logarithms of the series as being either trend stationary (TS) or difference stationary (DS). The first one is the GLS-DF test proposed by Elliot ª¨ø¥Ú(1996), which is a more powerful version of the well-known ADF test. The second one is the stationarity KPSS test proposed by Kwiatkowski ª¨ø¥Ú(1992). These tests (or similar ones) are jointly used in confirmatory analysis for the presence of a unit root in a series. [3]

It can be seen that in all cases but two (with three lags) the DF-GLS cannot reject the

[2]Exports and imports data are reported every month in current US dollars. For the calculations in the paper, I divide these numbers by the US CPI. From 1980 to 1990 maquila exports were treated differently from the rest of exports and were reported as a separate item. Since 1991 maquila exports are regarded as part of total exports and are also reported separately but the data were elaborated with a different methodology.

[3]The first test has the presence of a unit root as the null while the KPSS test has stationarity as the null. If GLSDF rejects and KPSS accepts, then the series is classified unambiguously as TS; while if GLSDF accepts and KPSS rejects the series is considered stationary. When both tests accept, then we conclude there is not enough information in the series to classify it. When both reject (an unusual situation), it is probably the case that a linear specification for the series is not a good approximation for its stochastic behavior.

Table 1: Unit Root Tests and Stationarity

Variable	DF-GLS Test		KPSS Test	
	3 lags	6 lags	3 lags	6 lags
Levels				
x	-1.8	-0.9	1.3**	0.8**
$x^{\{-QP\}}$	-1.7	-1.3	0.5**	0.3**
$x^{\{Q\}}$	-2.9**	-2.2	0.2**	0.2**
m	-1.5	-1.8	0.7**	0.4**
$m^{\{cap\}}$	-1.5	-1.5	0.7**	0.4**
$m^{\{cons\}}$	-1.8	-2.0	0.6**	0.3**
$m^{\{int\}}$	-1.7	-1.6	0.7**	0.4**
$m^{\{int_Q\}}$	-3.2**	-2.5	0.2**	0.1
$m^{\{int\_Q\}}$	-1.7	-1.7	0.7**	0.4**
$IPI^{\{USA\}}$	-1.1	-1.4	0.7**	0.4**
$ivpi$	-1.8	-1.7	0.8**	0.5**
tcr	-1.6	-1.9	0.5**	0.3**
Differences				
x	-8.0***	-3.7***	0.0	0.0
$x^{\{-QP\}}$	-8.1***	-3.7***	0.0	0.0
$x^{\{Q\}}$	-10.6***	-6.2***	0.0	0.0
m	-7.8***	-5.4***	0.1	0.1
$m^{\{cap\}}$	-5.2***	-2.8*	0.0	0.1
$m^{\{cons\}}$	-6.8***	-4.2***	0.1	0.1
$m^{\{int\}}$	-6.0***	-3.7***	0.0	0.0
$m^{\{int_Q\}}$	-10.1***	-6.1***	0.0	0.0
$m^{\{int\_Q\}}$	-5.7***	-3.8***	0.0	0.0
$IPI^{\{USA\}}$	-6.7***	-5.1***	0.1	0.1
$ivpi$	-9.5***	-5.6***	0.0	0.0
tcr	-8.3***	-5.5***	0.1	0.1

*** 1% significance

** 5% significance

* 10% significance

hypothesis for the presence of a unit root in the levels of the series. The result is confirmed by the KPSS test that rejects the hypothesis of stationarity in all but just one case (with six lags). For the differences of the series (rates of growth) the results are the opposite: the DF-GLS test rejects the hypothesis of a unit root in all cases and the KPSS test cannot reject the hypothesis of stationarity. Therefore, I consider all series to be $I(1)$.

Ì □ ø¥ß ± □ Æ ø˙a ” a® ø □±Æ Ã/ßº a

Mexico's geographical situation makes the variables that determine the level of its foreign trade easy to identify. Figure 1 shows, with a solid line in both panels, the Mexican trade balance, measured as $x - m$ instead of $X - M$. The dotted line in the upper panel represents the difference of the logarithm of the indexes of industrial production of Mexico ($ivpi$) and the US ($ivusa$), as a measure of relative income. The dotted line in the lower panel represents the path of the logarithm of the real exchange rate (rer).

It is clear that the trade balance worsens when the economic activity in Mexico increases faster than that in the US and the same happens when the real exchange rate appreciates.

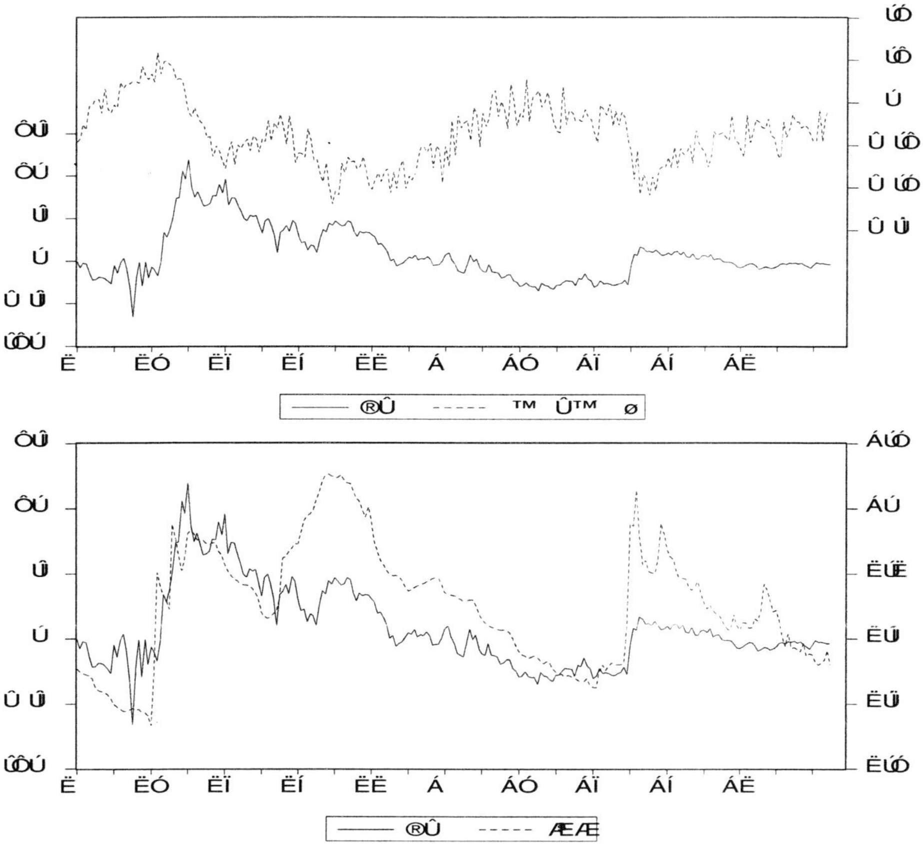

Figure 1. The Mexican Balance of Trade and its Main Determinants.

Therefore, to study the behavior of Mexican foreign trade it is enough to use scale and relative price variables with respect to the US. The choice of the econometric approach is also straightforward and consists of taking a vector $\mathbf{y}_t = (y_{1t}, \mathbf{y}_{2t})$ of k nonstationary economic variables forming a cointegrating system that can be interpreted as a demand y_1 of imports or exports depending on some other $k-1$ variables $\mathbf{y}_2$ in a linear fashion:

$$y_1 = \gamma' \mathbf{y}_2 \qquad (1)$$

where γ is the $k-1$ vector of long-run coefficients or elasticities.

In principle, one could try to model the equations for exports and imports simultaneously in the context of a VECM. I tried this approach but, due to the presence of structural changes (to be discussed later), the size of the workable sample was small relative to the number of parameters and, therefore, very sensitive to changes in the number of lags.[4] For

[4]The coefficients I obtain in the paper can be approximated by a VECM with nine lags and some restrictions that are rejected by the data.

this reason I study exports and imports separately.

ì ⓒ ¤® ±Æ

Since 1980 there have been some important changes in the composition, the rate of growth and the destination of Mexican exports, as illustrated by figure 2.

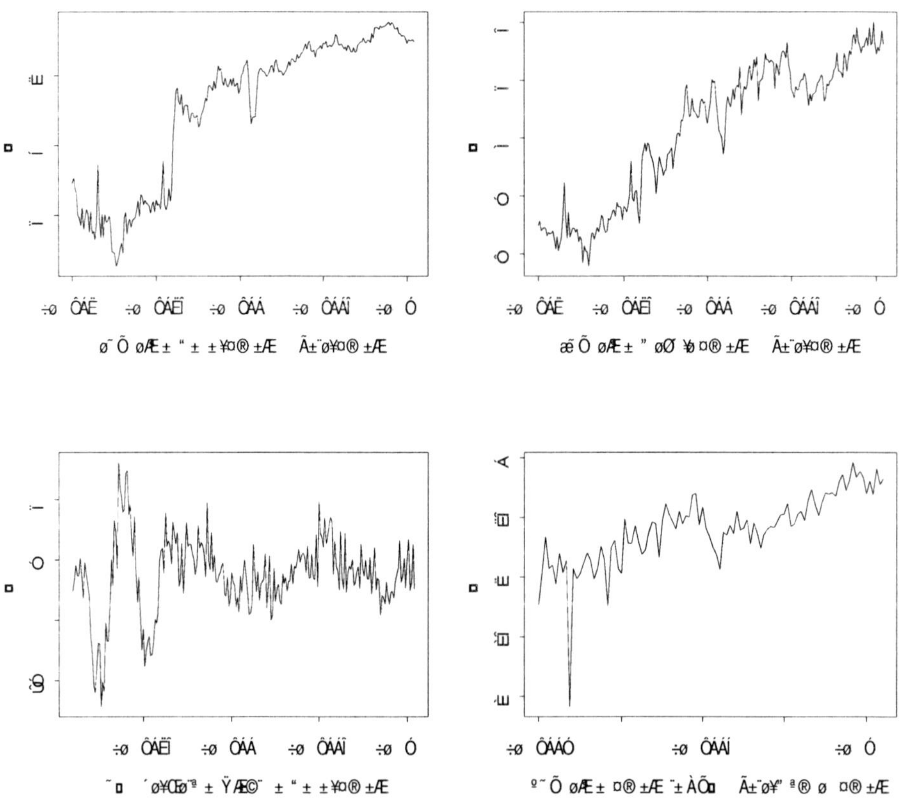

Figure 2: Changes in Mexican Exports.

Panel a) shows how nonoil-related exports have increased their share from about 50% in the early eighties to nearly 90% in 2000. Panel b) suggests a similar behavior of maquila exports, whose portion of total exports has reached nearly 50%, up from some 15% in the early eighties. Panel c) illustrates how the dynamics of exports have changed since the late eighties when Mexico entered into the GATT and gave up trade policy as a tool to correct macroeconomic imbalances. The long swings at the beginning of the sample are due to the implementation of several trade policies. This erratic behavior is reflected in the problem of estimating an export function for the whole sample. The final panel shows that the tendency of Mexican exports to concentrate in a single destination (the US) started before NAFTA.[5]

As a consequence of this complex behavior, it was not possible to obtain an equation for the whole sample period. To try to answer the main question posed by the paper, I modeled the long-run demand for Mexican exports (x) from 1990 to 2000 as a linear function of the US index of industrial production ($ivusa$) and the real exchange rate (rer). The rest of the sample is analyzed in a later section. In this section I apply the Johansen (1988) cointegration procedure to study the system formed by these three variables. The specification includes twelve lags and a constant in the cointegration space. I tried to correct the nonnormaility of the residuals with dummy variables but too many were required so I decided to run the VECM without them.[6] The results are shown in table 2:

Table 2: Maximum Likelihood Analysis for Exports 1990-2000

(i) Cointegration Analysis				
Eigenvalues	0.215	0 .054	.	0.027
Null Hypothesis	$ran.= 0$	$ran.\leq 1$	.	$ran.\leq 2$
λ_{trace}	41.280**	10.520	.	3.460
Critical Values (95%)	29.700	15.400	.	3.800
(ii) Standarized Cointegration Vector and Coefficientes of Adjustment				
Variable	x	$IPI^{\{USA\}}$		rer
Norm. Coint. Vec.γ	1.0000	-2.80	.	-0.318
Coeff. of Adjust.α	-0.399	-0.017	.	0.043
(iii) Significance and Weak Exogeneity Tests for a Given Variable				
Variable	x	$IPI^{\{USA\}}$		rer
Exclusion $\chi^2(1)$	21.247**	19.382**	.	10.656**
Weak Exogeneity $\chi^2(1)$	16.100**	5.168*	.	0.455
(iv) Specification Tests				
Equation	x	$IPI^{\{USA\}}$	rer	Joint Test
AR F(7,102)	4.40[.00]**	0.75[.63]	1.11[.37]	F(63,257)=2.01[.00]**
Normality $\chi^2(2)$	0.99[.61]	5.36[.07]	73.98[.00]**	$\chi^2(6)$ =76.44[.00]**
Heterosk. F(12,96)	1.35[.20]	1.59[.11]	3.08[.00]**	F(72,500)=1.47[.01]*

p-values are between parentheses
* Significant at 10%
** Significant at 5%
*** Significant at 1%
See Hendry (1995) for a detailed description of the tests.

Part (i) shows the trace statistics for the sequential hypotheses of zero, at most one and at most two cointegration vectors. Only in the first case is the hypothesis rejected, so I conclude there is only one long-run relationship. This fact reduces the identification efforts to give a unitary coefficient to one of the variables, which I conveniently choose to be exports. This makes the other coefficients interpretable as long-run elasticities.

Part (ii) shows the normalized cointegration coefficients. The coefficients have the correct signs and turn out to be very similar to the ones obtained with other methods. These coefficients imply the long-run export demand function:

[5]No data of Mexican exports to the US are available for previous years.

[6]This is a serious problem because many of the tests are based on the assumption of normality. All the results shown in this section have to be interpreted with this caveat in mind.

$$x = c + 2.80\, ivusa + 0.32\, rer \tag{2}$$

Part (iii) shows the exclusion and weak exogeneity tests. The results show that none of the three variables can be excluded from the long-run relationship and that only total exports reject the hypothesis of weak exogeneity. The results shown so far justify the more detailed analysis I carry out in later sections utilizing single-equation methods. Part (iv) shows several specification tests. The problems detected by them might render the conclusions invalid, therefore the results of this section should be interpreted cautiously. I used other estimation methods and the results were not very different. In a later section I will show other estimates and tests.

Finally, a simple test can be applied to decide whether NAFTA, or any other event, caused a structural change in the behavior of Mexican exports during the sample period. The procedure consists in recursively estimating the system, and at each step testing, with a likelihood ratio, the hypothesis of the recursive coefficients being statistically equal to the ones obtained for the whole period. Figure 3 shows the sequence of test statistics. The level of significance is determined by a χ^2 distribution with one degree of freedom.

The hypothesis of stable parameters is easily accepted by the data. On the basis of this result, one can claim that there was no structural change in the behavior of Mexican exports during the nineties; however, this result can be a byproduct of the aggregate level in which the estimation is taking place. Therefore, a more disaggregated analysis is necessary. As an example, one can consider the behavior of oil-related exports, which probably do not respond to market factors the way other kinds of exports do. The stability and constancy of the short-run dynamics is demonstrated later. The accuracy of the model is demonstrated graphically in figure 4.

The goodness of fit is acceptable in spite of not including the short-run dynamics or seasonal components. From these results one can make some calculations that explain the fact that the rate of growth of Mexican exports has been much higher since the beginning of NAFTA. For the 1994-1999 period, the growth of the equilibrium level of Mexican exports is due almost completely (97%) to the expansion of the American economy (as measured by its index of industrial production) and only 4% of this growth is related to a modest depreciation of the real exchange rate. From 1990 to 1993 exports grew less because of the American economy's much slower pace and the revaluation of the real exchange rate. For this period, the appreciation of the real exchange rate offset about one third of the positive effect of the scale variable.

ÌÓ ±Æ

During the eighties, imports were often subject to a restrictive trade policy and a strategy of recurrent devaluations in order to face balance-of-payments problems. After Mexico entered the GATT in the mid eighties, most nontariff restrictions were removed and tariffs were considerably lowered. The effect of all these changes can seen in figure 5.

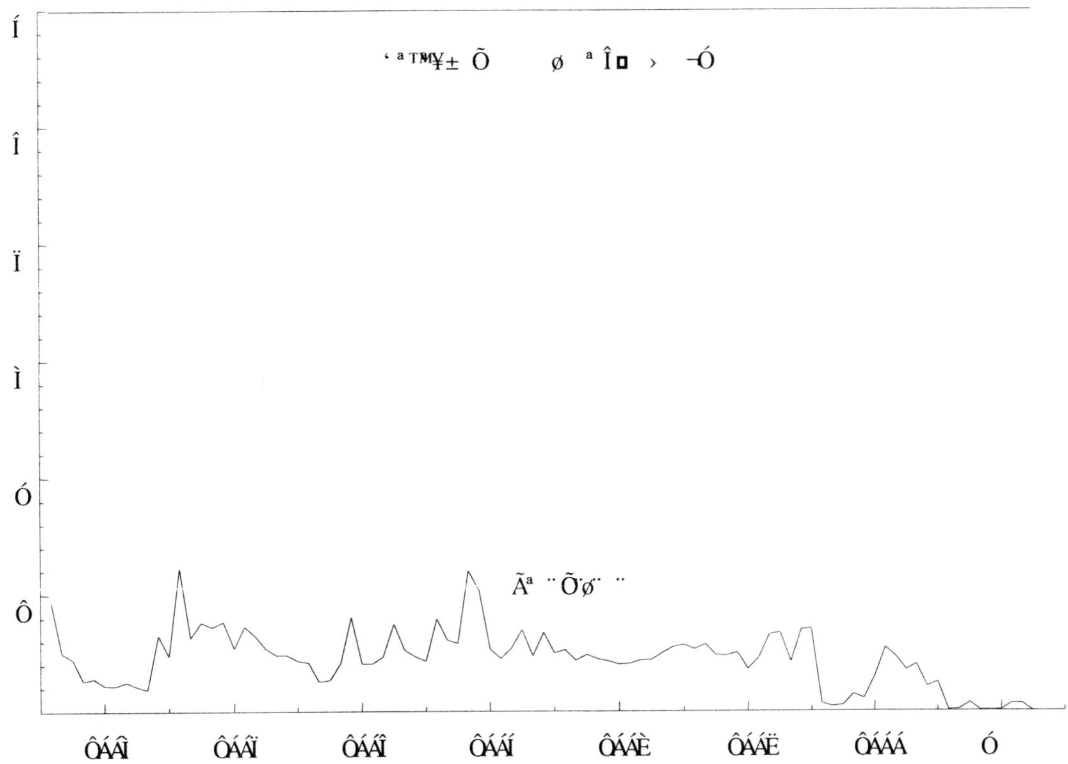

Figure 3: Recursive Test of Stability for Exports.

Panel a) shows the annual rate of growth of total imports. Major devaluations have always had a strong impact on imports and sometimes they came bundled with severe economic contractions and a discretionary trade policy. The large drop in 1983 corresponds to the beginning of the debt crises that left the country with a low level of foreign currency and a deep economic recession. Panel b) shows the share of consumption imports in the total. This type of imports presents the highest income effect. The economic expansion and the consumption boom from the beginning of the nineties coincides with the largest shares of this type of imports in the total. Panel c) represents the participation of intermediate goods, the most important component of imports. It has been growing since the beginning of the sample and currently makes up nearly 80% of the total. The last panel represents the share of intermediate goods imported by the maquilas. This is by far the most dynamic component of Mexican imports and currently approaches 30% of the total. This fact suggests that Mexican exports must be considered as an explanatory variable for Mexican imports.

I applied the Johansen procedure to a system that includes Mexican total imports (m),

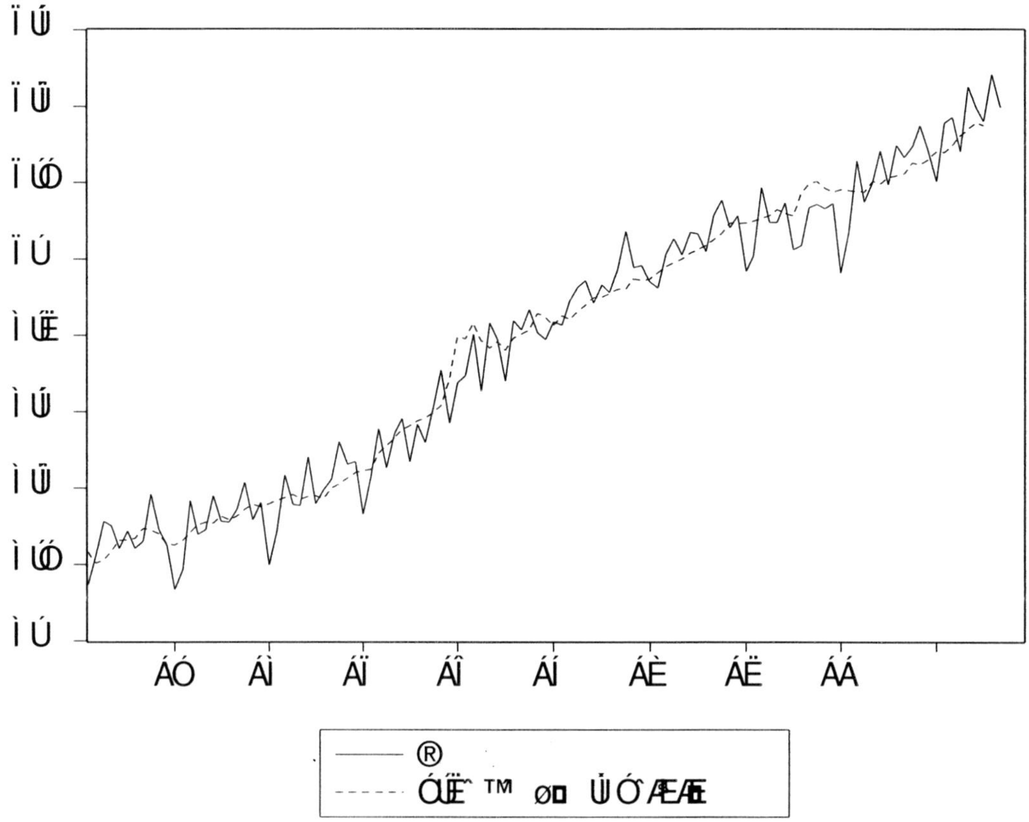

Figure 4: Exports (x) and its Long-Run Level ($2.8\, ivusa + 0.32\, rer + c$).

the Mexican index of value of industrial production ($ivpi$), the real exchange rate (rer) and the level of total Mexican exports (x). The results are shown in table 3.

The results are very similar to the ones obtained in the case of exports: there is only one cointegration vector; the long-run elasticities have the correct sign; none of the variables can be excluded, and only imports reject the hypothesis of weak exogeneity. There are also specification problems as neither autocorrelation nor normality are jointly accepted. The long-run demand for imports turns out to be:

$$m = c + 0.94\, ivpi - 0.41\, rer + 0.53\, x \tag{3}$$

The outcome of the stability test, however, is different. As figure 6 shows, the sequence of likelihood-ratio statistics crosses the significance line.

This result could be interpreted as indicative of a structural change in Mexican imports during the nineties, but a more detailed analysis is necessary. In spite of the apparent

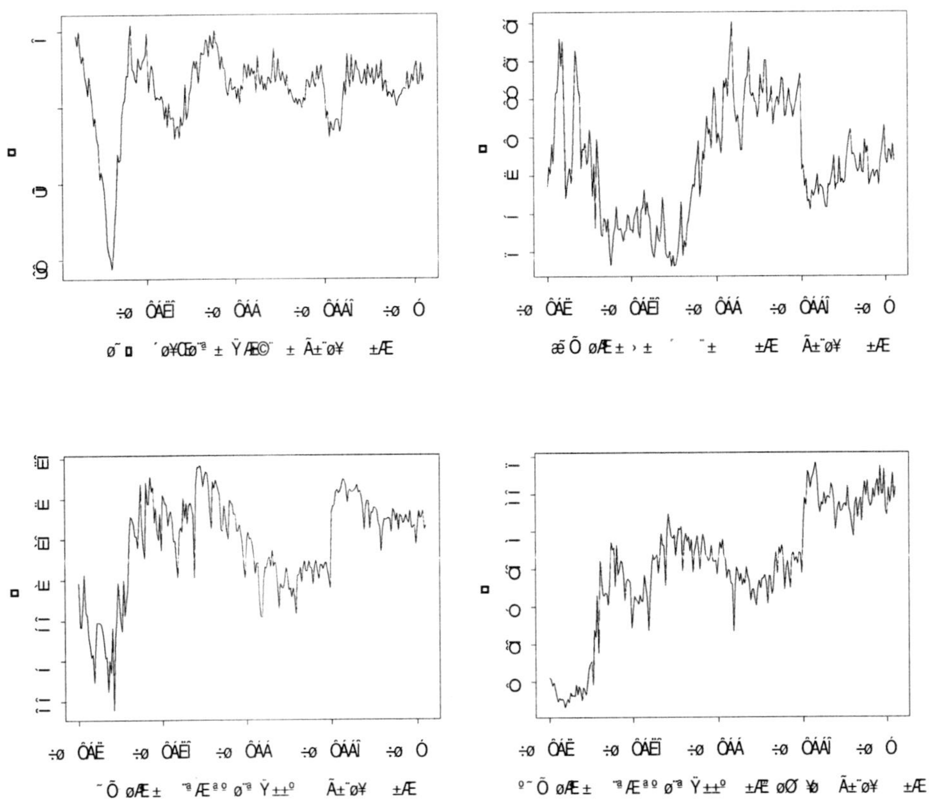

Figure 5: Evolution of Mexican Imports.

instability shown above, the long-run equation fits the data very well, as figure 7 shows. The fit is quite good even without short-run dynamics or seasonal components.

Ï ¤®ª º ·· ª ◻ ø¥ß ¨±‹ ø Æ ø¨ª ‹ ø¨ø

The results for exports and imports could be affected by either the shortened sample, the level of aggregation or even the inclusion of oil-related exports, which do not necessarily respond directly to free market forces. To control for all these factors, I estimated and tested the stability of export and import functions for the whole sample and the periods 1980-1989 and 1990-2000. I also disaggregated the data according to some reasonable criteria. Because of the large number of relationships being estimated, I used a single-equation framework. Two methods were used: OLS applied to unrestricted error-correction models and the Fully Modified Least Squares (FM-LS) method proposed by Phillips and

Table 3: Maximum Likelihood Analysis for Imports 1991-2000

		(i) Cointegration Analysis			
Eigenvalues	0.222	0 .136	.	0.29	0.002
Null Hypothesis	$ran.=0$	$ran.\leq 1$	.	$ran.\leq 2$	$ran.\leq 3$
λ_{trace}	48.590**	20.17	.	3.599	0.250
Critical Values (95%)	47.200	29.700	.	15.400	3.800
		(ii) Standarized Cointegration Vector and Coefficientes of Adjustment			
Variable	m	$ivpi$		rer	x
Norm. Coint. Vec.γ	1.000	-0.937	.	0.410	-0.530
Coeff. of Adjust.α	-0.713	-0.178	.	0.113	-0.365
		(iii) Significance and Weak Exogeneity Tests for a Given Variable			
Variable	m	$ivpi$		rer	x
Exclusion $\chi^2(1)$	27.980**	24.990**	.	17.290**	26.230**
Weak Exogeneity $\chi^2(1)$	16.630**	4.840	.	1.230	4.140
		(vi) Specification Tests			
Equation	m	ivpi	rer	x	Joint Test
AR F(7,97)	2.43[.03]*	2.29[.03]*	2.00[.06]	4.97[00]**	F(112,292)=1.83[.00]**
Normality $\chi^2(2)$	0.12[.94]	1.35[.51]	62.46[.00]**	0.61[.74]	$\chi^2(6)$ =67.74[.00]**
Heterosk. F(16,87)	1.10[.37]	1.58[.09]*	3.36[.00]**	1.84[.04]*	F(160,685)=1.59[.00]

p-values are between parentheses

* Significant at 10%

** Significant at 5%

*** Significant at 1%

See Hendry (1995) for a detailed description of the tests

Hansen (1990). The latter is more suitable when the normality assumption is not met but in all cases both methods yielded similar results. I first studied the cointegration property for the different types of exports and imports in each subsample and then I checked the stability properties with the Hansen (1992) tests in the cases where a long-run function was found.

Ï̂ÛÕ ¤® ·ª ª ± ' ± ÛŒ Œ¥ő¨ ± ‹ ø Æ ø·ª ‹ ø¨ø

This section presents separately the results of cointegration tests based on the ECM statistic for disaggregate data on exports and imports. The p-values in the tables were obtained from the Ericsson and MacKinnon (1999) program. I divided exports in maquila ($x^{\{Q\}}$), oil-related ($x^{\{O\}}$) and the rest ($x^{\{-QO\}}$). Imports are disaggregated in consumer goods ($m^{\{c\}}$), capital goods ($m^{\{k\}}$) and intermediate goods ($m^{\{i\}}$). I also considered imports of intermediate goods for maquila ($m^{\{iq\}}$) and the rest ($m^{\{i-q\}}$). For each category I estimated unrestricted error correction models in each subsample.

Ï̂ÛÕÕ › ± ·ª Æ̈ ± Ãª ¨ ±Æ ø Æ ø·ª ¤® ±Æ

Table 4 reports only the cases where there was evidence of cointegration for the different types of exports. Because the estimates of the unrestricted cointegration vectors are very similar to the ones obtained by FM-LS, shown in table 6, I do not present the corresponding equations.

Several parameters are needed to run the test. Column 3 gives the number of variables in

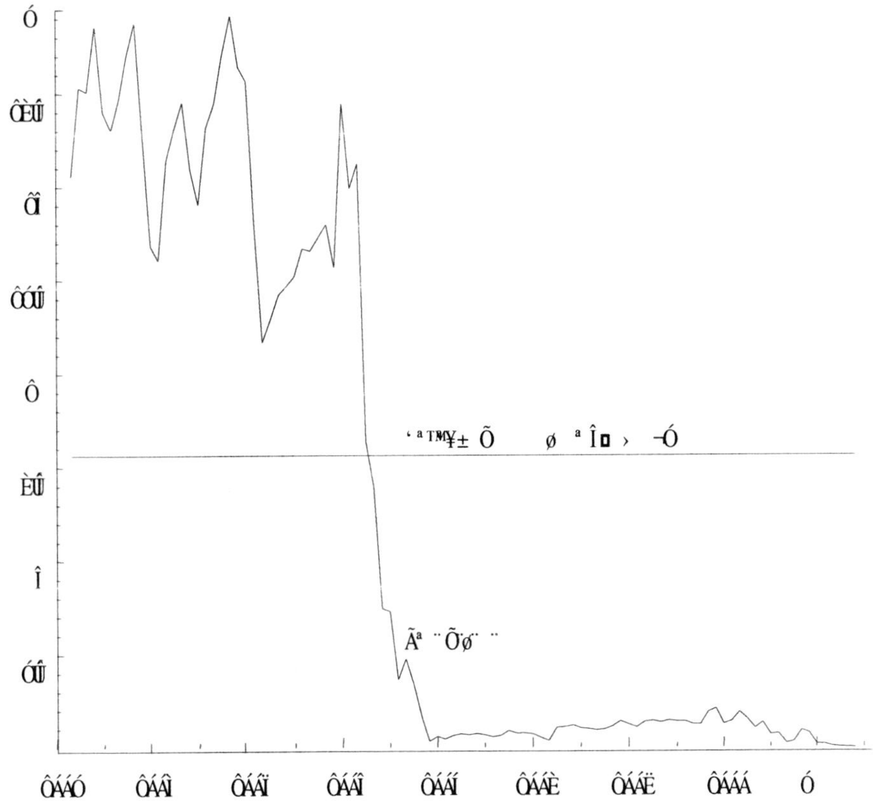

Figure 6: Recursive Test of Stability for Imports.

the cointegration relationship k. Column 4 gives the number of deterministic components d. Column 5 contains the sample size T and column 6 the number of total regressors h. Column 7 contains the ECM statistic (which is the t-statistic for the level of the lagged dependent variable). The final column provides the p-value for each ECM statistic generated by the Ericsson and McKinnon (1999) program. Each case is interesting in itself.

For total exports (x) I could find cointegration only for the period 1990-2000 (p-value=0.0) and not for the whole sample. The analysis of the case of maquila exports ($x^{\{Q\}}$) can explain the situation. First of all, the cointegration relationship excludes the real exchange rate (therefore $k = 2$). Second, for the whole sample the ECM statistic is not significant (-2.72 with p-value=0.15); however, for each subsample the ECM statistic is significant. This illustrates a likely structural break (as I will show, the cointegration vector is very different for each subsample) of the type suggested by Gregory and Hansen (1996),

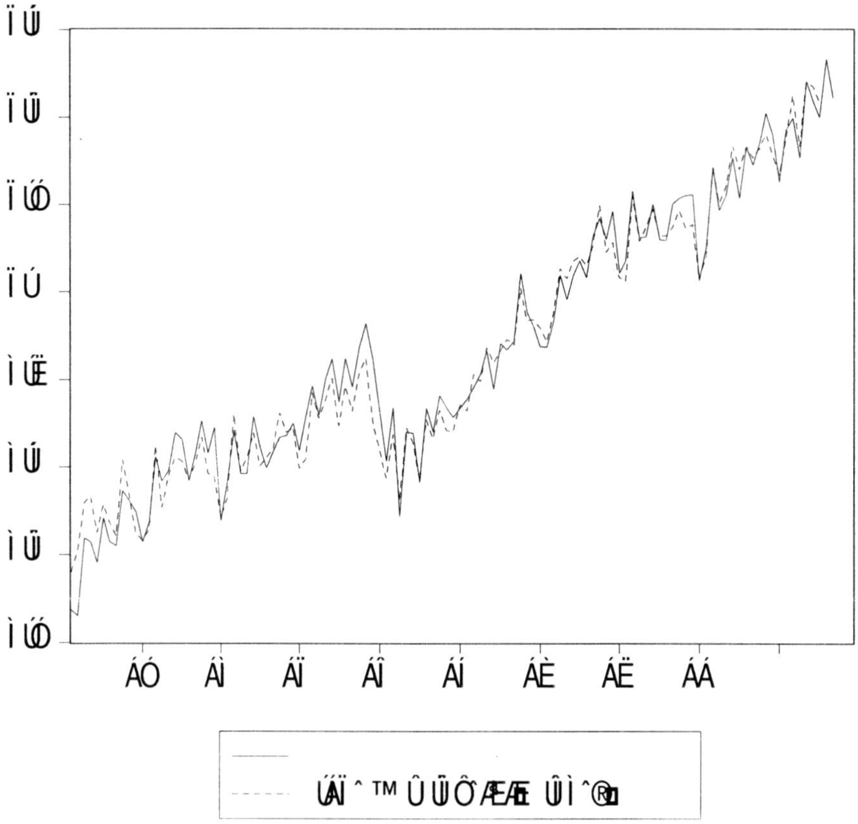

Figure 7: Imports (m) and its Long-Run Level $(0.94\,ivpi - 0.41\,rer + 0.53\,x + c)$.

where a structural change hides the existence of a long relationship among $I(1)$ variables.[7] These characteristics of the maquila exports explain the problem of finding cointegration for total exports. The case of nonoil-nonmaquila exports ($x^{\{-QO\}}$) shows cointegration for the three periods and the cointegrating variables are the same as the ones for total exports.

[illegible]

Table 5 shows that for total imports there is cointegration only for the period 1990-2000. For this category, the cointegrating variables are the Mexican index of industrial production, the real exchange rate and exports (so $k = 4$). The same cointegrating variables appear in

[7] I applied their tests and the results, available upon request, were coincident with the ones I present. It was interesting to observe that their ADF* test had the tendency to reject the hypothesis of cointegration. The other two tests performed more in accordance with what I report.

Table 4: ECM Tests for Exports

Variable	Period	No. of variables in Coint. Vect. k	No. of Determ. Variables d	Sample Size T	No. of Regressors h	ECM Statistic t	p-value* p
x	90-2000	3	1	127	7	-6.38	0.00
$x^{\{-QP\}}$	80-2000	3	1	234	7	-3.67	0.04
	80-89	3	1	107	7	-3.38	0.07
	91-2000	3	1	114	7	-4.80	0.00
$x^{\{Q\}}$	80-89	2	1	107	6	-3.90	0.01
	91-2000	2	1	113	6	-4.88	0.00

*Critical values and p-values herein were obtained using the response surfaces in Ericsson and MacKinnon (1999), as implemented in the program ECMtest.xls (version 1.0).

the case of imports of intermediate goods, but exports are not in the equations of imports of capital goods and consumption goods (so $k = 3$).

Table 5: ECM Tests for Imports

Variable	Period	No. of variables in Coint. Vect. k	No. of Determ. Variables d	Sample Size T	No. of Regressors h	ECM Statistic t	p-value* p
m	91-2000	4	1	113	8	-5.46	0.00
$m^{\{cap\}}$	80-2000	3	1	243	6	-6.00	0.00
	80-89	2	1	116	6	-4.02	0.01
	91-2000	3	1	114	6	-6.85	0.00
$m^{\{cons\}}$	80-2000	3	1	234	8	-3.93	0.02
	80-89	3	1	107	8	-3.71	0.03
	91-2000	3	1	114	8	-5.20	0.00
$m^{\{int\}}$	91-2000	3	1	113	6	-6.37	0.00
$m^{\{int_Q\}}$	91-2000	3	1	113	9	-4.81	0.00
$m^{\{int\_Q\}}$	80-2000	3	1	245	7	-3.38	0.07
	91-2000	3	1	113	7	-6.82	0.00

*Critical values and p-values herein were obtained using the response surfaces in Ericsson and MacKinnon (1999), as implemented in the program ECMtest.xls (version 1.0).

The case of imports of capital goods ($m^{\{cap\}}$) is remarkable because the existence of cointegration for the whole sample hides the presence of a structural change of a special kind. It shows cointegration in the three periods but the cointegrating vectors for the two subsamples contain a different number of components: $k = 3$ for the 1990-2000 sample and $k = 2$ for the 1980-89 period. In the latter case, the variable absent from the cointegration relationship is the Mexican index of industrial production. This case of structural change, however, was detected by the stability tests I report below. For imports of consumption goods ($m^{\{cons\}}$) I find cointegration for the three samples and the same number of variables appear in each case. However, as I will show, there is also evidence of a structural break.

For intermediate goods ($m^{\{int\}}$) I only found cointegration for the 1991-2000 period. As this is by far the most important component of Mexican imports, this property is passed on to the total. Dividing this category between those that go to maquila (m^{intQ}) and the rest ($m^{\{int-Q\}}$) I find similar results.

ÏÜÖ Õ'øæ¥¨ß± ¨ ª ' ± ÛŒ Œ¥ø¨ ± ± ‹ ø Æ ø¨ª ‹ ø¨ø

In this section I tested the stability of the long-run relationships found above. For the same categories of imports included in table 4, I estimated cointegration coefficients with the method of Fully Modified Least Squares (FM-LS) and applied the three stability tests for $I(1)$ variables proposed by Hansen (1991). The three tests have constant cointegration coefficients for the whole sample as the null hypothesis; however, the first two (LC and mean-F) consider a random walk for the coefficients as the alternative hypothesis while the alternative for the third test (sup-F) is a one-time break at an unknown date.[8]

ÏÜ Õ'øæ¥¨ß Ãª ¨ ±Æ ø Æ ø¨ª ¤® ±Æ

Columns 3 to 5 of table 6 contain the FM-LS estimates of the long-run coefficients and standard errors for each of the cointegrating variables and a constant. Columns 6 to 8 contain the statistics and p-values to test stability.[9]

Table 6: Stability of the Long-Run Relationships for Exports

Variable	Period	Cointegrating Variables*			Stability Test**		
		$ivusa$	rer	C	LC	$Mean\ F$	$Sup\ F$
x	90-2000	2.867	0.234	-11.890	0.321	5.090	7.680
		(0.070)	(0.070)	(0.656)	p=0.200	p=0.107	p=0.200
$x^{\{-QP\}}$	80-2000	3.597	0.069	-14.756	0.884	10.759	20.371
		(0.105)	(0.100)	(1.046)	p=0.010	p=0.010	p=0.010
	80-89	2.917	0.163	-12.595	0.479	5.382	13.884
		(0.302)	(0.123)	(1.351)	p=0.111	p=0.088	p=0.082
	91-2000	2.945	0.702	-17.077	0.258	5.003	10.460
		(0.0712)	(0.067)	(0.608)	p=0.200	p=0.114	p=0.200
$x^{\{Q\}}$	80-89	4.564	.	-18.974	0.772	7.560	12.105
		(0.199)	.	(0.889)	p=0.018	p=0.010	p=0.055
	91-2000	3.279	.	-12.706	0.176	1.831	4.897
		(0.074)	.	(0.353)	p=0.200	p=0.200	p=0.200

*Standard errors between parentheses **p-value

The first thing to notice is that the long-run elasticities for total exports calculated with FM-LS are quite similar to those obtained with the Johansen method and to the ones obtained with an unrestricted error-correction model. The stability tests confirm the result obtained in section 3 that showed no evidence of instability in the long-run relationship: the p-value of each test statistics is above 0.20.

[8]See Hansen (1991) for a full description of these tests.

[9]All of the calculations for this table were generated with the program that B. Hansen wrote in Gauss code.

For nonoil-nonmaquila exports ($x^{\{-QP\}}$) I found a long-run relationship for the three periods; however, for the whole sample, the test statistics detect instability. For each of the two subsamples the cointegration vectors differ mostly in the coefficient for the real exchange rate. Actually, for the whole period and the first subsample, the real exchange rate has very low significance and probably should be excluded. The stability tests do not detect problems within each period. In this case there seems to be a structural break but not so drastic as to hide the existence of a long-run relationship.

Maquila exports present the case where the structural break hides the existence of a long-run relationship. For the whole sample I could not find any reasonable cointegration vector but for each subsample I did find one. The real exchange rate does not enter in either vector, and the elasticity of the US index of industrial production is higher in the first subsample. For the first subsample the statistics detect instability but that problem does not appear in the second period.

ÏÛ Õ'øæ¥'ß Ãª ¨ ±Æ ø Æ ø'ª ±Æ

Table 7 presents the corresponding results for imports. The number of columns for the cointegrating variables and constant is now four. The interpretation is the same as in table 6.

Table 7: Stability of the Long-Run Relationships for Imports

Variable	Period	Cointegrating Variables*				Stability Test**		
		ivpi	*rer*	*x*	*C*	*LC*	*Mean F*	*Sup F*
m	91-2000	1.124	-0.286	0.461	-0.676	0.863	12.054	24.897
		(0.131)	(0.061)	(0.043)	(0.922)	p=0.020	p=0.010	p=0.010
$m^{\{cap\}}$	80-2000	2.217	-1.570	.	5.141	1.518	9.624	22.547
		(0.151)	(0.141)	.	(1.623)	p=0.010	p=0.010	p=0.010
	80-89	.	1.966	.	18.300	0.762	5.561	11.455
		.	(0.237)	.	(2.082)	p=0.019	p=0.025	p=0.071
	91-2000	1.966	-0.734	.	-0.927	0.173	2.658	9.215
		(0.077)	(0.068)	.	(0.728)	p=0.200	p=0.200	p=0.200
$m^{\{cons\}}$	80-2000	3.506	-2.277	.	4.720	0.962	9.488	17.121
		(0.376)	(0.350)	.	(4.039)	p=0.010	p=0.010	p=0.023
	80-89	5.324	-2.188	.	-4.095	0.696	5.818	14.974
		(1.571)	(0.402)	.	(8.802)	p=0.035	p=0.066	p=0.054
	91-2000	1.753	-1.160	.	3.30677	0.086	1.537	7.990
		(0.150)	(0.132)	.	(1.411)	p=0.200	p=0.200	p=0.200
$m^{\{int\}}$	91-2000	.	-0.476	0.908	4.261	0.331	4.806	10.862
		.	(0.048)	(0.017)	(0.399)	p=0.200	p=0.129	p=0.200
$m^{\{intQ\}}$	91-2000	.	-0.206	1.224	-0.181	0.567	10.247	20.327
		.	(0.071)	(0.026)	(0.592)	p=0.067	p=0.010	p=0.010
$m^{\{int\_Q\}}$	80-2000	2.549	-0.719	0.036	-2.833	1.388	11.626	19.623
		(0.502)	(0.186)	(0.182)	(2.923)	p=0.010	p=0.010	p=0.264
	91-2000	1.200	-0.146	0.323	-2.523	1.000	10.014	15.524
		(0.158)	(0.074)	(0.053)	(1.118)	p=0.010	p=0.010	p=0.113

*Standar Errors between parentheses **p-value

For total imports I found a cointegration only vector for the 1991-2000 period. It is very similar to the one I obtained in section 3, and the stability tests agree with the evidence of instability shown by figure 6. For imports of capital goods it was possible to find a cointegration vector for each period. The one for the whole sample and that for the first period show instability but the second subsample seems very stable. For this category of imports, as well as for those of consumption goods, the level of exports does not enter in the long-run relationship, which is intuitively sound. Interestingly enough, the scale variable (the Mexican index of industrial production) did not enter into the first subsample. This is a case where a possible structural change does not hide the existence of a long-run relationship. The case for imports of consumption goods also shows an unstable cointegration vector for the whole sample, but the ones corresponding to the two subsamples are stable, especially that for the second period.

For imports of intermediate goods I only found cointegration for the second subsample. The cointegration vector, which was very stable, does not include the Mexican index of industrial production and the relevant scale variable is the level of exports. In fact, disaggregating this category further, I found that imports for the maquila industry only show a cointegrating relationship for the second subsample and this is unstable. For intermediate imports for nonmaquila industries I found cointegration for the two subsamples but not for the whole period. The stability of these vectors is not obvious since the results of the tests are contradictory (one of them suggests stability while the other two reject that hypothesis).

After analyzing the stability properties for the export and import functions at disaggregate levels some conclusions can be drawn. First, for the whole period 1980-2000 it is not possible to find a cointegration relationship for each of the types of exports and imports I analyze; however, for most of the categories I did find stable long-run relationships for the 1990-2000 period. The only exceptions seem to be the very disaggregate data for imports of intermediate goods. This is probably the source of the instability suggested by figure 6 for total imports.

Î ¤ÆÆÆ̂ ±ÆÆ ¨± ” ±º ª¥

In this section I analyze the statistical properties of the error-correction models associated with the long-run relationships for the 1990-2000 period. The error-correction terms are constructed with the coefficients from tables 6 and 7. The tables show the estimates for the short-run parameters and, at the bottom, several statistical tests. The variable with superscript $x^i = x, x^{\{-QP\}}, x^{\{Q\}}$ indicates that the explanatory variable should be understood as being specific to a given equation.

Î Ï̂ ¤ÆÆÆ̂ ±ÆÆ ¨± ” ±º ª¥ ±Æ ø Æ ø ª ¤® ±Æ

Table 8 contains the result for exports. The coefficients of speed of adjustment are all negative and quite significant, reinforcing the hypothesis of the existence of a long-run relationship. It is in all cases quite high, indicating that the adjustment process does not take a long time to complete. There are several lags of the dependent variable, mostly negative, that produce an oscillating adjustment process. In the case of total exports, the short-run coefficient of the change in the US economic activity is very high. The short-run effect of changes in the exchange rate appears only in the equation for nonoil-nonmaquila exports.

Table 8: Error Correction Models for Exports

Variables	Models		
	dx	dx^{-QP}	$dx^{\{Q\}}$
$Cex_{t-1}^{\{i\}}$	-0.314 (0.077)	-0.271 (0.085)	-0.592 (0.123)
$dx_{t-1}^{\{i\}}$	-0.420 (0.085)	-0.483 (0.081)	-0.444 (0.102)
$dx_{t-2}^{\{i\}}$	-0.237 (0.078)	-0.358 (0.073)	-0.303 (0.082)
$dx_{t-4}^{\{i\}}$	-0.231 (0.075)	. .	. .
$dx_{t-5}^{\{i\}}$	-0.294 (0.077)	. .	. .
$dx_{t-8}^{\{i\}}$	0.225 (0.072)	. .	. .
$dx_{t-10}^{\{i\}}$	. .	. .	-0.161 (0.062)
$dx_{t-11}^{\{i\}}$	. .	0.304 (0.075)	. .
$dx_{t-12}^{\{i\}}$	0.245 (0.071)	0.358 (0.069)	0.214 (0.062)
$drer_t$	. .	0.417 (0.121)	. .
$dipi_{t-5}^{\{USA\}}$	2.222 (0.897)	. .	. .
ECM Statistic	-6.380	-4.800	-4.880
R^2	0.769	0.713	0.839
$\bar{R}^2$	0.728	0.679	0.812
S.E	0.045	0.053	0.051
Asym. Coeff.	0.154	0.226	-0.072
Kurtosis Coeff.	3.472	3.583	2.656
Jarque-Bera Stat.	1.68	2.587	0.662
LM(12) AR	1.387	0.728	0.771
LM(12) ARCH	1.970**	0.627	0.786
White Test	1.502*	0.03	1.019
RESET	0.002	0.013	0.4744
Chow B (94:01)	1.016	0.793	1.901**
Chow Pred.(94:01)	1.224	0.839	0.967

$Cex_{t-1} = x_{t-1} - 2.867ipi_{t-1}^{USA} - 0.234rer_{t-1}$

$Cex_{t-1}^{\{-QP\}} = x_{t-1}^{\{-QP\}} - 2.945ipi_{t-1}^{USA} - 0.702rer_{t-1}$

$Cex_{t-1}^{\{Q\}} = x_{t-1}^{\{Q\}} - 3.279ipi_{t-1}^{\{USA\}}$

All of the the ECM statistics (obtained with an unrestricted model) are significant at the 1% level. The measures of goodness of fit are very good. There are no problems with the normality of the residuals and only the equation for total exports shows some evidence of ARCH effects. The Chow tests for structural break and prediction failure for January 1994 (the date of the beginning of NAFTA) are all nonsignificant with the exception of one case. I introduced a dummy variable that was equal to one from the beginning of 1994 (used by some authors as a proxy for the institutional change brought about by NAFTA) and it was strongly nonsignificant. Figure 8 shows the recursive analysis of the ECM for total exports.

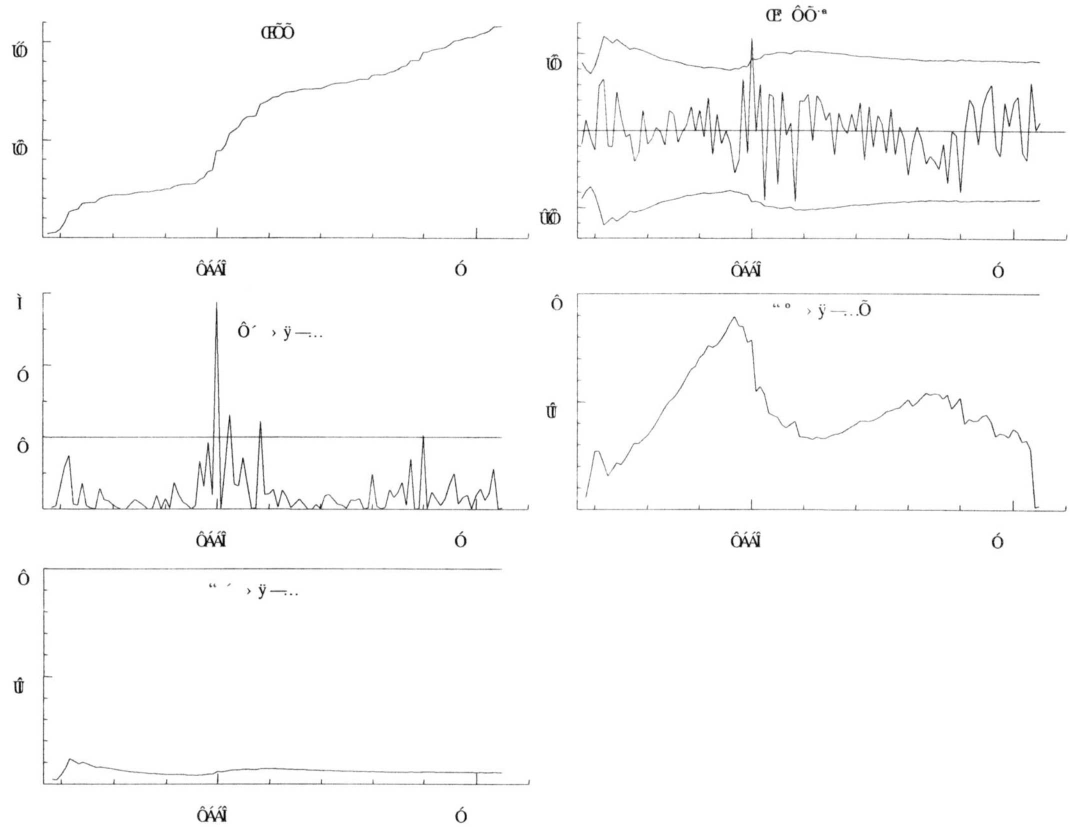

Figure 8: Recursive Stability Tests for Total Exports ECM

The first panel shows the sum of squares, which approaches a straight line; the second panel shows that the sequence of one-step residuals crosses the confidence band in just one month; the next panel shows the one-step Chow statistics that only detect three obvious cases of outliers; the last two panels show the n-step down and up Chow statistics of structural breaks. In both cases the sequence stays below the significance level of 5%. Figure 9 shows the sequence of recursive coefficients for the same ECM. Notice that the sequences for the seasonal dummy variables are also included. It can be seen that the short-run coefficients are constant. From these results it can be concluded that the short-run model does not seem affected by structural changes either.

ÎŬ ¤ÆÆÆ ±ÆÆ ¨± ” ±º ª¥ ±Æ ø Æ ø ±Æ

Table 9 shows the results for imports. The ECM statistics are all very high (significance level is above 1%). The measures of goodness of fit are similar to those found for exports. There are no problems with the residuals.

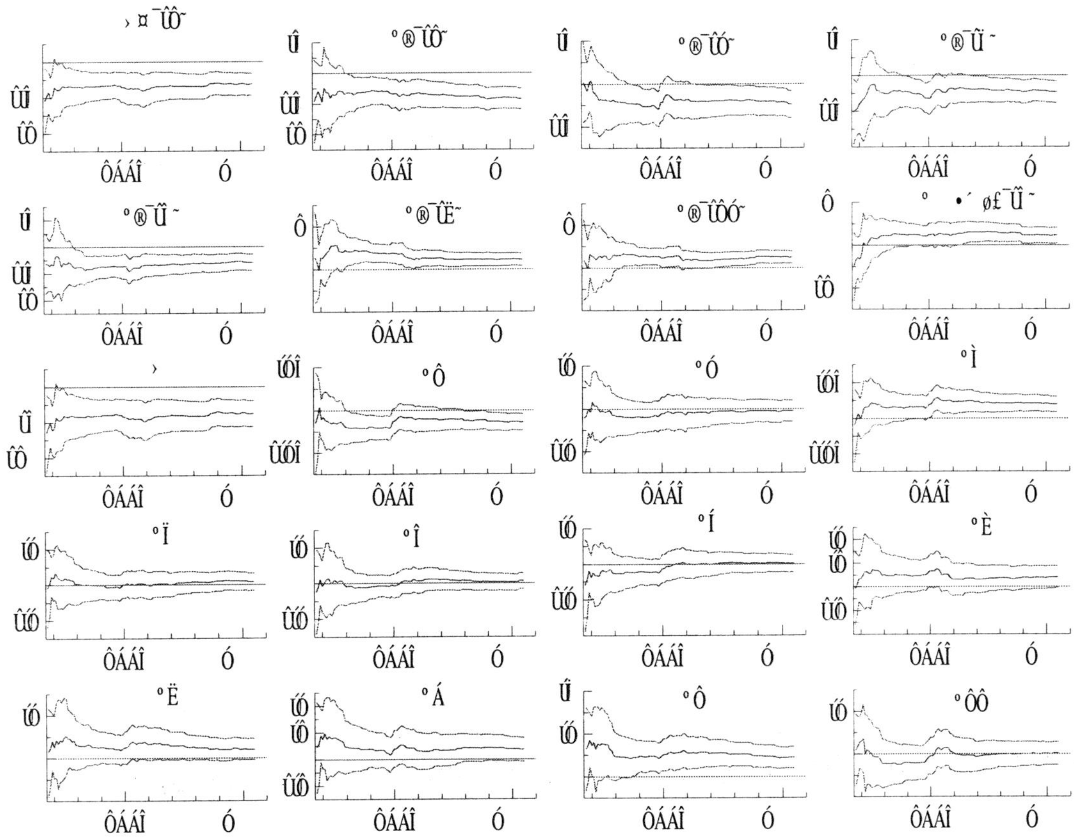

Figure 9: Recursive Coefficients for Total Exports ECM

The RESET test is easily passed by each equation; however, only the equations for consumption goods and capital goods pass both Chow tests of structural change for the beginning of NAFTA. Nevertheless, the rejection of stability with both tests occurs only with total imports.

Figure 10 completes the analysis of the ECM for total imports. The panels show the same recursive statistic as in the case of total exports (figure 8).

The sum of square residuals also approaches a straight line. The one-step residuals always stay within the bands except in one month. The one-step Chow sequence shows more outliers than in the case of exports but the n-step Chow statistics for structural change (up and down) do not show any problems since in no case do the sequences cross the 5% significance level. To complete the analysis, figure 11 shows the sequences of recursive statistics for the same ECM. The parameters seem to be constant throughout the sample period. The short-run model for imports does not seem to have serious stability problems in spite of the result for the long-run relationship.

Table 9: Error Correction Models for Imports

Variables	Models					
	dm	dm^{cap}	dm^{cons}	dm^{int}	dx^{int_Q}	dx^{int_Q}
$Cem_{t-1}^{\{i\}}$	-0.246 (0.057)	-0.343 (0.076)	-0.323 (0.063)	-0.313 (0.069)	-0.277 (0.080)	-0.331 (0.064)
$dm_{t-1}^{\{i\}}$	. .	-0.214 (0.067)	. .	. .	-0.440 (0.082)	. .
$dm_{t-2}^{\{i\}}$	. .	. .	. .	. .	-0.447 (0.089)	. .
$dm_{t-3}^{\{i\}}$	. .	. .	. .	. .	-0.374 (0.093)	. .
$dm_{t-4}^{\{i\}}$	. .	. .	. .	. .	-0.263 (0.078)	. .
$dm_{t-5}^{\{i\}}$	. .	. .	. .	. .	-0.195 (0.064)	. .
$dm_{t-7}^{\{i\}}$	0.101 (0.035)	. .	. .	. .	. .	. .
$dm_{t-10}^{\{i\}}$	-0.139 (0.037)	. .	-1.888 (0.060)	-0.130 (0.044)	. .	. .
dx_t	0.783 (0.043)	. .	. .	0.914 (0.048)	1.006 (0.088)	0.510 (0.054)
$divpi_t$	0.670 (0.091)	1.605 (0.201)	1.772 (0.205)	. .	. .	1.221 (0.122)
$drer_t$	. .	. .	-0.487 (0.156)	. .	. .	. .
$drer_{t-1}$	-0.199 (0.057)	-0.412 (0.161)	. .	-0.218 (0.076)	. .	-0.370 (0.077)
rer_{t-2}	. .	. .	. .	. .	. .	0.175 (0.072)
$drer_{t-3}$	. .	. .	. .	. .	0.342 (0.101)	. .
ECM Statistic	-5.460	-6.850	-5.200	-6.370	-4.810	-6.820
R^2	0.942	0.740	0.813	0.903	0.901	0.892
$\bar{R}^2$	0.932	0.705	0.787	0.888	0.881	0.875
S.E.	0.023	0.067	0.069	0.029	0.040	0.031
Asym. Coeff.	-0.095	0.056	0.239	-0.335	-0.103	-0.427
Kurtosis Coeff.	3.617	2.890	3.484	3.514	2.440	3.144
Jarque-Bera Stat.	1.959	0.130	2.430	3.390	1.691	3.537
LM(12) AR	1.555	1.533	0.839	0.695	1.042	1.106
LM(12) ARCH	0.701	0.779	0.888	1.096	0.919	0.540
White Test	1.065	0.956	1.459	1.169	1.570*	0.72
RESET	0.074	2.453	0.033	0.089	2.456	2.452
Chow B (94:01)	2.113**	1.183	1.201	2.209**	1.913**	1.850**
Chow Pred(94:01)	1.782*	0.533	0.625	0.938	1.271	0.999

$Cem_{t-1} = m_{t-1} - 1.124ivpi_{t-1} + 0.283rer_{t-1} - 0.461x_{t-1}$

$Cem_{t-1}^{int} = m_{t-1}^{int} + 0.476rer_{t-1} - 0.908x_{t-1}$

$Cem_{t-1}^{\{cap\}} = m_{t-1}^{\{cap\}} - 1.966ivpi_{t-1} + 0.734rer_{t-1}$

$Cem_{t-1}^{\{int_Q\}} = m_{t-1}^{\{int_Q\}} + 0.206rer_{t-1} - 1.224x_{t-1}$

$Cem_{t-1}^{cons} = m_{t-1}^{\{cons\}} - 1.753ivpi_{t-1} + 1.160rer_{t-1}$

$Cem_{t-1}^{\{int\_Q\}} = m_{t-1}^{\{int\_Q\}} - 1.200ivpi_{t-1} + 0.146rer_{t-1} - 0.323x_{t-1}$

Í › ± ¥ ±

Mexican Exports tripled their rate of growth from 1994 to 2000. Because this strong performance started around the time when NAFTA took place, it is rather common to interrelate both facts. I estimated long-run demand functions for exports and imports for the period 1990-2000 and obtained coefficients which are correctly signed and of reasonable magnitude. I found that the equation for exports is very stable for that period and, there-

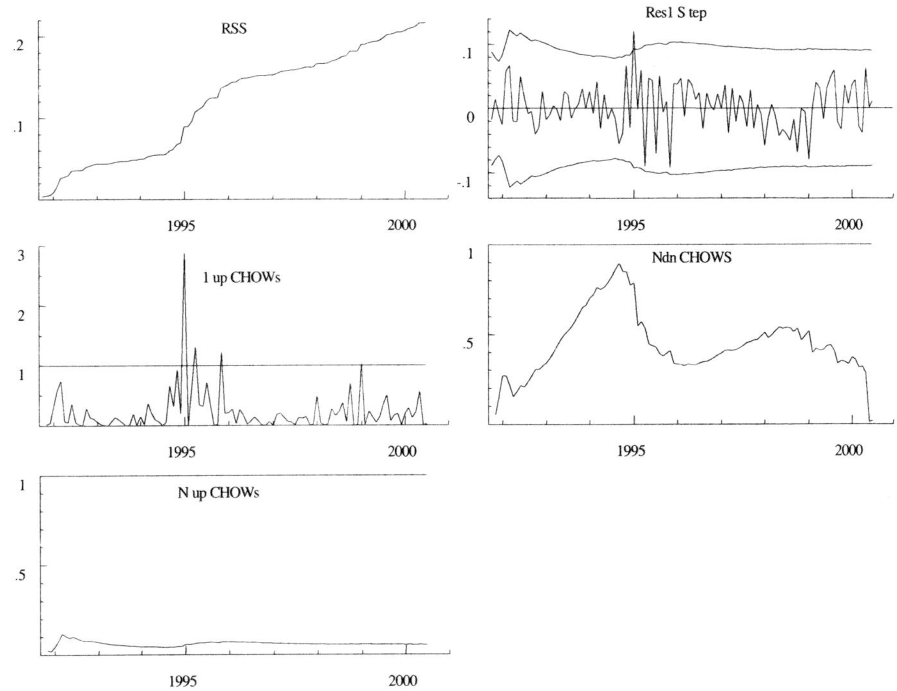

Figure 10: Recursive Stability Tests for Total Imports ECM

fore, NAFTA cannot account for the surge in foreign trade between Mexico and the US. The equation for imports demand, on the other hand, shows instability for the same period although it fits the data very well, even without considering seasonality and short-run dynamics.

I also used disaggregate data and extended the analysis for the period 1980-2000 and found cointegration for the whole sample only in a few categories of exports and imports. For each of the categories, I found a stable cointegration vector for the 1990-2000 period. Interestingly enough, the instability detected in the equation for total imports for the 1990-2000 subsample does not carry on to the equations with disaggregate data. In most cases a cointegration vector was also found for the 1980-1989 subsample, although those vectors do not show the stability found for the rest of the sample. I also obtained the error-correction models for the 1990-2000 period and found that they were stable and constant. These results confirm that a structural change in the demand for Mexican exports caused by NAFTA is extremely unlikely. The historical expansion of the American economy was by far the most important reason for the growth of Mexican exports.

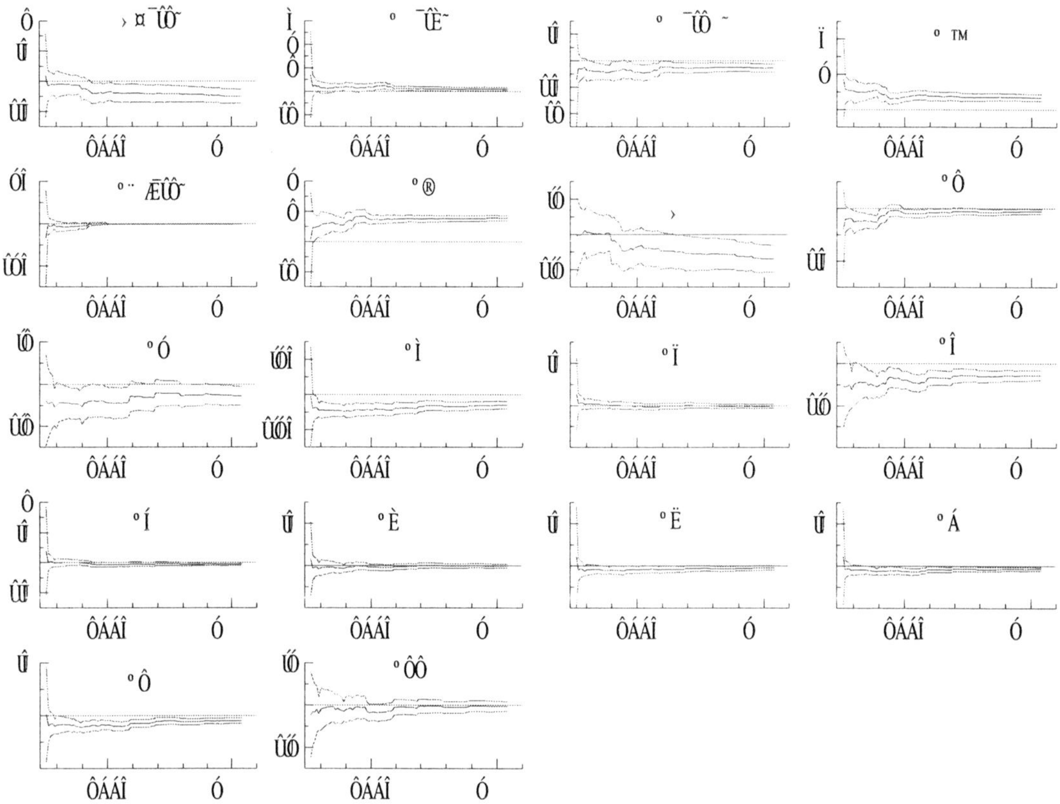

Figure 11: Recursive Coefficients for Total Imports ECM

A structural change probably occurred during the eighties and for that reason it is not possible to find long-run stable relationships for the whole period (1980-2000). This change is probably linked to the abandonment of the trade policy as a stabilization tool and the opening up of the economy when Mexico joined the GATT. This was quite important for Mexican exporters who depend heavily on the imports of intermediate and capital goods. This is the most likely reason for the lack of evidence of the effects of NAFTA on Mexican trade flows: most of the essential changes that helped Mexico to become an export powerhouse had already taken place as early as the mid eighties.

Œ ª Æ ª

[1] Ericsson, Neil R. and James G. MacKinnon, "Distributions of Error Correction Tests for Cointegration," International Finance Discussion Paper No. 655, Board of Gover-

nors of the Federal Reserve System, 1999.

[2] Gould, David M., "Has NAFTA Changed North America Free Trade,"¤ ± ± ŒÛ ™©, Federal Reserve Bank of Dallas, First Quarter 1998.

[3] Gruben, W.C. (2001) "Was NAFTA Behind Mexico's High Maquiladora Growth?," ¤ ± ± ø º ◘ ø ø¥Œ™©, Third Quarter, Federal Reserve Bank of Dallas.

[4] Hansen, B.E. (1992) "Tests for Parameter Instability in Regressions with I(1) Processes," ÷±´Æø¥± ◘´ ª ø º¤ ± ± Õø¨ ¨ , Ô, 321-335.

[5] Krueger, A. O., (1999) "Trade Creation and Trade Diversion Under NAFTA," NBER Working Paper No. 7429, December 1999.

[6] Kwiatkowski, D., P. Phillips, P. Schmidt and Y. Shin (1992): Testing the Null Hypothesis of Stationarity Against the Alternative of a Unit Root, ÷±´Æø¥± ¤ ± ± ª¨Æ Îï, 159-178.

[7] Phillips, P.C.B. y Bruce E. Hansen (1990), "Statistical Inference in Instrumental Variables Regression With $I(1)$ Processes," Œ™© ± ¤ ± ± Õ´º ª , ÎÈ, 99-125.

[8] Reinhart, C., 1995, "Devaluation, Relative Prices, and International Trade", " ◘ Õø –ø ªÆ, vol.42, No 2.

[9] Rose, A., 1991, "The Role of Exchange Rates in Popular Models of International Trade: Does the Marshall-Lerner Condition Hold?" ÷±´Æø¥± ªÆø¨± ø¥¤ ±Û ± , vol. 30, 301-16.

[10] Senhadji, A. (1998), "Time Series Estimation of Structural Import Demand Equations: A Cross-Country Analysis", " ◘ Õø –ø ªÆ, vol. 45, June.

[11] Senhadji, A. and C. Montenegro (1998), "Time Series Analysis of Export Demand Equations: A Cross-Country Analysis", " ◘ …±Æ –ø ªÆÁËÕÏ Á, October.

In: International Trade Issues
Editor: Robert. V. Weeks, pp. 171-204
ISBN: 1-59454-621-5

Chapter 8

FLUCTUATIONS IN THE DOLLAR: DO THEY MATTER?*

Magda Kandil
International Monetary Fund 700 Nineteenth St.,
Washington D.C., 20431
Ida A. Mirzaie
Department of Economics and Finance John Carroll University
20700 North Park Blvd. University Heights, OH 44118

Abstract

We examine the extent to which exchange rate fluctuations affect sectoral employment and wages in the United States. We introduce a theoretical rational expectation model that decomposes movements in the exchange rate into anticipated and unanticipated components. The model demonstrates the effects of demand and supply channels on the response of the nominal wage and labor employment to changes in the exchange rate. The evidence indicates that the deflationary effect dominates on industrial nominal wage in Manufacturing and Transportation industries in the face of dollar appreciation. More importantly, there is evidence of a decrease in employment growth in several industries in response to dollar appreciation, which is statistically significant in Construction and at the aggregate level. This evidence is consistent with a decrease in labor demand given the loss of competitiveness of U.S. products following dollar appreciation. Nonetheless, dollar appreciation is consistent with an increase in employment growth in the Mining sector where the share of imports is the largest among U.S. industries. There is also evidence of a positive spill over effect on employment in Transportation in the face of currency appreciation. Decomposing shocks in the exchange rate into appreciation and depreciation components yields symmetric, mostly insignificant effects, on employment and wages. Hence, the variability of the exchange rate appears to be neutral on employment growth and wage inflation.

* The views in the paper are those of the authors and should not be interpreted as those of the International Monetary Fund

I Introduction

Since the agreement to establish flexible exchange rates in the early 1970s, exchange rates of industrial countries, including the United States, have been highly fluctuating. Observed volatility in the exchange rate of the dollar has stimulated a debate in academia and policy arena over what the government response should be. Specifically, it was advocated that the dollar's appreciation may be responsible for the recession and increase in unemployment during the 1980s. The dollar appreciation decreases the price of foreign goods relative to home goods, decreasing the demand for home goods. In the labor market, the reduction in labor demand is likely to increase unemployment and moderate nominal wage inflation. Nonetheless, the dollar's appreciation, by pushing down the dollar's prices of intermediate imported goods, may increase the marginal product of labor and, hence, labor demand. This channel is likely to moderate the adverse effects of the dollar appreciation on employment and the nominal wage.

Concerns about the adverse effects on labor markets in the U.S. grew in the wake of the real appreciation of the dollar which appears to have been robust during the 1980s. To illustrate, Graph 1 depicts fluctuations in the nominal and real effective exchange rate of the US dollar between 1970-2000. The most striking aspect of fluctuations is the spike centered at 1985. The exchange rate of the dollar appreciated sharply. This appreciation was followed by a severe depreciation after the so-called Plaza Agreement in September 1985.[1] Nonetheless, the apparent robustness of the dollar appreciation during the 1980s prompted calls that the government should intervene systematically in foreign exchange markets to stabilize the dollar and protect employment and output against the adverse effects created by exchange rate fluctuations. More recently, the dollar has been depreciating against major currencies. Major U.S. trading partners have been advocating an intervention to stem dollar depreciation. In contrast, the position of the Fed has been against intervention, in favor of dollar depreciation. The competitiveness of U.S. products and higher cost of imports are likely to boost domestic demand and, therefore, stimulate economic activity.

At a disaggregate level, a number of recent studies have attempted to measure the effects of exchange rate fluctuations on economic conditions in industries of the United States. Specifically, empirical studies have considered the claim that sharp appreciation of the dollar after 1985 is responsible for the decline in tradable sectors like manufacturing, agriculture, and forestry products and the relative growth in non-tradable sectors such as services, construction, transportation, and public utilities. Along this line, Maskus (1990) examines the effects of exchange rate risk across major sectors of international trade. His results demonstrate that the exchange rate risk has a negative impact on trade. He also found that the agriculture sector is more sensitive to the exchange rate risk compared to the manufacturing sector.

Glick and Hutchison (1990) discuss that previous studies on the effect of the dollar appreciation on manufacturing fail to distinguish between exchange rate changes that are exogenous and changes that are endogenously determined by policy changes and other

[1] The Plaza Agreement involved a coordinated intervention policy among the "group of 5" (G5) countries- the United States, Japan, Germany, France, and the United Kingdom- in September 1985. Representatives of each country met at the Plaza Hotel in New York to announce a plan to coordinate foreign exchange-market intervention aimed at depreciating the dollar as a response to large U.S. trade deficits. The Plaza agreement had a strong impact on the market. The dollar fell rapidly because of both private and official sales of dollars.

shocks. For example, a policy-induced exchange rate appreciation arising from a fiscal expansion or monetary contraction has unclear effects on aggregate and sectoral movement. Accordingly, the nature of the disturbance moving the exchange rate in any particular period is essential in analyzing effects on the sectoral allocation of resources. Glick and Hutchison report evidence that the contractionary effect of the dollar appreciation on sectoral output is unstable and sample specific.

Revenga (1992) investigates the impact of increased import competition on employment and wages, using data for a panel of US manufacturing industries over the 1977-87 period. This period captures the dollar's appreciation during the early 1980s and its subsequent depreciation. Changes in import prices have had large and significant effects on both employment and wages. Nonetheless, the impact of an adverse trade shock on average wages in a particular industry is quite small where most of the adjustment occurs through employment.

Campa and Goldberg (1997) discuss that changes in the exchange rate can significantly influence the profitability and performance of US manufacturing industries.[2] To measure the sensitivity of domestic manufacturing industries to the dollar fluctuation, one must first examine the channels that transmit such shocks to production activity and, ultimately, to the economy as a whole. Capturing US industrial reliance on international markets involves measuring the extent to which manufacturers sell products to foreign markets, use foreign-made inputs, and more directly compete with foreign manufacturers in domestic markets.

The most widely used indicator typically calculated openness to trade by dividing (import+export) revenues of final products to domestic production revenues. This indicator fails to consider the growing use of foreign inputs in the manufacture of domestic goods. Campa and Goldberg (1997) use several measures to capture different industry's sensitivity to international shocks. The first measure is export shares. Producers with high export shares are likely to be more sensitive to international shocks than producers with a lower export share. They calculate the export share as the ratio of industry export revenues to industry shipments. This measure captures the portion of a producer's revenues that is generated in foreign markets. Second, import shares, or the ratio of imports to consumption of the industry's output captures foreign penetration in a particular industry. The industry's output and employment are also likely to be more sensitive to international shocks when there is a high degree of foreign penetration in domestic markets. Imported input share or imported inputs as a share of the value of production is the third measure for the degree of openness.[3] In contrast to the other two measures which provide guidance on the vulnerability of producer revenue to dollar fluctuation and other international forces, the imported input share measure provides a window into the potential sensitivity of a producer to shocks experienced through the cost side of its balance sheets. Finally, they present a measure of net external orientation defined as the difference between industry export share and import share.

Campa and Goldberg conclude that industries in the United States show the most volatile patterns in net external orientation. After remaining, on average, primarily export oriented in the 1970s, US industries experienced an increased international exposure in the early to mid

[2] Other relevant studies for the research of this paper include Branson and Love (1988), Bernard and Jensen (1995), Burgess and Knetter (1996), Campa and Goldberg (1998), and Goldberg and Tracy (1999).

[3] Because data on imported inputs are not available, they construct this series by combining industry import data with country input-output data that describe the expenditure on different categories of inputs by each manufacturing industry.

1980s through their reliance on imported inputs in production. In the late 1980s and in the 1990s, export shares grew faster than imported shares, raising the positive net external orientation of U.S. industries.

U.S. manufacturing industries have also steadily increased their use of imported inputs in production, on average from 4 percent in 1975 to more than 8 percent in 1995.[4] The increase in the imported input use across manufacturing was the greatest in the first half of the 1980s, when the U.S. dollar dramatically appreciated and reduced the cost of foreign-produced inputs relative to inputs produced domestically. By 1985, imported inputs as a share of total costs in the U.S manufacturing industries had risen to about 6 percent. Even after the dollar depreciated in the second half of the 1980s, the presence of imported inputs continued to increase in the United States. Overall, the imported input share has more than doubled in many manufacturing industries over the past two decades, creating concerns regarding the adverse effects of dollar appreciation on employment and production in the manufacturing sector of the US economy.

Table 1 Export share, import share, and imported input share of U.S. manufacturing

	1975			1995		
Industry	**Export Share**	**Import Share**	**Imported Input Share**	**Export Share**	**Import Share**	**Imported Input Share**
Tobacco products	6.9	0.6	1.4	14.9	0.6	2.1
Apparel and other textiles	2.0	8.5	1.3	7.4	31.4	3.2
Furniture and Fixtures	1.3	3.0	3.6	5.5	14.1	5.7
Chemical and allied products	10.1	3.6	3.0	15.8	11.0	6.3
Leather and leather products	3.9	17.7	5.6	14.4	59.5	20.5
Primary metal products	5.1	9.8	5.0	11.2	17.4	10.6
Industrial machinery and equipment	23.3	6.3	4.1	25.8	27.8	11.0
Electronic and other electric equipment	11.1	8.5	4.5	24.2	32.5	11.6
Transportation equipment	15.8	10.4	6.4	17.8	24.3	15.7
Instruments and related products	16.8	7.4	3.8	21.3	20.1	6.3
Total Manufacturing	8.4	6.3	4.1	13.4	16.3	8.2

[4]See Table 1. For more details, see Campa and Goldberg (1997).

Given demand and supply channels, what are the effects of the dollar appreciation on employment and the nominal wage? We examine the extent to which exchange rate fluctuations affect the US sectoral employment and wage.[5] Section II introduces a theoretical model that decomposes movements in the exchange rate into anticipated and unanticipated components using rational expectations. The solution of the model demonstrates the effects of demand and supply channels on labor employment and the nominal wage responses to changes in the exchange rate. Based on these solutions, we formulate, in Section III, an empirical model for sectoral nominal wage and employment. The model incorporates demand and supply shifts as well as exchange rate shifts. Given fluctuations in the value of the dollar over time, we decompose shocks to the exchange rate into appreciation (positive) and depreciation (negative) shocks. We then test asymmetry in the effects of these fluctuations on variables in the labor market.

The data under investigation are for average earnings and total hours of all persons by industry according to the Standard Industrial Classification (SIC) in the National Income and Product Accounts of the United States. Section IV presents the empirical results. The estimation highlights the relative importance of exchange rate fluctuations in determining sectoral labor employment and the nominal wage. Section V concludes.

Overall, the evidence indicates that the deflationary effect dominates on industrial nominal wage in Manufacturing and Transportation industries in the face of dollar appreciation. More importantly, there is evidence of a decrease in employment growth in several industries in response to dollar appreciation, which is statistically significant in Construction and at the aggregate level. This evidence is consistent with a decrease in labor demand given the negative effect of dollar appreciation on foreign demand for U.S. products, raising concerns about the negative effects of dollar appreciation on labor market conditions in the United States. Nonetheless, dollar appreciation is consistent with an increase in employment growth in the Mining industry, where the share of imports is the largest among U.S. industries.

II Theoretical Background

In the real world, stochastic uncertainty may arise on the demand or supply sides of the economy. Economic agents are assumed to be rational. Accordingly, rational expectations of demand and supply shifts enter the theoretical model. Economic fluctuations are then determined by unexpected demand and supply shocks impinging on the economic system.

We build a macroeconomic model that incorporates exchange rate fluctuations attributed to the dollar appreciation. Uncertainty enters the model in the form of disturbances to both aggregate demand and aggregate supply. Within this framework, the appreciation of the dollar determines aggregate demand through exports, imports, and the demand for domestic currency, and determines aggregate supply through the cost of imported intermediate goods. We show theoretically that the effect of appreciating the US dollar on the American economy

[5] In Kandil and Mirzaie (2002), we examine the effects of dollar appreciation on sectoral output and price in the United States.

is expansionary via the effect of the supply side. However, the effects of the dollar appreciation on aggregate demand make the final outcome inconclusive.[6]

II-A Aggregate Demand

The demand side of the economy is specified using standard IS-LM equations with a modification for an open economy. The demand side of the economy combines equilibrium conditions in the Goods and Money markets. In the specifications below, all coefficients are positive and throughout the paper, lower case denotes the logarithm of the corresponding level variable. The subscript t denotes the current value of the variable.

$$c_t = c_0 + c_1 y_{dt}, \quad 0 < c_1 < 1 \tag{1}$$

$$y_{dt} = y_t - t_t \tag{2}$$

$$t_t = t_0 + t_1 y_t, \quad t_1 > 0 \tag{3}$$

$$i_t = i_0 - i_1 r_t, \quad i_1 > 0 \tag{4}$$

$$R_t = \frac{S_t P_t}{P_t^*} \tag{5}$$

$$x_t = x_0 - x_1 log(R_t), \quad x_1 > 0 \tag{6}$$

$$im_t = m_0 + m_1 y_t + m_2 log(R_t), \quad m_1, m_2 > 0 \tag{7}$$

$$y_t = c_t + i_t + g_t + x_t - im_t \tag{8}$$

$$m_t - p_t = -\lambda[r_t + (E_t p_{t+1} - p_t)] + \phi y_t + \theta(E_t s_{t+1} - s_t), \quad \lambda, \phi, \theta > 0 \tag{9}$$

Equations (1) through (8) describe equilibrium conditions in the Goods market. In equation (1), real consumption expenditure, c, varies positively with real disposable income, y_d. In equation (2), disposable income is defined to be the net of real income, y, minus taxes, t. In equation (3), real taxes are specified as a linear function of real income. In

[6] Agenor (1991) introduces a theoretical model for a small open economy with a fixed exchange rate and distinguishes between anticipated and unanticipated movement in the exchange rate. He derives an aggregate output equation from a rational expectation macro model with imported intermediate goods. In this framework, he demonstrates that devaluation can be contractionary. Devaluation has a negative impact on aggregate supply by making the intermediate imported goods more expensive even if the net effect on aggregate demand is expansionary. Assuming the intermediate imported good is a necessary input in the production process, more expensive inputs decrease the demand for the product and the amount to produce.

equation (4), real investment expenditure, i, varies negatively with the real interest rate, r. In equation (5), let the domestic price level be represented by P and the foreign price level in foreign currency by P^*. The spot price of the dollar is denoted by S and defined as the number of foreign currency units per units of domestic currency. R is the price of domestically produced goods and services relative to the prices of foreign produced goods and services, i.e., the real effective exchange rate of the dollar. When R increases, the domestic currency appreciates in real terms. The value of R measures the degree of competitiveness of domestically produced goods and services relative to those abroad.[7] In equation (6), real exports are related to an autonomous element, x_0, which rises when the income level abroad rises, and to relative prices. The inverse relationship between R and x, in (6), refers to the fact that when the domestic price is higher relative to abroad, exports will decrease. In equation (7), real imports, im, are assumed to rise with the level of real income and the real effective exchange rate of the dollar. Equation (8) describes the equilibrium condition in the goods market. Real government spending, g, is assumed to be exogenous. The total expenditure by domestic residents in real terms (y) is the sum of real consumption expenditure (c), real investment (i), real government spending (g), and net exports (the real value of exports, x, minus the real value of imports, im).

After substituting all equations into the equilibrium condition for the goods market, we obtain the expression for real income, which is a function of the exchange rate, the domestic price level, the foreign price level, and the domestic interest rate. This expression is the IS equation which describes the negative relationship between real income and the real interest rate (See Appendix A).

In equation (9), equilibrium in the money market is obtained by equating the demand and supply of real money balances. The real money supply is equal to an exogenously nominal balances, m, deflated by price, p. The demand for real money balances is positively related to real income and inversely related to the nominal interest rate. The nominal interest rate is defined as the sum of the real interest rate and inflation expectation at time t. $E_t s_{t+1}$ is the expected future value of the dollar at time t. We assume that citizens in each country must hold domestic money for transactions purposes but they may speculate by holding foreign money.[8] An increase in the future expected value relative to the current value of the dollar (e.g., a temporary depreciation of the dollar) increases the demand for money. Consequently, agents decrease the speculative demand in the face of a temporary dollar appreciation,[9] establishing a negative relationship between the demand for real money balances and current shocks to the exchange rate of the currency.

The LM equation is determined by the equilibrium condition in the money market, establishing a positive relationship between real income and the real interest rate. Solving for the interest rate, r, from the LM equation and substituting the result into the IS equation gives us the equation for aggregate demand (See Appendix A).

[7]For a similar definition, see (Shone 1989).
[8] For a similar discussion, see (Buiter 1990).
[9]Agents are inclined to sell dollars to capitalize on the temporary appreciation in its value.

II-B Aggregate Supply

On the supply side, output is produced using a production function that combines labor, capital, energy and imported intermediate goods. When the currency appreciates, it is cheaper to buy intermediate goods from abroad. The price of energy is paid in dollars. That is, the change in the exchange rate of the dollar does not affect the cost of imported energy to the United States.

To illustrate, the level of gross domestic output, Q, is produced using a production function that combines imported intermediate goods, N, labor, L, and the capital stock, K. The production function is Cobb-Douglas in N and L, assuming fixed capital stock.[10] In addition, the production function is dependent on changes in the energy price, Z. Accordingly, the supply-side of this economy can be summarized in equations (10) through (14) as follows:

$$Q_t = L_t^{\delta} N_t^{1-\delta} e^{-Z_t} \tag{10}$$

$$Y_t = Q_t - \frac{1}{R_t} N_t \tag{11}$$

$$l_t^d = n_t - \eta\{w_t - p_t + z_t - log\delta\}, \quad \eta = \frac{1}{1-\delta} > 0 \tag{12}$$

$$n_t = l_t + \frac{1}{\delta}\{log(1-\delta) - z_t + log(R_t)\} \tag{13}$$

$$l_t^s = \eta log\delta + \omega\{w_t - E_{t-1}p_t\}, \quad \omega > 0 \tag{14}$$

Equation (10) specifies the level of gross domestic output produced, assuming complementary relation between the labor input and imported intermediate goods. Equation (11) defines domestic value added (output supplied) or the difference between gross domestic output and the amount of real intermediate imports.[11]

The demand for inputs is derived by calculating the marginal product of L and N and equating the results with the real cost of labor (the real wage) and the real price in domestic currency of imported intermediate goods (the inverse of the real exchange rate). Taking log transformation of the first-order conditions and rearranging produces equations (12) and (13). The demand for labor varies negatively with the real wage and positively with imported intermediate goods. Similarly, the demand for imported intermediate goods increases with the labor input. Dollar appreciation reduces the real price of imported intermediate goods and,

[10] By fixing the capital stock, we exclude the possibility that depreciation may increase labor productivity by stimulating capital accumulation. That is, investment aims at replacing capital depreciation.

[11] This definition follows Agenor (1991) where he introduces a model and assumes intermediate goods are necessary for the production process and cannot be produced domestically.

hence, increases the demand for these goods. Subsequently, the marginal product of labor increases and, hence, the demand for labor. Further, a rise in the energy price decreases the marginal product of labor, decreasing the demand for labor and imported intermediate goods.

Equation (14) hypothesizes a positive log-linear relationship between labor supply and expected real wage. Supply of labor increases with an increase in the nominal wage relative to workers' expected price at time $t-1$.[12]

Equating labor demand and labor supply, we solve for the nominal wage. Substituting the result into labor demand, we solve for employment and, in turn, imported intermediate goods. Substituting for l and n into the log transformation of equation (10), we obtain an equation for gross domestic output supplied (see Appendix A). Substituting the result into the log transformation of equation (11), we obtain an equation for aggregate supply of domestic value added (See Appendix A).

Aggregate supply has a direct positive relationship with output price surprises. Workers decide on labor supply based on their expectation of the aggregate price level. An increase in aggregate price relative to workers' expectations increases the demand for labor and, hence, the nominal wage. A rise in the expected real wage increases employment and, hence, the output supplied. In addition, aggregate supply moves positively with the foreign currency price of the dollar. Dollar appreciation decreases the cost of imported goods and increases the output supplied. Further, the output supplied varies negatively with changes in the energy price.

II-C Market Equilibrium

Internal balance requires that aggregate demand for domestic output be equal to aggregate supply of domestic output at full employment. We assume that demand and supply shifts in the model are constructed of two components: anticipated (steady-state) component and an unanticipated (random) component (See Appendix A). The combination of demand and supply-side channels indicates that real output depends on unanticipated movements in the exchange rate, the money supply, government spending, and the energy price. In addition, supply-side channels establish that output varies with anticipated changes in the exchange rate and the energy price.

Given demand-side channels, aggregate demand increases with an unexpected increase in government spending or the money supply, creating positive price surprises and, hence, increasing output and price in the short-run. Changes in the energy price, both anticipated and unanticipated, increase the cost of the output produced, decreasing output and raising prices.[13]

The effects of real exchange rate fluctuations on labor employment and the nominal wage are complicated by demand and supply channels as follows:

---

[12]The constant term is equal to that in the labor demand function to simplify mathematical derivation.

[13]The price level may rise unexpectedly in response to energy price shocks, creating incentives to increase the output produced. This channel moderates the reduction in output and the rise in price in response to energy price shocks. For a detailed theoretical illustration, see Kandil and Woods (1997). The moderating effect of the rise in price is further reinforced in our model through the rise in the real effective exchange rate, reducing the cost of intermediate imported goods.

1. In the goods market, an unexpected appreciation of the dollar will make exports more expensive and imports cheaper. As a result, the competition from foreign markets will decrease the demand for domestic products, decreasing labor demand and, hence, employment and the nominal wage.[14]
2. In the money market, an unexpected temporary increase in the value of the dollar, relative to its anticipated value in the future, prompts agents to hold less dollars and decreases the interest rate. This channel moderates the negative effect of the exchange rate shock on aggregate demand, labor demand, and, hence, employment and the nominal wage.[15]
3. On the supply side, changes in the exchange rate, both anticipated and unanticipated, determine the cost of importing intermediate goods. As the dollar appreciates, producers are inclined to increase imports of intermediate goods, increasing the marginal product of labor and, hence, labor demand, employment, and the nominal wage.[16] Concurrently, the reduction in price decreases the cost of living and, hence, workers' demand for higher wages.[17]

III Empirical Models

Our empirical investigation analyzes annual time-series data for sectoral employment and the nominal wage according to the SIC System in the United States (see Table 2). The time period covered is from 1961 to 2000. Over this span, we assume that industrial employment growth and nominal wage inflation fluctuate in response to aggregate domestic demand

[14] Guitian (1976) and Dornbusch (1988) have stated that devaluation increases production of tradables through its expenditure switching effects. Devaluation modifies the direction of demand by increasing the international competitiveness of domestic industries, thus diverting spending from foreign goods to domestic goods. The success of these policies in promoting trade balance largely depends on switching demand in the proper direction and amount as well as on the capacity of the home economy to meet the additional demand by supplying more goods. Empirical support of this proposition for Group 7 countries over the 1960-89 period is provided in Mendoza (1992).

[15] It is expected that the contractionary effect on aggregate demand stemming from the goods market will be more dominant. The speculative effect of money demand is likely to be dominant in developing countries where agents' incentives to hedge against potential fluctuations in the exchange rate of their domestic currency are high. Given the strong international position of the dollar, agents in the United States are less concerned, in the short run, with switching between dollars and other foreign currencies.

[16] Hirschman (1949) argues that devaluation from an initial trade deficit reduces real national income and may lead to a fall in aggregate demand. The possibility that devaluation will provide a fall in output is discussed theoretically in a model by Meade (1951). Diaz-Alejandro (1963) introduced another argument for contraction following devaluation. The redistribution of income from wages to profit may lead to a reduction in real income. This point was later confirmed in a general equilibrium model by Cooper (1971). Krugman and Taylor (1978) and Barbone and Rivera-Batiz (1987) have formalized the same view. Bruno (1979) postulates that in a typical semi-industrialized country where inputs for manufacturing are largely imported and cannot be easily replaced by domestic production, firms' inputs cost will increase following a devaluation or depreciation. Gylfason and Schmid (1983) provide evidence that the final effect of devaluation depends on the magnitude in which demand and supply curves shift because of devaluation. Hanson (1983) provides a theoretical approach on the impact of devaluation on output suggesting that the outcome depends on the assumptions regarding the labor market. Solimano (1986) studies the effect of devaluation and focuses on the relative intensity of domestic value added with respect to imported inputs in production. Wijnbergen (1989) explains that devaluation may cause an adverse effect on output while it is inflationary.

[17] The effect on the nominal wage will be dependent on the slope of the aggregate demand curve. The less elastic the aggregate demand curve is, the bigger the reduction in price following the increase in the output supplied. Hence, workers may accept lower nominal wages despite the increased marginal product of labor attributed to dollar appreciation.

shocks, energy price shocks, and exchange rate shocks. Shocks are randomly distributed over the time span under investigation. Detailed econometric methodology is provided in Appendix B. A detailed description and sources of all data are described in Appendix C.[18]

We formulate empirical models that approximate the solutions for employment and the nominal wage in the theoretical model. Accordingly, the empirical model for employment is specified as follows:

$$Dl_t = A_0 + A_1 E_{t-1}Dz_t + A_2(Dz_t - E_{t-1}Dz_t) + A_3 E_{t-1}Dm_t + A_4(Dm_t - E_{t-1}Dm_t)$$
$$+ A_5 E_{t-1}Dg_t + A_6(Dg_t - E_{t-1}Dg_t) + A_7 E_{t-1}Ds_t + A_8(Ds_t - E_{t-1}Ds_t) + A_9 EC_{t-1} + v_t^l \quad (15)$$

We test for the non-stationarity of industrial employment (see Table A1).[19] Given these results, the empirical model for employment is specified in first-difference form where $D(.)$ is the first-difference operator.[20] Accordingly, all variables in the model enter in first-difference form. Further, we test for cointegration between the non-stationary employment and non-stationary variables that enter the model (see Table A2). Given evidence of cointegration, the empirical model includes an error correction variable.[21]

Theory predicts that employment varies with unanticipated demand shifts in the economy. Agents are expected to negotiate higher wages in anticipation of expansionary demand shifts, neutralizing the effects of these shifts on employment. Nonetheless, anticipated demand shifts may determine employment through their effects on anticipated real effective exchange rate.[22] Consequently, anticipated demand shifts may increase employment.

---

[18] In addition to the references employing sectoral data in the introduction, other empirical literature on the effects of exchange rate fluctuations can be summarized as follows. Agenor (1991) uses annual data for a group of 23 countries in the 1978-87 period. The result shows that an anticipated devaluation of the real exchange rate has a negative effect on economic activity, while an unanticipated depreciation has a positive impact on output. Karras (1993) employs the structural autoregression approach (VAR) to investigate the importance of different kinds of shocks for the macroeconomic fluctuations of the US economy over the period 1973-1989. The result shows that supply and demand disturbances have important role for output fluctuations in both the short-run and the long-run.

[19] For details, see Kwiatkowski et.al. (1992).

[20] We first-difference the employment series in Manufacturing and Mining to maintain consistency of model specification. For these sectors, we also estimate the empirical model of employment in level (without first-difference). These results are similar to the evidence in Table 3 and available upon request.

[21] This is the lagged residual from the cointegration regression in which the non-stationary level of employment is regressed on the level of variables that enter the model: the energy price, the money supply, government spending, and the real exchange rate. See Table A2 for details. Note that this variable accounts for the short-run adjustment toward full-equilibrium. Additionally, it captures the effects of sector-specific variables that are likely to contribute to short-term deviation in sectoral employment from its trend growth path in the long-run.

[22] In the real world, institutional rigidity may interfere with agents' ability to adjust fully to anticipated demand shifts. In the labor market, contracts may be longer than one year, preventing wages at time t from adjusting fully to anticipated demand shifts at time $t-1$. Accordingly, anticipated demand shifts are not absorbed fully in wages. Alternatively, institutional rigidity may be attributed to price rigidity in the product market. Given the cost of adjusting prices, producers may resort to adjusting prices at specific intervals over time. Given price rigidity, anticipated demand shifts at time $t-1$ may determine employment growth in the short-run. For a discussion of the implications of sticky-wage and sticky-price models, see Kandil (1996).

Table 2: Nonlinear 3SLS Parameter Estimates for Employment Using Government Spending and Monetary shocks.

	A0	A1	A2	A3	A4	A5	A6	A7	A8	A9	A10	A11	RH0
Aggregate Employment													
Model 1 .													
	0.04** -	0.03	0.04	-0.42	-0.19	0.17	0.10	-0.08	-0.09**			-0.55**	0.76
	(1.82)	(-0.45)	(1.25)	(-1.41)	(-1.43)	(0.85)	(0.49)	(-0.95)	(-1.72)			(-1.90)	(3.96)
	R-square: 0.30												
Model 2													
	0.01	-0.06	0.05	0.09	-0.14	0.18	-0.09	-0.03		-0.06	-0.08	-0.18	0.26
	(0.70)	(-0.90)	(1.40)	(0.41)	(-0.94)	(1.05)	(-0.36)	(-0.32)		(-0.04)	(-0.83)	(-0.49)	(0.41)
	R-square: 0.46												
Construction													
Model 1													
	0.13**	0.001	0.15** -	1.79** -	1.05*	0.08	0.37	-0.30	-0.34*			-0.48**	0.76*
	(1.76)	(0.00)	(1.74)	(-1.88)	(-2.64)	(0.13)	(0.54)	(-1.04)	(-2.15)			(-1.78)	(4.17)
R-square: 0.25													
Model 2													
	0.13	-0.19	0.16	-1.67	-1.09*	0.05	0.31	-0.02		-0.03	-0.40	-0.43	0.74*
	(1.58)	(-0.61)	(1.63)	(-1.58)	(-2.46)	(0.06)	(0.41)	(-0.05)		(-0.05)	(-1.52)	(-1.46)	(3.48)
	R-square: 0.35												
Finance													
Model 1													
	0.08** -	0.02	0.01	-0.90**	-0.27	0.07	0.33	-0.07	-0.09			-0.39	0.88
	(1.94)	(-0.23)	(0.40)	(-1.96)	(-1.67)	(0.27)	(1.23)	(-0.67)	(-1.45)			(-1.30)	(7.19)
	R-square: 0.32												
Model 2													
	0.08** -	0.01	0.02	-0.84	-0.25	0.12	0.36	-0.07		-0.18	-0.06	-0.41	0.86*
	(1.95)	(-0.13)	(0.42)	(-1.70)	(-1.40)	(0.41)	(1.22)	(-0.53)		(-1.15)	(-0.68)	(-1.19)	(5.83)
	R-square: 0.22												
Manufacturing													
Model 1													
	-0.02	-0.19		0.15*	0.29	-0.74*	0.52	-0.70	-0.04	0.13			0.06
	(-0.56)	(-1.08)		(2.09)	(0.64)	(-2.51)	(1.39)	(-1.14)	(-0.17)	(1.06)			(0.24)
	R-square: 0.41												

Table 2: Nonlinear 3SLS Parameter Estimates for Employment Using Government Spending and Monetary shocks. (continued)

	A0	A1	A2	A3	A4	A5	A6	A7	A8	A9	A10	A11	RH0
Model 2													
	-0.02	-0.16	0.15**	0.29	-0.75**	0.55	-0.61	-0.09		0.05	0.12		0.05
	(-0.57)	(-0.90)	(1.99)	(0.62)	(-2.52)	(1.39)	(-0.96)	(-0.37)		(0.15)	(0.66)		(0.21)
	R-square: 0.42												
<u>Mining</u>													
	Model 1												
	-0.06	0.75*	0.22**	0.14	0.38	0.19	-2.10*	-0.19	0.66*				0.20
	(-1.33)	(2.42)	(1.98)	(0.20)	(0.76)	(0.33)	(-2.31)	(-0.44)	(3.14)				(0.56)
	R-square: 0.57												
Model 2													
	-0.08	0.95*	0.25**	0.14	0.35	0.18	-1.99*	-0.43		0.73	0.59		0.14
	(-1.42)	(2.45)	(1.98)	(0.19)	(0.64)	(0.28)	(-2.04)	(-0.96)		(1.20)	(1.73)		(0.46)
	R-square: 0.55												
<u>Retail Trade</u>													
Model 1													
	0.04	-0.03	0.02	-0.25	-0.14	0.04	-0.06	-0.02	-0.06			-0.42	0.78*
	(1.52)	(-0.37)	(0.67)	(-0.73)	(-0.79)	(0.16)	(-0.24)	(-0.22)	(-1.00)			(-1.21)	(3.49)
	R-square: 0.47												
Model 2													
	0.04	-0.05	0.02	-0.20	-0.15	0.05	-0.05	0.02		0.005	-0.06	-0.40	0.76*
	(1.32)	(-0.62)	(0.57)	(-0.53)	(-0.77)	(0.21)	(-0.20)	(0.18)		(0.00)	(-0.54)	(-1.04)	(2.92)
	R-square: 0.49												
<u>Service</u>													
Model 1													
	0.06*	-0.001	0.03	-0.50** -	0.26**	0.14	0.04	-0.04	-0.05			-0.14	0.76*
	(2.67)	(-0.04)	(1.26)	(-1.77)	(-1.88)	(0.82)	(0.23)	(-0.49)	(-1.31)			(-0.67)	(5.05)
	R-square: 0.28												
Model 2													
	0.06** -	0.01	0.03	-0.52	-0.28**	0.18	0.04	-0.03		-0.08	-0.02	-0.10	0.75*
	(2.57)	(-0.14)	(1.00)	(-1.72)	(-1.92)	(0.99)	(0.23)	(-0.29)		(-0.65)	(-0.23)	(-0.47)	(4.59)
	R-square: 0.26												

Table 2: Nonlinear 3SLS Parameter Estimates for Employment Using Government Spending and Monetary shocks. (continued)

	A0	A1	A2	A3	A4	A5	A6	A7	A8	A9	A10	A11	RH0
Transportation													
Model 1													
	0.03	-0.11	0.09** -	0.26	-0.09	0.36	-0.57	-0.01	0.11			-0.03	0.17
	(1.66)	(-0.89)	(1.88)	(-0.95)	(-0.44)	(1.51)	(-1.44)	(-0.04)	(1.32)			(-0.18)	(0.55)
	R-square: 0.34												
Model 2													
	0.02	-0.07	0.10** -	0.20	-0.11	0.23	-0.34	0.06		0.44**	0.01	-0.17	0.33
	(0.75)	(-0.60)	(1.80)	(-0.58)	(-0.48)	(0.80)	(-0.72)	(0.30)		(1.88)	(0.04)	(-0.71)	(0.95)
	R-square: 0.10												
Wholesale Trade													
Model 1													
	-0.06**	0.06	0.07	-0.09** -	0.36*	0.15	0.23	-0.09	-0.06			-0.49	0.83*
	(-1.77)	(0.79)	(1.65)	(-1.85)	(-1.77)	(0.53)	(0.78)	(-0.66)	(-0.84)			(-1.53)	(5.17)
	R-square: 0.11												
Model 2													
	0.06	0.05	0.08	-0.84	-0.33	0.17	0.24	-0.03		0.01	-0.53	-0.05	0.83*
	(1.53)	(0.65)	(1.58)	(-1.66)	(-1.51)	(0.59)	(0.75)	(-0.21)		(0.05)	(-1.51)	(-0.42)	(4.76)
	R-square: 0.16												

A0	Intercept	A7	Anticipated Real Effective Exchange Rate
A1	Anticipated Energy Price	A8	Unanticipated Real Effective Exchange Rate
A2	Unanticipated Energy Price	A9	Positive Shock to Real Effective Exchange Rate
A3	Anticipated Money Supply	A10	Negative Shock to Real Effective Exchange Rate
A4	Unanticipated Money supply	A11	Error Correction
A5	Anticipated Government Spending	RH0	Serial correlation
A6	Unanticipated Government Spending		

* Significant at 5%.

** Significant at 10%.

t-ratios are in parentheses.

To illustrate, let z_t be the log value of the energy price. Agents' expectation of a variable at time t based on information available at time $t-1$ is denoted by E_{t-1}. Based on theory's forecast, employment growth is expected to vary negatively with changes in the energy price, both anticipated and unanticipated, at time $t-1$. Accordingly, A_1, A_2 <0.

We approximate demand shifts using two sources of domestic policies, government spending and the money supply. The log values of government spending and the money supply are denoted by g_t and m_t. Unanticipated growth in government spending and the money supply increase aggregate demand, creating positive price surprises. Hence, A_4, A_6 >0. Anticipated growth in government spending and the money supply may also increase employment growth. Accordingly, A_3, A_5 >0.

Finally, anticipated appreciation of the real exchange rate determines the cost of the output supplied. Let s_t be the log value of the exchange rate of the dollar.[1] As producers anticipate a lower cost of imported intermediate goods, they increase the demand for labor. Accordingly, $A_7>0$. Unanticipated change in the exchange rate is likely, however, to determine both aggregate demand and supply. The cheaper cost of buying intermediate imports increases the demand for labor and the output supplied. However, demand-side channels render the effect of exchange rate fluctuations indeterminate. Accordingly, $A_8 \leq 0$.

Finally, EC_{t-1} denotes error correction. The unexplained residual of the employment equation is denoted by v_t^l.

To demonstrate fluctuations in sectoral nominal wage, an empirical model is specified as follows:

$$Dw_t = B_0 + B_1E_{t-1}Dz_t + B_2(Dz_t - E_{t-1}Dz_t) + B_3E_{t-1}Dm_t + B_4(Dm_t - E_{t-1}Dm_t)$$
$$+B_5E_{t-1}Dg_t + B_6(Dg_t - E_{t-1}Dg_t) + B_7E_{t-1}Ds_t + B_8(Ds_t - E_{t-1}Ds_t) + B_9EC_{t-1} + v_t^w \quad (16)$$

Testing for stationarity, sectoral nominal wage is evident to be non-stationary for various industries under investigation. Accordingly, the empirical model is specified in first-difference form. Further, the results of cointegration tests support the hypothesis that the nominal wage for several sectors is cointegrated with variables that enter the model. Given evidence of cointegration, the error correction term, EC_{t-1}, enters the empirical model.

Energy price shifts, both anticipated and unanticipated, increase the cost of the output produced and, hence, prices and wages. Accordingly, B_1, B_2 >0. Nonetheless, the relationship between labor and capital determines the effect of a rise in the energy price on the nominal wage. If labor and capital are complements, a rise in the energy price decreases

[1] Empirically, we measure the exchange rate by the real effective exchange rate (see Appendix C). This measure captures shifts attributed to the nominal exchange rate, s, and the foreign price of imports, p^*, in theory.

the demand for labor and, hence, the nominal wage.[2] Both anticipated and unanticipated demand shifts increase price and wage inflation. Accordingly, B_3, B_4, B_5, $B_6 > 0$.

Given the effect of anticipated dollar appreciation in increasing labor demand, nominal wage inflation increases and $B_7 > 0$. In contrast, an unanticipated dollar appreciation decreases the cost of imported intermediate goods, increasing labor demand. Further, unanticipated dollar appreciation may expand aggregate demand (money demand effect) or contract aggregate demand (goods market effect). The former two channels increase labor demand and, hence, nominal wage inflation while the latter channel decreases wage inflation. Accordingly, $B_8 \leq 0$.

2 Testing for Asymmetry

Given the complexity of the theoretical channels, it is possible that the effects of exchange rate shocks may be asymmetric in the face of dollar appreciation and depreciation. To test for possible asymmetry, we decompose the exchange rate shock into positive and negative components, $poss$ and $negs$.[3] Accordingly, $poss$ and $negs$ capture unanticipated dollar appreciation and depreciation around an anticipated steady-state trend. The procedure followed to construct $poss$ and $negs$ is described in Appendix A.

The empirical models (15) through (18) are reestimated with a modification that decomposes unanticipated exchange rate shocks into positive and negative components. For example, model (15) is modified as follows:

$$Dl_t = A_0 + A_1 E_{t-1} Dz_t + A_2 (Dz_t - E_{t-1} Dz_t) + A_3 E_{t-1} Dm_t + A_4 (Dm_t - E_{t-1} Dm_t) +$$
$$A_5 E_{t-1} Dg_t + A_6 (Dg_t - E_{t-1} Dg_t) + A_7 E_{t-1} Ds_t + A_{8p} poss_t + A_{8n} negs_t + A_9 EC_{t-1} + v_t^y \quad (17)$$

A_{8p} and A_{8n} measure the effects of dollar appreciation and depreciation on employment growth.

VI Empirical Results

The results of estimating the empirical model for employment and the nominal wage are presented in Tables 2 and 3 for eight industries of the U.S. economy: Construction, Finance, Manufacturing, Mining, Retail Trade, Services, Transportation, and Wholesale Trade.

---

[2] If labor and energy are substitutes, a rise in the energy price increases labor demand and, in turn, the nominal wage. The steeper the aggregate demand curve is, the higher the rise in price following an increase in energy price. Accordingly, the inflationary effect of a rise in the energy price is likely to be dominant on the nominal wage.

[3] The analysis of asymmetry has gained attention recently. For evidence in the face of monetary shocks, see Kandil (1995). For evidence in the face of aggregate demand shocks, see Kandil (1996), (1998), and (1999b). For evidence in the face of government spending shocks, see Kandil (2002).

Table 3: Nonlinear 3SLS Parameter Estimates for Wage

	B0	B1	B2	B3	B4	B5	B6	B7	B8	B9	B10	B11	RH0
Aggregate wage													
Model 1													
	0.04	0.07	0.02	0.01	0.04	-0.09	0.15	0.03	0.01			-0.24	0.93*
	(1.54)	(1.62)	(1.08)	(0.06)	(0.45)	(-0.66)	(1.10)	(0.54)	(0.17)			(-1.58)	(9.04)
R-square: 0.92													
Model 2													
	0.04	0.07	0.03	0.01	0.04	-0.12	0.13	0.05		0.04	-0.02	-0.26	0.94
	(1.23)	(1.44)	(1.24)	(0.04)	(0.38)	(-0.79)	(0.94)	(0.67)		(0.44)	(-0.30)	(-1.65)	(8.44)
R-square: 0.92													
Construction													
Model 1													
	0.10*	0.05	0.01	-0.64	0.11	-0.43	-0.41	0.10	-0.02			-0.41	0.89*
	(2.05)	(0.56)	(0.16)	(-1.28)	(0.42)	(-1.08)	(-0.92)	(0.65)	(-0.20)			(-1.16)	(6.55)
R-square: 0.61													
Model 2													
	0.10*	0.07	0.01	-0.57	0.22	-0.41	-0.47	0.05		-0.19	0.01	-0.48	0.86*
	(2.04)	(0.75)	(0.14)	(-1.12)	(0.75)	(-1.23)	(-1.04)	(0.31)		(-0.92)	(0.09)	(-1.32)	(6.11)
R-square: 0.61													
Finance													
Model 1													
	0.04*	0.14	0.04	0.06	0.23	-0.06	-0.04	0.10	-0.03				0.16
	(2.77)	1.43	(1.06)	(0.28)	(1.37)	(-0.31)	(-0.14)	(0.73)	(-0.43)				(0.77)
R-square: 0.47													
Model 2													
	0.04	0.09	0.06	0.08	0.21	-0.08	0.01	0.14		-0.06	-0.13		0.15
	(2.79)	(1.07)	(1.54)	(0.37)	(1.31)	(-0.42)	(0.02)	(1.14)		(-0.28)	(-1.24)		(0.71)
R-square: 0.43													
Manufacturing													
Model 1													
	0.07**	0.05	0.04	-0.40	0.20	-0.07	0.50**	-0.01	-0.12**			-0.68*	0.86*
	(2.02)	(0.66)	(1.04)	(-1.03)	(1.14)	(-0.25)	(1.86)	(-0.09)	(-1.84)			(-2.9)	(5.47)
R-square: 0.80													
Model 2													
	0.08**	0.05	0.04	-0.43	0.17	-0.03	0.52**	0.01		-0.19	-0.10	-0.64*	0.86*
	(2.09)	(0.63)	(0.97)	(-1.09)	(0.98)	(-0.10)	(1.88)	(0.11)		(-1.01)	(-0.91)	(-2.9)	(5.47)
R-square: 0.78													
Mining													
Model 1													
	0.08	-0.12	0.08	-0.37	0.48**	-0.07	0.21	0.04	-0.11			-1.27*	0.83*
	(1.65)	(-0.94)	(1.32)	(-0.60)	(2.01)	(-0.20)	(0.59)	(0.32)	(-1.32)			(-4.14)	(3.91)
R-square: 0.78													
Model 2													
	0.07	-0.12	0.07	-0.23	0.52**	0.01	0.23	0.08	-0.16	-0.04		-1.27*	-1.23*
	(1.51)	(-0.91)	(1.10)	(-0.36)	(1.95)	(0.02)	(0.63)	(0.58)	(-0.75)	(-0.34)		(-4.14)	(3.83)
R-square: 0.77													

Table 3: Nonlinear 3SLS Parameter Estimates for Wage. (Continued)

	B0	B1	B2	B3	B4	B5	B6	B7	B8	B9	B10	B11	RHO
Retail Trade													
Model 1													
	0.06	0.08	0.05	-0.13	-0.08	-0.05	0.20	0.02	-0.05			-0.36	0.81*
	(1.55)	(1.20)	(1.41)	(-0.33)	(-0.48)	(-0.20)	(0.80)	(0.14)	(-0.71)			(-1.66)	(4.83)
R-square: 0.67													
Model 2													
	0.06	0.07	0.05	-0.11	-0.09	-0.03	0.22	0.04		-0.03	-0.04	-0.35	0.80*
	(1.46)	(1.04)	(1.32)	(-0.25)	(-0.50)	(-0.13)	(0.82)	(0.34)		(-0.21)	(-0.41)	(-1.5)	(4.49)
R-square: 0.67													
Service													
Model 1													
	0.02	0.08	0.09*	0.44*	0.13	-0.13	-0.46	0.10	0.03			0.07	-0.04
	(1.55)	(1.20)	(2.60)	(2.25)	(0.78)	(-0.86)	(-1.62)	(0.84)	(0.37)			(0.85)	(-0.70)
R-square: 0.63													
Model 2													
	0.02	0.07	0.10**	0.42*	0.13	-0.14	-0.40	0.11		-0.0001	-0.02	0.08	-0.04
	(1.46)	(1.10)	(2.64)	(2.04)	(0.70)	(-0.86)	(-1.43)	(0.86)		(-0.00)	(-0.20)	(0.94)	(-0.69)
R-square: 0.67													
Transportation													
Model 1													
	0.06**	0.003	0.08*	-0.18	0.31*	-0.38**	-0.24	-0.05	-0.11*			-1.02*	0.90*
	(1.93)	(0.06)	(2.56)	(-0.47)	(2.55)	(-2.05)	(-1.30)	(-0.60)	(-2.26)			(-3.84)	(7.51)
R-square: 0.88													
Model 2													
	0.06	0.01	0.09*	-0.01	0.36*	-0.39**	-0.35	-0.03		-0.14	-0.12	-1.02*	0.90*
	(1.37)	(0.13)	(2.61)	(-0.02)	(2.77)	(-1.89)	(-1.68)	(-0.34)		(-1.09)	(-1.56)	(-3.84)	(7.51)
R-square: 0.89													
Wholesale Trade													
Model 1													
	0.02	0.18	0.11*	0.26	-0.10	0.23	-0.93*	0.09	0.03			-0.17	-0.37
	(1.15)	(1.48)	(2.26)	(1.16)	(-0.53)	(1.08)	(-2.48)	(0.55)	(0.42)			(-1.36)	(1.67)
R-square: 0.38													
Model 2													
	0.02	0.02	0.16*	0.29	-0.16	0.07	-0.78**	0.25		0.24	-0.11	-0.31*	-0.35
	(1.18)	(0.14)	(2.99)	(1.22)	(-0.69)	(0.32)	(-1.79)	(1.36)		(0.89)	(-0.79)	(-1.97)	(1.50)
R-square: 0.27													

B0 Intercept
B1 Anticipated Energy Price
B2 Unanticipated Energy Price
B3 Anticipated Money Supply
B4 Unanticipated Money supply
B5 Anticipated Government Spending
B6 Unanticipated Government Spending
B7Anticipated Real Effective Exchange Rate
B8 Unanticipated Real Effective Exchange Rate
B9 Positive Shock to Real Effective Exchange Rate
B10 Negative Shock to Real Effective Exchange Rate
B11 Error Correction
RHO Serial correlation

* Significant at 5%.
** Significant at 10%.
t-ratios are in parentheses.

VI-A The Employment Model

The results of estimating the empirical model (15) for employment are presented in Table 2. For each series, two entries are reported. The first entry provides estimates of the empirical model in (15). The second entry employs positive and negative shocks to the exchange rate to test asymmetry.

Except for the Mining sector, there is no evidence of a statistically significant effect of anticipated energy price shifts on employment growth. Unanticipated energy price shocks have a positive and statistically significant effect on employment growth in Construction, Manufacturing, Mining, and Transportation. Contrary to theory's prediction, a rise in the energy price increases labor demand and, hence, employment growth significantly.[4]

Where anticipated monetary growth shifts are statistically insignificant, their effects are neutral on employment growth. Further, ineffectiveness of monetary policy is evident by the negative and statistically significant response of employment growth to anticipated and unanticipated monetary shifts.[5] Anticipated and unanticipated increase in the money supply decreases employment growth in Construction, Services and Wholesale Trade sectors. Anticipated increase in the money supply decreases employment growth in the Finance sector. Unanticipated increase in the money supply decreases employment growth in Manufacturing. Further, the growth of government spending, both anticipated and unanticipated, is generally insignificant in determining sectoral employment growth. Unanticipated increase in government spending decreases employment growth in Mining.

More importantly for the purpose of this investigation is to observe the effects of changes in the real exchange rate on employment growth. All coefficients appear statistically insignificant in the face of anticipated exchange rate shifts. Further, unanticipated dollar appreciation decreases employment growth in several industries, which is significant both at the aggregate level and in Construction industries. This evidence confirms the dominant contractionary effect of dollar appreciation on employment growth in the United States. Dollar appreciation decreases the demand for U.S. products, which has a negative effect on labor demand and, hence, employment growth. Interestingly, however, unanticipated dollar appreciation has a positive and significant effect on employment growth in mining.

To understand variation in the effects of exchange rate shifts on sectoral employment, Table 4 provides the export/import share of U.S. industries. It is interesting to note the large share of imports in Mining (30.51 percent) compared to other industries. Given this large share, an unanticipated appreciation of the dollar decreases the cost of imported goods, which has a positive and statistically significant effect on employment growth in Mining.

The results of model 2 indicate, that currency fluctuations, both appreciation and depreciation, appear insignificant on employment growth. The decomposition highlights, however, the positive effect of dollar appreciation on employment growth in transportation. In

[4] Underlying theoretical predictions is the assumption that labor and energy are complements in the production process. Accordingly, a rise in the energy price decreases the marginal product of labor and, therefore, employment growth. If labor and energy are substitutes in the production process, a rise in the energy price may increase the demand for labor. Further, the energy price is highly correlated with the price of output in the Mining sector. That is the demand for labor in the Mining sector increases with the rise in the energy price.

[5] In Kandil and Mirzaie (2002), we report evidence that sectoral output growth does not vary significantly in the face of monetary growth shifts, both anticipated and unanticipated. The present evidence further isolates the real sector from monetary shifts and challenges the effectiveness of monetary policy in the short-run.

general, the symmetric insignificant effects of exchange rate shocks rule out the importance of variability in the value of the dollar to job creation and employment.

Table 4 Export share, import share, and the degree of openness for the U.S. major industries.

	1987			1992		
Industry	Export Share	Import Share	Degree of Openness	Export Share	Import Share	Degree of Openness
Agriculture	6.99	3.48	10.47	8.43	6.20	14.63
Mining	4.77	27.74	32.51	5.56	30.51	36.06
Construction	0.02	0.00	0.02	0.01	0.00	0.01
Manufacturing	8.20	15.63	23.83	12.38	16.80	29.19
Transportation and Utilities	4.38	1.19	5.57	6.45	1.36	7.81
Wholesales Trade	6.21	3.67	9.87	16.63	6.81	23.44
Retail Trade	0.02	0.00	0.02	0.00	0.00	0.00
Finance	2.24	0.28	2.52	2.41	0.09	2.50
Service	0.38	0.10	0.47	0.83	0.17	1.00

VI-B The Wage Model

The results of estimating the empirical model (16) of the nominal wage are presented in Table 3. There is no evidence of a significant increase in nominal wage inflation in the face of anticipated energy price shifts. Nonetheless, unanticipated energy price shifts have a positive and statistically significant effect on nominal wage inflation in Services, Transportation, and Wholesale Trade industries.

Except for services, there is no statistically significant evidence of an increase in sectoral nominal wage inflation in the face of anticipated money supply shifts. Unanticipated monetary shocks increase nominal wage inflation significantly in Mining and Transportation industries. Except for Manufacturing, there is no evidence of an increase in nominal wage inflation in the face of government spending shifts, both anticipated and unanticipated. Where the response is negative and significant, nominal wage inflation is not rising despite policy shifts. There is a reduction in nominal wage inflation in the face of anticipated growth in government spending. decreases nominal wage inflation in the Transportation industry. Further, there is an increase in wage inflation in Manufacturing and a reduction in wage inflation in Wholesale Trade in the face of unanticipated growth in government spending. More importantly, are the effects of exchange rate fluctuations on the nominal wage. Anticipated appreciation of the dollar decreases the cost of imported intermediate goods, increasing the demand for labor and, hence, nominal wage inflation. The increased supply decreases price and, hence, the real effective exchange rate, moderating nominal wage inflation. Indeed, anticipated appreciation of the dollar is not statistically significant in determining sectoral nominal wage inflation. In contrast, unanticipated appreciation of the dollar enters the demand and supply sides of the economy. Indeed, there is evidence of a statistically significant deflationary effect of dollar appreciation on the nominal wage in Manufacturing and Transportation industries.

The deflationary effect of dollar appreciation on the nominal wage further confirms the effect of demand contraction on the labor market in the United States. Dollar appreciation, by raising the international price of U.S. exports and reducing the domestic price of imports, decreases the demand for labor and, hence, the nominal wage. Further, this evidence is consistent with earlier results (Kandil and Mirzaie (2002)), concerning the deflationary effect of dollar appreciation on industrial output price in the United States.[6] Dollar appreciation decreases foreign and domestic demand and the cost of imported intermediate goods, decreasing the output price. Workers are, therefore, more likely to accept a reduction in nominal wage inflation given the reduction in the cost of living.

Decomposing exchange rate shocks into positive and negative components does not produce significant evidence on wage inflation. The symmetric insignificant effects rule out the relevance of currency fluctuations to wages and the standard of living in the U.S.

VI-C An Assessment

Dollar appreciation, by decreasing the international competitiveness of U.S. industries, has a negative effect on employment growth in the majority of U.S. industries, which is statistically significant in Construction and at the aggregate level. Given the large share of imported goods in the mining industry, dollar appreciation decreases the cost of production and increases employment growth. Both the reduction in demand and the increased supply have a negative effect on wage inflation, which is statistically significant in Manufacturing and Transportation.

Given qualitative differences across industries of the U.S. economy, we offer the following observations. For a more detailed discussion, see *The Economic Effects of Significant U.S. Import Restraints,* (1995).[7]

As Campa and Goldberg (1997) pointed out (see Table 1), US industries experienced an increased international exposure in the early to mid 1980s through their reliance on imported inputs in production. The imported input share has more than doubled in many manufacturing industries over the past two decades. Dollar appreciation decreases the competitiveness of manufactured American products in the international market while increasing domestic demand for manufactured foreign products. Further in 1992, the manufacturing sector had the second highest export share among major U.S. industries (see Table 4). This market mechanism necessitated intervention through voluntary trade restraints.[8] Trade restraints are likely to have moderated the statistical significance of the effects of dollar appreciation on

---

[6]In Kandil and Mirzaie (2002), we provide a statistically significant evidence for the effect of dollar appreciation in slowing down price inflation in several U.S. industries.

[7]This report is on the economic effects of significant U.S. import restraints on the U.S. economy, prepared at the request of the United States Trade Representative as a direct successor to a similar report in 1993. The report addresses the economic effects of the liberalization of significant U.S. import restraints in Manufacturing, Agriculture, and Services. Within each sector, the authors look at those products which have the highest import restraints. The base year for the study is 1993. The import restraints examined are tariffs and quantitative restraints, such as quotas, Voluntary Restraints agreements (VRAs), and Voluntary Export Restraints (VERs). More specifically, tariffs are specified as the average Most Favored Nation (MFN) ad valorem tariff calculated for 1993.

[8]For example, for the years 1992/93 and 1993/94, a voluntary trade restraint of 1.65 million units per year was in place on imports of autos from Japan, imports in 1993 were at 97% of this quota.

manufacturing industries.[9] Nonetheless, dollar appreciation, by decreasing the international competitiveness of U.S. industries, has a negative and statistically significant effect on wage inflation in Manufacturing.

Consistent with the statistically significant negative effect of dollar appreciation on employment growth in Construction, the U.S. schedule of commitments effectively places no limitations on the provision of construction services by foreign firms. See Table 5 for some illustrative figures between 1990-1992. The degree of openness (see Table 4) is the lowest in Construction among major U.S. industries. Nonetheless, dollar appreciation, by decreasing the demand for U.S. products, slows down domestic activity. Hence, employment growth in construction decreases significantly as a result of dollar appreciation.

Trade constraints are less operative in the Finance industry, providing for a larger degree of openness. Although foreign firms claim that the U.S. regulatory systems for the financial sector are unnecessarily overlapping and expensive, foreign firms seem to be treated largely the same as domestic firms. Indeed, there is plenty of evidence that foreign firms can enter the U.S. financial market: over four hundred foreign-owned insurance companies, from 28 countries, operate in the United States. These firms write a minimum of 10% of the total insurance market. In the securities market, there are 63 foreign companies, from 12 countries. As to foreign banking penetration of the U.S. market, foreign companies have 21 percent of total assets in the U.S. commercial banking system. Table 5 summarizes statistics between 1990-1992, which illustrate openness in the Finance industry. Given the presence of foreign firms in the U.S. financial market, dollar appreciation decreases the international competitiveness of these firms, which is evident by the negative effect on employment growth in the Finance industry.

While the effect of dollar appreciation is not significant in the Services industry, U.S. imports restraints are not strongly operative in this industry. Despite claims that foreign providers of some services face constraints on operations in the United States, most of these barriers are, in fact, requirements that providers of foreign service adhere to some regulatory schemes faced by domestic providers of services.[10] Table 4 illustrates, however, that the degree of openness is relatively smaller in the Services sector compared to other major U.S. industries.

Within the transportation sector, the air transport industry has significant restraints in the form of restrictive regulations and bilateral agreements that effectively restrain international air transport services. Likewise, maritime transport is subject to significant import restraints

[9] Indeed, *The Economic Effects of Significant U.S. Import Restraints*, (1995) provide the following evidence of trade effects in the Manufacturing industry. The most significant changes in prices faced by consumers as a result of import liberalization are as follows: Rubber and Plastic Footwear (-12%), Nonrubber Footwear (-5.5%), China Tableware (-5.4%), Leather Gloves (-5.4%), and Ceramic Floor and Wall Tile (-4.9%). Similarly, removal of Most Favored Nation (MFN) tarrifs and Voluntary Export Restraints (VER) led to a decline of 2,098 full-time equivalent jobs and a reduction of 0.4% in domestic output in Motor Vehicles industries. Consistently, import prices fell by 1.8% which translates into a 0.9% decline in prices faced by U.S. consumers. The effects of lower import prices were illustrated by 1.4% increase in imports. However, exports expanded as well by $36 million, fueled by a number of factors, including lower input prices. In particular, auto producers took advantage of lower prices for blast furnace and steel mill products.

[10] These regulatory schemes are not considered discriminatory. For example, requirements that foreign financial firms maintain assets in the U.S. if they want to operate in the U.S. are not considered discriminatory as long as U.S. firms face the same requirements.

by means of restrictive regulations.[11] Maritime transportation has a tariff equivalent of 89.1%. Further, Table 4 illustrates that the import share in the Transportation industry is very small. Nonetheless, dollar appreciation, by decreasing the competitiveness of U.S. products, has a negative and statistically significant effect on wage inflation in the Transportation industry.

Table 5 Trade Statistics Compared to Total Output Value and employment: Selected Years

Sectors	Variables	1990	1991	1992	1993
Banking, Insurance	Production (billion dollars)	341	377	407	—
and Other	Exports (million dollars)	4,389	5,135	4,857	—
Financial Services	Imports (million dollars)	5,167	6,022	7,179	—
Construction	Production (billion dollars)	240	223	222	—
	Exports (billion dollars)	44	69	72	—
	Imports (billion dollars)	15	12	9	—
Non-Durable Goods					
Nonrubber	Employment(1000 workers)	—	67.3	64.3	62.9
footwear	Exports (million dollars)	—	305.6	341.9	330.8
	Imports (million dollars)	—	8,311.	98,587.5	9,256.2
Rubber footwear	Employment(1000 workers)	—	10.9	10.8	10.7
	Exports (million dollars)	—	110.8	120.2	119.5
	Imports (million dollars)	—	791.8	1,028.7	1,332.1
Leather gloves and	Employment(1000 workers)	—	2.8	2.5	12.3
mittens	Exports (million dollars)	—	13.1	12.2	14.0
	Imports (million dollars)	—	112.8	117.0	148.7
Ceramic Wall and	Employment(1000 workers)	—	9.5	9.0	9.0
Floor tile	Exports (million dollars)	—	21.0	19.3	22.6
	Imports (million dollars)		365.1	418.5	471.9
China Tableware	Employment(1000 workers)		6.0	5.3	5.3
	Exports (million dollars)	—	43.0	50.2	46.8
	Imports (million dollars)	—	290.1	307.8	316.6
Durable Goods					
Motor Vehicles	Employment(1000 workers)	—	316	314	319
	Exports (million dollars)	—	14,892	17,265	18135
	Imports (million dollars)	—	54136	56,042	61,760
Intermediate Goods					
Blast Furnaces and	Employment(1000 workers)	—	196	187	175
Steel Mills	Exports (million dollars)	—	3,728	3,041	2,821
	Imports (million dollars)	—	7,760	7,841	8,552

11 One of the more important set of restrictions is the Merchant Marime Act of 1920 (Jones Act), which prohibits foreign vessels from carrying domestic freight between U.S. ports.

V Summary

This investigation has focused on the effect of foreign trade in determining economic conditions in the labor markets of industries in the United States. Towards this investigation, we build a theoretical model that incorporates the effects of exchange rate fluctuations on the demand and supply sides of the economy. We identify three directions for the effects of an unanticipated appreciation of the dollar on the economy. The first channel is on the demand side through the effects of appreciation in increasing imports and decreasing exports. The result is a contraction of aggregate demand. The second channel is through the effect of appreciation in decreasing the demand for the dollar as agents expect the exchange rate to return to its anticipated steady-state value. The result is an expansion of aggregate demand. On the supply side, appreciation allows producers to buy cheaper intermediate goods. The result is an expansion of the output supplied. The combined effects of the three channels remain indeterminate on variables in the labor market, employment and the nominal wage.

We attempt to investigate these effects using sectoral employment and wage data for the United States. Despite the small degree of openness of industries in the United States, the evidence indicates that the deflationary effect of dollar appreciation is more dominant on the nominal wage in Manufacturing and Transportation industries. More importantly, dollar appreciation decreases the international and domestic demand for U.S. products. The resulting reduction in labor demand is evident by a reduction in employment growth in the majority of industries, which is statistically significant in construction and at the aggregate level. In contrast, the largest share of imports in the mining industry is consistent with a significant increase in employment growth in the face of dollar appreciation. There is also evidence of a positive spill over effect, i.e., an increase in employment in construction in the face of currency appreciation.

In general, decomposing shocks in the exchange rate into appreciation and depreciation components yield symmetric, mostly insignificant, effects on employment and wages. In light of this evidence, the variability of the exchange rate appears to be neutral on employment growth and wage inflation. That is, the short-term effects of positive and negative shocks cancel out over time without determining trend growth. Given the limited effects of dollar fluctuations on domestic activity in the U.S., it is no surprise the Fed has been reluctant to respond to calls to intervene to stabilize the dollar. Fluctuations in dollar value, while beneficiary in some cases, cannot substitute for domestic policies to stabilize economic conditions and moderate the severity of business cycles in the U.S.

Appendix A

Theory Appendix

After substituting equations (1)-(7) into the equilibrium condition for the goods market (8), we obtain the expression for real income, which is a function of the exchange rate, the domestic price level, the foreign price level, and the domestic interest rate:

$$y_t = \frac{1}{1 - c_1(1 - t_1) + m_1}\{c_0 - c_1 t_0 + i_0 + g_t + x_0 - m_0 - (m_2 + x_1)log(R_t) - i_1 r_t\}$$

This expression is the IS equation describing the relationship between real income and the real interest rate.

Solving for the interest rate, r, from the LM equation (9) and substituting the result into the IS equation gives us the equation for aggregate demand as follows:

$$y_t = A\{c_0 - c_1 t_0 + i_0 + g_t + x_0 - m_0 - (m_2 + x_1)log(R_t) + \frac{i_1}{\lambda}(m_t - p_t) + i_1(E_t p_{t+1} - p_t) - \frac{i_1\theta}{\lambda}(E_t s_{t+1} - s_t)\}$$

where,

$$A = \frac{1}{1 - c_1(1 - t_1) + m_1 + \frac{i_1\theta}{\lambda}} > 0$$

and $log(R) = p + s - p^*$.

Combining labor demand and supply in (12) and (13) and substituting for imported intermediate goods, n, and the nominal wage, w, into the labor demand equation, we are able to express labor employment as follows:

$$l = \frac{\eta\omega + \omega^2}{\eta + \omega}(p_t - E_{t-1}p_t) - \frac{\omega^2\eta\delta + \omega^2 + \omega\eta + \omega\eta^2\delta}{\eta\delta(\omega + \eta)}z_t + \frac{\omega}{\eta\delta}(s_t + p_t - p_t^* + log(1 - \delta))$$

Substituting the results into the log transformation of Q in (10), we obtain gross domestic output supplied as follows:

$$q_t = (\omega + \eta)log\delta + \frac{\omega+\eta(1-\delta)}{\eta\delta}log(1 - \delta) + \omega(p_t - E_{t-1}p_t)$$
$$+ \frac{\omega+\eta(1-\delta)}{\eta\delta}log(R_t) - \frac{\eta+\omega+\omega\eta\delta}{\eta\delta}z_t$$

Substituting the result into the log transformation of equation (11),

$$y_t = log(Q_t - \frac{1}{R_t}N_t)$$

Applying Taylor expansion and substituting for l and n, we obtain the equation for aggregate supply of domestic value added as follows:

$$y_t = (\omega + \eta)log\delta + \frac{\omega}{\eta\delta}log(1 - \delta) + \omega(p_t - E_{t-1}p_t) + \frac{\omega}{\eta\delta}log(R_t) - \frac{\omega\eta + \delta + \omega}{\eta\delta}z_t$$

Sources of demand and supply shifts are assumed to follow the following processes:

$$g_t = \overline{g} + \varepsilon_{tg}$$

$$m_t = \overline{m} + \varepsilon_{tm}$$

$$z_t = \overline{z} + \varepsilon_{tz}$$

$$s_t = \overline{s} + \varepsilon_{ts}$$

$$p_t^* = \overline{p^*} + \varepsilon_{tp^*}$$

where $\overline{g}$, $\overline{m}$, $\overline{z}$, $\overline{s}$, and $\overline{p^*}$ are anticipated (steady-state) changes and ε_{tg}, ε_{tm}, ε_{tz}, ε_{ts}, and ε_{tp^*} are random unanticipated changes that have zero means and constant variances.

Equating aggregate demand and supply, we calculate the price of output. We take expectation of the resulting expression at time t to calculate $E_t p_{t+1}$. Substituting for $E_t p_{t+1}$ back into the equilibrium condition, taking expectation at time $t-1$ and subtracting the results from the original condition, we solve for output price surprises:

$$p_t - E_{t-1}p_t = \frac{\eta\delta\lambda A}{B+\omega\eta\delta\lambda}\varepsilon_{tg} + \frac{\eta\delta\lambda A i_1}{B+\omega\eta\delta\lambda}\varepsilon_{tm} + \frac{\omega\lambda+\omega\eta\delta}{B}\varepsilon_{tz}$$

$$+\frac{BC}{B+\omega\eta\delta\lambda}\varepsilon_{tp^*} - \frac{BC\lambda - Ai_1\eta\theta\delta\lambda}{(B+\omega\eta\delta\lambda)\lambda}\varepsilon_{ts}$$

where,

$$B = \lambda\omega + A\eta\delta\lambda(x_1 + m_2) + Ai_1\eta\delta + Ai_1\eta\delta\lambda > 0$$

and,

$$C = \frac{A\eta^2\delta^2\lambda(x_1 + m_2) + \omega\eta\delta\lambda}{\eta\delta B} > 0$$

A positive shock to ε_{tg} or ε_{tm} increases the demand for domestic output, creating positive price surprises. A positive shock to ε_{tz} increases the cost of the output produced, creating positive price surprises. A positive shock to ε_{tp^*} increases the demand for domestic goods and increases the cost of imported intermediate goods, creating positive price surprises.

In contrast, a positive shock to ε_{ts} has indeterminate effect on price through demand and supply channels.

Substituting the solution for output price surprises into the equilibrium conditions we solve for price as follows:

$$p_t = constant_p + \frac{B+i_1\eta\delta\lambda}{B}\{\frac{A\eta\delta\lambda}{B}\overline{g} + \frac{Ai_1\eta\delta\lambda}{B}\overline{m} + c\overline{p^*} - c\overline{s} + \frac{\omega+\omega\eta\delta}{B}\overline{z}\}$$
$$+\frac{A\eta\delta\lambda}{B+\omega\eta\delta\lambda}\varepsilon_{tg} + \frac{Ai_1\eta\delta\lambda B}{B(B+\omega\eta\delta\lambda)}\varepsilon_{tm} + \frac{BC}{B+\omega\eta\delta}\varepsilon_{tp^*}$$
$$+\frac{(\omega+\omega\eta\delta)\lambda}{B+\omega\eta\delta\lambda}\varepsilon_{tz} - \frac{BC-Ai_1\theta\eta\delta-C\omega\eta\delta\lambda}{B+\omega\eta\delta\lambda}\varepsilon_{ts}$$

Substituting for $(p_t - E_{t-1}p_t)$ and p_t into the expressions for the nominal wage and labor employment, we solve for w and l as follows:

$$w_t = constant_w + \{\frac{(\eta^2\delta+\eta\omega\delta+\omega+\eta)(A\eta\delta\lambda)}{\eta\delta(\omega+\eta)(B+\omega\eta\delta\lambda)}\}(\varepsilon_{tg} + i_1\varepsilon_{tm})$$
$$+\{\frac{(\eta^2\delta+\eta\omega\delta+\omega+\eta)(BC)-(\omega+\eta)(B+\omega\eta\delta)}{\eta\delta(\omega+\eta)(B+\omega\eta\delta)}\}\varepsilon_{tp^*}$$
$$+\{\frac{(\eta^2\delta+\eta\omega\delta+\omega+\eta)(\omega\eta\delta\lambda+\omega\delta)-(\omega\eta\delta+\omega+\eta+\eta^2\delta)(B+\omega\eta\delta\lambda)}{\eta\delta(\omega+\eta)(B+\omega\eta\delta\lambda)}\}\varepsilon_{tz}$$
$$+\{\frac{(\eta^2\delta+\eta\omega\delta+\omega+\eta)(BC-Ai_1\theta\eta\delta-C\omega\eta\delta\lambda)-(\omega+\eta)(B+\omega\eta\delta\lambda)}{\eta\delta(\omega+\eta)(B+\omega\eta\delta\lambda)}\}\varepsilon_{ts}$$
$$+\{\frac{(\eta^2\delta+\eta\omega\delta+\omega+\eta)(B+i_1\eta\delta\lambda)(A\eta\delta\lambda)}{B^2\eta\delta(\omega+\eta)}\}(\overline{g} + i_1\overline{m})$$
$$+\{\frac{C(\eta^2\delta+\eta\omega\delta+\omega+\eta)(B+i_1\eta\delta\lambda)-B(\omega+\eta)}{B\eta\delta(\omega+\eta)}\}\overline{p^*}$$
$$+\{\frac{B(\omega+\eta)-C(\eta^2\delta+\eta\omega\delta+\omega+\eta)(B+i_1\eta\delta\lambda)}{B\eta\delta(\omega+\eta)}\}\overline{s}$$
$$+\{\frac{B(\omega+\eta)-C(\eta^2\delta+\eta\omega\delta+\omega+\eta)(B+i_1\eta\delta\lambda)}{B\eta\delta(\omega+\eta)}\}\overline{z}$$

$$l_t = constant_l + \{\frac{\eta\delta\lambda A(\eta^2\delta\omega+\eta^2\delta^2\omega^2+\eta\omega+\omega^2)}{\eta\delta(\eta+\omega)(B+\omega\eta\delta\lambda)}\}\varepsilon_{tg}$$
$$+\{\frac{\eta\delta B(Ai_1\eta\delta\lambda)(\eta\omega+\omega^2)+\omega Ai_1\eta\delta\lambda B(\eta+\omega)}{\eta\delta B(\eta+\omega)(B+\omega\eta\delta\lambda)}\}\varepsilon_{tm}$$
$$+\{\frac{\eta\delta BC(\eta\omega+\omega^2)-\omega(\eta+\omega)(B+\omega\eta\delta\lambda)+\omega BC(\eta+\omega)}{\eta\delta(\eta+\omega)(B+\omega\eta\delta\lambda)}\}\varepsilon_{tp^*}$$
$$+\{\frac{\eta\delta(B+\omega\eta\delta\lambda)(\eta\omega+\omega^2)(\omega\eta\delta+\omega\delta)+B\omega(\eta+\omega)(\omega+\eta\lambda\delta+\omega\lambda)-B(\eta+\omega)(\omega\eta\delta+\omega^2+\omega\eta+\omega\eta^2\delta)}{\eta\delta B(\eta+\omega)(B+\omega\eta\delta\lambda)}\}\varepsilon_{tz}$$
$$+\{\frac{\omega\lambda(\eta+\omega(BC-Ai_1\theta\eta\delta-C\omega\eta\delta\lambda)-\omega\lambda(\eta+\omega)(B+\omega\eta\delta\lambda)-\eta\delta(\eta\omega+\omega^2)(BC\lambda-Ai_1\eta\theta\delta\lambda)}{\eta\delta\lambda(\eta+\omega)(B+\omega\eta\delta\lambda)}\}\varepsilon_{ts}$$
$$+\{\frac{\omega(B+i_1\eta\delta\lambda)(A\eta\delta\lambda)}{\eta\delta B^2}\}(\overline{g} + i_1\overline{m}) + \{\frac{\omega C(B+i_1\eta\delta\lambda)-\omega B}{\eta\delta B}\}\overline{p^*} + \{\frac{B\omega-\omega C(B+i_1\eta\delta\lambda)}{\eta\delta B}\}\overline{s}$$
$$+\{\frac{\omega(\omega+\eta)(B+i_1\eta\delta\lambda)(\omega+\omega\eta\delta)-B^2(\omega^2\eta\delta+\omega^2+\omega\eta+\omega\eta^2\delta)}{\eta\delta B^2(\omega+\eta)}\}\overline{z}$$

where $constant_w$ and $constant_l$ are determined by constant terms on the demand and supply sides of the economy. Based on the model's solutions, we note the following:

- Anticipated changes in government spending and the money supply, $\bar{g}$, $\bar{m}$, shift aggregate demand, increasing price. Given a constant level of nominal effective exchange rate, the rise in domestic price increases the real effective exchange rate, reducing the real cost of imported intermediate goods and increasing the marginal product of labor. Accordingly, $\bar{g}$ and $\bar{m}$ have positive effects on employment, and the nominal wage.
- Anticipated changes in imports price, $\overline{p^*}$, the energy price, $\bar{z}$, and the exchange rate, $\bar{s}$, enter the production function. A rise in imports price and the energy price increase the cost of the output produced, decreasing the marginal product of labor and, hence, employment and the nominal wage. The reduction in output increases price and, hence, the real effective exchange rate, moderating the reduction in employment and the nominal wage in the face of $\bar{z}$ and $\overline{p^*}$.

In contrast, an anticipated rise in the foreign price of the dollar, $\bar{s}$, decreases the cost of imported goods, increasing the marginal product of labor and, hence, employment and the nominal wage. The increased supply decreases price and, hence, the real effective exchange rate, moderating the increase in employment and the nominal wage in the face of $\bar{s}$.

1. Unanticipated demand shifts in the face of goverment spending and the money supply, ε_{tg}, ε_{tm}, increase the demand for labor, increasing employment, and the nominal wage. The increased demand raises price and the real effective exchange rate, reinforcing the increased employment and the nominal wage in the face of ε_{tg} and ε_{tm}.
2. Unanticipated increase in the imports price, ε_{tp^*}, increases demand and decreases supply. Accordingly, the effect is indeterminate on employment and the nominal wage.
3. An unanticipated increase in the energy price, ε_{tz}, decreases the marginal product of labor, decreasing employment and the nominal wage. The rise in price increases the real effective exchange rate, moderating the reduction in employment and the nominal wage in the face of ε_{tz}.
4. Finally, ε_{ts}, enters the demand and supply sides of the economy. Specifically, ε_{ts} increases the output supplied and results in an indeterminate effect on aggregate demand (an increase in net exports and a decrease in money demand). Hence, the effects of ε_{ts} are indeterminate on employment and the nominal wage.

The following table summarizes theory's predictions concerning changes in the labor market in response to various shifts.

Dependent Variable	$\bar{g}$	$\bar{m}$	$\overline{p^*}$	$\bar{z}$	$\bar{s}$	ε_g	ε_m	ε_{p^*}	ε_z	ε_s
Employment	>0	>0	≤ 0	≤ 0	≥ 0	>0	>0	?	$\leq$	?
Nominal Wage	>0	>0	≤ 0	≤ 0	≥ 0	>0	>0	?	$\leq$	?

Where theory predicts a moderating effect, the positive or negative effects may prove to be zero. Where the outcome is indeterminate, theory's prediction cannot be identified and is denoted by ?.

Appendix B

Econometric Methodology

The surprise terms in models (15) and (16) are unobservable, necessitating the construction of empirical proxies before estimation can take place. Thus, the empirical models include equations describing agents' forecast of specific demand growth, the change in energy price, and the change in the price of the dollar in foreign currency (the exchange rate).

To decide on variables in the forecast equations for each of the demand and supply shifts, we follow a formal causality test. Each variable is regressed on two of its lags as well as two lags of all variables that enter the model: the change in the log value of the energy price, nominal GDP, aggregate productivity, the real effective exchange rate, government spending, and the money supply. We then test the joint significance of the lags for each variable. The results are reported in Table A3 of the Appendix. Accordingly, the forecast equations account for the lags of variables proven to be statistically significant.

Obtaining a proxy for ex-ante forecasts of the energy price and the exchange rate is complicated by the assumption that the generating process experienced a structural change between 1973 and 1974. This assumption is supported by the results of a formal test suggested in Dufour (1982). For both the period 1961-73 and the period 1974-00, the generating process is modeled as described above. Testing for structural break in the money supply and government spending proved insignificant.

We form surprises by subtracting forecasts from the actual change. Positive and negative shocks are constructed following the procedure described in Kandil and Mirzaie (2002). These shocks are employed as "generated regressors" in the final empirical models, which demands a special attention to estimation. To obtain efficient estimates and ensure correct inferences (i.e., to obtain consistent variance estimates), the empirical models are estimated jointly with the equation that determines the proxy variables following the suggestions of Pagan (1984 and 1986). To account for the endogeneity of forecasted variables, instrumental variables are used in the estimation of the empirical models. The instrument list includes four lags for each of the first-difference of the log value of the energy price, the exchange rate, the money supply, government spending, nominal GDP, and aggregate productivity.

Following the suggestions of Engle (1982), the results of the test for serial correlation in simultaneous equation models are consistent with the presence of first-order autoregressive errors for some industries. To maintain comparability, it is assumed in all models that the error term follows an AR(1) process. The estimated models are transformed, therefore, to eliminate any possibility of serial correlation. The estimated residuals from the transformed models have zero means and are serially independent.

The qualitative results remain robust with respect to a number of modifications that include varying variables and the lag length in the forecast equations and the instruments list and modifying the final model specification to include sector-specific variables.

Appendix C

Data Sources

Sample Period: 1961-00.

The following annual data were taken from: The *National Income and Product Accounts of the United States (NIPAA), 1929-82 Statistical Tables,* U.S. Department of Commerce/Bureau of Economic Analysis. Updates for the years 1983-00 are provided in the July issues of *Survey of Current Business.*

1. Nominal GDP by industry, Table 6.1.
2. GDP by industry in constant dollars (1982=100), Table 6.2.
3. Sectoral price level=nominal output by industry/constant dollar output by industry.
4. Full-time equivalent employees by industry, Table 6.6B.
5. Sectoral productivity=the ratio of constant dollar output to the full-time equivalent employees by industry.

Other series are as follows:

1. Sectoral wage: Average earnings of production or non-supervisory workers on private nonfarm payrolls, by major industry, 1964-1966, *Employment and Earnings,* U.S. Department of Labor, Bureau of Labor Statistics, December 1997. For 1961-63, same source, various issues.
2. Sectoral Employment: Total hours of all persons, data bank: jobs, hours, and output, 1958-2000, Bureau of Labor Statistics, Office of Employment Projection.
3. Producers Price Index (1982=100) for Fuels, Power and Related Products- *Historical Series 1926-2000,* the U.S. Department of Labor, Bureau of Labor Statistics.
4. Real Effective Exchange Rate: Real weighted exchange rate (1980=100), Gordon (1993), Appendix A, Table A-2, Quarterly data for 1961-1974 of real weighted exchange rate (1980=100). Data are transformed to annual in E-View statistical package. Updates for the years 1975-00 are from *International Financial Statistics.* We follow a standard splicing procedure to combine the series from both sources.
5. Government Spending: Government expenditure on consumption and gross investment, *NIPAA.*

6. Money Supply: M3, monthly data from the Federal Reserve Bank of St. Louis. Annual data are obtained by averaging monthly observations.

Table A1 The KPSS Statistics for Null of Level Stationary.(The 5% critical value is 0.463)

	Lag Truncation Parameter				
Variables	0	1	2	3	4
Aggregate					
Employment	3.99	2.07	1.42	1.10	0.90
Wage	3.97	2.05	1.40	1.08	0.88
Construction					
Employment	3.55	1.90	1.34	0.06	0.89
Wage	3.88	2.01	1.38	1.06	0.87
Finance					
Employment	3.95	2.04	1.40	1.08	0.89
Wage	4.02	2.08	1.43	1.10	0.91
Manufacturing					
Employment	0.53	0.31	0.24	0.20	0.18
Wage	3.97	2.05	1.40	1.08	0.88
Mining					
Employment	0.81	0.42	0.29	0.23	0.19
Wage	3.93	2.03	1.38	1.06	0.87
Retail					
Employment	3.96	2.05	1.41	1.09	0.90
Wage	3.95	2.04	1.40	1.08	0.88
Service					
Employment	3.96	2.06	1.42	1.10	0.91
Wage	3.85	2.02	1.39	1.08	0.90
Transportation					
Employment	3.83	2.01	1.39	1.09	0.90
Wage	3.92	2.02	1.38	1.06	0.87
Whole Sale Trade					
Employment	3.90	2.03	1.40	1.08	0.89
Wage	4.00	2.06	1.41	1.09	0.89
Exchange rate	2.24	1.17	0.83	0.66	0.56
Energy price	3.46	1.78	1.21	0.93	0.77
Money supply	3.96	2.05	1.41	1.09	0.89
Gov. spending	3.83	2.01	1.39	1.08	0.89
Nominal GDP	4.01	2.08	1.42	1.10	0.90

Test description:

The KPSS (Kwiatowski, Phillips, Schmidt, and Shin) stationarity test procedure examines the null hypothesis of stationarity of a univariate time series. The KPSS test assumes that a time series variable X_t could be decomposed into the sum of a deterministic trend, a random walk, and a stationary error. Then the random walk term is assumed to have two components: an anticipated component and an error term. The stationarity of the error term is established by testing if the variance of the error is zero.

If the calculated lag truncation variable is greater than 0.463, we reject the null hypothesis of stationarity.

Table A2 Cointegration Test Results, ADF test statistics for the null hypothesis of non-stationary residuals. Cointegration regression includes energy price, real exchange rate, money supply, and government spending.

Sectors	Employment	Wage
Aggregate	-3.34	-3.60
Construction	-4.26	-3.25
Finance	-3.45	-2.18
Manufacturing	-2.58	-3.34
Mining	-1.78	-4.31
Retail Sale Trade	-3.27	-3.35
Services	-3.07	-3.53
Transportation	-3.01	-5.19
Whole Sale Trade	-3.05	-2.78

Test Description:

If we have n endogenous variables, each of which is first-order integrated (that is, each has a unit root or stochastic trend or random walk element), there can be from zero to n-1 linearly independent cointegrating vectors. If there is one cointegrating equation, the regression models of the text include a lag of error correction term as reported in tables 2-3.

To check for cointegration, we apply the ADF unit root test to the residual from the cointegration regression in which the non-stationary level of employment and wage are regressed on the level of variables that enter the model. The results reject the null hypothesis of non-stationarity at the 10% level for all residuals except for employment in manufacturing and mining and wage in finance sector.

Table A3 The Results of Endogeniety Tests.

Forecasted Variables

	Dz	Ds	Dm	Dg
Energy price (Dz)		3.27*	0.35	1.01
Real exchange rate (Ds)	2.51*		0.69	1.04
Money Supply (Dm)	1.84	1.25		1.01
Government Spending (Dg)	5.68*	5.53*	5.81*	

* The F-value is greater than the critical value of F at 10%.

References

[1] Agenor, Pierre-Richard, "Output, Devaluation and the Real Exchange Rate in Developing Countries," *Weltwirtschaftliches Archive,* 1991, Band 127.

[2] Barbone, Luca and Francisco Rivera-Batiz, "Foreign Capital and the Contractionary Impact of Currency Devaluation, with an Application to Jamaica," *Journal of Development Economics,* Vol. 26, June 1987, pp. 1-15.

[3] Branson, W., and J. Love, "United States Manufacturing and the Real Exchange rate," in R. Marston, ed., *Misalignment of Exchange Rates: Effects on Trade and Industry,* University of Chicago Press, 1988.

[4] Bruno, M., "Stabilization and Stagflation in a Semi-Industrialized Economy," in R. Dornbusch and J. Frankel, eds. *International Economic Policy,* Johns Hopkins University Press, Baltimore, MD, 1979.

[5] Burgess, S. and M. Knetter, "An International Comparison of Employment Adjustment to Exchange Rate Fluctuations," *NBER Working Paper,* **5861**, (December 1996).

[6] Buiter, William H. *International Macroeconomics,* 1990, Oxford University Press.

[7] Campa, Jose and Linda S. Goldberg, "The Evolving External Orientation of Manufacturing: A Profile of Four Countries," *Economic Policy Review,* Federal Reserve Bank of New York, July 1997.

[8] Cooper, Richard N. "Currency Devaluation in Developing Countries," *Essays in International Finance,* No. 86, International Finance Section, Princeton University, 1971.

[9] Diaz-Alejandro, Carlos F., "A Note on the Impact of Devaluation and Redistributive Effect," *Journal of Political Economy,* Vol. 71, August 1963, pp. 577-580.

[10] Dornbusch, Rudiger, *Open Economy Macroeconomics,* 2nd edition, New York, 1988.

[11] Dufour, Jean-Marie, "Generalized Chow Tests for Structural Change: A Coordinate Free Approach," *International Economic Review,* **23** (1982), 565-75.

[12] Engle, R. R. "A General Approach to Lagrange Multiplier Model Diagnostics," *Journal of Econometrics,* (1982) 20, 83-104.

[13] Goldberg, Linda and Joseph Tracy, "Exchange Rates and Local Labor Markets," Federal Reserve Bank of New York, *WP* 67, 1999. Gylfason, Thorvaldur and Schmid, Michael, "Does Devaluation Cause Stagflation?" *Canadian Journal of Economics,* Vol. XV1, November 1983.

[14] Gordon, Robert J. *Macroeconomics,* Sixth Edition, Harper Collins College Publishers, 1993.

[15] Glick, Reuven and Michael Hutchison, "Does Exchange Rate Appreciation 'Deindustrialize' the Open Economy? A Critique of U.S. Evidence," *Economic Inquiry,* Vol. 28, January 1990, pp. 19-37.

[16] Guittian, Manuel, "The Effects of Changes in the Exchange Rate on Output, Prices, and the Balance of Payments," *Journal of International Economics,* Vol. 6, 1976, pp. 65-74.

[17] Hanson, James A., "Contractionary Devaluation, Substitution in Production and Consumption, and the Role of the Labor Market," *Journal of International Economics,* **14**, 1983, pp. 179-89.

[18] Hirschman, Albert O. "Devaluation and the Trade Balance: A Note," *Review of Economics and Statistics,* **31**, 1949, pp. 50-53.

Kandil, Magda, ``Asymmetry in the Effects of Monetary and Government Spending Shocks: Contrasting Evidence and Implications," *Economic Inquiry,* Vol. 40, No. 2, April 2002, pp. 288-313.

Kandil, Magda, ``Asymmetric Nominal Flexibility and Economic Fluctuations," *Southern Economic Journal,* (January 1995), Vol. 61, No. 3, pp. 674-695.

[19] Kandil, Magda, "Sticky Wage or Sticky Price? Analysis of the Cyclical Behavior of the Real Wage," *Southern Economic Journal,* (October 1996).

Kandil, Magda, ``Supply-Side Asymmetry and the Non-Neutrality of Demand Fluctuations," *Journal of Macroeconomics,* Vol. 20, No. 4, Fall 1998, pp. 785-810.

[20] Kandil, Magda and Mirzaie, Aghdas, "Exchange Rate Fluctuations and Disaggregate Economic Activity in the United States: Theory and Evidence," *Journal of International Money and Finance,* Vol. 21, No. 1, February 2002, pp. 1-31.

[21] Kandil, Magda and Woods, Jeffrey, "Cyclical Comovements in Industrial Labor and Product Markets: Theory and Evidence," *Economic Inquiry,* (1997).

[22] Karras, Georgios, "Sources of Macroeconomic Fluctuations: 1973-1989," *Journal of Macroeconomics,* Vol. 15, Winter 1993, pp. 47-68.

[23] Krugman and Taylor, "Contractionary Effects of Devaluation," *Journal of International Economics,*, Vol. 8, pp. 445-456.

[24] Kwiatkowski, Denis, Peter C. B. Phillips, Peter Schmidt, and Yongcheol Shin, "Testing the Null Hypothesis of Stationarity Against the Alternative of a Unit Root: How Sure Are We That Economic Time Series Have a Unit Root?" *Journal of Econometrics,* **54**, 1992, pp. 159-78.

[25] Manuel, Jose and Linda S. Goldberg, "Employment Versus Wage Adjustment and the U.S. Dollar," Federal Reserve Bank of New York, *WP* **56**, 1998.

[26] Maskus, Keith E., "Normative Concerns in the International Protection of Intellectual Property Rights," *World Economy,* 13:387-409, September 1990.

[27] Meade, James E. *The Theory of International Economic Policy, I: The Balance of Payment,* Oxford University Press, Oxford.

[28] Mendoza, E. G., "The Effect of Macroeconomic Shocks in a Basic Equilibrium Framework," *IMF Staff Papers,* **39** (4), 1992, 855-89.

[29] Pagan, Adrian, "Econometric Issues in the Analysis of Regressions with Generated Regressor," *International Economic Review,* 1984, 25, 221-47.

[30] Pagan, Adrian, "Two Stage and Related Estimators and Their Applications," *Review of Economic Studies,* 1986, 53, 517-38.

[31] Revenga, Ana L. "Exporting Jobs? The Impacts of Import Competition on Impolite," *Quarterly Journal of Economics,* Vol. 107, February 1992, pp. 255-285.

[32] Shone, Ronald, *Open Economy Macroeconomics,* Harvester Wheatsheaf, 1989.

[33] Solimano, Andres, "Contractionary Devaluation in the Southern Cone- The Case of Chile," *Journal of Development Economics,* 1986, 23, pp. 135-51.

[34] U.S. International Trade Commission, *The Economic Effects of Significant U.S. Import Restraints: First Biannual Update,* Publication 2935, December 1995, Washington D.C.

[35] Wijnbergen, Sweder Van, "Exchange Rate Management and Stabilization Policies in Developing Countries," *Journal of Development Economics,* **23**, 1989, pp. 227-47.

In: International Trade Issues
Editor: Robert. V. Weeks, pp. 205-226
ISBN: 1-59454-621-5

Chapter 9

EXPORTING, CROSS-BORDER INVESTMENT AND EMPLOYMENT DYNAMICS: AN EMPIRICAL INVESTIGATION

Sourafel Girma [*]
Department of Economics, University of Leicester
Leicester LE1 7RH
Yundan Gong [**]
Department of Economics, University of Leicester
Leicester LE1 7RH

Abstract

This chapter provides a systematic analysis of the impact of cross-border investment and exporting on firm level employment growth in the U.K manufacturing industry for the period 1990-1998. Economically significant employment growth effects are identified following entry into export markets, whereas the job creation effects of foreign direct investment are found to be more modest.

I Introduction

Does international commerce exert a causal influence on employment growth? This is the main question addressed in this chapter, and we believe that this would be of interest to policy-makers and academic economists alike.

There is now a large body of empirical evidence that points to robust correlation between multinationality, exporting and business performance[1]. Formal economic models that attempt to explain this empirical regularity have been developed recently [e.g. Helpman et al (2003)

[*] E-mail address: sourafel.girma@le.ac.uk
[**] E-mail address: yg13@le.ac.uk
[1] See for example Conyon et al (2002) and Griffith and Simpson (2002) for the UK; Doms and Jensen (1998) and Bernard and Jensen (1999) and Clerides et al (1998) for Columbia, Mexico and Morocco.

and Melitz (2003)]. These models suggest that because of the existence of sunk costs, firms engaged in foreign direct investment (FDI) activity are more efficient than those servicing foreign markets through arms-length exporting alone, while the least efficient firm will operate only in the domestic market. Since employment (or size) is a good proxy for firm performance, the present study will provide vigorous empirical tests of the theoretical predictions of these models.

It is well documented that governments the world over intervene to attract foreign direct investment by offering incentives such as trade policy concessions, financial assistance, and tax breaks to multinational firms [see Blomström and Kokko (2003) for a recent discussion]. For example, between 1991 and 1995 some half a billion pounds was paid in grants for internationally-owned companies by the UK government under the Regional Selective Assistance scheme[2], costing around £17,500 per net job created. In the US, the government of Alabama paid the equivalent of $150,000 per employee to Mercedes for locating its new plant in the state in 1994 (Head, 1998).

Exports are also high on many policy-makers agenda. This has resulted in extensive export promotion activity of one form or another, ranging from trade promotion schemes, through to export subsidies to state trading monopolies. For example, *UK Trade & Investment* is the government organisation that supports UK companies trading internationally, and it has active branches in over 200 countries across the globe.

One prominent motivation for encouraging inwards FDI and international trade is the presumption that multinational and exporting firms stimulate productivity and employment, either directly through their own higher productivity and employment growth or through indirect spillover effects. It is therefore important to subject this optimistic prognosis by policy makers to systematic empirical investigation. Furthermore, it would be interesting to quantify the relative employment generating potential of foreign multinationals and domestic exporters in view of the fact that governments seek to attract inward investment, often with the use of substantially more public funds than are devoted to encouraging domestic firms to export.

The empirical setting of the paper is the U.K manufacturing industry. Given that the UK is the second largest host of FDI after the USA[3] and the fifth largest exporter of merchandise exports globally, it is a good test case for research designed to assess the relative importance of exports and foreign direct investment in promoting economic welfare. Accordingly this study undertakes a detailed micro-econometric analysis of the employment dynamics of domestically oriented firms relative to multinational and exporting enterprises, based on a firm-level panel data over the period 1990-1998. To reflect heterogeneity even amongst firms with the same international commerce orientation, multinational enterprises (MNE) are trichotomised as U.K[4], US and other multinationals[5], whereas exporters are distinguished by their exporting intensity.

---

[2] See the official report at http://www.dti.gov.uk/regional/evaluationRSA91-95.pdf

[3] The UK has a total of $400bn of direct foreign investment, and attracted $78bn in 1999 according to the United Nations Conference on Trade and Development. It is estimated that more than one-third of the UK's manufacturing sector is now foreign owned. The UK is home to over 22% of all foreign direct investment in the EU. This includes over 40% of both US and Japanese investment.

[4] Between 1996 and 2000, U.K. multinational corporations have spent £42.6 billion in foreign direct investment, and by the end of this period they owned a staggering £600 billion worth of assets abroad.

[5] This tricotomisation of foreign acquisitions was essentially driven by the preponderance of US and UK acquirers. Unfortunately, the number of acquirers from most countries was too small for meaningful analysis

Our empirical investigation adds to the existing literature in two respects. Firstly instead of focusing on average employment differentials, it evaluates the effects of multinationality on the entire productivity distribution with the aid of the Kolmogorov-Smirnov nonparametric testing procedure. This technique is based on the notion of stochastic dominance to rank the cumulative distribution functions of employment. We also attempt to quantify the employment growth differentials across the various groups of firms via standard conditional mean models, as well as least absolute deviations (median) and outlier-robust regressions. Secondly, the chapter contrasts the job creating potential of exporting and cross-border investment by looking at the employment growth trajectories of new export markets entrants and newly acquired subsidiaries of multinational firms[6], with the view of establishing the direction of causality between international commerce and employment growth.

Our findings from the nonparametric test statistics indicate that the employment *level* distribution of exporters stochastically dominates the employment distribution of non-exporters. Amongst exporters, those selling a higher share of their output abroad do not always dominate other exporters. On the other hand, the employment distribution of exporters is dominated by the distribution of multinational enterprises. However, controlling for a host of firm-level and industry-wide factors, the results from the employment *growth* regressions suggest that firms that export a high proportion of their output experience higher employment growth than any other group of firms, including multinationals.

We also uncover evidence that firms exhibiting higher than average employment growth tend to enter the export markets for the first time, and exporting appears the boost employment growth still further. In sharp contrast, multinational acquirers in our sample appear to target firms with average employment growth, and we fail to identify any subsequent improvements to the employment prospects of the acquired firms. On the strength of our results we therefore conclude that although both exporting status and multinationality are positively correlated with employment growth, only exporting exerts a causal influence on job creation.

This rest of the chapter proceeds with Section II, which briefly considers the theoretical literature that seeks to establish the connection between business performance, multinationality and exporting. Section III presents a selective review of the existing empirical literature that has explored the impact international commercial activity on employment dynamics. Section IV describes the database used in this study and presents some descriptive statistics. Section V discusses the results from the nonparametric Kolmogorov-Smirnov tests, while Section VI reports the findings from the parametric regressions designed to assess the correlation between export intensity, multinationality and employment growth. Section VII examines the employment growth trajectories of new export market entrants and newly acquired subsidiaries of multinational firms in order to isolate the causal effects of international commerce on employment creation. Finally Section VIII concludes.

---

[6] Like most developed economies, foreign direct investment via the acquisition of indigenous establishments is an increasingly important component of inward investment in the U.K. It is interesting to note that two-thirds of foreign-owned projects that received public grants in the period 1900-95 involved expansion at existing sites, acquisitions or buy-outs rather than new start-ups and branch plants.

II Multinationality, Exporting and Business Performance: Some Theoretical Issues

Theories concerning foreign direct investment (FDI) emphasise that foreign firms must have inherent firm-specific advantages that allow them to overcome the higher costs of becoming a multinational (Hymer, 1976; Kindleberger, 1969)[7]. Higher costs result because domestic firms have pre-existing familiarity with suppliers, demand conditions, culture, language, the legal environment and product standards, while foreign firms do not. The firm-specific advantages of multinationals may be tangible – for instance an improved production process or a product innovation – or intangible. The latter include brand names, better management structures or the technical knowledge of employees. But firm-specific assets are frequently intangible, which provides one motivation for firms internalising transactions and becoming multinationals rather than licensing their assets to local firms. The intangible nature of the assets means that a market may not exist for them, increasing the difficulty of writing contracts and entering into licensing agreements. It is a combination of these factors that leads to FDI – the advantages of the firm, the need to internalise the transaction, and the advantages of the country in which the FDI is located (Dunning, 1977).

The assumption that multinational firms have firm-specific assets implies that they may also possess substantial competitive advantages over their purely domestic rivals. A number of arguments are advanced in the literature linking multinationality with performance advantages over otherwise comparable firms operating in the domestic market alone [see *inter alia*, Kogut (1985), Benvignati (1987); Grant (1987); and Gomes and Ramaswamy (1999)]. These include: (i) better access to technological knowledge and foreign product innovation; (ii) wider international networks and management structure to meet domestic competition; (iii) benefits from economies of scale and scope; (iv) dampening domestic business fluctuations by using foreign market outlets; (v) taking advantage of factor cost differentials across multiple locations; (vi) tapping into corporate specific strategies such as transfer pricing and tax accounting practices; and (vii) greater geographic dispersion which facilitates the undertaking of domestic ventures that are high-risk but also highly profitable.

But the literature has also identified several reasons as to why the costs associated with expanding abroad might outweigh the potential benefits. Grant (1987) suggests that limits to the capacity of managers to cope successfully with greater complexity associated with multinationality may exert a negative impact on performance. Hitt et al (1997) also argue that multinationality may generate a decline in performance due to excessive spreading of managerial capabilities and co-ordination problems. Greniger et al. (1989) conjecture that an inverted-U relationship exists between the degree of multinationality and performance, where beyond an optimal degree of internalisation, profit advantages start to be eroded. In the same vein, Gomes and Ramaswamy (1999) contend that above a threshold level of multinationality, transactional and informational costs may exceed the benefits of diversification. However, Mathur et al. (2001) point out that due to potentially high initial costs of establishing abroad, there might be an initial performance decline followed by improvements, as average costs decline once economies of scale and scope are achieved. This line of argument predicts that the relationship between the degree of multinationality and performance is a U-shaped one.

[7] The development of the concept of firm-specific or proprietary assets can be attributed to a number of authors. See also Dunning (1977), Buckley and Casson (1976) and Caves (1971).

It is widely accepted that the starting point for explaining why some firms export and others do not is sunk costs. Entry costs associated with, for example, market research, product modification and compliance mean that profit maximising firms will only enter export markets if the present value of their profits exceeds the fixed costs of entry. Building on the work of Dixit (1989) and Krugman (1989), Roberts and Tybout (1996), Clerides, Lach and Tybout (1998) and Bernard and Jensen (2001) have developed dynamic optimising models to analyse entry and exit decisions of exporting firms. The sunk costs/entry models also offer a framework for gaining insight into an important dimension of firm behaviour, namely learning. There are plausible reasons for thinking that, having entered export markets, firms experience further growth. The central idea behind this is that a combination of learning from buyers, competition with other firms and generally gaining greater exposure to best practice results in cost improvements. As a consequence, exporters that were more efficient to start with become even more efficient by virtue of their presence in export markets. This then generates a testable proposition, that exports boost performance.[8]

Recently Helpman et al. (2003) have developed a model that allows for three *modi operandi* for firms: serving only the domestic market, exporting, or investing abroad to sell on the foreign market (FDI). The properties of the model of interest are generated through the assumptions of different costs (largely fixed costs) associated with serving the domestic market, and serving foreign markets (through FDI or exports), along with heterogeneity in the level of productivity across firms and imperfect competition. Before a firm can enter the industry it pays a fixed cost f_D. Upon entry it receives a level of labour productivity a drawn from a known distribution $G(a)$. Using its knowledge about the level of labour productivity the firm then chooses whether to serve the domestic market only, in which case it bears the fixed cost f_D, or to bear additional costs and serve foreign markets also. A productivity draw below the level necessary to make positive profits (zero for the marginal firm) leads the firm to exit the industry. Helpman et al (2003) show that in equilibrium the most efficient firms will engage in FDI while the least efficient will operate only in the domestic market. Firms with medium efficiency levels will become exporters, but not undertake FDI. This conclusion is consistent with Rugman (1974)'s early conjecture that multinationals are likely to enjoy greater competitive advantages than exporters since they diversify in both product and factor markets.

While this clear-cut ordering of firm's performance according to their involvement in international commerce emerges from the theory, one may of course not expect it to hold in all practical situations[9]. For example, due to uncertainty, firms may not immediately enter into exporting even if they have the necessary level of efficiency. Recently Head and Ries (2004) argue forcefully that factors other than the structure of international commerce should also be taken into account if one is to fully understand heterogeneous firm behaviour.

---

[8] This proposition has been exposed to micro level investigation in a number of recent studies. For example Aw and Hwang (1995) on Taiwan; Bernard and Jensen (1995) (1999) on the US; Clerides, Lach and Tybout (1998) on Colombia, Mexico and Morocco; Bernard and Wagner (1997) on Germany; Kraay (1999) on China; Castellini (2001) on Italy; Delgado, Farinos and Ruano (2002) on Spain and Girma at al (2004) on the U.K.

[9] Although this model is quite recent, it is already the subject of a number of empirical tests. These include Girma at al (2003) using UK data, Girma et al (2004a) using Irish data and Head and Ries (2004) based on Japanese firms.

III Multinationality Exporting and Employment: A Selective Review of the Empirical Literature

This section takes a brief look at the more recent empirical literature that examined the effects of multinational enterprises and exporting on employment growth. Two papers have tried to assess the causal impact of exporting on firm performance, including employment growth, with the aid of propensity score-matching techniques (e.g. see Rosenbaum and Rubin, 1983), which are often employed in the microeconometric evaluation problems[10]. These are Wagner (2002) for Germany and Girma et. al (2004b) for the U.K. Let Δy represents the growth rate of employment, and let $EXP_{it} \in \{0,1\}$ be an indicator (dummy variable) of whether firm i entered the export markets for the first time at time period t, and denote by Δy^1_{it+s} employment growth at time t+s, $s \geq 0$ following export markets entry. Also denote by Δy^0_{it+s} the outcome of firm i *had it not* started exporting. The causal effect of exporting for firm i at time period t + s is defined as:

$$\Delta y^1_{it+s} - \Delta y^0_{it+s} . \quad (1)$$

The fundamental problem of causal inference is that the quantity Δy^0_{it+s} is unobservable. Thus the analysis can be viewed as confronting a missing-data problem. In common to most of the microeconometric evaluation literature (cf. Heckman ET al, 1997), the *average* effect of exporting on export market entrants is defined as:

$$E\{\Delta y^1_{t+s} - \Delta y^0_{t+s} \mid EXP_{it} = 1\} = E\{\Delta y^1_{t+s} \mid EXP_{it} = 1\} - E\{\Delta y^0_{t+s} \mid EXP_{it} = 1\} \quad (2)$$

Causal inference relies on the construction of the counterfactual for the last term in equation (2), which is the outcome entrants would have experienced, on average, had they not participated in export markets. The counterfactual is estimated by the corresponding average value of firms that remain non-exporters: $E\{\Delta y^0_{it+s} \mid EXP = 0\}$.

An important feature in the construction of the counterfactual is the selection of a valid control group. We assume that all the difference in Δy (bar that caused by exporting) between exporters and the appropriately selected control group is captured by a vector of observables X and the pre-entry *level* of the outcome variable y_{it-1}. The basic idea of matching is then to select from the reservoir of non-exporters those firms in which the distribution of the variables affecting the outcome variable is as similar as possible to the distribution of the exporting firm. To do so, the 'propensity score matching' method of Rosenbaum and Rubin (1983) is adopted. For example, Girma et. al (2004b) identify the probability of exporting (or 'propensity score') for all firms using the following probit model

[10] For a comprehensive review on the microeconometric evaluation literature see Blundell and Costa Dias (2000). Matching techniques are especially popular in applied labour economics, where, for example, the aim of the study is the evaluation of training programmes on earnings.

$$P(EXP_{it}=1)=F(TFP_{it-1}, size_{it-1}, ownweship_{it-1}, wages_{it-1}) \tag{3}$$

Here F is the normal cumulative distribution function, and the full set of regional, sectoral and time dummies is also included[11]. Let P_{it} denote the predicted probability of exporting at t for firm i, which is an actual (eventual) exporter. A non-exporting firm j, which is 'closest' in terms of its 'propensity score' to an exporting firm, is then selected as a match for the former, using the 'nearest-neighbour' matching method. More formally, at each point in time and for each new exporter i, a non-exporting firm j is selected such that[12]

$$\left|P_{it}-P_{jt}\right|=\min_{k\in\{EXP_{kt}=0\}}\left\{P_{it}-P_{jt}\right\} \tag{4}$$

This type of matching procedure is preferable to randomly or indiscriminately choosing the comparison group because it is less likely to suffer from selection bias by picking firms with markedly different characteristics.

The upshot from these studies is as follows: In the case of the U.K Girma et al (2004b) report that export market entrants typically exhibit higher employment growth than non-exporters before they start exporting, but their employment growth is further boosted as a direct result of exporting. However this beneficial effect of exporting appears to be confined to the first post-entry year. This finding is consistent with Wagner (2002)'s finding that exporting has positive influence on employment growth for Germany. This has led him to conclude that "... to export seems a good thing to do ".

Using a more traditional regression analysis framework, Bernard and Jensen (1997) show that not only fast growing U.S plants tend to self-select themselves into exports markets, but they also experience higher employment growth than non-exporters once they start exporting. Bernard and Jensen (1997) also identify a reward from exporting, namely it increases the probability of plant survival, hence contributing to the stability of many jobs.

A separate strand of the literature has sought to establish whether foreign direct investment leads to employment growth. Although it has long been known that multinational firms are generally bigger than domestically owned enterprises (see Cave, 1996 for an extensive review), the issue of establishing a causal relationship between multinationality and employment growth is still an under-researched topic. However there are two papers that made some progress in this direction. Conyon et al (2002) examine the productivity, wage and employment effects of the foreign acquisition of existing UK manufacturing firms. They assume that foreign take-over leaves most industry and plant characteristics unchanged, at least for the medium term. Accordingly, by observing employment changes before and after the event of acquisition, they argue that it should be possible to isolate that component of performance that is solely due to a multinationality status. Their paper employs a panel design that allows firms subject to domestic acquisition and those subject to no ownership changes to be used as controls, firm level fixed effects to be removed, and for the inclusion of year dummies to control for cyclical factors. Conyon et al (2002) report the labour demand of the

[11] It goes without saying that the success of the matching method depends on correctly identifying the variables that determine export participation.

[12] A non-exporting firm can be match to more than one exporting firms

typical firm decreased by 6.2 percent during the years following foreign acquisition. In a similar vein, Girma and Görg (2002) investigate whether the acquisition of a domestic establishment by a foreign owner has any effects on the survival prospects and employment growth of that plant. Their analysis uses plant level data for the UK electronics and food industries for the period 1980 to 1993, and possible endogeneity is controlled for using a matched sample of plants and appropriate instrumental variables. Based on estimates from a standard hazard model, Girma and Görg (2002) conclude that foreign take-over reduces the lifetime of the acquired plant in both the electronics and food sectors. Furthermore, an analysis of the determinants of employment growth in domestic plants provide some evidence that the incidence of foreign take-over *reduces* employment growth, in particular for unskilled labour in the electronics industry. However, no significant post-acquisition employment effect was found in the food sector.

As the above brief review of the existing literature shows there are no studies that deal with the effects of cross-border investment and exporting on employment dynamics in a unified framework. The present chapter is partly motivated by the desire to bridge this gap in the literature. In the next section we describe the database we used in our attempt to deal with this issue.

IV Database Construction and Some Sample Characteristics

The primary source of information for this study is the *OneSource* database of private and public companies, which is derived from the accounts that companies are legally required to deposit at Companies House. All public limited companies, all companies with employees greater than 50, and the top companies based on turnover, net worth, total assets, or shareholders funds (whichever is largest) up to a maximum of 110,000 companies are included in the database. Companies that are dissolved or in the process of liquidation are excluded. Thus the database is heavily biased towards the larger firms. This may or may not be a major problem depending on the purpose at hand. We believe that the fact that *OneSource* under-represents firms with less than 50 employees is not too problematic for the purpose of this paper. Multinational and exporting firms generally employ more than 50 workers, and comparing their performance with similar (in terms of size) domestic firms actually makes sense.

The database provides information on employment, physical capital and output in a consistent way both across firms and across time. It is also one of the very few databases with firm level export data. However, each edition of *OneSource* contains foreign-ownership indicators for the latest year alone[13], so that it is not possible to identify when a firm became a subsidiary of a foreign multinational. To track the dynamics of ownership, we matched the population of manufacturing firms in the database to a list of U.K. firms acquired by foreign multinationals[14]. *OneSource* does not provide any information on the multinational activity of U.K-owned firms either. Fortunately enough we were able to merge it with a newly created database of foreign multinational activity: the European Linkages and International

[13] For this study we used the *OneSource* CD-ROM entitled "UK companies, Vol. 1", for October 2000.

[14] This information, which is in hard copy format, is obtained from the Office of National Statistics upon special request. The matching process required considerable effort, and Girma wishes to thank Mehtap Hisarciklilar for helping him in this regard.

Ownership Structure (ELIOS) database built at the University of Urbino[15]. The information obtained from ELIOS was also complemented with a list of U.K firms that made foreign acquisitions, compiled from various issues of *Acquisitions Monthly*.

We focus on manufacturing subsidiaries of domestic and foreign companies, and independent domestic producers that do not own any subsidiaries[16]. Firms with annual employment or output growth exceeding 100% were omitted, given doubts about the reliability of these extreme data points. Our final sample contains information on an unbalanced panel of more than 11000 firms over the period 1990 to 1998, and it was divided into seven types of firms: domestic non-exporters, low exporters (defined as domestic firms with export intensity less than 5%), medium exporters (defined as domestic firms with export intensity between 5% and 33%), high exporters (domestic firms that export more than a third of their output), UK-owned MNEs, US-owned MNEs and MNEs from all other countries. Table 1 gives the frequency distribution of these firms by type of ownership and year, ranging from 4801 in 1990 to 8929 is 1998.

Table 1: Frequency of firms by type of ownership

	Exporters				Multinationals			
Year	**Non**	**Low**	**Medium**	**High**	**U.K.**	**USA**	**Others**	**Total**
1990	2778	309	471	278	247	226	492	4801
1991	3041	351	584	332	262	236	513	5319
1992	3258	398	635	384	268	244	528	5715
1993	3442	423	692	445	287	259	546	6094
1994	3594	441	760	485	304	267	566	6417
1995	3734	467	825	539	333	277	580	6755
1996	3829	531	895	586	354	302	591	7088
1997	4722	727	1323	888	390	310	483	8843
1998	4874	749	1290	869	393	290	461	8926

Table 2 presents the number of firm observations in each of the two-digit manufacturing sectors, and Table 3 provides summary statistics of some variables of interest by type of international commerce activity.

The raw data show that within exporting firms, medium exporters enjoy the highest level of employment and labour productivity. It can also be seen that multinationals are on average bigger than exporters and non-exporters.

V Non-parametric Analysis

To test whether employment patterns are different across exporters, multinationals and firms that serve domestic markets alone, we adopt the nonparametric one-sided and two-sided Kolmogorov-Smirnov tests (e.g. Covonor, 1999; Sprent 1989). These tests rank the

---

[15] Girma wishes to express his gratitude to Davide Castellani and Antonello Zanfei for allowing him to use some information from this database.

[16] Parent companies were omitted if they have consolidated accounts as this leads to double counting.

employment distributions using the concept of stochastic dominance. To establish stochastic dominance requires that the employment level of each type of firms differ across all moments of the distribution. This therefore provides a stricter test of equality than simply comparing mean levels of employment.

Table 2: Number of observation by 2-digit SIC industry

	Exporting Status				Multinationals			
2-digit SIC92 industry	**Non**	**Low**	**Medium**	**High**	**U.K.**	**USA**	**Others**	**Total**
15: Food and beverages	3010	310	284	134	161	120	380	4399
17: Textiles	1346	288	508	222	119	56	99	2638
18: Clothing	950	173	264	117	59	6	39	1608
19: Leather, Luggage and footwear	346	22	40	47	22	9	18	504
20: Wood, straw and plaiting materials	988	105	113	11	25	7	55	1304
21: Pulp, paper and paper products	875	115	134	99	60	95	307	1685
22: Publishing, printing and media	5823	334	439	337	125	202	395	7655
23: Coke, refined petroleum and nuclear fuel	81	2	7	4	2	18	25	139
24: Chemicals and chemical products	1470	201	503	468	220	259	376	3497
25: Rubber and plastic products	2099	402	681	135	190	105	444	4056
26: Other non metallic mineral products	1011	91	201	105	128	30	145	1711
27: Basic metals	1043	157	356	163	94	59	182	2054
28: Fabricated metal products	4533	699	926	302	430	234	359	7483
29: Machinery and equipment	2905	411	1034	1008	416	400	576	6750
30: Office machinery and computers	474	65	83	110	43	36	123	934
31: Electrical machinery and apparatus	1178	185	450	248	180	152	197	2590
32: Radio, TV and communication equipment	709	116	262	266	158	159	227	1897
33: Medical, precision and optical instruments	1016	90	336	554	210	188	317	2711
34: Motor vehicles, trailers and semi-trailers	918	147	254	133	96	90	249	1887
35; Other transport equipment	740	92	196	207	48	96	155	1534
36: Manufacturing not classified elsewhere	1757	391	404	136	52	90	92	2922

Table 3: Summary Statistics

	Exporting Status								Multinationals					
	Non		Low		Medium		High		U.K.		USA		Others	
Variable	**Mean**	**Std. Dev.**	**Mean**	**Std. Dev.**	**Mean**	**Std. Dev.**	**Mean**	**Std. Dev.**	**Mean**	**Std. Dev.**	**Mean**	**Std. Dev.**	**Mean**	**Std. Dev.**
Log Labour Productivity	4.1939	0.7926	4.2652	0.7022	4.48[illegible]9	0.6866	4.4696	0.6895	4.2385	0.6589	4.2181	0.6378	4.3331	0.7756
Log Employment	4.2848	1.3117	4.8967	0.2883	5.36[illegible]7	1.3979	5.085	1.2061	4.5378	1.0562	4.6839	1.1339	4.5898	1.2514
Log Wage	2.6715	0.4559	2.6936	0.3375	2.83[illegible]3	0.316	2.7791	0.3641	2.6578	0.3464	2.6728	0.3191	2.7575	0.5024
Capital Labour Ratio	7293.5	320053	2826.2	19970	2582[illegible]3	4466.1	2356	3121	1760.5	5101	1579.7	2936.7	1714.3	3140.4

To perform this test we define two cumulative distribution functions F and G. F corresponds to the group of interest, for example domestically owned exporters, and G the comparison group, for example US multinationals. First-order stochastic dominance of F with respect to G is defined as: $F(z)-G(z)\leq 0$ uniformly in $z\in\Re$, with strict equality for some z. The two-sided Kolmogorov-Smirnov statistic tests the hypothesis that both distributions are identical, and the null and alternative hypotheses can be expressed as:

$$H_0 : F(z)-G(z)=0\ \forall z\in\Re \text{ vs. } H_1 : F(z)-G(z)\neq 0 \text{ for some } z\in\Re. \quad (5)$$

By contrast, the one-sided test of stochastic dominance can be formulated as:

$$H_0 : F(z)-G(z)\leq 0\ \forall z\in\Re \text{ vs. } H_1 : F(z)-G(z)> 0 \text{ for some } z\in\Re. \quad (6)$$

For the one-sided test, for example, the Kolmogorov-Smirnov statistic is given by $KS=\sqrt{\frac{n.m}{N}}\max_{1\leq i\leq N}\left|F_n(z_i)-G_m(z_i)\right|$, where n and m are the sample sizes from the empirical distributions of F and G respectively, and $N = n+m$. Acceptance of the null hypothesis (6) implies that the distribution of F is to right of G. In this case, F is said to stochastically dominate G.

Because the limiting distribution of the Kolmogorov-Smirnov statistics is only known under independence of observations, it is more appropriate to apply the testing procedure on cross section by cross section basis, rather on the pooled panel where within-firm dependence is likely to exist. For two selected years (the first and last years in the sample) Table 4 summarises the findings from the Kolmogrov-Smirnov tests for employment level differentials between the various comparison groups.

In general we find a strong support for the heterogeneous firm model, there is a clear ordering of employment levels according to the type of commerce. The cumulative employment distribution of multinational firms lies to the right of that of exporting firms, which in turn is to the right of that of non-exporting enterprises. But there are also significant differences within multinationals. For example, the employment distribution of U.S multinationals dominates that all other multinationals. By contrast the difference within exporters is not that clear cut, although for 1998 medium exporters appear to have the most dominant size distribution.

We have presented graphical depictions of selected pairs of estimated distribution functions to allow for easy visual comparisons of employment distributions.

Figure 1 (Figure 2) shows that the cumulative distribution function of US multinationals (medium exporters) is well to the right of the distribution function of high exporters (non-exporters), implying that distribution of the former stochastically dominates that of the latter. By contrast Figures 3 and 4 offer examples of non-dominance of one distribution by another, as the distribution functions overlap at least.

Table 4: Kolmogorov-Smirnov test statistics of employment level differences for selected years

Dominant group						
UK MNEs	**US MNEs**	**Non-US MNEs**	**High exporters**	**Medium exporters**	**Low exporters**	**Non-exporters**
Dominated group in 1990:						
High exporters	Non-US MNEs	High exporters	Non-exporters	Non-exporters	Non-exporters	
Low exporters	UK MNEs	Low exporters				
Medium exporters	High exporters	Non-exporters				
Non-exporters	Low exporters					
	Medium exporters					
	Non-exporters					
Dominated group in 1998:						
High exporters	Non-US MNEs	UK MNEs	Non-exporters	High exporters	Non-exporters	
Low exporters	UK MNEs	High exporters		Low exporters		
Non-exporters	High exporters	Low exporters		Non-exporters		
	Low exporters	Non-exporters				
	Medium exporters					
	Non-exporters					

Note: Inference is based on tests with 5% level of significance.

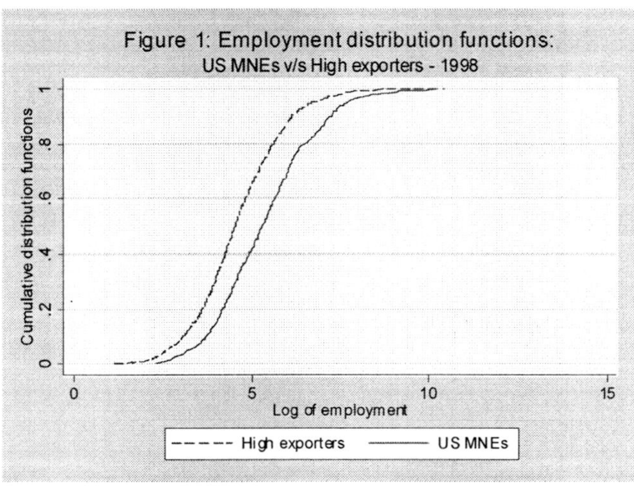

Figure 1: Employment distribution functions: US MNEs v/s High exporters - 1998

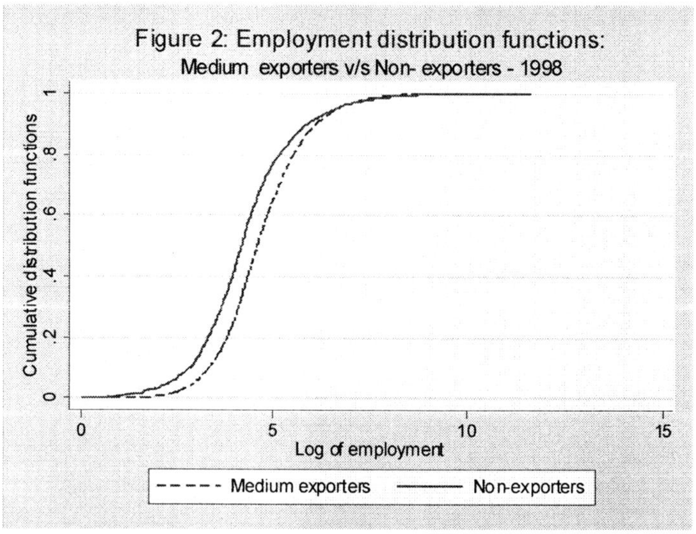

Figure 2: Employment distribution functions:
Medium exporters v/s Non- exporters - 1998
Cumulative distribution functions
0
.2
.4
.6
.8
1
0
5
10
15
Log of employment
Medium exporters
Non-exporters

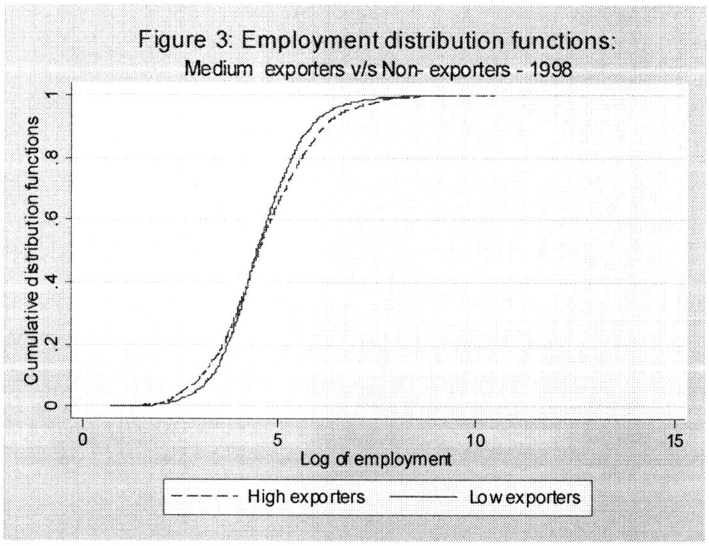

Figure 3: Employment distribution functions:
Medium exporters v/s Non- exporters - 1998
Cumulative distribution functions
0
.2
.4
.6
.8
1
0
5
10
15
Log of employment
High exporters
Low exporters

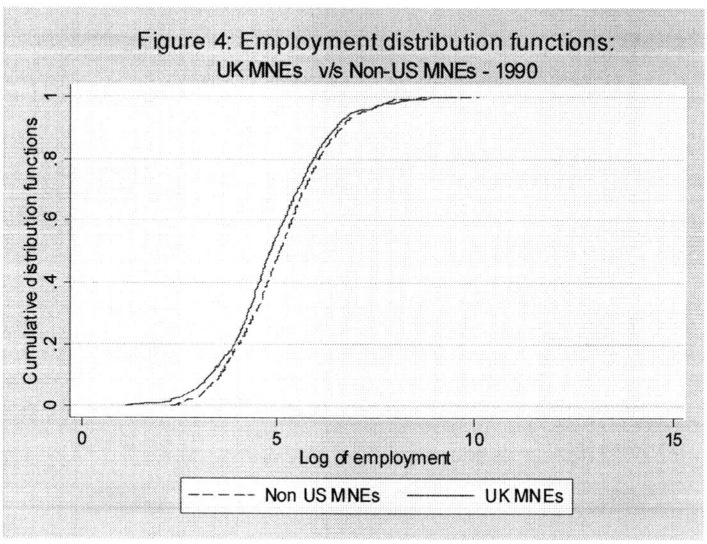

Figure 4: Employment distribution functions:
UK MNEs v/s Non-US MNEs - 1990
Cumulative distribution functions
0
.2
.4
.6
.8
1
0
5
10
15
Log of employment
Non US MNEs
UK MNEs

VI Modelling Employment Growth Differentials

In order to investigate the role of the structure of international commerce in mediating firm growth we estimate the following employment growth (ΔEMP) equation:

$$\Delta EMP_{it} = \alpha EMP_{it-1} + \beta' X_{it-1} + \sum_{k=1}^{6} \gamma_k TYPE_k + D_t + D_j + \varepsilon_{it} \tag{7}$$

In the above equation *i, t* and *j* index firms , time periods and two-digit industries respectively, EMP_{it-1} captures initial level of employment[1]. On the other hand, *X* is a vector of variables hypothesised to impact on firm level employment growth trajectories, namely firm level wage growth , capital growth and the age of the firm. The higher the rate of growth of the wage faced by the firm, the lower employment growth is expected to be. Also to the extent that capital and labour are complements, a positive association between employment and capital growth rates is expected. The inclusion of age in the list of covariates is motivated by the finding in the literature that younger firms tend to grow faster than older ones.

The vectors D_j and D_t in Equation (7) denote the full set of industry and time dummies respectively, and ε is a random error term. The use of industry dummies helps mitigate concerns that firm growth rates might be a function of unobserved industry characteristics, whereas time dummies are designed to capture aggregate labour demand shocks.

The TYPE variables in our estimating equation are defined as the relevant dummies for the six types of firms (domestic non-exporters are chosen to be the base group). Thus the γ's are the main parameters of interest in this study as they capture the employment growth rate differentials across the various firm types.

We start by estimating Equation (7) via OLS with heteroskedasticity and within-firm serial correlation robust standard errors. This is essentially a conditional mean regression, and the resulting estimates can be interpreted as the average employment growth differences with respect to the average domestic non-exporting firm. However, standard techniques that concentrate on the conditional mean function of the dependent variable are unlikely to be adequate analytical tools in the presence of heterogeneous employment growth processes. It is more appropriate (and arguably more interesting) to examine the dynamics of employment productivity at different points of the distribution rather than "average" properties (i.e. conditional means). To address this concern, we also consider median regression technique that is a special case of the semiparametric method of quantile regressions (see Buchinski,1998, for an excellent review of the literature). Subsuming all regressors in a matrix Z, the median regression estimator solves the following minimisation problem:

$$\min_{\beta} \frac{1}{n} \left\{ \sum_{i,t} \left| \Delta EMP_{it} - Z'_{it} \beta \right| \right\} \tag{8}$$

[1] Thus a negative α would imply that larger firms grow less rapidly than smaller ones, consistent with the reversion to mean hypothesis.

Thus in contrast to OLS, the sum of the absolute values of the residuals is minimised, and for this reason this method is also known as the Least Absolute Deviations regression.

Another problem frequently encountered in estimation relates to outliers. There are two definitions according to which an observation can be considered an outlier. A 'response outlier' occurs when the dependent variable (y_i) takes on a value that is unusual, given the explanatory variables (x_i's). In other words, y_i is not close to $E(y/x_i)$ - it is in the tail of the distribution of y given $x = x_i$. A 'design outlier' occurs when an explanatory variable is much different, either very small or very large, in comparison to the remainder of the data, that is, x_i is not close to other observations on x. The inclusion or exclusion of outliers, especially if the sample size is small, can substantially alter the results of regression analysis. If useful generalisations are to be drawn, it is important to ensure that the results reflect what is going on in the majority of the sample rather than being driven by a few outlying observations only. For this reason we also deploy a third estimation strategy in this study: outlier robust regression.

In the empirical literature, various approaches have been used to address the issue of outliers. In some cases, the regression model is re-estimated iteratively omitting one observation at a time with the aim of identifying the one that exerts a significant influence on the set of estimates. This is known as the 'deletion method'. But this would clearly be quite a cumbersome process, especially for a large data se like ours. Another approach is to exclude observations with high residuals from the sample. Both procedures can be seen as part of a sensitivity analysis after the main results have been obtained. It is also quite common to omit data points with extreme values of the explanatory variables, where for example observations that are three standard deviations away from the mean value are defined as extreme values. There is of course an element of subjectivity associated with this definition. In this chapter we have chosen an alternative method – robust regression (Rousseeuw and Leroy, 1987), a three-step procedure to deal with outliers. The first step involves estimating the regression and calculating Cook's Distance measure of influence. Cook's D for the ith observation is a measure of the distance between the coefficient estimates when observation i is included and when it is not, and it is defined as

$$D_i = \frac{\hat{e}_{si}^2 (s_{pi} / s_{ri})^2}{k} \tag{9}$$

where $\hat{e}_{si}$ refers to standardized residuals, s_{ri} to standard error of the residuals and s_{pi} to standard error of prediction. k represents the number of independent variables including the intercept term.

High values of Cook's D imply that the ith observation has significant influence on estimation results, therefore, can be deemed to be an outlier. The second step in robust regressions is to screen data points in search of such outliers and eliminates observations for which Cook's distance exceeds 1 – these are the gross outliers. Thereafter, robust regression involves an iterative weighted least squares method whereby the outliers are identified and weights are assigned to the observations.

The results from the three estimation strategies outlined above are reported in Table 5. The estimated coefficients of initial employment are negative in all specifications. This is consistent with the notion of convergence in size (or reversion to the mean). Conditional on initial employment, older firms grow at a slower rate, but the magnitudes of the point estimates imply that the between-ages difference might not be practically important. The results also suggest that capital growth exerts an employment enhancing influence. As expected, firms level employment demand is negatively correlated with wage growth.

Table 5 The relationship between international commerce and employment growth

	Dependent variables: Employment Growth		
	OLS with robust standard errors	Median regression	Outlier robust regression
Initial employment	-0.037	-0.015	-0.015
	(23.67)***	(33.44)***	(34.46)***
Wage growth	-0.185	-0.084	-0.072
	(8.40)***	(33.87)***	(29.63)***
Capital growth	0.150	0.111	0.093
	(14.36)***	(97.85)***	(83.06)***
Age *1000	-0.576	-0.369	-0.399
	(10.04)***	(14.68)***	(16.20)***
Non US MNEs	0.008	0.001	0.002
	(1.68)*	(0.40)	(1.14)
UK MNEs	0.018	0.003	0.002
	(3.26)***	(1.12)	(0.92)
USA MNEs	0.032	0.006	0.003
	(5.22)***	(2.03)**	(0.99)
High exporters	0.012	0.006	0.006
	(2.81)***	(2.90)***	(2.82)***
Medium exporters	0.017	0.004	0.003
	(4.69)***	(2.03)**	(1.53)
Low exporters	0.005	0.001	0.004
	(1.24)	(0.70)	(1.93)*
Constant	0.201	0.100	0.104
	(26.68)***	(37.72)***	(39.71)***
Observations	47374	47374	47374
R-squared	0.15		0.20

Notes:
Robust t-statistics in parentheses
significant at 10%; ** significant at 5%; *** significant at 1%
All regressions control for time and industry effects.

Although the conditional mean model suggests a positive correlation between multinationality and employment growth, this result is not robust to alternative specifications. In the outlier robust model, for example, none of the multinationality indicators attracts a statistically significant coefficient. By contrast high exporters (i.e. exporters that ship more than a third of their output abroad) are associated with higher employment growth, *ceteris paribus,* and this conclusion is not sensitive to the estimation technique that is deployed. Medium exporters are also associated with higher growth, expect in the outlier robust model.

Interestingly, low exporters appear to have a higher than average employment growth in the outlier robust model only. Overall our regression estimates point to the conclusions that (i) multinationality and employment growth are not necessarily positively correlated, and (ii) the more a firm exports, the stronger the exporting-employment growth nexus seems to be.

But clearly the above conclusions do not allow us to make any causal inference regarding the relationship between multinationality, exporting and employment growth. In the next section we make an attempt at identifying the direction of causality between international commerce and employment dynamics.

VIIIn Search of a Causal Relationship between Exporting, Cross-Border Investment and Employment Growth

The results reported in the previous section are supportive of the notion that international commerce activity and firm growth are positively correlated. In this section we refine the analysis further and isolate the causal impact of multinationality and exporting on the growth of employment. The following equation is estimated to this end:

$$\Delta EMP_{it} = \alpha EMP_{it-1} + \beta' X_{it-1} + \sum_{k=1}^{4} \gamma_k PRE_k + \sum_{k=q}^{4} \delta_k POST_k + D_t + D_j + \varepsilon_{it} \quad (10)$$

Most of the variables in this equation are defined as in Equation (7) above. However here we have introduced two 4×1 vectors of dummies designed to capture the international commerce entry effects (POST) and the pre-entry employment growth characteristics (PRE). The four distinct entry modes considered in this study are: acquisition by US, non-US and UK multinationals and new export market participation. The PRE dummies help identify whether the employment growth rates of the newly acquired firms or new exporters are different from the average sample value in the pre entry period. For example, a positive coefficient on the pre-export entry variable would be consistent with the hypothesis that faster growing firms self-select themselves into exporting. On the other hand, the POST variables isolate the causal impact of international commerce on employment. For instance, a positive coefficient on the post-US MNE acquisition variable would indicate that firms acquired by US multinationals benefit in the form of higher employment growth as a direct result of becoming multinational subsidiaries.

The sample for this exercise is restricted to new export market entrants, to new multinational subsidiaries and to non-exporting domestically owned firms. The latter group of firms are used a control group, and the remaining firms can be seen as the "treatment" group. The sample of acquired firms was screened for data availability for at least two years before and after the acquisition/entry event, and in the final analysis we identified 639 new export markets entrants and 758 multinational acquisitions. The frequency distribution of these events is given in Table 6. The control group consists of about 3600 domestic non-exporting firms that did not experience any type of ownership change. Three versions of Equation (10) are also estimated: OLS with robust standard errors, least absolute deviations (median) and outlier robust regressions, and the parameter estimates are reported in Table 7.

Table 6 Frequency distribution of firms by mode of international commerce entry

		Acquired by:		
Year	*New Exporters*	*UK MNE*	*USA MNE*	*Non-Us MNE*
1990	0	49	12	47
1991	119	44	21	52
1992	105	48	5	64
1993	104	30	19	32
1994	95	41	30	64
1995	95	32	33	47
1996	121	30	20	38
Total	639	274	140	344

Table 7 The causal effects of international commerce on employment growth

	Dependent variables: Employment Growth		
	OLS with robust standard errors	*Median regression*	*Outlier robust*
Initial employment	-0.036	-0.014	-0.015
	(18.41)***	(26.68)***	(25.69)***
Wage growth	-0.227	-0.104	-0.089
	(8.09)***	(34.94)***	(27.83)***
Capital growth	0.163	0.114	0.093
	(12.07)***	(81.01)***	(60.85)***
Age *1000	-0.647	-0.401	-0.432
	(8.30)***	(12.95)***	(12.94)***
Pre US acquisition	0.018	-0.002	0.007
	(1.06)	(0.22)	(0.66)
Pre non US acquisition	-0.001	-0.011	-0.012
	(0.13)	(1.83)*	(1.74)*
Pre UM MNE acquisition	-0.025	-0.005	-0.001
	(1.67)*	(0.68)	(0.12)
Pre export market entry	0.035	0.009	0.010
	(3.28)***	(1.98)**	(2.07)**
Post US acquisition	0.037	0.008	0.004
	(3.11)***	(1.45)	(0.62)
Post non US acquisition	0.020	0.012	0.012
	(2.34)**	(2.99)***	(2.80)***
Post UM MNE acquisition	0.012	0.009	0.007
	(1.02)	(1.82)*	(1.26)
Post export market entry	0.044	0.022	0.023
	(5.72)***	(7.05)***	(6.90)***
Constant	0.208	0.104	0.109
	(21.35)***	(32.98)***	(32.20)***
Observations	28996	28996	28996
R-squared	0.17		0.19

Notes: Robust t-statistics in parentheses
significant at 10%; ** significant at 5%; *** significant at 1%
All regressions control for time and industry effects.

Starting our discussion with the causal impact of exporting, it can be seen from Table 7 that export markets entry led to a significant increase in both average and median employment growth among exporters. Employment growth is an estimated 4.4 and 2.2% per cent per annum higher for the average and median exporters compared to non-exporting firms. Even after controlling for the influence of extreme observations, the employment creating effect of exporting is found to be as impressive. This result is the more remarkable given that new exporters exhibited higher than average or median employment growth prior to entering the export markets. For example according to the outlier robust model, the growth rate of these firms was one percentage point higher compared with otherwise equivalent enterprises.

The results from the multinational acquisitions are not as impressive though. We find weak evidence that U.K multinationals tend to target firms with below average employment growth, and the post-acquisition median employment growth of these targets is higher by about one percentage point. However this result is not robust when one takes into account of the effect influential observations. Non-US acquirers also appear to take over relatively slow growing firms, but unlike the case with acquisition by U.K multinationals we detect a robust employment enhancing effects. The average (median) non-US MNE acquired firm grows by more than 2 (1.2) percentage points than would otherwise been the case. Finally we find that acquisition by US multinationals appears to lead to a higher than average employment growth. But this apparent positive result is driven by outliers, as no discernible employment generating impact is found when the median and outlier robust models are estimated.

So what are we to make of the results? On the basis of the present evidence exporting is the most important source of employment growth, and this appears to vindicate U.K policy makers effort to encourage domestic firms to export. Our findings also suggest that the causal role of cross border investment in employment creation should perhaps not be overestimated.

VIII Conclusion

The research described in this chapter has provided a systematic microeconometric analysis of the impact of multinationality and exporting on firm level employment growth in the U.K manufacturing industry for the period 1990-1998. It has identified an economically significant employment growth following export markets entry, and a modest job creation effect following acquisitions by non-U.K and non-US multinationals.

One caveat of this study is that it did not examine the causal impact of international commerce on firm survival, hence the stability of the jobs. It is therefore important to consider this issue in future work in order to get a more complete picture of the long-term effects of exporting and cross-border investment on employment dynamics.

References

Aw, B.Y. and Hwang, A.R. (1995), Productivity in the export market: A firm level analysis, *Journal of Development Economics*, **47**, pp.131-332.

Benvignati, A.M. (1987), Domestic profit advantages of multinational firms. *Journal of Business*, **60**, pp. 449-461.

Bernard, A. and Jensen, J.B. (1995), Exporters, jobs and wages in US manufacturing: 1976-1987, *Brookings Papers on Economic Activity, Microeconomics 1995*, pp.67-119.

Bernard, A. and Jensen, J. (1999), Exceptional exporters performance: cause, effect or both? *Journal of International Economics*, **47**, pp. 1-25.

Bernard, A. and Jensen, J. (2001), Why Some Firms Export, *NBER Working Paper* No. **8349**.

Bernard, A. and Wagner, J. (1997), Exports and success in German manufacturing, *Weltwirtschaftliches Archiv*, **133**, pp. 134-157.

Blomstrom, M and Kokko, A. (2003), The economics of foreign direct investment incentives, *NBER Working Paper* No. **9489**

Buchinski, M. (1998). Recent advances in quantile regression models. *Journal of Human Resources*, **33**, pp. 88-126.

Buckley, P.J. and Casson, M. (1976). *The future of the Multinational Enterprise*. London: Macmillan.

Castellani, D. (2002), Export behaviour and productivity growth: Evidence from Italian manufacturing Firms, *Weltwirtschaftliches Archiv*, **138**, pp.605-628.

Caves, R.E. (1971). International comparisons: the industrial economics of foreign investment. *Economica*, **38**, pp. 1-27.

Caves, R. E. (1996), *Multinational enterprise and economic analysis*, Cambridge Surveys of Economic Literature, 2nd Edition, Cambridge University Press.

Clerides, S., Lach,S. and Tybout, J. (1998), Is learning by exporting important? Micro-dynamic evidence from Columbia, Mexico and Morocco, *Quarterly Journal of Economics*, **113**, pp.903-948.

Conover, W. J. (1999), *Practical Nonparametric Statistics*, New York: John Wiley &Son

Conyon, M.J., Girma, S., Thompson, S. and Wright, P.W (2002). The productivity and wage effects of foreign acquisition in the United Kingdom. *Journal of Industrial Economics*, pp. 85-102

Delgado, M., Farinas, J. and Ruano, S. (2002) Firm productivity and export markets: A Non-Parametric approach, *Journal of International Economics* **57**(2), pp. 397-422

Dixit, A. (1989), Entry and exit decisions under uncertainty, *Journal of Political Economy,* Vol. 97, No.3, pp. 620-638

Doms, M.E. and. Jensen, J.B (1998), Comparing wages, skills, and productivity between domestically and foreign-owned manufacturing establishments in the United States. In R. Baldwin, R. Lipsey and J.D. Richardson (eds.), *Geography and Ownership as Bases for Economic Accounting*, Chicago: Chicago University Press.

Dunning, J.H. (1977), Trade, location of economic activity and MNE: a search for an eclectic approach. In B. Ohlin, P.O. Hesselborn and P.M. Wijkman (eds.) *The international allocation of economic activity*, London: Macmillan

Girma, S. and Görg, H. (2002), Blessing or curse? Domestic plants employment and survival prospects after foreign acquisitions, *CEPR Discussion Paper DP 2994*

Girma, S., Görg, H., and Strobl, E. (2004a), Exports, international investment, and plant performance: Evidence from a non-parametric test, Forthcoming in *Economics Letters*.

Girma, S., Greenaway, D and Kneller, R. (2004b), Does exporting lead to better performance? A microecometric analysis of matched firms, *Review of International Economics,* Forthcoming.

Girma, S., R. Kneller and M. Pisu (2003), "Exports versus FDI: An empirical test", Research Paper 2003/21, University of Nottingham

Grant, R.M (1987), Multinationality and performance among British manufacturing companies. *Journal of International Business Studies,* **18** , 79-89.

Greniger, J.M., Beamish, P.W., and da Costas, R.C. (1989), Diversification strategy and internalization: implication for MNE performance. *Strategic Management Journal,* **10**, 109-119.

Griffith, R. and Simpson, H. (2002), Characteristics of foreign-owned firms in British manufacturing. In R. Blundell, D. Card and R. Freeman (eds.), *Creating a Premier League Economy*, Chicago: Chicago University Press.

Gomes, L. and Ramaswamy, K. (1999), An empirical examination of the form of the relationship between multinationality and performance, *Journal of International Business Studies,* **30**, pp. 173-188.

Head, K. and Ries, J., (2004), Heterogeneity and the FDI versus export decision of Japanese manufacturers, Forthcoming in *Journal of the Japanese and International Economics.*

Heckman, J., Ichimura, H., Smith, J. and Todd, P. (1997), Matching as an econometric evaluation estimator: Evidence from evaluating a job training programme, *Review of Economic Studies* Vol. 64, pp.605-654.

Helpman E., Melitz M.J., and S.R. Yeaple (2003), Export versus FDI with heterogeneous firms, *American Economic Review*, forthcoming.

Hitt, M.A., Hoskisson,R.E and Kim, H. (1997), International diversification: effects on innovation and firm performance in product diversified firms. *Academy of Management Journal*, **40**, pp. 767-798.

Hymer, S.H. (1976), *The International Operations of National Firms: A Study of Direct Foreign Investment.* Boston: MIT press.

Kindleberger, C.P. (1969). *American Business Abroad: Six Lectures on Direct Investment.* New Haven: Yale University Press.

Kogut, B (1985), Designing global strategies: profiting from operational flexibility. *Sloan Management Review*, **26**, pp. 27-38.

Kraay, A. (1999), Exports and economic performance: Evidence from a panel of Chinese enterprises, mimeo World Bank.

Krugman, P. (1989), *Exchange rate instability*, MIT press, Cambridge MA.

Mathur, I., Singh, M. and Kinberly, C.G. (2001), The evidence from Canadian firms on multinational diversification and performance. *The Quarterly Review of Economics and Finance*, **41**, 561-578

Melitz M.J. (2003), The impact of trade on intra-industry reallocations and aggregate industry productivity, *Econometrica,* Forthcoming

Roberts, M. and Tybout, J. (1997), The decision to export in Columbia: An empirical model of entry with suck costs, *American Economic Review* **87**(4), pp. 545-564.

Rosenbaum, P. and Rubin, D.B (1983). The central role of the propensity score in observational studies for causal effects, *Biometrika*, **70**, pp.41-55.

Rousseeuw, P. J. and A. M. Leroy (1987), *Robust Regression and Outlier Detection*, John Wiley, New York

Rugman, A.M. (1974), Motivation for foreign investment: The market imperfections and risk diversification hypotheses. *Journal of World Trade Law*, **9**, pp. 567-673.

Sprent P. (1989), *Applied Nonparametric Statistical Methods*, Chapman and Hall: London.

Wagner, J (2002), The causal effects of exports on firm size and labour productivity: first evidence from a matching approach, *Economic Letters,* Vol. 77, 287-292.

In: International Trade Issues
Editor: Robert. V. Weeks, pp. 227-249

ISBN: 1-59454-621-5

Chapter 10

ARBITRAGE IN FOREIGN EXCHANGE MARKETS WITHIN THE CONTEXT OF A TRANSACTIONAL ALGEBRA

Rodolfo Apreda *
University of Cema, Buenos Aires,
Argentina

Abstract

This chapter sets forth the foundations for a transactional approach for the performance of arbitrage in foreign exchange markets. Firstly, we review both the standard model of financial arbitrage and the so-called covered-interest arbitrage environment, and we also lay bare striking shortcomings in these points of view, mainly grounded on wide- ranging empirical evidence. Next, we move on to what we have labeled in previous research work papers a transactional algebra, from which we expand on its main tools of analysis, namely differential rates, residual information sets, arbitrage gaps and transaction costs functions. Afterwards, we establish and prove the minimal conditions under which a successful arbitrage can be carried out within a transactional algebra.

JEL: F30, F31, G15
Kew words: transactional algebras, arbitrage, covered-interest arbitrage, differential rates, residual information sets, arbitrage gaps.

Introduction

Before the 70s, current practice and standard books on International Finance had been resorting to a very simple and intuitive framework of analysis to deal with foreign exchange

* Professor Rodolfo Apreda holds a Ph. D in Economics (University of Buenos Aires). Currently, he is Chair of Corporate Finance and Director of the Center for the Study of Private and Public Governance at the University of Cema. Address: Av. Cordoba 374, Room 612. Phone number: (5411) 6314 000. E-mail addres: ra@cema.edu.ar

arbitrage. However, as the 70s evolved, many academics and practitioners were feeling at variance with mainstream opinions and started not only pursuing different points of view but also shaping a new toolbox that included transaction costs, comparative economics, conflicts of interests, the so-called institutional approach, asymmetric information problems and even corporate governance issues.

In this chapter, I want to review the old model of foreign currency arbitrage, and to also make a humble contribution to its expansion and upgrading through the notion of transactional algebras.

To begin with, I introduce the standard model of financial arbitrage, which will be followed by the so-called covered interest arbitrage, still widely used to teach and discuss foreign exchange key points arising in trade and MBAs' syllabuses. The description of both standpoints will also include an outline of their shortcomings.

Afterwards, I will introduce a my own standpoint, which derives from the frame of mind that has been in construction since the 70s. To attain our goals, the substantive notions of arbitrage gap, differential rates of return, residual information sets, and transactional algebras are laid bare to reshape the covered interest arbitrage into a sensible picture that entails market institutions and frictions, ultimately leading to the core task of intermediaries: the brokerage of asymmetric information[1] by means of a set of minimal conditions to be met so as to grant a successful arbitrage within transactional algebras.

Summing up, a non standard approach to arbitrage in International Finance is the central claim of this chapter. It certainly furthers our previous research work[2] and takes advantage of an outstanding job done by distinguished scholars who are going to be referred in due course.

1 The Standard Financial Arbitrage Model

A middle-of-the-road intuition about what is meant by arbitrage is usually framed this way: "You buy cheap, hold on[3], and then sell to reap the profit arising from the gap in both prices." We could not deny that for some currently round-off transactions this stands up well as a suitable explanation. Moreover, such way of dealing with this issue seems misleading, to say the least, since from many transactions we are not able to get any profit[4], in spite of a stark difference in prices. Even worse, when we define transactions that involve buying firstly and selling later, we leave out of the picture the reversal situation, in which we set up good arbitrage processes by selling firstly and repurchasing the good later at a lower price. That is why the standard viewpoint of financial arbitrage calls for a tighter semantics[5].

Definition 1

Financial Arbitrage *is a decision-making process whose main features are:*

---

[1] As far as our knowledge, the expression "brokerage of asymmetric information" was firstly coined and fully developed in Apreda (2001).

[2] See Apreda (2004, 2003, 2001a, 2001b, 2000a, 2000b, 2000c).

[3] If the span of the holding period were very small, then the dealer would usually carry out an "spatial arbitrage", whereas the longer the span the more "temporal" the arbitrage becomes.

[4] This is attributable to the costs of running a transactional algebra, an expansion of which the reader will find in section 3.

[5] A perspective that stems from Microeconomics can be found in Varian (1987).

i) the trade of a financial asset g_1*, at an expected moment* t_1 *and in a certain market* m_1*, at the value* $V(g_1; m_1; t_1)$ *;*
ii) the trade of a financial asset g_2[6]*, at an expected moment* t_2 *and in a certain market* m_2*, at the value* $V(g_2; m_2; t_2)$, with $t_1 \leq t_2$ *;*
iii) making a profit from round-off transactions with g_1 and g_2 , either the long-short or the short-long types, that is to say, the payoff functions $\Pi(.)$ become positive:

$$\begin{cases} \Pi(\text{long-short}) = V(g_2; m_2; t_2; s) - V(g_1; m_1; t_1; l) > 0 \\ \Pi(\text{short-long}) = V(g_1; m_1; t_1; s) - V(g_2; m_2; t_2; l) > 0 \end{cases}$$

iv) no investment is required for bringing both transactions to completion;
v) risks of rounding off both transactions are null[7].

An equivalent statement for condition *iii)* will become useful later[8]:

$$\begin{cases} \Pi(\text{long-short}) = V(g_2; m_2; t_2; s) \,/\, V(g_1; m_1; t_1; l) > 1 \\ \Pi(\text{short-long}) = V(g_1; m_1; t_1; s) \,/\, V(g_2; m_2; t_2; l) > 1 \end{cases}$$

To avoid misunderstandings, definition 1 deserves two further qualifications, one linked with the concept of substitution, the other with the arbitrage process itself:

a) Whereas non-financial arbitrage always requires of an asset g_1 (or two close substitutes, g_1 and g_2) to be mispriced, financial arbitrage takes place within a much more encompassing setting. In fact, to what extent can we regard two financial assets as close substitutes? A sensible approach qualifies two assets or portfolios to be substitutes if the following features hold outright:

- their stream of expected future cash flows makes them indistinguishable from each other,
- some relevant measure of risk, when applied to both stream of cash flows puts them into the same risky category[9].

It is when the foregoing remarks are carried on to their full swing that financial economists will regard such assets as equivalent and following the law of one price[10]. A trading-off between expected return and some risk measure underpins the substitution issue[11].

---

[6] It is frequent in practice that $g_1 = g_2$; otherwise, close substitutes match the deal. Spatial-like types of arbitrage ask for $m_1 = m_2$, as well.
[7] In real practice, it is enough to ask for a negligible level of risk, even in a model so-constrained as the standard one.
[8] Mainly in definition 3 and through section 4.
[9] More background on cash flows valuation in Ross (1978), and Elton-Gruber (1995) comes in handy for financial assets and portfolios.
[10] Froot et al. (1995) review the performance of the law of one price over 700 years, while Rogoff (1996) deals with the purchasing power parity puzzle. On the other hand, Isard (1977) remains a classic on the topic.
[11] By all means, this is a key issue, of which more details will follow in section 2.

b) We can also perform arbitrage successfully by selling the asset at a certain moment, waiting for a while, and purchasing it later at a lower price. If we have the asset, that means opening a short position. If we do not, we open a short-selling position, a procedure seldom used in financial markets since there are many restrictions to the activity, albeit short-selling comes up as a crucial assumption in many Financial Economics models[12] and classroom settings.

In financial environments, risk can only sparingly be dispensed with, and we say that in such cases a pure arbitrage is under way. But coping with risk is just a fact of life in capital markets. Moreover, whenever the purchase of a security at date $\mathbf{t}_1$ involves its selling at a later date $\mathbf{t}_2$, the arbitrage is risky, because at the starting point we do not know the value

$$\mathbf{V}\ (\mathbf{g}_2;\ \mathbf{s}_2;\ \mathbf{t}_2\ )$$

that the underlying financial asset $\mathbf{g}_2$ will have at date $\mathbf{t}_2$ – unless we held some assets like zero-coupon bonds or had eventually hedged our position with derivatives.

1.1 Shortcomings in the Standard Financial Arbitrage Model: Empirical Evidence

It is hardly surprising that intensive research has been undertaken to uncover drawbacks of such oversimplified world like the one depicted in the standard financial arbitrage model. On this side of empirical research, let us highlight some contributions worthy of record and comment.

a) In practice, arbitrageurs are able to draw up arbitrage opportunities through the exchange of substitutes that convey a legal right to acquire or dispose of, and conversely an obligation to provide or accept, securities identical with an existing one under known terms and contracts. Henderson and Martine (1986) studied this issue, mainly through the following examples:

- Asset substitutes by risk grades, term to maturity, coupons, duration and convexity.
- Convertible bonds and new issues of ordinary shares.
- Options and futures.
- ADRs and US Treasury Strips.
- Risk arbitrage: by opening positions in stock from companies in the threshold of mergers or acquisitions, to profit later arbitraging between them.

b) In real-life environments, it is very difficult to carry out a complete arbitrage with financial assets, because of quantities, terms to maturity, regulations, marginal accounts balances linked with leverage and short-selling positions, as it was proved by Larkman (1986).

---

[12] The fact is that in many countries such mechanism is forbidden. But dealers can attain similar outcomes by carrying out repos and reverses so as to synthesize short-selling positions (an introductory grounding in Blake, 2000).

c) Bralsford (1986), working with both currencies and interest rate swaps, highlights some facts that enhance discrepancies between prices and returns, namely mismatching of regulations, foreign exchange policies, minimal sizes required for any trade. That is to say, the sort of features that hinge upon market microstructure.

d) Metcalf (1990) has done econometric research on departures from pure arbitrage. In the United States, there is a tax exemption granted to municipal and state bonds that has allowed municipal and state governments to profit from arbitrage opportunities in a consistent and lasting way. Accordingly, they issue tax-exempted bonds at a rate r(m) and invest the proceeds at taxable rate r(t). This is a clear example of how much influential microstructure, transaction costs and creative accounting could become in the capital markets. Although the practice is illegal, the Internal Revenue Service has not been able to prevent state and local governments from earning arbitrage windfalls. Even the so-called Gram-Rudman-Hollings Law (that deals with balanced budgets) has proved very difficult of being enforced. In fact, Metcalf singles out two kinds of arbitrage:

- *Financial Arbitrage*: like the one above-mentioned.
- *Savings Arbitrage*: by raising taxes to invest the proceedings in securities with higher returns. The interest from investments is paid to taxpayers under the guise of lower taxes expected in the future.

e) There is an interesting case of the law of one price violation in the bonds market, provided in an empirical research by Daves y Ehrhardt (1993). Interest coupons and principal coupons are not perfect substitutes, since when reconstructing them after the moment they had entered the market as strips, there is a positive differential in favor of the principal coupon. By the same token, they are not equivalent as regards liquidity concerns. Dealers rebuild the bond and sell it a higher price than the one they could get by adding up the prices of single coupons. Furthermore, the spread at the selling side is not the same as the spread at the buying side; in general, it is higher.

f) As it was argued by Shleifer and Summers (1990), arbitrage is risky and therefore limited. This approach helps to explain available and noteworthy anomalies in the efficient markets model, and also key patterns of market behavior such as trading volumes and actual investment strategies. They singled out two types of economic agents in the capital markets, namely arbitrageurs (also labeled smart money, rational speculators) and noise traders (liquidity traders, irrational agents)[13]. The former are exceedingly proficient in building-up portfolios on fully rational expectations about financial assets returns. The latter, on the contrary, are subject to systematic biases, acting on psychological impulse (noise). It is for the arbitrageurs to bring prices towards fundamentals. Ultimately, two types of risk actually limit arbitrage in real markets:

- *Fundamental risk:* selling short to repurchase later at a lower price may fail whenever expectations on that asset improve; that is to say, prices may never revert to fundamental values eventually.

[13] In spite of the labels, they are both rational actors. In the case of liquidity traders, their rationality is contestant of the one on the side of arbitrageurs. They have adversarial information sets, and take advantage of asymmetric information [a development around these topics in Apreda (2001a)]

- *Unpredictability of the future resale price*: at the time of liquidating his position in the future, the arbitrageur would bear the risk for the asset of being overpriced. This type of risk is financial by nature because, even if prices converge to fundamentals, the path could be uncertain and bumpy.

Although risk makes arbitrage ineffective, pervasive constraints in actual arbitrage are also to be found in the imperfect knowledge about fundamental values, and even in the ability to detect price changes that reflect deviations from fundamentals. That is to say, there are problems with mispricing identifications as well as with the risk of betting against them. News alone does not fully explain price changes, because uninformed changes in demand also have a word along the process. Finally, capital requirements mean that money cannot be indefinitely raised, neither costlessly nor unfettered by regulations.

g) Whenever both investors and securities are subject to differential taxation, there might be a lack of referential prices to rule out tax arbitrage (Dammon and Green,1987). We should bear in mind that in ideal models the existence of "no-tax-arbitrage" prices ensures the existence of equilibrium prices. Identical securities that contribute to taxable income to different degrees will, in general, be valued differently and equilibrium will fail to exist unless short-sale restrictions are imposed that prevent investors from exploiting such arbitrage opportunities.
h) Mitchell and Pulvino (2000) followed a sample of 4,750 stock-swap and cash mergers, cash mergers and cash tender offers during 1963 – 1998, so as to single out the risk and return in risk arbitrage processes, finding out excess returns of 4 % per year. The risk arbitrage came out from the difference between the target's stock price and the offer price, that is to say, a distinctive arbitrage spread. Those results suggest that financial markets exhibit systematic inefficiency in the pricing of firms involved in mergers and acquisitions.
i) Arbitrage is very active between spot and future markets, with offsetting positions so that the law of one price holds. In the real world, however, mispricings are not infrequent and market frictions prevent arbitrage from taking place. Kempf (2001) did research on short-selling restrictions and early unwinding opportunities. He found out a major impact on the mispricing behaviour, mainly on index arbitrage trading by using the German stock index DAX and the DAX futures. The paper showed that

- arbitrageurs faced trading and holding costs, and market impact costs as well;
- there was a pervasive influence of asymmetric holding costs and early unwinding.

j) Mitchell, Pulvino and Stafford (2001) studied hindrances to arbitrage in equity markets between 1985 and 2000, any time when the market value of a company is less than the sum of its publicly traded parts. There were arbitrage opportunities, they persisted, and prices did not converge to fundamental values. Moreover, in 82 situations they found out that cross holdings had brought about this environment in which transaction costs stemmed from imperfect information and actual trades.
k) The late 1990s wave of mergers and acquisitions was intended to consolidate industries. It can be explained as a response to market misvaluation of potential acquirers, potential targets and their combinations (Shleifer and Vishny, 2001). This approach sees managers

as completely rational, conversant with market inefficiencies, and ready to arbitrage to their profit.

l) The activity of arbitrageurs impact prices, and they back their trading with their own capital (capital adequacies for trading books of banks and securities firms, the margin levels imposed by clearing brokers, margins on futures and on leveraged equity accounts). On this issue, Attari and Mello (2001), conclude that "persistent price deviations occur and then they are the result of arbitrageurs being financially constrained."

m) With costly arbitrage and active noise traders, assets prices will be at variance of fundamental values,as Gemmill and Thomas (2002) proved in connection with a huge number of closed-end funds, which performed with an average discount to fundamental values in the long run, mainly because managers set high charges eventually.

2 The Standard Covered Interest Arbitrage Model

Without loss of generality, let us suppose that we make an educated guess that it is in the foreign market where a chance may arise for grabbing up a good net trading profit.

Stage 1 There is a local alternative to consider by which, at valuation date **t**, we buy a security in the domestic market. Let us assume that it is a term deposit with maturity at **T**, when we will sell the security at that date[14].

Formally, if we plan to invest **V(t, $)** dollars in the local market **D**, at an annual nominal rate of interest equal to **TNA** $_{\mathbf{D}}$, then the effective rate of interest for the horizon **[t ; T]** is given by[15]

$$\mathbf{r_D\,(t, T) \;=\; TNA_D\,.\,(T - t)\,/\,Year\text{-}basis_D}$$

Therefore, the final value **V(T, $, D)** in dollars will be

$$\mathbf{V(t, \$, D)\,.\,[\;1\;+\;r_D\,(\,t, T\,)\,]\;\;=\;V(T, \$, D)}$$

Stage 2 On the other hand, there is also a path of action that involves buying the term deposit in a foreign market. Let us imagine, for the sake of argument, we choose London. If we were to follow this choice, we should firstly purchase pounds, at valuation date **t**.

Let us assume that at that date, the selling quotation for pounds[16] provided by a forex dealer is

---

[14] In point of fact, when we make a term deposit we buy it spot from an authorized bank and, at the same moment, we sell it forward to the issuing bank. This round-trip exchange involved in the process is a plain swap of cash-flow positions.

[15] In most markets the year-basis equals 360 days, although in some others 365 is a frequent input. We are assuming that the same year-basis convention is used in both markets. Otherwise, an easy adjustment would give us the equivalent rate of interest that matches our target.

FX (t, $ / £, a)

that means how many dollars we need to buy from the broker a unit of pound sterling.

Hence, our starting capital in dollars could be translated to pounds the following way:

V(t, $, D) / FX (t, $ / £, a)

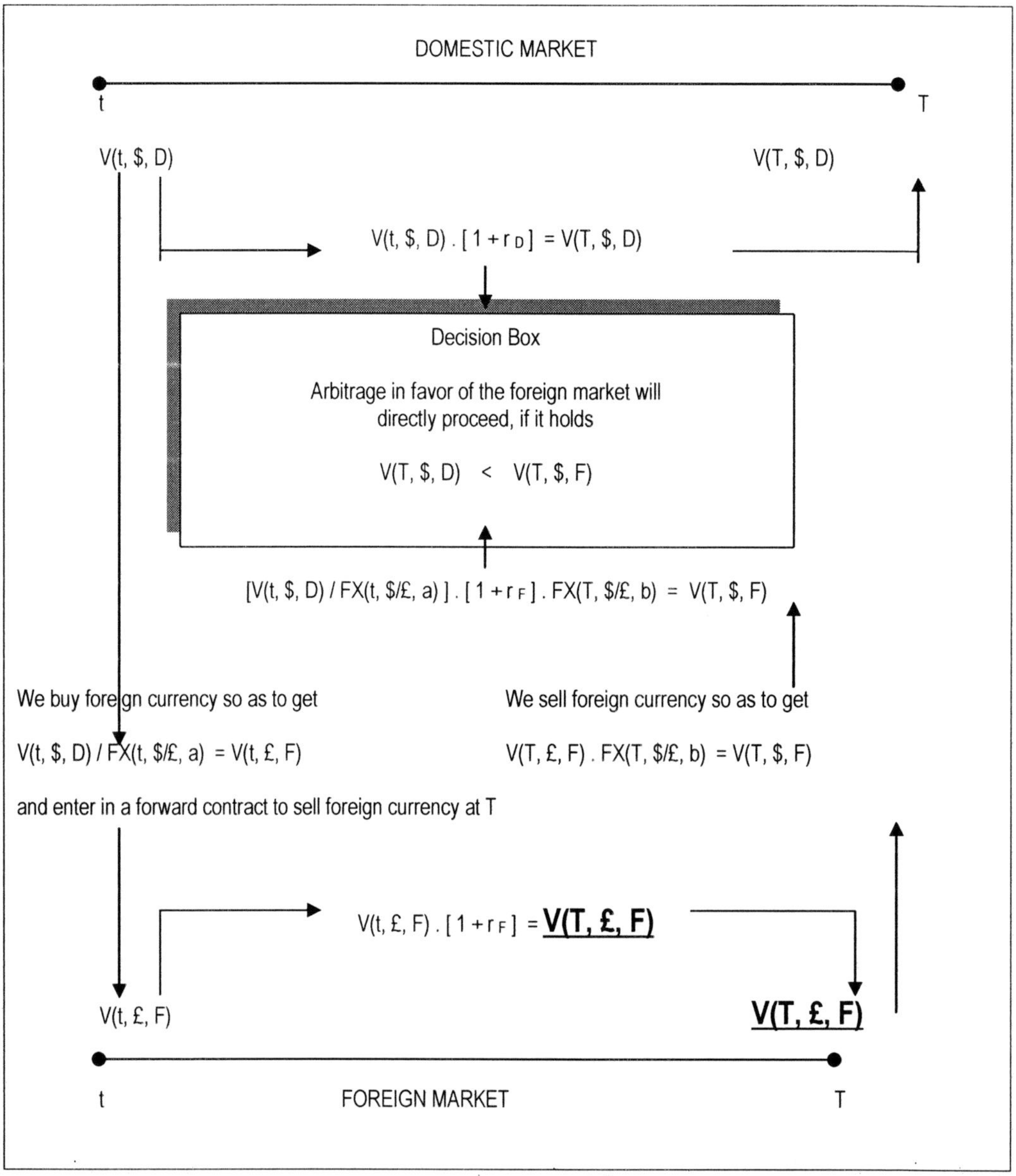

Exhibit 1 Covered- interest arbitrage

[16] "Offer" or "asked" are here used as synonyms. Besides, the "direct quotation" format is the one we use. That is to say, the quotation that tells us how many units in our own domestic currency are needed to buy or sell a unit of foreign currency.

We intend to illustrate through Exhibit 1the standard case for a covered arbitrage of interest rates between a domestic and a foreign market, from which we could make a riskless benefit[17].

Stage 3 After buying the currency, we proceed to purchase the security issued in the foreign market, matching the same class of risk and maturity that conveys the one we could have chosen in the domestic market.

If the foreign money market is offering for term deposits an annual nominal rate of interest equal to TNA_F, then the effective rate of interest for the investment horizon will be

$$\mathbf{r_F\,(t, T) = TNA_F\,.\,(T - t) \,/\, Year\text{-}basis_F}$$

At maturity, the amount of foreign currency brought about by the deposit adds up to[18]

$$\mathbf{[\ V(t, \$, D) \,/\, FX\,(t, \$ \,/\, £, a)\ ]\ .\ [\ 1 + r_F\,(t, T)\ ]\ =\ V(T, £, F)}$$

Stage 4 Lastly, we should sell this foreign currency. This leads to two distinctive settings: either we wait till maturity to sell, or we cover our ex ante position with some derivative, mainly through a forward contract to sell the foreign currency. As ours is an ex ante decision-making process, we proceed to cover.

Hence, at date **t** the buying quotation for future dollars to sell at date **T** is given by[19]

$$\mathbf{FX\,(T, \$ \,/\, £, b)}$$

therefore, the amount to collect in dollars will be equivalent to

$$\mathbf{[\ V(t, \$, D) \,/\, FX\,(t, \$ \,/\, £, a)\ ]\ .\ [\ 1 + r_F\,(t, T)\ ]\ .\ FX\,(T, \$ \,/\, £, b)\ =}$$

$$\mathbf{=\ V(T, \$, F)}$$

Stage 5 The decision-making process to invest the money in any of these markets is very simple. We are going to agree that the best market is the one that offers the higher amount of money to us.

For instance, the foreign market will be more profitable whenever it holds that

---

[17] An earlier attempt to handle this issue is to be found in Frankel-Levich (1973); for a unified approach to covered arbitrage of interest rates, see Apreda (1993). An excellent outline of arbitrage and speculation with financial assets can be read in Blake (2000). From another line of analysis, Spraos (1959) provides a helpful development about speculation and arbitrage with foreign currency.

[18] Bear in mind that D or F should be stressed as we did in the expressions above, since we could do a transaction in dollars outside the United States. One thing is the currency adopted as benchmark, quite another the market where we are going to use it.

[19] If no coverage is achieved, we might have written this quotation as **E[FX (T, $ / £, b)]**.

$$\mathbf{V(t, \$, D)\ .\ [\ 1\ +\ r_D\ (\ t, T\ )\ ]\ <}$$

$$\mathbf{<\ [\ V(t, \$, D)\ /\ FX\ (t, \$\ /\ £, a)\ ]\ .\ [\ 1\ +\ r_F\ (\ t, T\ )\ ]\ .\ FX\ (T, \$\ /\ £, b)}$$

Stage 6 As we can see, **V(t, $, D)** can be left out from both sides of the inequality, so as to get

$$\mathbf{[\ 1 +\ r_D\ (\ t, T\ )\ ]\ <}$$

$$\mathbf{<\ [\ FX\ (T, \$\ /\ £, b)\ /\ FX\ (t, \$\ /\ £, a)\ ]\ .\ [\ 1\ +\ r_F\ (\ t, T\ )\ ]}$$

Now, if we give heed to the first expression within square brackets on the right side of the latter inequality, we realize that it entails a return to be reaped for holding pounds (at **t** we purchase the currency, and after holding it along the horizon, we sell it at **T**, and this amount to a swap of cash flow positions in currencies, dollars-to-pounds-to-dollars). This return is usually denoted as the swap return, r_{SWAP}. All in all,

$$\mathbf{[\ FX\ (T, \$\ /\ £, b)\ /\ FX\ (t, \$\ /\ £, a)\ ]\ =\ [\ 1\ +\ r_{SWAP}\ (\ t, T\ )\ ]}$$

In conclusion, and by running stages 1 through 6, we have already proved the following statement.

Lemma 1 ***For a profitable arbitrage in the foreign market, it must hold that:***

$$\mathbf{[\ 1\ +\ r_D\ (\ t, T\ )\ ]\ <\ [\ 1\ +\ r_F\ (\ t, T\ )\ ]\ .\ [\ 1\ +\ r_{SWAP}\ (\ t, T\ )\ ]}$$

Otherwise, the domestic market will provide the arbitrage opportunity.

Once the arbitrage opportunity fades away, it is said that the market becomes arbitraged; in such an extreme case, the outcome turns out to be

$$\mathbf{[\ 1\ +\ r_D\ (\ t, T\ )\ ]\ =\ [\ 1\ +\ r_F\ (\ t, T\ )\ ]\ .\ [\ 1\ +\ r_{SWAP}\ (\ t, T\ )\ ]}$$

which is usually known as **covered-interest arbitrage** (or parity theorem)[20].

Finally, and for the sake of clarity, it's worth giving heed to the source of the swap return. To begin with, we should wonder about the nature of the expected return arising from the process of purchasing, holding and selling foreign currency. When we handle foreign currency that way, it amounts to the holding of any financial asset, which usually provide a return that can be broken down into a holding return on the one hand, and a financial return[21] on the other hand. The latter component is missing with currencies; therefore, they provide a holding return, positive or negative, as a matter of course.

---

[20] More on this topic can be followed in Blake (2000), in particular the international Fisher effect and the purchasing power parity. A related article in the New Palgrave Dictionary of Money and Finance proves to be useful to practitioners.

[21] Often, this is conveyed through payment of interest, dividends or the like to the investor, who had bought any asset in the financial market, from where it derives the label of "financial asset".

If we firstly recall how to work out the return of any financial asset, next we could attempt to assess the return of holding currencies. By the rate of return **r(t, T)**, for certain financial asset and throughout a planned investment horizon **H = [t ; T]**, is meant the following expression:

$$r(t, T) = [\, V(T) - V(t) + I(t, T) \,] / V(t)$$

where **V(T)** stands for the value of the asset at date **T**, **V(t)** for the one at date t, **I(t, T)** for any cash flow to reward the investor under the guise of interest, dividends, and the like.

In dealing with foreign currency, the equation above turns out to be

$$r_{SWAP}(t, T) = [FX(T, \$/£, b) - FX(t, \$/£, a)] \; / \; FX(t, \$/£, a)]$$

that is equivalent to

$$[\; 1 + r_{SWAP}(t, T) \;] = [\; FX(T, \$/£, b) / FX(t, \$/£, a) \;]$$

2.1 Driving Forces and Constraints behind Real Markets

The standard model of covered interest arbitrage disregards the actual constraints behind real markets. It is true that the dynamics provided by supply and demand, on the one hand, and the adjustment process provided by arbitrage, on the other, point to real market forces. But this only entails a first level of understanding for the market dynamics; indeed, this seems to be the standard approach arising from the neoclassical standpoint, of which Lemma 1 is a direct heir.

As a matter of fact, a second level of understanding for the market dynamics, and a deeper one by all intents and purposes, tracks down the underpinnings of forces that the first level has rather neglected, namely the institutional arrangements [rules of the game, distinctive laws and regulations, law enforcement and transparency]; transaction costs [on which we are going to expand further in section 3.1]; different endowment of information claimed by economic agents [asymmetric information]; opportunistic behavior, and the essential role intermediaries perform in the markets[22]. By choosing such level of research and analysis, we take advantage of a positive approach we have called "transactional algebras" that comes in handy to bring about arbitrage in down-to-earth settings.

3 Transactional Algebras[23]

We are going to introduce the toolbox required to handle our proposal, namely differential rates, residual information sets, arbitrage gaps, transactional algebras and enlarged transaction costs.

---

[22] We have dealt with this issue in depth elsewhere (Apreda, 2001).

[23] To the extent of our knowledge, the expression "transactional algebra" was firstly coined in Apreda (2003).

3.1 Differential Rates and Residual Information Sets

For the time being, let us assume that the information set[24] claimed by a decision-maker **k** at date **t**

$$\Omega(t ; k)$$

allows him to handle a rate of return linked to any distinctive economic variable[25] that comes defined along the investment horizon **H** = **[t ; T]**, contingent upon such information set. If we could assess another information set $\Omega_1 (t ; k)$ such that it would hold

$$\Omega_1 (t ; k) \subseteq \Omega(t ; k)$$

and which would explain reasonably well the value of a rate of return

$$r_1 (t, T, \Omega_1 (t ; k))$$

then, we could also attempt to measure up for how much of the starting rate value it still remains unexplained by this new one[26].

This is the logic behind the complementary notions of differential rates of return and residual information sets. We are going to provide a simplified definition of both concepts, but good enough for the purposes of this paper. But the reader should keep in mind that when we try to deal with more than two differential rates and residual information sets, the mathematics of the subject become more intricate and we have to deal with algebras of sets, a complete development of which was provided elsewhere (Apreda, 2000a, 2004).

Definition 2 Differential Rates and Residual Information Sets

The rate of return ***g(.)*** *that solves the following equation*

$$[1 + r(t, T, \Omega(t ; k))] =$$
$$= [1 + r_1 (t, T, \Omega_1 (t ; k))] . [1 + g(t, T, \Omega_R (t ; k))]$$

is called the ***differential rate*** *of* ***r(.)*** *given* $r_1 (.)$ *, whereas the underlying information set for this rate*

$$\Omega_R (t ; k)$$

gets the label of ***residual****.*

[24] That is to say, all the information available to the decision-maker. Whereas the conventional models assume all the economic actors share the same information (symmetric information), as from the 70s the stress is laid upon different endowments of information (asymmetric information).

[25] It could be, for instance, either a price, a rate of return, or the value of a certain market index.

[26] In the case of a financial asset, we mean here the rate of return of that financial asset. But there are other natural examples, as in the foreign exchange market when dealing with the appreciation or depreciation of the foreign currency against the domestic one. Also we could point to the rate that measures the change undergone by certain index.

3.2 Arbitrage Gaps

At this juncture, I introduce a concept that will help us to keep the further discussion within operational bounds[27]. We are speaking about the arbitrage gap, which intends to measure up the expected return from an arbitrage opportunity, in nominal terms.

Definition 3

*By **Arbitrage Gap** is meant the rate of return brought about either in long-short or short-long arbitrage processes, springing from the following equations:*

$$\begin{cases} 1 + r(\text{arbitrage; long-short}) = V(g_2; m_2; t_2; s) \,/\, V(g_1; m_1; t_1; l) \\ 1 + r(\text{arbitrage; short-long}) = V(g_1; m_1; t_1; s) \,/\, V(g_2; m_2; t_2; l) \end{cases}$$

For any arbitrage to be successful both rates must be positive. The problem arises when the transaction costs and microstructure features of the market are not taken into account, therefore preventing the economic agent from eventually seizing the arbitrage opportunity.

3.3 Transactional Algebras

The concept of a transactional algebra summons not only a framework for the analysis of financial trading, including arbitrage processes within an institutional context, but also two matching tools: firstly, a suitable transaction costs function and, secondly, the concept of residual information sets.

Definition 4

*By a **Transactional Algebra** it is meant a complex structure whose distinctive features are:*

i. *Existence of one or more markets where financial assets can be traded either in public or private settings.*
ii. *The institutional framework and the market microstructure are set up by means of*

   - *trading and regulatory institutions;*
   - *intermediaries, investors, and regulators;*
   - *enforceable laws and rules of the game;*
   - *contractual arrangements about the property rights attached to each transaction.*

iii. *A total transaction costs function is explicitly given[28] which includes all relevant and computable enlarged transaction costs.*

---

[27] Actually, it has been introduced implicitly when, after definition 1, a remark was made about condition iii of such definition.

[28] Section 3.4 labors this issue in length.

iv. The metrics for this structure comes out of differential rates, which are conditional upon their respective residual information sets

3.4 Enlarged Transaction Costs: The Costs of Running Transactional Algebras

Transaction costs have been usually neglected for decades. Even worse, as it is stated in some quarters, most transaction costs would become negligible as communication devices improve. To say the least, this belief is misplaced because transaction costs are the costs of running nothing less than a transactional algebra, as next remarks intend to bring to light:

- Firstly, what it is customarily meant by transaction costs points only at some particular types of trading costs, mainly linked with purchasing and selling securities. Although in some markets trading costs are being curbed, in other places they are not. The sensible question to elicit is about the structure of those trading costs, which is not so simple as it seems at first sight.
- Secondly, enlarged transaction costs encompass a broad variety of items[29], which refer to manifold sources of distinctive costs:

- *intermediation (INT),* which stem from the actual trading stages of purchasing or selling financial assets;
- *microstructure (MICR),* which stand for those costs stemming from market regulations, dealers trading arrangements to meet their intermediary roles; and restrictions on capital movements;
- *information (INF),* which involves the search of all kinds of information needed by investors and dealers; also the costs of drafting, implementing, monitoring and improving the underlying contracts to enforce transactions (Flood et al., 1998);
- *taxes (TAX);*
- *financial costs (FIN)* associated with the purchase, selling or holding securities or foreign currencies.

Although these five categories are neither exhaustive nor the only ones to work out, we believe that they pave the way for a sensible assessment of the transaction costs rate denoted by[30]

$$\mathbf{TC}\,(\,t_1\,;\,t_2\,;\,m_1\,;\,m_2\,;\,x)$$

which is a construct with the following features:

---

[29] More background on this subject can be found in Apreda (2000a, 2004).

[30] In the format that follows, a vectorial frame is used by which t_1 and t_2 stand for starting and maturity dates for the transaction; m_1 and m_2 for the markets in which the involved transactions can be carried out at those dates; x for long or short position at the current date. It goes without saying that if we worked out costs at the starting date and in certain market, we should drop the remaining date and market, as we are going to do below.

a. it comes by the side of every single transaction;
b. it amounts to a rate of change that may be expressed in percentage points;
c. and it may be framed out of the functional relationship provided by a multiplicative model:

$$< 1 + TC(t, T, \Omega^{TC}{}_t) > = < 1 + int(t, T, \Omega^{INT}{}_t) > . < 1 + micr(t, T, \Omega^{MICR}{}_t) > .$$
$$. < 1 + tax(t, T, \Omega^{TAX}{}_t) > . < 1 + inf(t, T, \Omega^{INF}{}_t) > . < 1 + fin(t, T, \Omega^{FIN}{}_t) >$$

with the restriction

$$\Omega^{k}{}_t \subseteq \Omega^{TC}{}_t \quad \text{for } k: \text{int, micr, inf, fin, tax}$$

Bearing in mind definition 4, we can see that the transaction cost rate gives account not only of any distinctive cost to be attributed to transactions and trades, but also their contractual costs and those that arise from underlying institutional settings. In fact, the role and essence of intermediation can be explained out of transaction costs (Benston and Smith, 1976).

We are interested here in applying this functional relationship to arbitrage processes, distinguishing long from short positions, as shown next[31].

$$\begin{cases} \textbf{short position:} \quad 1 + TC(t_2; m_2; s) = \\ = [1 - int(s)] . [1 - micr(s)] . [1 - tax(s)] . [1 - inf(s)] . [1 - fin(s)] \\ \textbf{long position:} \quad 1 + TC(t_1; m_1; l) = \\ = [1 + int(s)] . [1 + micr(s)] . [1 + tax(s)] . [1 + inf(s)] . [1 + fin(s)] \end{cases} \quad (1)$$

When selling, costs lessen the cash flows to be finally collected. When purchasing, they add to incurring outflows[32].

Before concluding this section, we need to take a step further and embed each transaction cost rate pertaining the short and long position into a comprehensive differential rate that might account for the costs of running transactional algebras.

Definition 5

In a transactional algebra environment, let us denote with

---

[31] See footnote 20.

[32] Although decision-making in (1) requires an ex ante setting, we leave out the expectations operator symbol, E[.], for ease of notation. Each component has its own functional structure, which does not come up as linear, necessarily. In fact, non-linearity is customary and useful in latest research, which take advantage of piece-wise linear functions, or still better, the so-called simple or step functions, so as to approximate more complex relationships. [For instance, Levy-Livingston (1995) on portfolio management; Day (1997) in nonlinear dynamics applied to economics; Apreda (1999) on chaotic patterns for the arbitrage gap in capital markets]

diff TC (long-short)

*the **differential transaction costs rate** that solves the equation*

$$1 + \textit{diff TC(long-short)} = $$
$$= [1 + TC(t_2; m_2; s)] / [1 + TC(t_1; m_1; l)]$$

In other words, the differential transaction costs rate measures up the whole impact of the costs of running the transactional algebra involved with an arbitrage. It will prove functional to the main statements conveyed by Lemmas 2 and 3, which are going to be proved in next section.

By the same token, if the transaction is of the type short-long, the equation in the definition should become

$$\mathbf{1 + diff\ TC(short\text{-}long) =}$$
$$\mathbf{= [1 + TC(t_2; m_2; l)] / [1 + TC(t_1; m_1; s)]}$$

4 Arbitrage within Transactional Algebras

Rates of return can be broken down into the cost components on the one hand, and a return netted from them, on the other hand. Two lemmas are needed to cope with this matter.

Lemma 2 ***In a transactional algebra, and for every arbitrage opportunity, it holds true that:***

i. ***there is an arbitrage return net of transaction costs.***
ii. ***there are diferential rates to translate each type of transaction costs arising from the rounding-off trades;***

Proof:

Using (1), the money to collect when selling the asset (all-in-cost basis) would amount to

$$\mathbf{V(s) . [1 - int(s)] . [1 - micr(s)] . [1 - tax(s)] . [1 - inf(s)] . [1 - fin(s)] =}$$
$$\mathbf{= V(s) . [1 + TC(t_2; m_2; s)]}$$

and when purchasing the asset (all-in-cost basis):

$$\mathbf{V(l) . [1 + int(l)] . [1 + micr(l)] . [1 + tax(l)] . [1 + inf(l)] . [1 + fin(l)] =}$$
$$\mathbf{= V(l) . [1 + TC(t_1; m_1; l)]}$$

The return from this arbitrage yields (either trading or financial, and in nominal terms) follows from

$$\mathbf{V(s) / V(l) = 1 + r(arbitrage)}$$

When taking into account transaction costs arising from the rounding-off exchanges we can put forth the equation

$$\mathbf{V(s)\,.\,[\,1 + TC\,(\,t_{2};\, m_{2};\, s\,)\,]\ /\ V(\,l\,)\,.\,[\,1 + TC\,(\,t_{1};\, m_{1};\, l\,)\,] = 1 + r_{net}\ (arbitrage)} \qquad (2)$$

and solving for $\mathbf{r_{net}}$ **(arbitrage)** we ultimately have a measure of the return in an arbitrage process that embodies transaction costs.

Furthermore, by resorting to definition 5, the differential transaction costs rate follows from

$$\mathbf{1 + diff\ TC(long\text{-}short) = [\,1 + TC\,(\,t_{2}\,;\, m_{2}\,;\, s\,)\,]\ /\ [\,1 + TC\,(\,t_{1}\,;\, m_{1}\,;\, l\,)\,]}$$

therefore, the relationship (2) can now be rewritten in a much more compact format:

$$\mathbf{[\,V(s)\ /\ V(\,l\,)\,]\,.\,[\,1 + diff\ TC(long\text{-}short)\,] = 1 + r_{net}\ (arbitrage)}$$

and, last of all, we get

$$\mathbf{[\,1 + r(arbitrage)\,]\,.\,[\,1 + diff\ TC(long\text{-}short)\,] = 1 + r_{net}\ (arbitrage)}$$

ii) Let us substitute now the labels t_k (k: 1, 2, 3, 4, 5) for the enlarged transaction costs labels trad, micr, tax, inf, and fin, respectively. Then,

$$\mathbf{1 + g_{k} = [\,1 + t_{k}\,(s)\,]\ /\ [\,1 + t_{k}\ (l)\ ]}$$

where $\mathbf{g_k}$ performs as a differential rate drawn out of $\mathbf{t_k}$ **(s)** and $\mathbf{t_k}$ **(l)** .

On the other hand, we can replace in (1) to get the equivalence:

$$\mathbf{1 + diff\ TC(long\text{-}short) = [\ \prod\ (\,1 + g_{k}\,)\ ] = [\,1 + TC\,(\,t_{2}\,;\, m_{2}\,;\, s\,)\,]\ /\ [\,1 + TC\,(\,t_{1}\,;\, m_{1}\,;\, l\,)\,]} \quad \text{[END]}$$

Whereas in the standard financial arbitrage model arbitrage opportunities can be grabbed once the conditions of definition 1 are met, in a transactional algebra structure this cannot be warranted. In fact, arbitrage will only be feasible if the arbitrage gap overrides the constraints of the transactional algebra, as the following lemma makes clear.

Lemma 3 ***In a transactional algebra, the fulfillment of the standard financial arbitrage conditions does not grant that an arbitrage opportunity remains profitable.***

Proof:

Whenever an investor takes advantage of arbitrage opportunities, he tries to lock in a sure profit that follows from definition 3:

$$1 + r(\text{arbitrage; long-short}) = V(g_2; m_2; t_2 ; s) \ / \ V(g_1; m_1; t_1 ; l)$$

$$1 + r(\text{arbitrage; short-long}) = V(g_1; m_1; t_1 ; s) \ / \ V(g_1; m_2; t_2 ; l)$$

Let us analyze each relationship at a turn.

a) the long-short type of arbitrage

If we included transaction costs, according with Lemma 1, we would get a net arbitrage return:

$$1 + r_{net}(\text{arbitrage}) = [\, 1 + r(\text{arbitrage}) \,] \,.\, [\, 1 + \text{diff TC(long-short)} \,]$$

For the arbitrage to become successful, it must hold:

$$[\, 1 + r(\text{arbitrage; long-short}) \,] =$$
$$= [\, V(g_2; m_2; t_2 ; s) \ / \ V(g_1; m_1; t_1 ; l) \,] > 1$$

but this is not a sufficient feature, because differential transaction costs could lead to

$$1 + r_{net}(\text{arbitrage; long-short}) =$$
$$= [\, 1 + r(\text{arbitrage}); \text{long-short} \,] \,.\, [\, 1 + \text{diff TC(long-short)} \,]) < 1$$

thus yielding a negative return on the net rate of return for the arbitrage.

b) the short-long type of arbitrage

By the same procedure as in a) we would get that is not enough the fulfillment of

$$[\, V(g_1; m_1; t_1 ; s) \ / \ V(g_2; m_2; t_2 ; l) \,] > 1$$

because the transaction costs structure could bring about the following outcome:

$$1 + r_{net}(\text{arbitrage; short-long}) =$$
$$= [\, 1 + r(\text{arbitrage}); \text{short-long} \,] \,.\, [\, 1 + \text{diff TC(short-long)} \,] < 1$$

giving forth a negative return on the net rate of return for the arbitrage. [END]

It is from Lemma 2 that we can frame a definition of what is meant by financial arbitrage within a transactional algebra[33].

[33] See footnotes 7 and 8.

Definition 6

Financial Arbitrage within a transactional algebra *is a decision making process whose main features are:*

i. *the trade of a financial asset* $\mathbf{g}_1$*, at an expected moment* $\mathbf{t}_1$*, in a certain market* $\mathbf{m}_1$*, at the value* $V(g_1; m_1; t_1)$ *;*
ii. *the trade of a financial asset* $\mathbf{g}_2$*, at an expected moment* $\mathbf{t}_2$*, in a certain market* $\mathbf{m}_2$*, at the value* $V(g_2; m_2; t_2)$, with $t_1 \leq t_2$ *;*
iii. making a sure profit from round-off transactions with $\mathbf{g}_1$ and $\mathbf{g}_2$, either the long-short or the short-long types, that is to say, the payoff functions $\Pi(.)$ are positive:

$$\begin{cases} \Pi(\text{long-short}) = 1 + r(\text{arbitrage; long-short}) = \\ \quad = V(g_2; m_2; t_2; s) \ / \ V(g_1; m_1; t_1; l) > 1 \\ \\ \Pi(\text{short-long}) = 1 + r(\text{arbitrage; short-long}) = \\ \quad = V(g_1; m_1; t_1; s) \ / \ V(g_1; m_2; t_2; l) > 1 \end{cases}$$

iv. *no investment is required for setting up both transactions;*
v. *risks of rounding off both transactions are null.*
vi. *it meets the following boundary conditions*

$$\begin{cases} 1 + r_{net}(\text{arbitrage; long-short}) = \\ = [\,1 + r(\text{arbitrage}); \text{long-short}\,] \, . \, [\,1 + \text{diff } TC(\text{long-short})\,] > 1 \\ \\ 1 + r_{net}(\text{arbitrage; short-long}) = \\ = [\,1 + r(\text{arbitrage}); \text{short-long}\,] \, . \, [\,1 + \text{diff } TC(\text{short-long})\,] > 1 \end{cases}$$

5 Covered Interest Arbitrage within a Transactional Algebra

Henceforth, I assume that the trade of financial assets and currency will proceed between a domestic and a foreign market within the context of a transactional algebra. It's worth giving heed to what this fact actually amounts to, by noticing the following remarkable issues:

a) There is, on the one hand, an institutional setting consisting of the rules of the game (laws, regulations and conventions) as well as exchange arrangements. On the other hand, there are watchdogs that make for the fairness of the whole game (Central Banks and Securities Exchange Commissions).
b) Investors, dealers, brokers and international banks, work out transaction cost functions[34].
c) Asymmetric information is the name of the game, and hand in hand with this feature, we may face opportunistic behavior with guile on the side of the players.

---

[34] Although this may be done either approximately or as an educated guess, the key point is that transaction costs are embedded in the entirety of the analysis.

d) Lemma 1 amounts to a valid statement in a world of perfect competition and symmetric information, with a boundless arbitrage activity. Therefore, it should be only regarded as a benchmark that provides technical and helpful approximations.
e) Broadly speaking, Lemma 2 holds by and large, granting that arbitrage opportunities are meaningful only when transactions costs are embedded in the analysis, and become translated as differential rates.
f) Lemma 3 also holds by and large, pledging that arbitrage opportunities, as discovered by applying Lemma 1, might not ultimately lead to net profits eventually.

Being this one the last section of this chapter, let us move on to give due regard to transaction costs, stemming both from the foreign exchange markets and the securities markets.

However, we know that enlarged transaction costs must also include those arising from the market microstructure, the financing of positions in foreign currency, taxes and information costs. With such a broad viewpoint, we are going to trace the round-trip involved with this arbitrage process.

Domestic securities market: When buying, holding and selling a security in the domestic market, the return can be broken down into a net rate of return, and a differential rate

$$g_D(t, T)$$

that stands for transaction costs. Hence:

$$[1 + r_D(t, T)] = [1 + \text{net } r_D(t, T)] \cdot [1 + g_D(t, T)] \quad (3)$$

*Foreign securities market*By the same token, when buying, holding and selling a security in the security market, we get

$$[1 + r_F(t, T)] = [1 + \text{net } r_F(t, T)] \cdot [1 + g_F(t, T)] \quad (4)$$

*Foreign exchange markets*Last of all, buying foreign currency, holding it under the guise of a security, and selling it eventually, leads to a return decomposable in a net rate of return and a differential rate of transaction costs

$$[1 + r_{SWAP}(t, T)] = [1 + \text{net } r_{SWAP}(t, T)] \cdot [1 + g_{SWAP}(t, T)] \quad (5)$$

The preceding line of analysis has paved the way for a simple but powerful outcome.

Lemma 4 ***In a transactional algebra, and conditional upon an information set Ω_t, covered interest arbitrage against the domestic exchange in favor of the foreign exchange requires the fulfillment of the following inequality:***

$$[1 + \text{net } r_D(t, T)] <$$
$$< [1 + \text{net } r_F(t, T)] \cdot [1 + \text{net } r_{SWAP}(t, T)] \cdot [1 + g(t, T)]$$

where $g(t, T)$ translates the round-trip transaction costs gap.

Proof: By plugging (3), (4) and (5) into the main outcome of lemma 1, the arbitrage will be granted in favor of the foreign market whenever it holds:

$$[\,1 + \text{net } r_D(t,T)\,] \cdot [\,1 + g_D(t,T)\,] <$$
$$< [\,1 + \text{net } r_F(t,T)\,] \cdot [\,1 + g_F(t,T)\,] \cdot$$
$$\cdot [\,1 + \text{net } r_{SWAP}(t,T)\,] \cdot [\,1 + g_{SWAP}(t,T)\,]$$

if we build up the round-trip transaction costs gap this way

$$[\,1 + g(t,T)\,] =$$
$$= \{\, [\,1 + g_F(t,T)\,] \cdot [\,1 + g_{SWAP}(t,T)\,] \,\} \,/\, [\,1 + g_D(t,T)\,]$$

we could grant that the foreign market is better, even when we take transaction costs into account. If the transaction costs gap does not meet the latter inequality, then it will mean that the arbitrage is not advisable because it comes short of covering costs. [END]

Conclusions

Although the standard financial arbitrage model and the covered-interest arbitrage's proposition provide an extreme framework of analysis, they have proved more of a hindrance than a help in real financial markets.

In line with the new theoretical and empirical viewpoints that have evolved in Financial Economics since the 70s, this chapter puts forth a proposal to overcome the constraints of the standard models by means of the notion of Transactional Algebra, which is a construct that adds to arbitrage the institutions that rule the markets, also the transaction costs structure that stems from such setting, and a new toolbox to address these issues, namely differential rates, residual information sets, arbitrage gaps and the differential transaction cost rate.

The main outcome of this chapter sets up the conditions to be fulfilled in order to successfully carry out an arbitrage with foreign currencies in a transactional algebra.

References

Apreda, R. (2004) Differential Rates, Residual Information Sets and Transactional Algebras. Working Papers Series, University of Cema, number 256, Buenos Aires, Argentina (downloadable from *www.cema.edu.ar/publicaciones*).

Apreda, R. (2003) On the Extent of Arbitrage Constraints within Transaction Algebras (A Non-Standard Approach), Working Paper Series, University of Cema, number 239, Buenos Aires, Argentina (downloadable from *www.cema.edu.ar/publicaciones*)

Apreda, R. (2001a) The Brokerage of Asymmetric Information. Working Papers Series, The University of Cema, number 190, Buenos Aires, Argentina (downloadable from *www.cema.edu/publicaciones*).

Apreda, R. (2001b) Differential Rates and Residual Information Sets. Working Papers Series, S-01-3, New York University, Stern School of Busines.

Apreda, R. (2000a) A Transaction Costs Approach to Financial Assets of Return. Working Papers Series, The University of Cema, number 161, Buenos Aires (downloadable from *www.cema.edu.ar/publicaciones).*

Apreda, R. (2000b) Differential Rates and Information Sets: A Toolkit for Practitioners, Financial Economists and Accountants. Working Papers Series, The University of Cema, number 166, Buenos Aires, Argentina (downloadable from *www.cema.edu.ar/pub licaciones*)

Apreda, R. (2000c) Differential Rates and Residual Information Sets. Working Papers Series, The University of Cema, number 177, Buenos Aires, Argentina (downloadable from *www.cema.edu.ar/publicaciones*).

Apreda, R. (1999) Dynamic Arbitrage Gaps for Financial Assets in a Nonlinear and Chaotic Adjustment Price Process. *Journal of Mathematical Financial Management*, volume 9, pp. 441-457.

Apreda, R. (1993) An Unified Approach to Foreign Exchange Arbitrage. *The Journal of Argentine Financial Executives,* April, pp. 29-34 (in Spanish).

Attari, M. and Mello, A. (2001). Financially Constrained Arbitrage in Illiquid Markets. SSRN Working Papers, ID 27628.

Benston, G. and Smith, C. (1976). A Transaction Costs Approach to the Theory of Financial Intermediaries. *Journal of Finance*, volume 31, May, pp. 215-231.

Blake, D. (2000). *Financial Market Analysis*. John Wiley, second edition, London.

Bralsford, M. (1986). *Interest Rate and Currency Swaps*. (In Arbitrage, Rudi Weisweiller)

Chen, Z. and Knez, P. (1995). Measurement of Market Integration and Arbitrage. *Review of Financial Studies*, volume 8, number 2, pp. 287-325.

Dammon, R. and Green, R. (1987). Tax Arbitrage and the Existence of Equilibrium Prices for Financial Assets. *Journal of Finance*, volume 42, number 5, pp. 1143-1166.

Daves, P. and Ehrhardt, M. (1993). Liquidity, Reconstitution and the Value of US Treasury Strips. *The Journal of Finance*, volume 48, pp. 315-329.

Day, R. (1994). *Complex Economic Dynamics*, volume 1. The MIT Press, Massachusetts.

Elton, J. and Gruber, M. (1995). *Modern Portfolio Theory and Investment Analysis*. Wiley, New York.

Flood M. et al. (1998). *Search Costs: The neglected Spread Component*. Institute of Business and Economic Research, RPF. 285, University of California.

Frankel, J. and Lench, R. (1975) Covered Interest Arbitrage: Unexploited Profits? *Journal of Political Economy*, volume 83, number 2, pp. 325-329.

Froot, K.; Kim, M. and Rogoff, K. (1995). The Law of One Price over 700 years. *National Bureau of Economic Research*, Working Paper 5132.

Gemmill, G. and Thomas, D. (2002). Noise Trading, Costly Arbitrage, and Asset Prices: Evidence from Closed-end Funds. *The Journal of Finance*, volume 57, number 6, pp. 2571-2594.

Henderson, M. and Martine, R. (1986). *Securities Arbitrage*. (In Arbitrage, Rudi Weisweiller)

Isard, P. (1977). How Far Can We Push the "Law of One Pice". *The American Economic Review*, volume 67, number 3, pp. 942-948.

Kempf, A. (1996). *Short Selling, Unwinding and Mispricing*. Working Paper, University of Manheim.

Larkman, B. (1986). *Financial Futures*. (In Arbitrage, Rudi Weisweiller)

Levy, A. and Livingston, M. (1995). The Gains from Diversification Reconsidered: Transaction Costs and Superior Information. *Financial Markets, Institutions and Instruments*, volume 4, number 3, pp. 1-58.

Metcalf, G.(1990). Arbitrage and the Savings Behaviour of State Governments. *The Review of Economics and Statistics*, volume 72, number 3, pp. 390-396.

Mitchell, M. and Pulvino, T. (2000). Characteristics of Risk and Return in Risk Arbitrage. SSRN, Working Paper ID 268144.

Mitchell, M. ; Pulvino, T. and Stafford, E. (2001). Limited Arbitrage in Equity Markets. Social Sciences Research Network, Working Paper 267998.

Rogoff, K. (1996). The Purchasing Power Parity Puzzle. *Journal of Economic Literature*, volume 34, number 2, pp. 647-668.

Ross, S. (1978). A Simple Approach to the Valuation of Risky Streams. *Journal of Business*, volume 51, number 3, pp. 453-475.

Shleifer, A. and Summers, L. (1990). The Noise Trader Approach to Finance. *Journal of Economic Perspectives*, volume 4, number 2, pp. 19-33.

Shleifer, A. and Vishny, R. (2001). Stock Market Driven Acquisitions. *NBER*, Working Paper 8439.

Spraos, J. (1959). Speculation, Arbitrage and Sterling. *The Economic Journal*, volume 69, number 273, pp. 1-21.

Varian, H. (1987). The Arbitrage Principle in Financial Economics. *Journal of Economic Perspectives*, volume 1, number 2, pp. 55-72.

Weisweiller, R. (1986). *Arbitrage: Opportunities and Techniques in the Financial and Commodity Markets.* John Wiley, New York.

In: International Trade Issues
Editor: Robert. V. Weeks, pp. 251-267
ISBN: 1-59454-621-5

Chapter 11

IS INTERNATIONAL TRADE GUILTY FOR AN ENLARGING WAGE DIFFERENTIAL? A DYNAMIC INTERTEMPORAL GENERAL EQUILIBRIUM MODEL

Hsiao-chuan Chang*,‡
Department of Economics, The University of Melbourne
Victoria 3010 Australia

Abstract

There is much literature on the link between international trade, productivity growth and wage differential of skilled and unskilled labour. The theoretical and empirical research is mainly based on the Heckscher-Ohlin framework. This paper constructs a dynamic intertemporal general equilibrium (DIGE) model incorporating endogenous skill formation. Both the short- and long-run transition with shocks can be illustrated.

The result supports the argument that trade has a responsibility for an increased wage differential. A cut in government education investment tends to enlarge the wage differential. Productivity growth may not be the cause of an enlarged wage differential in the long run.

JEL classification: C61; F10; F41; H52; J22; J24; J31
Keywords: Dynamic Intertemporal General Equilibrium Model, International Trade, Wage Differential

---

* I am greatly indebted to Warwick McKibbin for his valuable comments in writing this paper. I would like to thank John Freebairn, David Vines, Pan-Long Tsai, Bruce Chapman, Rod Tyers, Prema-Chandra Athukorala, Neil Vousden, and Dominic Wilson for their helpful discussions and comments on earlier drafts of this paper.
‡ E-mail address: changh@unimelb.edu.au

1 Introduction

The cause of changes in the wage differential between skilled and unskilled labour has been an important issue of debate for several decades. One viewpoint proposes that international trade is responsible for the enlarging wage differential between skilled and unskilled labour. For example Wood (1995) suggests that trade is the main cause of wage inequality.[1] The other view is that trade is not the main cause of this phenomenon. For example Krugman and Lawrence (1994) point out that skill-biased productivity growth is the main cause of increasing wage inequality.[2] Extensive research has contributed to large country cases.[3] Only limited research has been based on small open economies.[4] This debate is ongoing. Both labour economists (such as Katz and Autor, 1999; Wood, 1994) and trade theorists (such as Bhagwati and Dehejia, 1994; Leamer, 1994) contribute to the literature, theoretically and empirically, by proposing compelling arguments from various angles and by elaborating different methodologies. However, the more investigation one does the less conclusive the debate becomes.

Katz and Autor (1999) have developed a supply-demand-institutions (SDI) framework to assess the role of market forces (supply and demand shifts) and institutional factors in changes in the wage structure. In their discussion of market forces they analyze skill-biased technological change, globalization and de-industrialization in the determination of the wage differential. Deardorff and Hakura (1994) conducted a selective survey of the empirical literature on trade and wages, and categorized the discussion into trade volumes, prices, and measures of protection. A role for technological innovation (sometimes also referred to loosely as productivity growth) was introduced when research, for example Bound and Johnson (1992), Lawrence and Slaughter (1993), and Tombazos (2003), failed to find that trade has a significant impact on wages. The majority of existing research focuses on developed or large countries and is based either theoretically on a Heckscher-Ohlin-Samuelson framework or empirically on econometric models. Under the assumption of the Heckscher-Ohlin-Samuelson model, the endowments of skilled and unskilled labour are fixed. Therefore, an increased demand for skilled labour, moving into a situation that skilled labour become scarce relative to unskilled labour, increases the skilled-unskilled wage differential. Allowing numbers of labour endogenized in a general equilibrium system may raise a situation which fails the above concomitant of assuming fixed endowments, especially in the long run. The econometric approaches use either reduced forms from relatively simple theoretical models or somewhat ad hoc forms, neither of which is sufficiently comprehensive.

Since the empirical data come from a dynamic time frame, a theoretical model as playing a leading role in the empirical research should equip a dynamic essence. This paper constructs a dynamic intertemporal general equilibrium (DIGE) model with three-sectors (exports, imports, and non-traded), two kinds of labour (skilled and unskilled) plus another input of capital, and three-agents (firms, households, and government). This model features a more complicated framework than the Heckscher-Ohlin model and in which the amount of input factors are endogenous, i.e. they are not fixed. The skilled-unskilled wage differential varies

---

[1] Murphy and Welch (1991), Leamer (1992), and Sachs and Shatz (1994) support this strand.

[2] Bound and Johnson (1992), Katz and Murphy (1992), Lawrence and Slaughter (1993), Berman, Bound, and Griliches (1994), and Slaughter and Swagel (1997) support this point,

[3] Krugman (1995) debating Leamer (1994) is an impressive example.

[4] Chen and Hsu (2001) is a recent contribution for a case study of Taiwan.

along with the change of supply and demand of skilled and unskilled labour. The process of skill formation is essential when considering both skilled and unskilled labour. Education is the fundamental input to skill formation.[5] Hence, education production and consumption play important roles in this model. The simulation provides a dynamic transition of the skilled-unskilled wage differential in both the short- and long-run.

The main results from this study are that, in the long run, productivity growth and/or an increase in government education investment decrease the wage differential. At most productivity growth raises the wage differential in the short run. An increase in trade creates the wage differential. Furthermore, in the long run, an increase in government education investment has a relatively larger effect on the wage differential than the shocks of productivity growth and international trade. These theoretical simulation results have been substantiated by an empirical case study of Taiwan conducted by Chang (2003) in which the error correction model (ECM) is used.

A general picture of the modeling methodology is presented in Section 2. Section 3 illustrates the theoretical framework. Section 4 frames the simulation results. Section 5 shows the sensitivity test of the model and Section 6 concludes.

2 Modeling Methodology

Firms employ physical capital, skilled and unskilled labour, to produce three types of goods, i.e. exports, import substitutes, and non-traded,[6] and sell these goods to households for consumption, to government for education capital investment, and to themselves for physical capital investment. The export good is sold abroad based on foreign demand in exchange for imports. Households supply unskilled labour to firms and skilled labour to both firms and government in order to gain wages. Households also own the physical capital and earn financial dividends. Households purchase goods from firms and purchase education from government. Households also consume leisure with an opportunity cost of not working, and maximize utility by distributing consumption optimally on both goods and leisure. To incorporate the issue of leisure enables this model to take account of the income effect and the substitution effect between working and not working, which is seldom discussed by the existing literature. Government buys goods from firms and transforms them into education capital, together with skilled labour, to produce education. The role of government as an education supplier is essential. This model captures the reality of government supplying education in consideration of the associated beneficial externalities. The government balances its budget by collecting labour income tax and selling education to households.[7] The accumulation of physical capital, skill formation, education capital and financial assets drives the dynamic evolution of the economy over time.

The numbers of workers in the two categories of skilled and unskilled labour can vary over time. In addition to government investment in education and training facilities, the motivation of households to pursue higher skills is an important factor when considering

[5] Bhagwati and Srinivasan (1977) indicate education confers skills.

[6] Three types of goods are also characterized as skilled labour intensive, unskilled labour intensive, and capital intensive.

[7] To avoid unnecessary complexities, a subsidy rate on investment and a tax rate on financial dividends is assumed to balance.

changes in the proportions of labour in different categories. The main incentive for acquiring skills is higher future income. This motivates candidates to forsake current unskilled wage, and to invest, by time consumption and direct cost (tuition), in upgrading their education level.[8] To model the transformation of unskilled into skilled labour, the method assumes a representative agent who reflects the aggregate labour force in the economy. A portion of the person serves as skilled labour and the remaining portion as unskilled labour. In each period of time, this representative person makes a choice to invest in education to gain skill, which is subject to an increasing convex cost of adjustment function. The skilled labour faces no transformation cost to work as unskilled labour. The equilibrium skill formation depends on the fixed skill formation, skill depreciation rate, and the skill stock as well as the demand for skilled labour. Due to the assumption of the mobility of labour internally, there is a single nominal wage for skilled workers and a single nominal wage for unskilled workers.

The elasticity of the skilled labour supply, with respect to the wage of skilled labour, is greater than zero, since the supply of skilled labour is not fixed. It is less than infinity in the short run, because the transformation from unskilled to skilled labour is not fully free. Some skills are specific or patented, and training facilities are not always established quickly. It is also not perfectly elastic in the long run. There are four main reasons proposed on this point by Wood (1994), but only two are appropriate in this model.[9] First, the imperfection of capital markets, which means the opportunity to acquire loans for schooling is not equal for all unskilled labour, emerges the issue of unequal availability of skill acquisition. While becoming a full time student means only a decrease in savings for some, it can mean starvation for others. Second, variations in trainability amongst unskilled labour arise from differences in innate ability and family background (Phelps 1977). These two factors provide the accuracy of embodying a positive and limited elasticity of skilled labour supply in the model.

3 The Model

This model follows the general approach of the G-Cubed model (McKibbin and Wilcoxen 1999) but with the first time to incorporate issues of education and of skill formation.

3.1 Firms

There are three representative firms in the economy respectively from the export sector, the import substituting sector, and the non-traded sector. A Cobb-Douglas production function is employed,[10]

$$Q_i = A_{Q_i} \cdot K_i^{\alpha_i} \cdot L_{s,i}^{F\ \beta_i} \cdot L_{u,i}^{\ 1-\alpha_i-\beta_i}\,, \tag{3.1}$$

[8] In the ensuing model, education is the necessary channel for acquiring skills. Learning by doing is treated as a skill improvement in the same category, not jumping into a high level. Spill over effect is embedded into the education investment function.

[9] The other two reasons are that skill transformation is increasing returns, and external, which are proper to explain the enduring gap of skill levels between North and South.

[10] Every variable implicitly carries a subscript of time.

where Q_i is the gross output, A_{Qi} is the sectoral technology variable, i is the sector index and i = 1, 2, 3. The three inputs are capital K_i, skilled labour $L^F_{s,i}$, and unskilled labour $L_{u,i}$, and α_i, β_i, $(1- \alpha_i - \beta_i)$ are, respectively, the shares of employment of capital, skilled labour, and unskilled labour in production.

The sector with a larger share of skilled labour is defined as a relatively skilled intensive sector. The sector with a larger share of unskilled labour is defined as a relatively unskilled intensive sector. And the sector with a larger share of capital is defined as relatively capital intensive. To initialize the model, it is assumed sector 1 is relatively skilled labour intensive, sector 2 is relatively unskilled labour intensive, and sector 3 is relatively capital intensive. It is also assumed this small open economy exports good 1, imports good 2 and good 3 is non-traded. That is, the representative firms export the relatively skilled intensive and import the relatively unskilled intensive goods. Table 1 illustrates this characteristic. Other combinations of trade attributes and factor intensities are tested in Section 5 to see if the result from this designation is robust.

Table 1 Sector Characteristic

Sector	Factor Intensive	Trade
1	Skilled	Export
2	Unskilled	Import substitute
3	Capital	Non-traded

Exports demand by foreigners (X) is a function of foreign income (Y^*) and the inverse of terms of trade as follows,

$$X = (\frac{P_2}{P_1})^{\rho} \cdot Y^*, \tag{3.2}$$

where ρ is a positive parameter. Equation (3.2) states that exports of the domestic country are boosted by an increase in foreign income, a decrease in export price (P_1), and an increase in import price (P_2). Exports decrease when the opposite is true. This model makes a case that the exported good is an imperfect substitute for foreign goods, whereas the imported good is a perfect substitute for the domestic good 2. To simplify, it is assumed that trade is balanced in all periods.

Capital accumulation in each sector depends on the rate of gross fixed capital formation (J_i) and the rate of depreciation (δ_i),

$$\frac{dK}{dt} = J_{t,i} - \delta_i \cdot K_{t,i} . \tag{3.3}$$

Under the assumption of rising marginal costs of installation in the investment process, the total investment expenditure (I_i) in sector i is

$$I_i = J_i \cdot [1 + (\frac{\phi_i}{2} \cdot \frac{J_i}{K_i})], \tag{3.4}$$

where ϕ_i is a positive parameter, and $(\phi_i/2)(J_i/K_i)$ is the unit costs of adjustment, which is assumed to be a linear function of the rate of capital formation.

The firms maximize intertemporal profit, and choose L_s^F, L_u and J subject to equations (3.3) and (3.4) by solving the current value Hamiltonian function with λ_i being the shadow price of capital. The first order conditions state that the real return to factors is equal to its marginal productivity under perfect competition. The shadow price of capital is greater than one due to the adjustment cost. By solving the first-order differential equation and applying the transversality condition, the shadow price of capital becomes

$$\lambda_i(t) = \int_t^\infty (Q_{Ki} + \Theta_i)\, e^{-(r + \delta_i) \cdot s} \cdot ds, \tag{3.5}$$

where $\Theta_i = (\phi_i/2)(J_i/K_i)^2$ and r is the discount rate. Equation (3.5) states that the shadow price of capital is equal to the present discounted value of future marginal products. It consists of two parts: Q_{Ki} is the marginal product of capital and Θ_i is the marginal product of capital in reducing adjustment costs in investment at each point in time. Therefore, λ_i is the increment to the real value of the firm from one unit of installed capital at time t.

3.2 Household

The household distributes after-tax labour income and dividends to consumption of the three goods, financial asset accumulation for future consumption and education investment, together with the choice of leisure, to maximize utility. The objective function of the household, the intertemporal budget constraint, a dynamic accumulation of skilled labour, the financial assets ownership, and education investment are shown as follows,

$$\text{Max.} \int_0^\infty U(C_{1,t}, C_{2,t}, C_{3,t}, l_t) \cdot e^{-\theta \cdot t} \cdot dt \tag{3.6}$$

Subject to

$$\frac{dF_t}{dt} = r_t \cdot F_t + (1-\tau_t) \cdot (\frac{W_{s,t}}{P_{2,t}} \cdot L_{s,t} + \frac{W_{u,t}}{P_{2,t}} \cdot L_{u,t}) - [(\frac{P_{1,t}}{P_{2,t}}) \cdot C_{1,t} + C_{2,t} + (\frac{P_{3,t}}{P_{2,t}}) \cdot C_{3,t} + (\frac{P_{E,t}}{P_{2,t}}) \cdot S_{E,t}], \tag{3.7}$$

$$\frac{dL_{s,t}}{dt} = J_{s,t} - \delta_s \cdot L_{s,t}, \tag{3.8}$$

$$F_t = (\frac{P_{1,t}}{P_{2,t}}) \cdot \lambda_{1,t} \cdot K_{1,t} + \lambda_{2,t} \cdot K_{2,t} + (\frac{P_{3,t}}{P_{2,t}}) \cdot \lambda_{3,t} \cdot K_{3,t}, \tag{3.9}$$

$$S_{E,t} = J_{s,t} \cdot [1 + \frac{\Phi}{2} \cdot (\frac{J_{s,t}}{L_{s,t}})], \tag{3.10}$$

where $C_{i,t}$ is the consumption of goods, l_t is leisure, θ is the rate of time preference, F_t is financial assets, τ_t is the tax rate on labour income, $P_{E,t}$ is the price of one unit of education, $S_{E,t}$ is the amount of education buying, $J_{s,t}$ is the fixed skill formation, δ_s is the depreciation rate of skill, and Φ is the adjustment cost parameter.

Equation (3.7), the budget constraint, states that the accumulation of the household's financial assets depends on financial dividends, total after-tax labour income and total spending on goods and education. Equation (3.8) states that the net skill formation is the skill depreciation subtracted from the fixed skill formation. Equation (3.9) shows the contents of financial assets, which includes the value of capital in each sector, so-called equity. Equation (3.10) states that education investment depends on fixed skill formation and an adjustment cost. The adjustment cost reflects the foregone production and relies on the rate of skill formation. If skilled labour increases, the adjustment cost decreases. It is plausible due to the spillover effect among labour. Leisure is defined as the remaining time after deducting total labour hours.

The current value Hamiltonian function is employed to solve the above autonomous two-state variables system with μ_1 and μ_2 being the shadow prices respective to the financial assets and skill. The first order conditions imply $\mu_1 = MU_1/P_1 = MU_2/P_2 = MU_3/P_3$, where MU_i stands for the marginal utility of consuming good 1, good 2 and good 3, respectively. It demonstrates that marginal utility should be the same for each good to achieve optimality. The shadow price of skill is greater than the shadow price of the financial asset due to the adjustment cost of skill formation. If the shadow price of skill is not greater than that of the financial asset, the household would defer spending on skill formation instead of accumulating financial assets for future consumption.

Applying the transversality condition to the shadow price of skill, μ_2, results in

$$\mu_2(t) = \int^{\infty} \{\mu_1 \cdot [(1-\tau_1) \cdot \frac{W_{s,t}}{P_{2,t}} + \frac{P_{E,t}}{P_{2,t}} \cdot \frac{\Phi}{2} \cdot (\frac{J_{s,t}}{L_{s,t}})^2] + U_{L_s,t}\} \cdot e^{-(\theta+\delta_s)\cdot t} \cdot dt, \tag{3.11}$$

where $U_{Ls,t}$ is the partial derivative of the utility function with respect to skilled labour. The transversality condition asserts that, in an infinite time horizon, the present value of the shadow price of one additional skilled labour formed is equal to zero. It eliminates the case of infinite accumulation of skilled labour. This assertion is plausible because the variation of the skilled wage initialized by the movement of the skilled labour supply and demand can tie down infinite accumulation of skilled labour. Equation (3.11) states that the shadow price of skill is equal to the present discounted value of future marginal utility. The first component of the shadow price of skill contains the marginal utility of consuming goods, the after-tax skilled wage, and the reduction of adjustment cost in education investment. It provides the gross increment of utility the household gains from supplying one additional unit of skilled labour. The second part is the marginal disutility of offering one unit of skilled labour. Combining these two gives the net utility the household can achieve by supplying one unit of skilled labour, which substantiates the essence of μ_2.

To derive consumption on goods and leisure, a Cobb-Douglas utility function with γ_i, i =1,2,3 as corresponding shares is assumed, resulting in

$$C_i = \frac{\gamma_i \cdot U \cdot P_2}{\mu_1 \cdot P_i}, \tag{3.12}$$

$$l = \frac{(1-\gamma_1-\gamma_2-\gamma_3)\cdot U \cdot P_2}{(1-\tau)\cdot \mu_1 \cdot W_u}. \tag{3.13}$$

Equations (3.12) and (3.13) state, ceteris paribus, that when the price P_i or net unskilled earnings increases, the household decreases demand for good i or leisure. Also, when consumption increases with fixed prices, the marginal utility μ_1 decreases, i.e., the law of diminishing return. This is an outcome of the concave utility function. Equation (3.13) also shows that, if income tax increases, leisure increases. This corroborates that heavy taxation lessens the motivation for working in a partial equilibrium.

3.3 Government

The government collects income tax and sells education ($P_{E,t} \cdot S_{E,t}$) to finance total spending, and also buys good 1 ($I^G_{E,1}$), good 2 ($I^G_{E,2}$), and good 3 ($I^G_{E,3}$) to produce education capital ($K_{E,t}$). Total government investment on education capital is represented by I^G_E. It is assumed that I^G_E is exogenously controlled by the government. To produce education, the government employs skilled labour (L^G_s) as well as using education capital,

$$S_{E,t} = K^{\xi}_{E,t} \cdot L^{G^{1-\xi}}_{s,t}, \tag{3.14}$$

where ξ is the input share parameter.

The accumulation of education capital results from the total investment of government after subtracting depreciation,

$$\frac{dK_{E,t}}{dt} = I^G_{E,t} - \delta_E \cdot K_{E,t}, \tag{3.15}$$

where δ_E is the rate of depreciation and I^G_E is defined as follow,

$$I_E^G = \frac{1}{P_E^G} \cdot (P_1 \cdot I_{E,1}^G + P_2 \cdot I_{E,2}^G + P_3 \cdot I_{E,3}^G), \tag{3.16}$$

where P_E^G is the weighted price index defined as below,

$$P_E^G = P_1^{\varepsilon_1} \cdot P_2^{\varepsilon_2} \cdot P_3^{\varepsilon_3}, \tag{3.17}$$

where ε_i is the weight of this pooled index.

Government spending on each good for education investment follows $I_{E,i}^G = \varepsilon_i \cdot \frac{P_E^G \cdot I_E^G}{P_i}$. To assure the model is consistent, as well as the economy is in equilibrium, the rule of demand equal to supply is applied on both sides of the goods and factor markets.

3.4 Steady State

Table 2 summarizes this model in the steady state. It should be highlighted that the rate of time preference is equal to the rate of interest in the steady state. If the rate of time preference is greater than the interest rate, the household will decumulate financial assets instead of increasing consumption. This will raise the interest rate till it reaches the level of time preference. The adjustment reverses if the interest rate is greater than the rate of time preference. Hence, those two rates have to be equal in equilibrium.[11]

The shadow price of capital is well known as marginal *Tobin's q*, noted as q_i^M. In the steady state, it follows

$$q_i^M = 1 + \delta_i \cdot \phi_i. \tag{3.18}$$

Hence, without subsidy of investment, the marginal *Tobin's* q is greater than 1 when an adjustment cost exists, and equal to 1 when the adjustment cost is zero.[12] Similarly, the marginal *Tobin's* q of skill,[13] noted as q_s^M, has a relationship with the shadow price μ_2. That is $q_s^M = \mu_2$, and in the steady state,

$$q_s^M = \mu_1 \cdot P_E \cdot (1 + \delta_s \cdot \Phi). \tag{3.19}$$

[11] This result is consistent with the argument in chapter two of Blanchard and Fischer (1989).

[12] After the subsidy of investment is embedded, the marginal *Tobin's* q is smaller when the rate of subsidy is higher. That is to say, if the government subsidizes investment with a higher rate, the investment cost is lower and will encourage firms to invest.

[13] It can be regarded as human capital.

Table 2 Model in the Steady State

Equations
$Q_i = A_{Q_i} \cdot K_i^{\alpha_i} \cdot L_{s,i}^{F\ \beta_i} \cdot L_{u,i}^{1-\alpha_i-\beta_i}$
$J_{t,i} = \delta_i \cdot K_{t,i}$
$I_i = J_i \cdot (1 + \phi_i \delta_i/2)$
$Q_{i,Ls} = W_s/P_i$
$Q_{i,Lu} = W_u/P_i$
$\lambda_i = 1 + \phi_i \cdot \delta_i$
$Q_{Ki} = (r + \delta_i)\lambda_i - \phi_i \cdot \delta_i^2/2$
$P_{2,t} \cdot M_t = P_{1,t} \cdot X_t$
$X = (P_2/P_1)^{\rho} \cdot Y^*$
$0 = r_t \cdot F_t + (1-\tau_t) \cdot [(W_s/P_2) \cdot L_{s,t} + (W_u/P_2) \cdot L_{u,t}] - [(P_1/P_2) \cdot C_{1,t} + C_{2,t} + (P_3/P_2) \cdot C_{3,t} + (P_{E,t}/P_2) \cdot S_{E,t}]$
$J_{s,t} = \delta_s \cdot L_{s,t}$
$F_t = (P_1/P_2) \cdot \lambda_{1,t} \cdot K_{1,t} + \lambda_{2,t} \cdot K_{2,t} + (P_3/P_2) \cdot \lambda_{3,t} \cdot K_{3,t}$
$I_{E,t} = J_{s,t}(1 + \Phi \cdot \delta_s/2)$
$l_t = T - L_{s,t} - L_{u,t}$
$U_{Ci} = (P_i/P_2) \cdot \mu_1$
$U_{Lu,t} = -\mu_1 \cdot (1-\tau) \cdot W_u/P_2$
$\mu_2 = \mu_1 \cdot P_E \cdot (1 + \Phi \cdot \delta_s)/P_2$
$r_t = \theta$
$U_{Ls} = (\theta + \delta_s) \cdot \mu_2 - \mu_1 \cdot [(1-\tau) \cdot W_s + P_E \cdot (\Phi \cdot \delta_s^2)/2]/P_2$
$S_E = K_E^{\xi} \cdot L_s^{G^{1-\xi}}$
$I_E^G = \delta_E \cdot K_E$
$I_E^G = (P_1 \cdot I_{E,1}^G + P_2 \cdot I_{E,2}^G + P_3 \cdot I_{E,3}^G)/P_E^G$
$P_E^G = P_1^{\varepsilon_1} \cdot P_2^{\varepsilon_2} \cdot P_3^{\varepsilon_3}$
$P_E^G \cdot I_E^G + W_s \cdot L_s^G = \tau \cdot (W_s \cdot L_s + W_u \cdot L_u) + P_E \cdot S_E$
$Q_{1,t} - X_t = C_1 + I_{E,1}^G + I_1$
$Q_{2,t} + M_t = C_2 + I_{E,2}^G + I_2$
$Q_{3,t} = C_3 + I_{E,3}^G + I_3$

Equation (3.19) states that, marginal *Tobin's* q of skill is equal to the shadow price of financial assets, i.e., the marginal utility of consuming goods, times the total cost of one unit of skill formation. It asserts that skill generates higher wages, hence, more utility. The product of education price and the parenthesis is equivalent to the total price of upgrading one unit of skill. Hence, the multiple on the right-hand side is the marginal utility the household can have after gaining one unit of skilled labour. To maximize utility, the household will invest in skill formation untill its generation of marginal utility is equal to its marginal cost.

3.5 Wage Differential

Due to the complexity of the above model, there is no reduced form that can be derived to present the wage differential. A possible simple expression of the wage differential in the steady state is as follows,

$$W_s = W_u + \frac{P_E}{(1-\tau)} \cdot (\theta + \theta \cdot \Phi \cdot \delta_s + \delta_s + \frac{1}{2} \cdot \Phi \cdot \delta_s^2) . \tag{3.20}$$

The expression of equation (3.20) is independent of the functional form of utility and production function.[14] It provides a rigorous theoretical result of the wage differential. The relationship between the skilled and unskilled wage depends on the rate of time preference, the depreciation rate of skill, the skill adjustment cost parameter, the tax rate, and the price of education. A higher skill adjustment cost and a higher skill depreciation rate tend to boost the cost of skill formation, therefore leading to a higher skilled wage. The rate of time preference counts because an investment in skill formation takes time to repay. A larger time preference involves a larger adjustment cost for skill formation, therefore a patient household will expect a higher skilled wage. The education price and the tax rate are endogenous in this model. Theoretically, each endogenous variable can be solved and substituted by the exogenous variables and parameters, then turn the equation (3.20) to the following,

$$\frac{W_s}{W_u} = f(A_{Q_i}, I_E^G, Y^* \mid parameters) . \tag{3.21}$$

The wage differential equation (3.20) illustrates both the importance of, and the transmission channel of, education in the determination of the wage differential. This is the reason for the inclusion of education in the debate on the wage differential, in addition to the traditional arguments of international trade and productivity growth. The government, as an education supplier and tax collector, has the ability to influence the wage differential to a certain extent. What matters in a general equilibrium outcome is the interactive effect of the education price and the tax rate. Simulation becomes necessary to explore the short- and long-run transitions of each endogenous variable and so establish the policy implications.

4 Simulation Results

A number of simulations are considered in this section in order to explore the long run, defined as the steady state, and the short run relationships between investigated variables in the model. The exogenous variables are technology (A_{Q_i}), time (T), government investment

[14] A detailed proof is available from the author.

on education (I_E^G), and foreign income (Y^*). All other variables are endogenous. The setting of the parameters and exogenous variables is presented in the Appendix 1.[15] The experiment is to investigate the transition of all endogenous variables between steady states in five cases: a 10% improvement in technology in each sector, a 10% increase in government education investment, and a 10% increase in foreign income. It should be noted that this model simultaneously provides the cases of total factor productivity (TFP) and input efficiency growth in each sector. The dynamic path of input efficiency shock is not shown because it is similar to the shocks of TFP.[16] An aggregation of three sectors leads to a case of factor biased productivity growth, a reason emphasized by Krugman and Laurence (1994) of causing enlargement of the wage differential. However, this model allows the supply and demand of skilled labour to determine the skilled wage rather than the scenario in their paper, which asserts the demand in skill dominates the jump of skilled wage.[17]

The simulation paths are presented in Figure 1. Table 3 summarizes the results. The main results from this model are that, in the long run, productivity growth and an increase in government education investment lessen the wage differential.[18] Generally speaking, increased education investment also lessens the wage differential in the short run, albeit with a fluctuation at the early stage. (The fluctuation occurs because the adjustment process of skill formation takes time and households make optimal choices between working and leisure.) Productivity growth, at most, raises the wage differential only in the short run: it may reduce the wage differential in the short run if productivity growth is biased towards the sector which is intensive in unskilled labour. An increase in international trade via an increase in foreign income raises the wage differential to a larger extent in the short run than in the long run.[19]

Intuitively, an increased demand for skilled labour resulting from a growth in productivity or in exports can eventually be filled in the long run as skill supply plays an important role in the wage determination. In the short run, the created demand cannot be filled immediately due to the time required for skill formation. By using equation (3.20), the transitions are as follows. Productivity growth pushes down goods prices. This reduces the costs of government purchases and motivates the government to cut the tax rate which , in turn, decreases the wage differential. If the government increases education investment, thereby decreasing the education price, it can cause diminution of the wage differential. While the international trade factor is not explicitly shown in equation (3.20), its effect is transmitted from production to wages through the education price. An increase in skill-intensive exports boosts the price of exports and the demand for skilled labour. This increases the demand for education and, hence, the price of education. Therefore, the wage differential rises.

---

15 The calibration is based on good empirical knowledge albeit subjective.

16 This model can easily pull in the input efficiency factor. The production function becomes $Q_i = A_{Qi} \cdot (c_{k,i} \cdot K_i)^{\alpha i} \cdot (c_{s,i} \cdot L_{s,i}^F)^{\beta i} \cdot (c_{u,i} \cdot L_{u,i})^{1-\alpha i-\beta i}$, where $c_{j,i}$, j = k, s, u, represents the relative efficiency of factor K, L_s, L_u in sector i. Obviously, the upgrade of input efficiency reaches a similar result, but in a different level of TFP growth.

17 To adapt this model to the scenario in Krugman and Laurence (1994), either to increase the adjustment cost of skill to a fairly high extent to make it very hard for households to transform skill, or to increase the shares of skilled labour in all sectors to force the skill demand dominating the skilled wage.

18 Productivity growth lessens the wage differential to a small but non-zero extent.

19 In the long run, the wage differential is enlarged to a small but non-zero extent.

From a theoretical perspective it is unconvincing that productivity growth raises the wage differential in the long run since skill formation eventually catches up with the progress of technology as long as the adjustment cost is affordable for the unskilled labour.

Table 3 The Results of the Wage Differential to Each Shock

Wage Differential	**Tech 1**	**Tech 2**	**Tech 3**	**Education**	**Trade**
Short Run	Increase	Decrease	Increase	Decrease	Increase
Long Run	Decrease 0.03%	Decrease 0.03%	Decrease 0.02%	Decrease 0.76%	Increase 0.02%

Note: Each shock is 10% up.

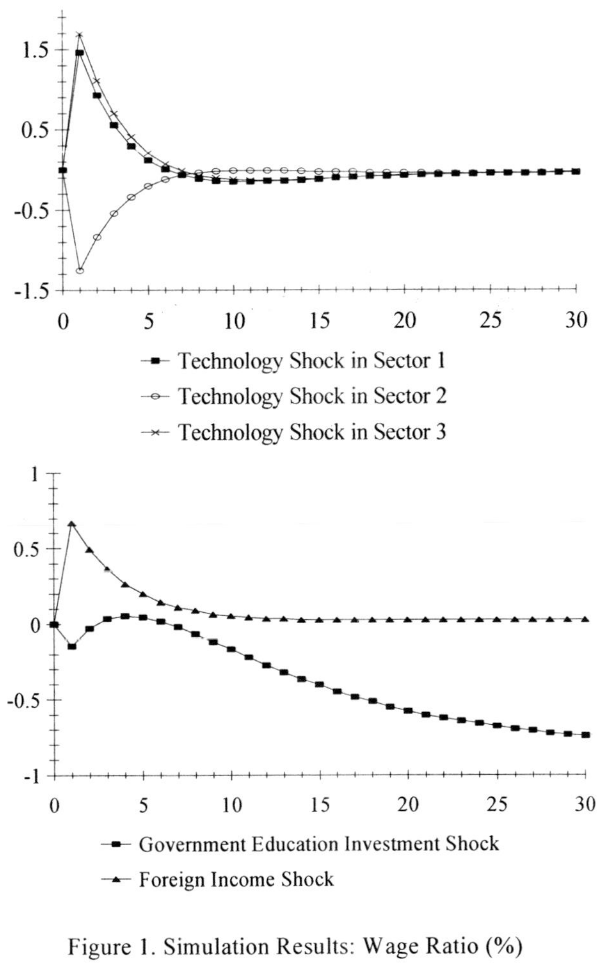

Figure 1. Simulation Results: Wage Ratio (%)

5 Sensitivity Test

Since there are three sectors with a different intensity of each factor, and five different shocks— technological progress in sectors 1, 2 and 3, government education investment and foreign income, there is a total of thirty cases within this framework. Sector 1 is designated the export sector, sector 2 the import sector, and sector 3 the non-traded sector. The key variable investigated is the change of the wage ratio between the steady states. The results, set out in Table 4, show that this model is fairly robust. In Table 4, the first column gives the combination of three sectors with different intensities of inputs. Numbers stand for sectors and letters stands for inputs, for example 1U2S3K represents sector 1 as unskilled-labour intensive, sector 2 as skilled-labour intensive and sector 3 as capital intensive. The second to sixth columns respectively stand for an improvement in technology in sectors 1, 2 and 3, an increase in government education investment and an increase in foreign income. A minus sign (-) means a decreased wage differential and a plus sign (+) means an increased wage differential.

Table 4. Sensitivity Test: The Long-run Effect of Shocks on the Wage Differential

	Tech 1	Tech 2	Tech 3	Government Education Invest	Foreign Income
1S2U3K	-	-	-	-	+
1S2K3U	-	-	-	-	+
1U2S3K	-*	-*	-	-	-
1U2K3S	-	-	-	-	-
1K2S3U	-	-	-	-	-
1K2U3S	-	-	-	-	+

*When the share of education capital in education production is equal to or greater than 0.5, the sign becomes +.

To summarize, on the one hand, the effect on the wage differential of an improvement in technology in any of the sectors or of increased government investment in education is insensitive to different combinations of sectors, that is, in each case the wage differential decreases in the long run, whereas, on the other hand, the effect on the wage differential of a foreign income shock that raises exports is sensitive to different combinations of sectors. If the export sector is skilled intensive, an increase in export boosts the wage differential; if the export sector is unskilled intensive, an export expansion reduces the wage differential; if the export sector is capital intensive, an increase in exports may either boost or reduce the wage differential.

6 Conclusion

This paper discusses the relationship between productivity growth, international trade, education, and the wage differential by constructing a DIGE open economy model. The main insight of this model is the choice of the household to undertake skill formation. This varies the endowment of skilled labour from short to long run. The result provides a comparison to a standard result from the Heckscher-Ohlin model in which skill endowments are fixed. Education is shown to be quite important yet its effect on the wage differential is seldom discussed in the literature. It would be biased to only focus on the external trade effect in this issue. At the same time, an internal education policy should be recruited into the debate. The education issue is especially important when a developing country is investigated, due to the scarcity of skilled labour relative to a developed country. It is crucial to embed the dynamic adjustment process for guiding future econometric modeling in which data is used from a dynamic adjustment period. This model also shows the steady state relation which underlies the literature, can be misleading in the short run.

The main results from this model are that, in the long run, productivity growth and/or an increase in government education investment decrease the wage differential. At most productivity growth raises the wage differential in the short run. An increase in trade creates the wage differential. Furthermore, in the long run, an increase in government education investment has a relatively larger effect on the wage differential than the shocks of productivity growth and international trade. This model shows that a 10% increase in government education investment reduces the wage differential by about 0.76%. A 10% improvement in technology reduces the wage differential by around 0.02 to 0.03% and a 10% increase in foreign income enlarges the wage differential by about 0.02%. To summarize the results and policy implications from thirty cases by combining factor intensity in each sector with trade characteristic and shocks, the wage differential tends to decrease with a productivity upgrade. It is also found that if the export sector is skilled labour intensive, an increase in export boosts the wage differential; if the export sector is unskilled labour intensive, an export expansion reduces the wage differential; if the export sector is capital intensive, an increase in exports may either boost or reduce the wage differential. This model implies that a developed country's trade with a developing country enlarges the wage differential in the developed country and reduces the wage differential in the developing country. The result also tends to substantiate the argument that international trade has a responsibility for an enlarging wage differential. From a theoretical perspective it is unclear how productivity growth raises the wage differential in the long run due to skill formation eventually catching up with the progress of technology.

A couple of extensions of this model can be undertaken in future research to explore other interesting issues. For example, the effect of tariffs can be included. A test of the impact of unskilled labour immigration would be important for some countries. The model could also be extended to the case of an open capital account which may have important implications for the adjustment process to a range of shocks.

Appendix 1

The parameters and exogenous variables settings are as follows:

$\alpha_1 = 0.3$;	$\beta_1 = 0.5$;	$\delta_1 = 0.1$;	$\phi_1 = 5$;	
$\alpha_2 = 0.3$;	$\beta_2 = 0.2$;	$\delta_2 = 0.1$;	$\phi_2 = 5$;	
$\alpha_3 = 0.5$;	$\beta_3 = 0.3$;	$\delta_3 = 0.1$;	$\phi_3 = 5$;	
$\delta_s = 0.05$;	$\gamma_1 = 0.3$;	$\gamma_2 = 0.2$;		$\gamma_3 = 0.2$;
$\theta = 0.1$;	$\xi = 0.5$;	$\delta_E = 0.1$;	$\Phi = 10$;	
$\varepsilon_1 = 1/3$;	$\varepsilon_2 = 1/3$;	$\rho = 0.5$;	$T = 8760$;	
$A_{Qi} = 1$;	$I_E^G = 100$;	$Y^* = 100$;		

References

Bhagwati, J. and Dehejia, V.H. 1994. "Freer Trade and Wages of the Unskilled- Is Marx Striking Again?," in Bhagwati, J. and Kosters, M.H. (eds.), *Trade and Wages: Leveling Wages Down?,* Washington, D.C., AEI Press.

Bhagwati, Jagdish H. and T.N. Srinivasan. 1977. "Education in a 'Job Ladder' Model and the Fairness-In-Hiring Rule", *Journal of Public Economics*, **7**: p.1-22.

Berman, Eli, John Bound, and Zvi Griliches. 1994. "Changes in the Demand for Skilled Labor Within U.S. Manufacturing Industries: Evidence from the Annual Survey of Manufacturing." *Quarterly Journal of Economics* **109**(2): p.367-97.

Blanchard, Olivier Jean and Fischer, Stanley. 1989. *Lectures on Macroeconomics*, The MIT Press, Cambridge, Massachusetts.

Bound, J. and Johnson, G. 1992. "Changes in the Structure of Wages in the 1980s: An Evaluation of Alternative Explanations," *American Economic Review* **82**: 371-392.

Chang, Hsiao-Chuan. 2003. "International Trade, Productivity Growth, Education and the Wage Differential: A Case Study of Taiwan" *Journal of Applied Economics*, Vol. VI, No.1, p. 25-48.

Chang, Hsiao-Chuan. 2000. International Trade, Productivity Growth, Education, and Wage Differentials in General Equilibrium, Ph.D. Thesis, the Australian National University.

Chen, B.L. and Hsu, M. 2001. "Time-Series Wage Differential in Taiwan: The Role of International Trade," *Review of Development Economics* **5**: 336-354.

Deardorff, A.V. and Hakura, D.S. 1994. "Trade and Wages- What Are the Questions?," in Bhagwati, J. and Kosters, M.H. (eds.), *Trade and Wages: Leveling Wages Down?*, Washington, D.C., AEI Press.

Katz, L.F. and Autor, D.H. 1999. "Changes in the Wage Structure and Earnings Inequality," in Ashenfelter, O. and Card, D. (eds.), *Handbook of Labor Economics*, Volume 3: 1463-1555.

Katz, Lawrence F. and Kevin M. Murphy. 1992. "Changes in Relative Wages, 1963-1987: Supply and Demand Factors." *Quarterly Journal of Economics*, **107**: p.35-78.

Krugman, Paul and Lawrence, Robert. Z. 1994. "Trade, Jobs and Wages" *Scientific American*, **270**, p.22-27.

Krugman, Paul. 1995. "Technology, Trade, and Factor Prices" *NBER Working Paper*, No. **5355**. November, 1995.

Lawrence, R.Z. and Slaughter, M.J. 1993. "Trade and U.S. Wages: Giant Sucking Sound or Small Hiccup?," Brookings Papers on Economic Activity, *Microeconomics* **2**: 161-210.

Leamer, Edward E. 1992. "Wage Effects of a U.S. – Mexican Free Trade Agreement" *National Bureau of Economic Research Working Paper*, No. **3991**.

Leamer, Edward E. 1994. "Testing Trade Theory" *Surveys in International Trade*, edited by Greenaway, David and Winters, L. Alan. Blackwell Publishers, Oxford.

McKibbin, Warwick J. and Wilcoxen, Peter J. 1999. "The Theoretical and Empirical Structure of the G-Cubed Model" *Economic Modelling*, **16**, p. 123-148.

Murphy, Kevin M. and Finis Welch. 1991. "The Role of International Trade in Wage Differentials." In Marvin H. Kosters, editor, *Workers and Their Wages*. Washington D.C.: American Enterprise Institute.

Phelps Brown, E. H. 1977. The Inequality of Pay, Oxford University Press, Oxford.

Sachs, Jeffrey D. and Shatz, Howard J. 1994. "Trade and Jobs in U.S. Manufacturing" *Brookings Papers on Economic Activity*, Vol. 1, p. 1-84.

Slaughter, Matthew J. and Swagel, Phillip. 1997. "The Effect of Globalization on Wages in the Advanced Economies" *IMF Working Paper*, WP/97/43, April, 1997.

Tombazos, Christis. 2003. "A production Theory Approach to the Imports and Wage Inequality Nexus" *Economic Inquiry*, Vol. 41, No. 1, p. 42-61.

Turrini, Alessandro. 1998. "Endogenous Education policy and Increasing Income Inequality between Skilled and Unskilled Workers" *European Journal of Political Economy*, Vol. 14, p. 303-26.

Wood, Adrian. 1994. North-South Trade Employment and Inequality, Changing Fortunes in a Skill-Driven World, *IDS Development Studies Series*, Clarendon Press, Oxford.

Wood, Adrian. 1995. "How Trade Hurt Unskilled Workers" *Journal of Economic Perspectives*, Vol. 9, No. 3, p.57-80.

INDEX

A

B

E

F

G

H

I

J

K

L

M

N

O

P

Q

R

S

T

U

V

W